Senior Examiner

John M. Lindquist

NYS BD

International Banking

SIXTH EDITION

PETER K. OPPENHEIM

EDUCATION POLICY & DEVELOPMENT

AMERICAN
BANKERS
ASSOCIATION

1120 Connecticut Avenue, N.W.
Washington, D.C. 20036

This publication is designed to provide accurate and authoritative information in regard to the subject matter covered. It is sold with the understanding that the publisher is not engaged in rendering legal, accounting, or other professional service. If legal advice or other expert assistance is required, the services of a competent professional person should be sought.

—From a Declaration of Principles jointly adopted by a Committee of the American Bar Association and a Committee of Publishers and Associations.

Library of Congress Cataloging-in-Publication Data

Oppenheim, Peter K.
    International banking / Peter K. Oppenheim. — 6th ed. p. cm.
    Includes bibliographical references and index.
    ISBN 0-89982-369-6
    1. Banks and banking, International. I. Title.
HG3881.06   1991
332. 1'5—dc20   91-10638
                                                                          CIP

1993 Printing

Printed in the United States of America

This edition is dedicated in appreciation and with my personal gratitude to **William H. Baughn**. Legions of international bankers learned their business through his 18 years as director of the School for International Banking and as co-editor of the *International Banking Handbook*, as well as more overall banking knowledge from his work as co-editor of the *Bankers Handbook*, as director of the Stonier Graduate School of Banking, and as Professor of Finance and Dean of the School of Business Administration at the University of Colorado.

Contents

Figures

Tables

Boxes

ABOUT THE AUTHOR

Peter K. Oppenheim began his banking career in 1957 in foreign exchange trading in Los Angeles with Bank of America N.T. & S.A. In the following years he had a variety of international operational, credit, and training assignments, including five years in New York. He retired in 1987 as a Vice President in that bank's World Banking Division in San Francisco.

He began authoring the American Bankers Association's *International Banking* in 1968 with the second edition and has continued with each subsequent edition. He is also the author of *The Language of International Finance in English: Money and Banking,* published in 1976. His articles have been published by the Committee for Economic Development, American Peoples Encyclopedia Yearbook, Verbatim, and Scott's Monthly.

Mr. Oppenheim holds a credential as an instructor in the California Community Colleges in Banking, Finance, and Government. He has taught at the Stonier Graduate School of Banking, School for International Banking, San Francisco City College, University of California Extension, and the American Institute of Banking. He has testified as an expert witness on international banking in U.S. Federal Court.

He graduated from the University of California at Berkeley with a Bachelor of Arts degree in English. Following service in the U.S. Air Force in Europe, he earned a Master of Arts degree at Berkeley in International Relations.

He is now designing, developing, and presenting seminars on international operations and credit for U.S. banks, a field in which he has had extensive experience in recent years.

PREFACE

This is the sixth edition in a series that began in 1966. I joined the project with the second edition in 1968. It is now ABA's longest running title under the same author.

This longevity may surprise some who have written off international banking in the past decade. However, as the prologue suggests, it is not that the business needs of the bank's customers have changed, but rather that banks have pulled back in a reaction of caution from what was perhaps an excess of enthusiasm in the 1970s. As my friend Steve Davis noted in the opening of his book *Managing Change in the Excellent Banks*, "Innovation and experimentation are rare in a business where learning from others' mistakes is a virtue."[1] Today's reality is that many bankers find themselves responsible for meeting their customers' demands without the presence any longer of the international specialists.

To meet this need, this sixth edition has been broadened to address not only the specialist in the remaining international banking departments, but also the domestic banker seeking insight into the operational and credit products the customer needs and the risks to the bank that these entail. We hope this book will make them more comfortable with these responsibilities.

In light of the negative impact of some international activities on banks in recent years, this edition has added material to identify the place of such activities in a bank's financial statement, particularly the implications as the risk-based capital guidelines become fully effective, which will bring more international banking activities into the overall capital calculations of a bank. Other changes from the previous edition include the updating of banking practices and the addition of more background on the evolution of many of these practices and products. This is done both in the text as well as with a new feature—boxes containing extracts from contemporary articles or books to illustrate specific uses of these products.

I want to acknowledge my great indebtedness to the assistance of many people.

First, to George T. Martin who has managed this edition for the ABA, my appreciation for his support and guidance. This is our fourth edition together.

Second, to the members of the advisory committee who were very generous with their limited free time in reviewing the manuscript and providing suggestions from their experience in this field as well as from having taught the course at AIB chapters using the fifth edition. These were

Ralph Charbonneau
Vice President and Manager (Retired)
Seattle First National Bank
Seattle, Washington

Lori Clos Fisher
Manager, Community Banking Support
International Division
C & S Sovran Corporation
Atlanta, Georgia

Denise C. Gaudy
Vice President
Corporate Banking Department
Mellon Bank, N.A.
Philadelphia, Pennsylvania

David Glowacki
Foreign Exchange Trader
NBD Bank, N.A.
Detroit, Michigan

Rosanna Gomez-Moreno
Personal Banking Officer
Frost National Bank
San Antonio, Texas

Peter Senica
Vice President
World Banking Group
Maryland National Bank
Baltimore, Maryland

Third, I want to thank those who were kind enough to respond to inquiries about specific activities: Robert R. Bench, formerly Deputy Comptroller of the Currency and now Partner, Price Waterhouse, Washington, D.C., for background on the development of the risk-based capital guidelines and the role of the BIS; William M. Walsh, Senior Vice President, New York Clearing House for details on CHIPS; the public relations people at S.W.I.F.T., La Hulpe, Belgium, for the massive material about the details of their operations; and to Edwin M. Truman, Staff Director, Division of International Finance, Board of Governors of the Federal Reserve System for several details on bankers' acceptances.

Notwithstanding all of the assistance acknowledged above, I remind the reader that the opinions expressed are my own and that any errors that remain should be attributed solely to the carelessness or stubbornness of the author.

Peter K. Oppenheim
December 1990

1.   Steven I. Davis, *Managing Change in the Excellent Banks* (London: Macmillan Press Ltd., 1989) p. 1.

Prologue

AN OPENING WORD:

Who is an international banker?

Twenty-five years ago that was comparatively easy to answer: An international banker was a specialist working in a separate department of a commercial bank called *foreign* or *international*. The international banker's customers were corporations, governments, and banks in other countries; the international banker's local customers bought and sold goods in other countries, traded pounds or yen for dollars, and transferred funds from one country to another. The local customer's other business was the domain of a domestic banker.

In mid-1982 this was all changed by the onset of what has come to be called "the international debt crisis." When the scheduled repayments of loans made to borrowers in many countries were delayed, U.S. commercial banks increased their loan loss reserves out of current earnings, which resulted in lower net profits or year-to-year losses for the entire bank. In reaction, virtually every U.S. bank reduced the number of their international bankers or eliminated those specialized departments. Bank strategic long-term plans now often focus only on segments of the domestic market.

International banking thus may seem to be an activity in peril. Not so. While banks were turning away from specialized international banking units, the banks' U.S. customers were increasing their participation in global markets: over 100,000 U.S. companies make at least seven export sales a year; $200 billion of foreign exchange is traded each day in the U.S. market; money and stock market funds offer individuals a wide range of attractive yields in foreign markets; foreign investment in U.S. real estate, factories, and government debt expands each year; U.S. companies manufacture in a variety of countries and assemble these parts in a few locations for worldwide sales; and U.S. imports doubled from 1982 to 1989 to $475 billion, accounting now for 22 percent of what Americans buy.[1]

Because U.S. business is more involved in the world than a decade ago, the demand today from a bank's customers for international banking skills and expertise has grown to match their global business outlook. What has changed in the commercial bank, therefore, is not the activity of international banking, but rather the bankers who are now doing it. For many banks, it is the domestic banker.

Federal Reserve Board Chairman Greenspan described this change to Congress: "The international role of the [U.S.] banks has changed from one of simply extending credit to one of facilitating transactions... U.S. banks have tended to cut back on those activities that result in assets that must be booked on a balance sheet. For example, they have chosen to reduce drastically their interbank lending business, which is essentially a high-volume, low-spread business. U.S. banks have devoted their resources instead to banking services that often do not result in assets held by the bank. These activities, such as risk-management involving relatively high-tech, sophisticated products, are also the areas in which U.S. banks remain among the world's leaders."[2]

Whether today's domestic bankers want to or not, they must understand international risks if they are to serve their customers' needs and reflect their banks' policies and goals. There are no longer as many international banking specialists to carry that burden.

U.S. banks do not have a monopoly in their own country. As the 1990s begin, the reality is that 20 percent of lending to U.S. businesses is already being done by foreign banks. While the U.S. bank may have decided to reduce or withdraw from the supposed perils of the international arena, the foreign banker is ready to offer such services to local U.S. customers. This competitor is not thousands of miles away; it is already established for business in the U.S.

Who, therefore, is today's international banker? It is every banker who has a customer doing business in the global marketplace.

It is increasingly difficult to continue thinking of domestic and international business as separate activities. The U.S. company has only one financial statement that interlocks its domestic and foreign risks. Managing foreign exchange risk, for example, is as integral a part of corporate finance today as managing the accounts receivable. The president of one major investment banking firm "recalls that the 'single best thing' [it] ever did was to abolish its international division in the late 1970s, telling all those running a business that they were responsible for it worldwide."[3] The reality of today is that "firms compete with truly global strategies involving selling worldwide, sourcing components and materials worldwide, and locating activities in many nations to take advantage of low cost factors. They form alliances with firms from other nations to gain access to their strengths."[4]

Businesses think globally; their bankers must do no less. This is a challenge for bankers of this decade and the focus of this book. In the chapters that follow we shall examine what all bankers, whether they consider themselves to be domestic or international, need to know today about global banking.

Notes

1. *Los Angeles Times*, "America's Import Addiction," November 19, 1989, p. D1.

2. Statement, April 4, 1990. *Federal Reserve Bulletin*, June 1990, p. 441.

3. *The Economist*, September 30, 1989, p. 86.

4. Michael E. Porter, *The Competitive Advantage of Nations* (New York: The Free Press, 1990), p. 14.

1

The World of International Banking

No modern nation can prosper relying solely on its own resources—mineral, human, manufacturing, or capital. Transactions, with other countries, therefore, are a national business necessity. Adam Smith writing in *The Wealth of Nations* in 1776 commented: "When the produce of any particular branch of industry exceeds what the demand of the country requires, the surplus must be sent abroad and exchanged for something for which there is a demand at home. Without such exportation a part of the productive labour of the country must cease, and the value of its annual produce diminish."[1] Professor Michael Porter's description of the modern world in 1990 is remarkably similar: "No nation can be competitive in (and be a net exporter of) everything. A nation's pool of human and other resources is necessarily limited. . . . A nation can thereby specialize in those industries and segments in which its firms are relatively more productive and import those products and services where its firms are less productive than foreign rivals, in this way raising the average productivity level in the economy. Imports, then, as well as exports, are integral to productive growth."[2]

A nation's international economic activities are broadly grouped into three categories: the movement of goods (raw materials, manufactured goods), the movement of services (engineering, scientific, personal, processing), and the movement of capital (from long-term plant investments to short-term financing). Because the bank's customers are engaged in such activities, the banker is asked to provide the skills and products that those customers need in order to do their business. This is the basis for the myriad array of international banking products. Banks and businesses both benefit when the banker offers the products the customer needs. The determination of which products a bank should offer begins with examining what that bank's customers do, what they need, then what products and services the banker has to meet those needs, and lastly how to deliver the products to the customers.

One of the myths about international banking has been that only a bank with a network of overseas branches and a large staff can furnish the services a customer may need. This is not so. Every bank, no matter what its size, can meet the needs of its local customers through a knowledgeable local banker and the technical operational capacity of a correspondent bank.

This chapter will examine the background activity out of which the needs from customers will develop. In the chapters that follow, you will examine the individual products that compose international banking. Even though these are discussed as a series of separate topics, they are, in business practice, interrelated and interdependent. To put these into practice requires the banker's ability to recognize and apply them to the particular customer's needs. Even though we will speak of what "nations" do, one should remember that "Firms, not nations, compete in international markets."[3]

The objectives of this chapter are to
- describe the history of business transactions between nations
- survey the basic international activities in which customers are engaged
- introduce basic definitions that form the basis of the language of international banking

HISTORY

The history of trade parallels the history of human development. "Archeologists have . . . concluded that the people of [9000 years ago] traded goods across long distances. It has been possible. . . to trace the obsidian trade more or less all over the Near East . . . [and] through the analysis of trace elements in pottery to identify the pottery's origin and conclude that it was made and traded out of a particular central site."[4] Within the span of written knowledge there is vast evidence that the spread of trade has been a catalyst for development, change, and the rising standard of living.

In the sixteenth and seventeenth centuries the Portuguese, Dutch, and British went to Asia, initially to trade for spices, later building what were to become colonial bases in order to monop-olize and develop the sources of supply. Along the way they traded textiles from India for pepper in Sumatra and then other spices, coral, elephants, and silk to Europe. This trade interlock-ed with trade for other goods from the Baltic and from America as Venice, Amsterdam, and London became great trading centers and subsequently financing centers.[5] Trade was big business.

"Until about 1670 the Dutch East India Company was the richest corporation in the world. . . . [It] mustered 150 trading ships and 40 ships of war, with 20,000 sailors, 10,000 soldiers and nearly 50,000 civilians on its payroll."[6] With trade automat-ically went finance and credit.

In the seventeenth, eighteenth, and nineteenth centuries one of the great trade commodities was tea. A look at some of the details of this commerce, which eventually was to have such an impact on the American Colonies, shows how trade in one commodity affected the growth of other industries and how these changed the ways people lived.

Tea replaced wine as the everyday temperate drink when a cheap supply of a sweetener became available. Before sugar was plentiful, the tea drinker relied on a very limited supply of honey. Sugar cane at that time could be grown on a large scale only in the tropics, but for Europeans to be able to live and work there, a control for malaria, which was widespread, was needed. The discovery in 1638 by the court physician to the Spanish Viceroy in Lima of the native Andean bark, quinquina (quinine), made control of this disease possible.

Once tea trade began on a large scale, other trade developed. Porcelain, for example, came to Europe in quantity because ships bringing tea and silk from China needed ballast, provided by the porcelain which helped improve the stability of ships. With 4,000 tons of tea being imported each year in the eighteenth century into England, 240 tons of porcelain were simultaneously being imported (at an average 2.8 ounces per piece).[7]

Trade with Asia traditionally demanded gold and silver for payment. "China and India [became] bottomless pits for the precious metals in circulation."[8] Thus the silver and gold mines of the Americas became crucial for Europe's ability to buy from Asia. Europe paid for these metals, and for tobacco, by selling the colonists processed goods, such as furniture, and foods, among which was tea.

This trend has continued. In 1989 world trade was $3.1 trillion. "The volume of world trade rose by 50 percent in the last decade and by about 75 percent in dollar terms."[9] Of this total,

20 industrial countries accounted for over $2 trillion, with the United States being the world's largest importer and exporter. In the U.S. and most industrialized countries, this trade is generally conducted by individuals and companies. In some other countries it is done by government entities, such as government-owned development banks, utilities, steel companies, and so forth.

VISIBLE TRADE

Trade between nations takes place today for a number of reasons. This movement of goods, whether raw materials or manufactured goods, is referred to as *visible* trade. It consists of *imports* (what a nation buys from abroad) and *exports* (what a nation sells abroad). A nation pays money for its imports; it earns money from its exports. Obviously one nation's imports are another nation's exports; one nation's income is another nation's expense. The principal reasons for trade are as follows:

A nation does not have a particular item. For example, the United States still does not grow tea or cocoa. For people in the United States to have these commodities, the country must buy them from countries that do grow them. The same is true for every country and for a whole range of foods and minerals that are unevenly distributed in the world. Some countries manufacture specialized goods and can sell them to those that do not manufacture them. Agriculture, mining, and manufacturing require many different resources, and therefore trade to acquire what one needs but does not have is an absolute necessity for all countries. No modern nation can completely eliminate foreign trade. In fact, nations that actively import and export generally have higher standards of living than those who, for political or cultural reasons, limit foreign trade to a bare minimum. Complete self-sufficiency has few benefits.

A nation does not have enough of a particular item. The United States grows some coffee beans and sugar beets, but not enough to meet its internal demands. Some countries have large iron ore reserves but only small coal deposits. In this case they must trade in order to have the capability to produce steel.

A nation can produce an item at a lower cost than can other nations. Economic theory suggests that foreign trade should take place because one nation has a comparative advantage in producing an item. Thus, each nation should produce what it most efficiently can and trade the surplus for another nation's product. In recent years internal political pressures have often made this difficult to do. Part of the problem has been assessing whether one country's lower cost is the result of more efficient production or because of favorable tax or subsidy treatment by a government.

A nation produces items with a desirable style or innovation. In the United States many consumers prefer foreign-made automobiles or electronic products. Both are produced in the United States, but the consumer's selection is based on a style preference or innovative feature. Sometimes an item labeled "finest imported" is bought solely on snob appeal.

Features of Trade

The difference between what a nation imports and exports is its *balance of trade*. When a nation buys more than it sells, it is said to have an "unfavorable" or "deficit" balance of trade; when it sells more than it buys, it has a "favorable" or "surplus" balance of trade. A favorable balance of trade brings with it net international income.

A nation often has a choice about where to obtain its imports. This *direction of trade* can be determined by availability, comparative cost from each source of supply, or political factors such as alliances or former colonial ties. The former colonies of England and France continue to do much of their trade with their previous colonial rulers because of long-standing relationships, established customer preferences, or reduced tariffs granted by the former parent country. Other factors such as regional animosity or availability of transportation affects the pattern of trade. "Even though a number of East African nations have a preferential trade agreement, jealousies are pervasive. Thus neighboring Tanzania prefers to buy its sports equipment in Europe rather than 'make Kenya rich' [a Kenyan trader] said. 'They pay 45 percent more for Adidas in Europe, and then the freight back, even though the products are made next door'.... Also the idea of doing business across the continent—from Kenya in the east to the Ivory Cost in the west [is almost impossible]. 'If I want to export to the Ivory Coast, it's often easier out of Paris'.... There is no direct flight to the Ivory Coast from Kenya."[10]

Trade Protectionism

When a country determines that it wishes to reduce imports, it may do so by imposing a *tariff* or a *quota*. A tariff is a tax levied by a government on imported goods. Thus, a buyer of an import will have to pay the seller's price plus a charge to the government.

The intent is to raise the overall price to such an extent that the buyer will not purchase the foreign-made goods because of their high price. If the buyer still makes the purchase, then the government has produced income for itself. A quota is a limit on the absolute amount of a particular product that can be imported. The intent is to prevent the local buyer from having access to foreign-made goods. In some cases the effect of a quota or tariff can be accomplished indirectly. "If a powerful government is worried about the harm imports are doing to its producers. . . it requires another government, on pain of retaliation, to restrict its country's exports of the good in question."[11] Both the tariff and the quota will protect the domestic industry and encourage the purchase of its goods rather than those made in other countries.

Governments have other means to discourage imports or raise their cost, such as requiring the importer to deposit the money in advance, imposing surcharges, and conducting special inspections. France, for example, tried to discourage imports of VCRs by requiring that each machine be inspected several hundred miles inland from the port by a small staff of examiners.

Trade protectionism is as much a complex political decision as an economic one. One historic argument in support of trade barriers is to shelter infant industries. This means giving a new industry a chance to develop within the country before having to compete against similar imported goods from another country where the industry may be established and able to sell at a lower cost. The problem becomes how long to continue this and the difficulty in identifying at what point it is no longer an infant industry but has become instead inefficient.

Likewise, foreign trade protectionism may be sought to counteract sales by foreign producers who are perceived to be receiving government subsidies or other unfair economic support that might lead to the destruction of a domestic industry. The term *dumping* is used to describe such sales. It can become very difficult to differentiate between dumping and the results of comparative efficiency. Strong political forces can be marshalled to support protectionism. When protection is maintained for a long period it can encourage high costs and inefficient local businesses who thrive behind such trade walls. Thus, any protection, whether through tariffs, quotas, or administrative means, has a cost to consumers and consequently to a country's economy. It can also lead to the development of new, or reestablished, industries in a country, which in time can compete locally and internationally, thereby benefitting a country's economy.

Nations apply different tariff rates to similar goods coming from two different countries. When nation A says it is granting country B *most favored nation* status, it means it is applying the tariff rate that it grants to its most favored trading partner, in other words, the lowest tariff it gives any nation. It is usually reciprocal. "That does not mean that B's tariffs will be identical to A's, merely that neither will give an advantage to any third country in the tariffs they impose on each other's products."[12]

Reducing imports can also be a goal when the country needs to reduce its foreign expenditures. Some goods are imported, however, to be processed into other goods, which are then exported. The United States facilitates this by giving a rebate, called *drawback*, of almost all of the tariff paid.

Effect of Trade

Exports and imports affect the economies of both the selling country and the buying country. The economic calculation for a country's gross national product (GNP) includes the net difference between exports and imports. For many countries, international trade is of greater consequence to their economy than it has been for the United States, where exports are only 8 percent of the GNP. For comparison, in recent years it was 15 percent for Japan; between 24 and 27 percent for Great Britain, Canada, Italy, and France; and 31 percent for West Germany.[13]

Imports and exports have both benefits and costs. A nation that generates exports creates jobs in its own economy. If a particular industry, such as steel, can export part of its output, then its cost per ton of steel may be lower because it can spread fixed costs over a larger production. This can benefit its domestic sales. The global market for a product can be very competitive, since some countries will subsidize an industry's costs in order to maintain a market share. It may have no other item to sell internationally to earn foreign currency, or it may want to keep local employment high, calculating that it is cheaper to do this than to pay the economic and political costs of domestic unemployment. Such subsidies end up being paid by the taxpayer.

Imports can benefit a country by supplying goods or commodities that it may not have or may not have enough of. When imports are cheaper than similar locally produced goods, the buyers benefit from the lower price. But the local competing industry will suffer through unemployment or low wages. This can be offset if there are new industries to provide employment for those displaced. The United States has had to wrestle with these competing effects in industries such as steel, copper, and other basic industries.

INVISIBLE TRADE

In addition to international trade in commodities and manufactured goods, there also exists trade in services, often referred to as *invisible* trade, which was estimated in 1989 to be "$680 billion, or nearly one-fifth of total world exports."[14]

One type of invisible trade is *transportation*. For example, when a tobacco farmer in Virginia sells the crop to a buyer in Great Britain, arrangements must be made to ship the tobacco from the seller to the buyer. The cheapest method for such bulk shipments is by ocean vessel. Many nations, such as Hong Kong and Norway, have large maritime fleets that provide such transport service. Space in an ocean vessel is rented for the cargo, and payment is made to the maritime nation for the service. The nation owning the vessel earns money by providing this service, just as it would if it had exported a commodity.

Insurance is another invisible trade item. While at sea, a cargo is vulnerable to many dangers, the most obvious of which is the ship's sinking. Cargo can also be damaged from leaking pipes or an accident at an intermediate port. To protect against financial loss from such occurrences, the international trader purchases insurance. Some nations, such as Great Britain with its Lloyd's of London, are major providers of maritime insurance. Again, the country providing the insurance earns money from this service, just as if it had sold a commodity.

Some countries do not have commodities to sell abroad, but they do have a healthy and attractive climate, preserved antiquities, unique vistas, or superior sporting locations that bring tourists from other countries. For example, during the winter the warm climate and attractive beaches of The Bahamas, Mexico, and the Caribbean countries attract many visitors from the northern United States. The money that tourists spend for hotel accommodations, restaurants, and personal purchases is another example of invisible trade. *Tourism* is estimated to be a $750 billion-a-year business, and it includes not only vacationers but also the business traveler. Tourist travel is very sensitive to political instability. Many countries have suffered sudden declines in the number of foreign visitors, and the consequent earnings, when there is an industrial accident, internal political violence, or war. The growth of international tourism expanded with the development of package tours in the 1960s, which combined charter flights and hotel block bookings to create

America's Place in the World

America remains the largest single participant in world commerce, though not by much. In 1987 our $410 billion of imports and $251 billion of exports accounted for 15 percent of the world's recorded international merchandise trade. America's share of world trade has declined irregularly ever since the end of World War II as other major trading nations have completed their postwar reconstruction programs and then gone on to achieve faster rates of overall economic growth, built in many cases around a special emphasis on producing for export. Even so, West Germany, the second largest participant in world trade, still accounted for only 14 percent in 1987, and Japan, the next largest, for just 9 percent. Though American exports have stagnated, our total international trade flows—including both exports and imports—remain the largest for any country, and by a sizable margin.

Moreover, because global trade patterns are uneven, America bulks especially large as a trading partner for particular countries and regions. Our $85 billion of imports from Japan in 1987 represented more than a third of Japan's total merchandise exports. The $74 billion of goods we bought from Canada accounted for more than three-fourths of all Canada's exports. Even for western Europe, which is far less dependent on sales to this country, America's $96 billion of imports in 1987 accounted for about a fifth of the total merchandise exports for the region considered as a whole.

The swing in America's trade balance required to stabilize our net international debt will amount to about 5 percent of our total income if the adjustment to a new equilibrium takes place by the end of the decade, and still more if—as is likely—it takes longer. In the context of the trade flows that occurred in 1987, a change equal to 5 percent of our income would have meant an American export-import *surplus* of some $65 billion instead of a $159 billion deficit. To have effected such an adjustment, we would have had to import $224 billion less or export $224 billion more or done some combination of the two. By 1990 or even later, the dollar totals involved will be correspondingly greater.

An adjustment in America's trade flows on this scale will not only lower our standard of living but also impose major burdens on many, if not most, other countries participating in international commerce. For some of these countries the implications of this realignment are profoundly threatening. Much of the prosperity of Japan and the newly industrialized Asian countries has resulted from their ability to sell to American buyers a large share of what they produce overall. In 1987 exports to America equaled more than a fifth of total economywide production in the four

Continued

economies of scale, thereby reducing the individual's costs.[15] Airlines and governments have also been major forces in expanding world tourism by creating new tourist complexes, the former to generate more ticket sales for their flights, the latter to expand earnings in foreign currencies.

Remittances, such as from immigrants and temporary workers, are another item in invisible trade that have been quite important for some countries. The United States has been described as a nation of immigrants. Many Americans regularly send money to relatives in the "old country." The past three

"Asian tigers": Taiwan, South Korea, Hong Kong, and Singapore. Canada is likewise dependent on U.S. markets, so much so that the two countries are for many practical purposes economically integrated. Even in western Europe, the industries that sell to American markets are in some cases heavily dependent on those sales, even if their economies more broadly are not. A dramatic decline in our imports from any of those countries would remove a basic pillar supporting their prosperity.

Eventually of course, these countries will presumably be able to redeploy their productive resources. But because of the huge amounts involved, what is at stake is more than the ordinary ebb and flow of world commerce. The implosion of our trade deficit from $26 billion in 1980 to $159 billion in 1987 bankrupted American companies, displaced American workers, in some cases eliminated entire industries, and depressed whole regions of the country. Reversing the process, and then some, by cutting back our imports by enough to deliver a substantial trade surplus, is likely to have corresponding effects on export industries abroad. And because no other country is as large as America and few countries are as economically diversified, balancing the damage to some industries against gains elsewhere will doubtless be an even more difficult challenge than it has been here.

These problems will be even more staggering for the 50 or so developing countries that already carry excessive debts denominated not in their own currencies but in dollars. The largest of these debtors, and the only ones whose defaults could plausibly endanger the world's financial structure, are in Latin America. These countries depend especially heavily on U.S. markets to earn dollars to service their debts. Brazil, for example, which suspended all interest payments to its foreign creditors in February 1987 (and then resumed payments a year later, after receiving a new $6 billion package of bank loans), heads the list of developing country debtors with $110 billion owed abroad. The $8 billion of goods we imported from Brazil in 1987 accounted for more than a fourth of Brazil's total exports. Mexico, with $100 billion of foreign debt, has thus far kept its payments current but only through an extraordinary series of special arrangements coordinated and supported by the U.S. government. In 1987 the United States imported $20 billion of goods (about half of which was oil and gas) from Mexico, accounting for more than two-thirds of Mexico's entire exports.

Portions of pp. 52-55 reprinted with permission of Benjamin M. Friedman, *Day of Reckoning* (New York: Random House, 1988).

decades have seen workers from Turkey going to work in Western Europe, from Southern Europe and Middle Eastern countries to work on construction projects in the Arabian peninsula, and from Latin America to work in the United States. These workers send money home to support their families. In some instances this has been a country's largest source of foreign revenue, and when work was no longer available, severe economic shock hits the workers' home country.

Invisible trade also occurs when one nation hires engineers and technicians from another country to plan and supervise the construction of large development projects such as dams, highways, and ports. These workers receive salaries and commissions for their services; their company receives fees. Likewise, banks earn fees by providing financial advisory services. Other sources of invisible trade include licensing fees for patents, motion picture rentals, dividends and interest from investments, and computer services.

INVESTMENTS

Of considerable importance to the world economy is the flow of investments. International investments represent the transfer of savings from one country to another where they are used for economic development that might otherwise not be possible because of the lack of savings in the second country.

Investments may take many forms. The money may be sent from one country, for example, for constructing a manufacturing plant, building a power generator, or developing a mine in another country. This is *direct investment.* The investors expect that the new manufacturing plant will in the future become profitable, after which they will receive a flow of dividends as their profit. Ultimately they may sell the plant and receive a higher price than they spent because the plant is now a profitable going concern. Everyone benefits from such investments. The investor shows a profit. The investor's country has a stream of income in future years. The receiving country gets the financial means to create a new manufacturing plant that will create jobs, perhaps increase exports or reduce imports, and represent wealth to that country. Singapore is a good example: "Foreign-owned companies accounted for 55% of Singapore's employment in the manufacturing industry . . . 63% of its manufacturing output and 90% of its exports of manufactured goods."[16]

Unlike a loan, a direct investment will not be paid back until it becomes profitable. Direct investments may be made to assure a source of supply of a raw material, to locate a plant inside a country in order to hold or gain a share of that market, or to take advantage of lower production costs made possible by lower labor costs, tax incentives, or proximity to a source of supply. "Debt can safely be used to finance investment only if the investment generates the revenues that will be needed to repay the loan."[17]

Another form of investment is *indirect* or *portfolio* investment. This may be for the purchase of shares of stocks or bonds that in turn provide funds to a business. Individuals or financial institutions may do this to acquire an asset with a higher yield than they could get in their own country, considering the dividends, the expected increased market value of the stock, and in some cases the appreciation of the value of the foreign currency in which the stock or bond has been issued.

Another reason for investing may be for *humanitarian* or *national security* purposes. These do not necessarily carry an expectation of a monetary profit and are usually made by governments instead of corporations or individuals.

BALANCE OF PAYMENTS

All of the foregoing activities take place continuously and represent flows of funds into and out of each country. To keep track of the impact of these flows in both directions, each nation records its *balance of payments.* A balance of payments shows a country's receipts from, and payments to, all other countries during a period of time.

Table 1.1 shows the activities represented in a balance of payments. The importance of the balance of payments is that it reflects how money earned in any category is available for any type of international expenditure. For example, a country that earns money from foreign tourists can use it to import raw materials; or an inflow of investment money for building a new factory can pay for machinery imports for that factory. The assessment of the balance of payments is discussed in greater detail in chapter 3.

Table 1.1 Activities Represented in a Balance of Payments

Income	*Payments*
Received for:	**Made for:**
Exports	Imports
Services we do for others	Services others do for us
Foreign tourists visting us	Our tourists in other countries
Money sent by people in other countries	Money sent to people in other countries
Others' investments in our country	Our investments in other country
Interest and dividends on our investments in other countries	Interest and dividends on others' investments in our country

The United States' Situation

The United States has had a substantial annual trade deficit for many years. Attempts to reduce this have been made through varied programs to restrict imports and encourage exports. Part of the problem in reducing imports is that "intra-company transactions represented about 17% of the nation's imports in recent years."[18] This is because for decades U.S. corporations have made direct investments in manufacturing plants overseas, in many cases to reduce their overall cost of a finished product by making components in lower-cost production areas and then centrally assembling them in another country.

These direct investments are part of the total U.S. investments in other countries that amounted to $1.25 trillion in 1988. In comparison, foreign investments in the United States were $1.8 trillion, of which the British are the largest direct investors followed by Japan, Holland, Canada, West Germany, and France.[19]

"In service trade, the deficit is growing the same way because Americans are beginning to pay foreigners more in interest, fees, royalties, rents, dividends and profits than they collect abroad. This trade in services—or 'invisibles,' as they are also called—had produced a surplus each year since 1970, as much as $35 billion in 1981 and still more than $6 billion [in 1987]. The crossover to a deficit came in [1988's] first quarter. The deficit was about $4 billion and the trend was clear."[20]

DEVELOPED AND DEVELOPING COUNTRIES

International bankers use economists' terms to refer to groups of countries. There are *developed* countries and *developing* countries. Expressions that are applied to the latter also include *underdeveloped country, less developed country (LDC), third-world country,* or *capital-importing developing country.* It is not always clear precisely which countries are being referred to. As a guide, the International Monetary Fund uses the term *industrial countries* to refer to the 23 member countries (Western Europe, Australia, Canada, Japan, New Zealand, United States). All others are *developing countries,* which it subdivides as either net creditors (8 countries) or net debtors (124 countries).[21]

Developing countries tend to be exporters of agricultural products or ore from mines. They generally are buyers of manufactured goods. Their economic development depends on them being able to produce more of these manufactured goods themselves. Developed countries generally have the capability to produce their own manufactured goods, while at the same time a number of them, such as the United States, are also major agricultural producers and exporters.

Since World War II there has been the assumption that moving from the status of a developing country to a developed country was a desirable goal. Such change has generally involved movement of people from the countryside where they practiced agriculture and mined ores to cities where factories were located. The benefits of such movement have not been without social costs, usually evidenced by the slums that surround most large cities in the developing countries, pollution, and the disruption of political and social structures. Moving an economy from a developing to a developed status has turned out to be more complex than many realized. "Carried away by the power of money to finance great capital undertakings, many people seem to think of such investments as being development itself. Build the dam and you have development! But in real life, build the dam and unless you also have solvent city markets and transplanted industries, you have nothing."[22] In subsequent chapters, we shall see how this has affected international banking.

SUMMARY

International banking exists to meet the needs of the bank's customers. These customers have business needs as they deal in a global economy. Newspaper stories and television reports of an international debt crisis do not change the fact that international business continues and is growing in many different ways. International trade continues to be a necessity, the growth of services may be expanding at an even faster rate, and investments continue unabated.

Because these customer needs are undiminished, the commercial banker must be able to respond. The world economy is becoming so interconnected that the banker cannot easily say where the domestic needs of a customer stop and the international needs begin.

The chapters that follow discuss the specialties that make up the world of international banking so that you can meet your customers' needs. When you have finished you should be able to answer four basic questions:

- What activities are my customers engaged in globally?

- Because they are, what services do they need from a bank in order to conduct their business?

- What products do banks have to meet these needs?

- How do we deliver these products to the customer to meet those needs?

Your customer may be a business, an individual, another bank, or even a government. Regardless of the size of your bank, your customer needs services and products from you.

QUESTIONS
1. Why does trade take place between countries?
2. What is invisible trade?
3. Why are foreign investments important to countries?
4. What is a tariff?

PROBLEM

Identify 10 items in your home that are imported. Are these items also made in the United States? If so, would you ever be willing to purchase them? If not, why not?

Notes

1.   Adam Smith, *An Inquiry into the Nature and Causes of the Wealth of Nations* (London: Strahan & Cadell, 1776). Reprint (London: Penguin Books Ltd., 1970), p. 472.

2.   Michael Porter, *The Competitive Advantage of Nations* (New York: The Free Press, 1990), p. 7.

3.   *Ibid.*, p. 33.

4.   *The New York Times*, "Prehistoric Society: A New Picture Emerges," December 16, 1986, p. 17.

5.   Fernand Braudel, *The Perspective of the World* (New York: Harper and Row, 1984).

6.   Henry Hobhouse, *Seeds of Change* (London: Sidgwick & Jackson, 1985), p. 100.

7.   *Ibid.*, p. 108; chapters 1, 2, 3.

8.   Fernand Braudel, *The Perspective of the World* (New York: Harper and Row, 1984).

9.   *The New York Times*, November 29, 1990, p. C13.

10. *The New York Times*, August 24, 1990, p. C2.

11. *The Economist,* Survey of World Trade, September 22, 1990, p. 8.

12. Rupert Pennant-Rea and Bill Emmott, *The Pocket Economist* (New York: Cambridge University Press, 1983), p. 121.

13. *The New York Times*, "Backdrop for the Debate," May 3, 1985, p. 6.

14. *The New York Times*, November 29, 1990, p. C13.

15. *The Economist*, October 16, 1982, pp. 118-119.

16.   *The Economist*, November 26, 1988, p. 73.

17.   The World Bank, *World Development Report 1990* (Washington, D.C.: Oxford University Press, 1990), p. 14.

18.   *The New York Times*, March 26, 1989, p . 13.

19.   *The New York Times*, June 13, 1990, p. C2.

20.   *The New York Times*, August 17, 1988, p. C2.

21.   International Monetary Fund, *World Economic Outlook, October 1990*, pp. 105-107. Since most of the communist countries were not IMF members they are not included in the country totals.

22.   Jane Jacobs, *Cities and the Wealth of Nations* (New York: Random House, 1984), p. 105.

2

Organization of U.S. Banks

" As with most other businesses, the size, nature, and strategies of banks are strongly affected by the needs and interests of customers. Consequently, banks have generally followed, rather than led their customers abroad."[1]

Before the enactment of the Federal Reserve Act in 1913, national banks had no authority to establish foreign operations or to accept drafts arising from international trade. Customers needing international banking services went to the few state-chartered banks that had overseas branches, to foreign banks, or to merchant banks. "During the nineteenth century London's merchant banks, while continuing to remain the foreign traders' chief source of commercial credits, also emerged as the dominant force in international finance."[2] It was not until after World War II that U.S. commercial banks began to expand their international capabilities with an array of organizational structures.

A bank may organize itself in a number of ways to conduct international activities. These ways include the establishment of international departments, overseas branches, Edge Act corporations, foreign representative offices, subsidiaries, and joint ventures. The appropriate combination of the many available elements will vary among banks, depending on the needs of a bank's customers and management's decision on how best to serve these needs. Even if a bank now has no international structure of its own, the account officer with a domestic customer can serve that customer's global needs through the bank's domestic correspondent banking relationships that have an international organization.

No matter how large and important an international department may become, it is still part of the parent banking institution; its operations must comply rather than conflict with the objectives of that bank. Presumably, the bank's paramount purpose is to combine service to customers with profit for stockholders. Consequently, the international department should not engage in exotic services for which its community has no need, nor should it permit the glamour of far-flung overseas relationships to obscure their possibly disproportionate cost.

The international activities of a commercial bank are combined with its domestic business into a single financial statement. Bank regulators apply ratios to the total bank to measure the adequacy of the level of the bank's capital to its assets. With the change to the risk-based capital guidelines (see appendix D), a greater number of international activities will be brought into that calculation. Bank management will need to assess their international business ventures and the borrower's country, not only for the present risk criteria and costs, but also for their differing impact on the level of bank capital each will require.

The objectives of this chapter are to
- describe the various organizational elements available to a bank for international banking
- analyze the advantages of these
- describe the placement of international activities in a bank's financial statement

---

INTERNATIONAL DEPARTMENTS

The move into international banking begins with establishing a section or department in the bank's head office for handling international business transactions. The organization of this international department should be tailored to meet particular needs. It may be small, with every individual capable of performing nearly every task, or it may be large and highly specialized. In any case, the international department must have a single responsible head with enough knowledge to coordinate the activities of the department as it expands and with the authority to share in the formulation of bank policy.

Until the volume of business becomes substantial, the international department can use the bank's existing domestic facilities. For example, domestic collection clerks can handle international collections until there are enough such collections to justify the assignment of personnel solely to international transactions. Foreign sections in the bookkeeping and audit-control divisions of the domestic organization are relatively easy to create. Use of the protection arrangements of large banks should make possible the maximum expansion of a money transfer capacity with minimum investment of time and capital. Unsuccessful and costly experiences can be avoided by proceeding slowly in the expansion of an international department.

Most banks active in international banking develop international departments in their head offices. Comparatively few of these banks establish overseas branches or Edge Act corporations, and then only after they have developed active international departments at home.

The international department of a bank active in overseas business is a miniature bank. An international department carries on nearly every operation performed by a commercial bank engaged in domestic banking. It accepts deposits and maintains its own deposits in other institutions. It pays checks against the accounts on its books and draws against its own funds abroad. It receives and pays out cash, makes funds transfers, has a collection section dealing with both incoming and outgoing items, lends money to its local customers and to borrowers abroad, and maintains credit information and correspondent bank relations.

All these functions have their counterparts, usually on a larger scale, in the bank's domestic activities, but an international department also handles numerous transactions with which the domestic divisions do not ordinarily have any contact. Among such transactions are the opening and negotiating of commercial letters of credit, trading in foreign exchange, purchase and sale of foreign currency banknotes, creation of bankers' acceptances, and lending to borrowers in other countries.

Examining an international department's operations reveals the kinds of the services it offers its customers. The international department can have a number of sections that carry on its major activities. The more important and active parts of the international department are examined in greater detail in succeeding chapters; these show not only what the various sections of the department do but also how they can serve the customer.

FOREIGN BRANCHES

U.S. banks were slow to develop foreign branches for several reasons. First, it was not until the passage of the Federal Reserve Act in 1913 that national banks were clearly permitted to establish foreign branches. Before that time, the few overseas branches that did exist had been formed under state banking laws. Second, the United States was a debtor country, with much of its developmental capital coming from foreign banks. Even though the foreign trade of the United States expanded after the Civil War, it was being financed by European banks that had well-established techniques and capabilities for financing trade, including accepting bills drawn on them.[3]

The first overseas office of a U.S. commercial bank was opened in 1887. By 1967, 15 U.S. banks had established a total of 295 branches overseas. Three of these banks accounted for approximately 75 percent of the branches. By the end of 1989 133 U.S. banks "were operating 845 branches in foreign countries and overseas areas of the United States."[4] This represented a decline from the peak in the early 1980s of 166 banks and a total of 917 branches.[5]

U.S. banks now have branches in virtually every foreign market. Many banks with only a few overseas branches have located these in the major money centers such as London or in locations like The Bahamas or the Cayman Islands, where laws permit a branch to be established at a low cost for special purposes. Many branches offer a full range of banking services to individuals and to local and U.S. companies. Some countries, however, prohibit U.S. banks from offering certain services, such as taking deposits. Likewise, some countries require that U.S. banks establish separate subsidiaries instead of a branch. Regardless of the form, to open a branch or subsidiary in another country, the U.S. bank must obtain permission of the host government as well as approval of the Board of Governors of the Federal Reserve System.

U.S. banks have expanded their overseas branch systems to serve clients whose foreign activities are increasing and, in many cases, to compete with local banks for local business. One incentive for the development of overseas branches in the 1950s and 1960s was the increasing amount of U.S. government funds held abroad, much of it generated by Public Law 480 (the law governing sales of U.S. surplus agricultural commodities payable in foreign currencies). While these funds could be deposited in central banks or private foreign banks, federal law required that if U.S. banking facilities were available they should be used as depositories.

The foreign branch must comply with all the banking rules, exchange controls, and regulations of the host country and is subject to examination by both the host country and U.S. banking authorities. U.S. banking regulations permit overseas branches more freedom than their head offices have. For example, overseas branches do not maintain reserves in a Federal Reserve Bank against their deposits (Federal Reserve Regulation D), may pay interest on demand deposits, and can issue certain guarantees, such as shipside bonds (see chapter 8), which the bank may not do in the United States. Deposits in overseas branches are not insured by the FDIC.

In most cases a branch's capital is segregated from that of its parent bank. The branch resembles a small unit bank in its operations. The branch must do its own hiring, complying with all the local labor laws and union regulations. Most overseas staff members are hired locally, and all, including the few officers from the head office, are expected to be fluent in both the local language and English. The branch clears its checks directly with the local clearing house, if one exists, or directly with other banks. Deposits at that branch are subject to local regulations. The branch is responsible for maintenance of premises, construction, and printing of forms and stationery. It deals in the local money market for placement of its short-term cash surplus and maintains reserves at the central bank. It must also comply with all the reporting requirements of the country's regulatory agencies.

These are just a few of the problems for which the local overseas manager is responsible. In the United States, most of these problems are handled by the head office on behalf of all its branches. In addition to all of the administrative responsibilities of operating the branch, the overseas manager is also the parent bank's representative in the foreign country, a position that necessitates attendance at official and nonofficial functions. The hours the overseas branch manager must devote to the job far exceed those of a domestic branch manager. With all this, the branch's basic objective is still to show a profit.

The overseas branch of a U.S. bank has a dual function. It is a foreign bank competing with the local banks in the local market for local customers. The lobby traffic in an overseas branch can often exceed what a banker is accustomed to in his own head office. In addition, it is the local link in the parent bank's international chain of offices. It is generating international financial business for its system and serves the bank's customers from other markets.

SHELL BRANCHES

Some overseas branches are established not for general banking in the local market but for a special purpose. Most U.S. branches in The Bahamas and Cayman Islands are domiciling units for Eurodollar deposits and loans originating through the efforts of the bank's head office or other overseas branches. They often have a tiny staff or, in some cases, only a designated local banker who serves the nominal role as manager. These are sometimes referred to as "shell branches."

Such branches, being in countries with low tax rates, can offer important tax savings for a bank. "The tax savings relate to foreign, rather than to U.S. taxes. Foreign branch. . . earnings are immediately attributable to the parent U.S. banks for U.S. tax purposes." Banks paying taxes on their earnings in some countries that have rates higher than the U.S. "attempt to lower their overall foreign tax rate by booking [some] loans in tax-free centers."[6]

Consequently, the use of these shell branches for tax or other reasons to "garage" or "warehouse" loans that originated in some other foreign country, results in misleading statistics. For example, in 1989 according to Federal Reserve figures, over 30 percent of the total U.S. foreign branch assets were in these branches, exceeding the assets in London branches.[7] By another calculation, the shell branches showed more international loans than in U.S. banking offices.[8]

RECENT CHANGES

The attractiveness of having an overseas branch has changed. The great expansion of U.S. banks with overseas branches occurred between 1968 and 1970, when the number of banks increased from 26 to 79, a period coincident with U.S. government programs for balance of payments restraint. At the end of 1981, 157 national banks had overseas branches; of these, 112 had only shell branches.[9] This indicates that the banks' interest was solely to have a Eurodollar capability and not for local or international trade development. Furthermore, two of the three banks that in 1967 accounted for 75 percent of the total branches had, between 1971 and 1977, actually reduced the number of foreign cities in which they had branches. The third bank followed this pattern shortly thereafter. It thus appears that the full-service overseas branch is an expensive and perhaps not always rewarding form of organization.[10] Since 1982 and the realization of the magnitude and consequences of the international debt crisis (see chapter 17), the number of foreign branches of U.S. banks has continued to contract. Many banks have closed or sold many of their branches. Those that remain are often concentrated in the larger business centers.

EDGE ACT CORPORATIONS

In 1919 the Federal Reserve Act was amended by the enactment of Section 25(a) to permit national banks to incorporate subsidiaries for international banking and investment. These subsidiaries are established in the United States and are called Edge Act corporations* after the bill's sponsor, Senator Walter Edge of New Jersey. Such corporations are permitted to establish domestic offices outside of their home state to transact only international business; hence, the Edge Act corporation can deal only with overseas customers and that portion of any local U.S. customer's business that is international, such as export-import financing. A number of such corporations were established immediately following the passage of the act. By the end of the 1920s, few remained. Following World War II, however, interest in Edge Act corporations revived. Edge Act corporations may be for banking or foreign investment purposes. Some banks therefore have one for each purpose. Banking Edge Act corporations constitute the majority by number and over 90 percent of the total by assets.

The International Banking Act of 1978 restated the purposes of Edge Act corporations in broad terms, with emphasis on these entities as a major instrument for U.S. competition in international finance and trade:

> [W]ith powers sufficiently broad to enable them to compete effectively with similar foreign-owned institutions in the United States and abroad; to afford to the United States exporter and importer in particular, and to United States commerce, industry, and agriculture in general, at all times a means of financing international trade, especially United States exports; to foster the participation by regional and smaller banks throughout the United States in the provision of international banking and financing services to all segments of United States agriculture, commerce, and industry and, in particular, small business and farming concerns; to stimulate competition in the provision of international banking and financing services throughout the United States; and, in conjunction with each of the preceding purposes, to facilitate and stimulate the export of United States goods, wares, merchandise, commodities, and services to achieve a sound United States international trade position.[11]

---

*State-chartered banks are permitted under an earlier amendment to Section 25 to create "agreement corporations," which are very similar to Edge Act corporations. The company "agrees" with the Federal Reserve to limit its activities to those permitted to Edge Act corporations.

The majority of Edge Act corporations are located in New York City, even though the parent banks are located in other states. Through these corporations, the parent bank can offer international clients and correspondent banks the services of an office in New York City in addition to the services available in its home state, a combination of services not possible under normal branch banking permits. Edge Act banks are now also located in many other cities, such as Chicago, Miami, San Francisco, and Los Angeles.

The law requires that "an Edge must have minimum equity capital of $2 million. Combined with the legal restriction that prevents any national bank from investing more than 10 percent of its equity in Edges, this requirement effectively limits the ownership of Edges to banks with assets exceeding $300 million."[12] Although Federal Reserve Regulation K generally governs the operations of Edges, they are not members of the Federal Reserve System nor are their deposits insured by the FDIC. They are required to maintain the same level of reserves against deposits as does any national bank.

An Edge Act bank may have a small staff or a large staff of more than 500 employees. In either case it is organized as a complete bank, providing all the services of a full-size foreign department. It may also establish branches in other states. The International Banking Act of 1978 also permitted foreign banks to establish Edge Act corporations. Thus the act's restrictions on the creation of multistate branching for foreign banks are alleviated by opening to them the route of Edge Act branches with exclusive focus on international banking. At the end of 1989 there were 110 Edge Act corporations with 47 branches. This total has been declining since 1983.

The basic difference, in summary, between a branch and an Edge Act corporation of a U.S. bank is that the branch is located outside the United States, while the Edge Act corporation is in the United States.

INTERNATIONAL BANKING FACILITY

Banks in the United States have been permitted since December 1981 to establish a separate set of accounts in their domestic office in order to participate in the Eurodollar market without incurring the expense of maintaining an overseas branch. This is an *International Banking Facility* (IBF). Essentially this has the attributes of an overseas shell branch while being physically located in the United States. It may take Eurodollar deposits from nonresidents and make Eurodollar loans free of Federal Reserve regulations on reserve requirements. Facilities are also exempt from the insurance coverage and assessments imposed by the Federal Deposit Insurance Corporation.[13] An IBF may be established by any U.S. bank, Edge Act corporation, or U.S. branch or agency of a foreign bank. Federal Reserve approval is not required, merely notification in advance and agreement to comply with Federal Reserve regulations. Even though an IBF is dealing in the Eurodollar market, it is located in the United States and thus is a U.S. country risk since it is under the laws of the United States. Various states have passed laws to exempt IBFs from state taxes.

Although exempt from some Federal Reserve regulations, IBFs were from the beginning bound by others. They may "conduct business only with foreign residents (including banks), other IBFs, or the IBF's own establishing entity. . . . Credit provided to foreign nonbank customers may be used only outside the United States."[14] The purpose of this regulation is to insulate them from the U.S. market, where reserve requirements must be followed. Deposits placed by corporations must remain for a minimum of 48 hours, whereas banks in foreign countries may place overnight deposits. The deposit minimum is $100,000. IBFs may not issue negotiable instruments, such as certificates of deposit.

The advantage of a bank establishing an IBF, or several in different offices, is that it reduces expenses by sharing them with other activities of the bank. The same staff can, during the day, negotiate and process international transactions for an IBF and perform other domestic money activities for the parent bank. It is a vehicle for attracting Eurocurrency activities to the United States. Many foreign customers, however, have continued to prefer to domicile their businesses in offshore banking areas, such as The Bahamas and Cayman Islands. "An IBF may have marginal cost and administrative advantages over shell branches, but it cannot reduce a bank's overall rate of foreign tax payments. Consequently, shell branches will most likely continue to play an important role in the activities of at least the larger and more internationally active U.S. banks."[15] As of the end of 1989, there were 533 IBFs, almost half of them established in the first months that IBFs were allowed.

"An entity that establishes an IBF does not obtain any new powers by doing so. . . . In meeting loan limitation requirements, establishing entities must include loans made by the IBF."[16]

REPRESENTATIVE OFFICES

A bank often establishes a *representative office* in a foreign city, usually the capital, when it wants to have a presence there but does not have sufficient business to justify the expense of a branch, or in countries where branches may not be permitted. The bank's assigned representative is usually an experienced officer from the head office of the U.S. bank who can develop new business for the bank and whose presence in the foreign country can help customers of the bank doing business in the country. The office staff is usually very small, often consisting of only the representative, an assistant, and a secretary. Representatives cannot do any banking business, such as taking deposits or making loans, but will direct business to the head office of the bank or its branches.

In many instances, establishment of a representative office has preceded establishment of a branch. In some countries, such as Mexico, new branches of foreign banks are prohibited; hence, many U.S. banks maintain their presence in such countries through representatives who have, in many cases, comparatively large staffs.

SUBSIDIARIES AND JOINT VENTURES

In addition to overseas branches, banks have *affiliates,* which may be *subsidiaries* or *joint ventures.* A foreign subsidiary is a foreign company in which a U.S. banking organization has majority ownership or some other form of control. A joint venture is a foreign company in which the U.S. banking organization does not have a controlling interest. Such definitions differentiate the two types of entities from a bank regulatory perspective; definitions for taxing and accounting purposes may vary.

"Banks establish foreign subsidiaries to improve their competitive position, to minimize foreign tax liabilities, and to take advantage of opportunities they would otherwise miss."[17] Although most banks prefer to operate through their own branches, the subsidiary may be used where branches are not permitted in order to develop local consumer business that should have a separate identity, such as with a finance company, or to perform functions prohibited to branches. These latter include such investment activities as security underwriting.

The joint venture can be a bank established by several different banks that share ownership and, in some cases, management of the bank. The joint venture allows foreign banks with local investors to establish a presence in a country that does not encourage foreign-owned branches or to specialize in certain fields. Each shareholder provides a prorated portion of the capital for the joint venture and has a proportionate representation on the board of directors. Daily management may be provided by the shareholders, who will "lend" officers, or by one of the shareholders under a management contract, or by a manager hired from outside the member banks. The joint venture, which is often a bank, has its own name and will function as an independent bank, usually receiving only policy direction from the shareholders through the board of directors. While most joint venture banks are owned by major international banks, the joint venture also provides a way for smaller banks, which might not feel they have the expertise or capacity to be in a country on their own, to have a presence in a particular foreign market.

EXPORT TRADING COMPANY

In late 1982 U.S. banks were permitted to establish, through a bank holding company, an *export trading company* (ETC). The purpose of these companies is to improve U. S. export capability in both goods and services, with corresponding benefits for U.S. balance of payments, employment, and economic growth. A wide range of export-related services is permitted an ETC: consulting, marketing, financing, insurance, freight forwarding, warehousing, and the like. Authority to create ETCs was thought to be necessary because the U.S. export business is fragmented among a large number of small businesses. Many businesses in the United States do not now export. To encourage them to do so, an ETC can bring together many fragmented export services along with financial resources and thereby offer a business a centralized source of all it will need to engage in exporting. As of the end of 1989, 47 such ETCs existed. However, the level of activity in these has been disappointingly low.

MERCHANT BANK

Merchant bank, originally a British term, describes what in the United States is referred to as an investment bank to distinguish it from a commercial bank. A merchant bank specializes in such corporate financing needs as underwriting stocks and bonds, handling mergers and acquisitions, and undertaking a range of other financial advisory services. Its antecedents in Europe, from about the fifteenth century on, were the initial providers of international banking services before commercial banks entered the field. The original merchant banks began as commercial trading companies, which then added banking services.

"Giovanni Medici (1360-1429) . . . headed an international trading and banking company that dealt in woolens, silks, furs, and leather; invested in and supervised a variety of domestic industries; financed a miscellany of overseas commercial ventures; and provided its many clients with most of the foreign exchange, banking, and credit facilities they required . . . . The growth of commerce, both in scope and volume, made international traders increasingly dependent upon the safe and efficient transfer of funds from one principality and kingdom to another. Europe's great merchant bankers with branches and agents in distant cities, such as the Medici, with a half-dozen offices outside Italy ["Headquarters in Florence and branches in Venice, Rome, Milan, Bruges, Avignon, London, and Geneva"],[18] enjoyed the confidence of large entrepreneurs and commanded the machinery to serve them efficiently."[19]

In the nineteenth century, particularly, and even into the 1930s, the larger merchant bankers had influence and power on a scale unknown today for companies and governments, internationally and domestically. The French prime minister in 1818 would say of one of them, "There are six great powers in Europe: England, France, Prussia, Austria, Russia, and Baring Brothers."[20] "By the time of the [American] Civil War, Barings was the agent bank for Russia, Norway, Austria, Chile, Argentina, Canada, Australia, and the United States."[21]

Many of the international services that were unique to the merchant banks are now done by commercial banks, so that today's merchant banks are focused on providing investment banking expertise that supplements the lending and operational capabilities of the commercial banks. Within the U.S. some investment and commercial banks used the name merchant bank as a public relations cachet endeavoring to tap the glamorous associations of this term.

FOREIGN BANKS IN THE UNITED STATES

Foreign banks have come to the United States for reasons similar to those motivating U.S. banks to expand overseas: to serve their customers, to develop a share in the largest business market in the world, and to have a direct means of attracting and investing U.S. dollars. This banking presence takes many forms. As of year-end 1989, 263 foreign banks operated 479 state-licensed branches and agencies, 86 branches and agencies licensed by the Office of the Comptroller of the Currency, 16 Edge Act corporations, and 10 commercial lending companies. "In addition foreign banks held a 25 percent or greater interest in one hundred and one U.S. commercial banks. Together, these foreign banks at year-end controlled approximately 22 percent of U.S. banking assets."[22] For comparison, the 82 foreign banks in Japan made less than 2 percent of all loans.[23]

With the passage of the International Banking Act of 1978, the United States aimed to create order out of the state and federal regulations for the establishment of foreign banking offices in the United States. The act provided for FDIC insurance for foreign-owned branches, controlled the opening of foreign branches in the future in more than one state, and permitted creation of branches and agencies licensed by the Comptroller of the Currency.

However, "the vast majority of branches and agencies of foreign banks. . . are not insured by the FDIC and do not accept consumer deposits."[24] The Federal Reserve has the overall responsibility for the supervision of these foreign branches and agencies although much of the examination may be done by other federal and state agencies. "It is important to keep in mind that branches and agencies are not U.S. banks. A branch or agency is an integral part of a foreign bank."[25] Therefore, the U.S. regulators work closely with the regulators of the foreign parent bank to ensure the sound operation of these United States-based units.

Foreign investment in U.S. banking can be traced to the beginning of this country's history, with the charter of the First Bank of the United States in 1809, which housed large foreign holdings. In the late nineteenth century, Japanese, Canadian, and British banks were established, initially on the West Coast. By 1911 Massachusetts, Oregon, California, and New York permitted foreign banking. The 1920s saw a boom in foreign banking, but that died out with the Great Depression, and it was not until the 1960s that the present rush of foreign bank openings in the United States began.[26]

Setting up a Foreign Bank in the United States

The steps by which foreign banks become involved in the United States are similar to the sequence that U.S. banks undertake when setting up their international business. For the foreign bank these are as follows:

- trade finance and correspondent banking
- medium-term lending to overseas corporations and governments as a participant in credits of other banks

- development of banking units with a dollar source of funds for disbursing dollar-denominated loans
- aggressive seeking out of banking relationships with prime international corporate and sovereign risk names through a growing overseas network
- development of specialist skills in an effort to establish a strategic competitive advantage[27]

Foreign banks now consider a presence in the United States vital to their global strategy in order to establish "a dollar funding base and . . . some form of international corporate lending and trade financing capability."[28] Thus U.S. banks find that their prime customers are exactly the same companies that foreign banks consider the best targets for their business development effort. "Fortune 500 names are almost universally regarded, at least initially, as the highest priority, although many banks subsequently focus on smaller, even middle-market, firms as they come up against the problem of developing a profitable relationship with these sought-after names."[29]

Most foreign banks in the United States have avoided the retail market—that is, soliciting accounts of the general public with the accompanying demand for personal loans—and have specialized in corporate customers. Concentration on the wholesale market, combined with a higher balance sheet ratio of loans to capital in many cases, has enabled these foreign banks to show a profit on lower rates than U.S. banks. This has constituted an additional competitive factor that will diminish with the uniform application of the risk-based capital guidelines.

GLOBAL MANAGEMENT

The decision about establishing which of the above entities, how many, or the location is based on a bank's overall global strategy. "Large, multinational banks are managed and operated on a worldwide consolidated basis. . . . Branches of [foreign] banks will be influenced by factors specific to their home country as well as to the local environment in which these branches are operating. In some cases, a foreign branch operating in a less regulated environment might engage in activities that otherwise would have been undertaken by the bank's home country office had it been less regulated, particularly in cases of limitations on interest rates or quantitative restraints on particular activities. In fact, Eurocurrency banking largely owes its existence to banks' seeking to avoid regulatory restraints in their domestic banking markets."[30]

This trend is evident in several ways. U.S. banks use overseas shell branches to warehouse loans for tax benefits or as sources of funding; merchant banks use the branches to conduct investment banking activities outside of the U.S. The expansion of branches in the 1960s followed by the contraction in the 1980s were both the result of the prevalent global strategy that prevailed during each of those decades.

It has also been true for foreign banks. For example, Japanese banks, the largest foreign banks as of the late 1980s, have substantial branch presences in both London and the United States. They use these branches differently, partly because there are restrictions in Japan on the rate of interest banks may pay on the bulk of their local deposits. "The main difference is that offices of Japanese banks in London serve as an important net funding source for their related offices in other countries [principally Japan to finance loans to local Japanese companies], while offices in the United States... are heavily concentrated in lending to locally based companies.... In the United Kingdom, Japanese banks lend largely to nonlocal borrowers in nonlocal currencies." In fact, "Little of the activity of Japanese banks in the United Kingdom is oriented toward the U.K. economy." In the United States "a large proportion of activity by Japanese banks is with customers identified as U.S. residents... many [of whom] are affiliates of Japanese entities. As of December 1988, [loans to] Japanese residents by U.S. agencies and branches of Japanese banks were $106 billion out of a total of $307 billion... When claims are reallocated to the country of the ultimate parent obligor, the total Japanese risk of the U.S. agencies and branches amounted to $208 billion—a clear indication that U.S. offices of Japanese banks are closely associated with Japan-based customers."[31]

BANK ACCOUNTING FOR INTERNATIONAL BANKING

The *balance sheet* of a U.S. commercial bank is a statement of the financial position of that bank as of a stated date. International banking transactions are merged with domestic ones to be presented in a single balance sheet. The balance sheet has four general categories of accounts: assets, liabilities, capital, and contingent (sometimes referred to as "off-balance sheet" items).

The *income statement* or *statement of operations* "measures the flow of revenues and expenses over a period of time, usually one year."[32] It likewise combines the international and domestic business.

By the latter 1980s, U.S. bank regulators required commercial banks to have minimum *primary capital* equal to 6 percent of assets. Primary capital generally meant the total of shareholders' equity, retained earnings, and reserve for loan losses. Each asset was counted in full in the formula regardless of the risk; contingent accounts (many of which reflect international banking transactions) were excluded. These were the rules applicable to United States' banks.

Each country had its own set of regulations and capital definitions for their banks, which were often inconsistent with those of other countries, creating inequalities as banks spread globally. Some banking activities were excluded by some countries from capital requirements but included by others.

Risk-Based Capital

To address these problems, meetings were held over several years in Basle, Switzerland, at the Bank for International Settlements by bank regulators from 12 countries: Belgium, Canada, France, Germany, Italy, Japan, Luxembourg, Netherlands, Sweden, Switzerland, United Kingdom, and United States. Out of this came the *Risk-Based Capital Guidelines*, which each country's bank regulators agreed to apply to banks under their jurisdiction. Each country fully retains all of its sovereign powers to regulate and supervise their banks. What has occurred is that each country has agreed to substitute these commonly agreed-upon guidelines in place of their separate previous rules and thereby achieve greater global consistency than at present. There is no international organization with power to regulate and supervise the banks of any country.

These became effective in the U. S. on March 15, 1989, to be phased in by December 31, 1992. As applied to the U. S., "the guidelines are designed to achieve certain important goals: Establishment of a uniform capital framework, applicable to all federally supervised banking organizations; encouragement of international banking organizations to strengthen their capital positions; and reduction of a source of competitive inequality arising from differences in supervisory requirements among nations.

"The guidelines establish a systematic analytical framework that makes regulatory capital requirements more sensitive to differences in risk profiles among banking organizations, takes off-balance sheet exposures into explicit account in assessing capital adequacy, and minimizes disincentives to holding liquid, low-risk assets."[33]

The *Risk-Based Capital Guidelines* (see appendix D) redefine capital, increase the amount of required bank capital, and assign a risk-weighting to each asset so that a bank will have to allocate more capital for higher risk assets. Each asset is multiplied by a risk weight percentage (0, 20, 50, or 100 percent) and the resulting total determines the base for calculating required capital. Contingent account categories are now brought into this calculation.

The impact of these guidelines falls heavily on a bank's international transactions. For example, a bank will have to hold more capital for its loans to some foreign governments than to others; certain international business transactions that did not require capital in the past, now will. When it is fully effective "banking organizations will be required to have capital equivalent to 8 percent of assets, weighted by risk."[34]

In the chapters that follow, its applicability and impact for international banking business will be examined in detail for each of the types of assets.

SUMMARY

The U.S. bank seeking to expand its international banking activities has a number of options, each with its advantages and costs. It is therefore prudent to proceed only when there is business capable of supporting it. Organizing an international department in the head office is the logical first step. The establishment of an Edge Act office, overseas branches, and a joint venture can be justified only when there is enough business or potential profit to cover the very substantial expenses. With the authorization of International Banking Facilities, many banks may be able to participate in Eurodollar activities without the expense of establishing a branch overseas.

Regardless of its organization, a bank can meet the international banking needs of its customers with just a capability in its head office, or solely through the international organization of a major city correspondent bank.

While U.S. banks were expanding their presence in foreign markets, the U.S. market has been attracting foreign banks in growing numbers. U.S. banks now find themselves facing new competitors in their own serving area. This will certainly continue in future years.

QUESTIONS
1. What is the difference between a foreign branch and an Edge Act corporation?
2. Does a U.S. bank need to have overseas branches in order to provide international banking business to its customers?
3. Why do foreign banks have banking offices in the United States?
4. What is an International Banking Facility?

PROBLEMS
1. Prepare a chart showing the organization of your bank's international department.
2. Looking at the area that your bank serves in the United States, identify the competition from foreign banks through local banking offices and other efforts.

Notes

1. James V. Houpt, *International Trends for U.S. Banks and Banking Markets,* Staff Study 156, Board of Governors of the Federal Reserve System (Washington, D.C., 1988), p. 5.

2. Vincent P. Carosso, *The Morgans: Private International Bankers 1854-1913* (Cambridge: Harvard University Press, 1987), p. 11.

3. Harry Guenther, *Banking and Finance in North America* (London: Financial Times Business Publishing Ltd., 1981), p. 125 and following.

4. Board of Governors of the Federal Reserve System, *Annual Report* (Washington, D.C., 1989), p. 181.

5. Houpt, *op. cit.*, p. 7.

6. Houpt, *op. cit.*, p. 9.

7. *Federal Reserve Bulletin*, December 1989. Statistical table 3.14.

8. *The Economist*, December 16, 1989, p. 100, quoting data of Bank for International Settlements.

9. James V. Houpt and Michael G. Martinson, *Foreign Subsidiaries of U.S. Banking Organizations*, Staff Studies, Board of Governors of the Federal Reserve System (Washington, D.C., 1982), p. 5.

10. Peter Merrill Associates, *The Future Development of U.S. Banking Organizations Abroad* (Washington, D.C.: American Bankers Association, 1981), chapter 1.

11. *International Banking Act of 1978*, Sec. 3(b).

12. James V. Houpt, "Edge Corporations," *International Banking: U.S. Laws and Regulations* (Washington, D.C.: American Bankers Association, 1984), pp. 10-14.

13. *Federal Reserve Bulletin*, October 1982, p. 565.

14. Houpt, *op. cit.*, p. 16.

15. Houpt, *op. cit.*, p. 17.

16. *Federal Reserve Bulletin*, October 1982, p. 567.

17. Houpt and Martinson, *op. cit.*, p. 1.

18. Samuel L. Hayes and Philip M. Hubbard, *Investment Banking: A Tale of Three Cities* (Boston: Harvard Business School Press, 1990), p. 10.

19. Carosso, *op. cit.*, pp. 3-4.

20. Philip Ziegler, *The Sixth Great Power: Barings 1762-1929* (London: Collins, 1988), p. 10.

21. Ron Chernow, *The House of Morgan* (New York: Atlantic Monthly Press, 1990), p. 25.

22. Board of Governors of the Federal Reserve System, *op. cit.*, p. 174.

23. *The New York Times*, March 21, 1990, p. C1.

24. Statement by William Taylor, Staff Director, Division of Banking Supervision and Regulation, Board of Governors of the Federal Reserve System, October 16, 1990. *Federal Reserve Bulletin*, December 1990, p. 1,032.

25. *Ibid.*, p. 1,033.

26. Peter Merrill Associates, *op. cit.*, p. 14.

27. *Ibid.*, p. 22.

28. *Ibid.*, p. 23.

29. *Ibid.*

30. *Federal Reserve Bulletin*, February 1990, pp. 41-44.

31. *Ibid.*

32. Fred M. Frankston, Charles D. Mecimore, and Michael F. Cornick, *Bank Accounting* (Washington, D.C.: American Bankers Association, 1985), p. 61.

33. Board of Governors of the Federal Reserve System, Press Release, January 19, 1989.

34. *Ibid.*

3

Country Risk Assessment

The essence of international banking is dealing with customers in another country. The banker is in one country; the customer or borrower is in another—subject to the consequences of changes in their economic conditions, social structures, and political events. Events in that country can delay or prevent a borrower from repaying a bank. The effect of such changes represents a risk in addition to the credit risks the banker has in dealing with a customer. This is referred to as *country risk*. The bank incurs similar risks when it establishes a branch in another country or when it conducts transactions through a foreign correspondent bank.

Country risk for the banker can be direct or indirect. Direct country risk exists when the banker directly lends to a borrower who actually lives in the country at risk. Indirect country risk exists when the banker finances a local borrower who is dealing with a customer in a country at risk. That local borrower's financial health would be affected if his foreign customer did not pay for a purchase, or a supplier could not provide the goods or components that the local customer depended on for his production. Bankers may often ignore such indirect country risk. However, a local bank's customer has only one financial statement and any problems that customer has with country risk will affect all of his or her commitments with the local banker.

Country risk assessment begins with a banker's analysis of a country's economic information: the internal elements, such as inflation and government deficits, as well as the country's international payments and receipts as expressed in the balance of payments. The assessment also considers the effect of political, historical, social, and cultural factors on the business a bank would be doing with that country. Such risk analysis may have several elements: the risks associated with *cross-border* lending, that is, from one country to another; the *transfer risks* associated with repayment, which will require the borrower to be able to transfer funds from one country to another; and risks associated with the general factors that would affect a local branch in making loans in that currency.

Country risk assessment is done in a series of analytical steps: what are the conditions in that country now; what is the likelihood of change; and what effect would such change have on a borrower's ability to repay the bank in the future.

Country risk analysis is not only a defensive assessment in which a bank tries to identify problems that may have a negative effect; it can also be an offensive strategy for a bank's business development. Country risk assessment can identify the markets the bank would want to grow in and where a bank can find new customers. Trade follows the flag. It is equally true that banking business follows trade.

The objectives of this chapter are to

- outline the analytical elements in developing a country risk assessment
- describe the elements of a balance of payments assessment
- review the effect of political, cultural, and social factors on a country's business environment
- describe how banks manage country risk exposure

BACKGROUND

Each time a bank extends credit to a foreign borrower, it is exposed to country risk regardless of whether the borrower is the government, a private company, or a bank. It incurs country risk whenever it finances a local business that, in turn, depends on a foreigner as the source of repayment. It also experiences country risk when it has funds on deposit in another country, buys or sells foreign exchange, or establishes a branch in another country. *Country risk* is the risk that any changes in economic, political, or social conditions in that country will adversely affect the repayment of a loan, access to foreign funds, or the safety of an investment. Although this definition focuses on adverse change, bankers should likewise consider the impact of favorable changes. These can offer opportunities for developing new business or commencing business in a previously unsatisfactory area.

The risk that a banker has in doing business in another country is nothing new. In 1867, a distinguished British economic writer stated the problem: "Many persons have not a distinct perception of the risk of lending to a country in a wholly different state of civilization. They can hardly imagine the difficulties with which such a country struggles, and the dangers to which it is exposed. They forget that national good faith is a rare and recent thing . . . [or] how little do facts . . . prove that a debt will be paid, or that interest on it will be paid when new borrowings cease to be possible."[1]

Country risk assessment is difficult because it is an attempt to forecast the future. Banking decisions are made today; their success depends on conditions in the future, which is ultimately unpredictable. The banker has to evaluate not only the credit risks of the borrower's future business prospects but also how changes in political and economic conditions in that country may affect the borrower's business and ability to pay its debts as scheduled. Likewise, the banker financing a local customer, who in turn is selling to a foreign buyer, has to consider the impact on the local customer's overall financial health if that foreign buyer cannot make timely payments. What would be the effect on the local customer dependent on buying materials or goods from a foreign source if that supplier fails to deliver at the agreed-upon price or even fails to deliver at all? The failure of the foreign supplier may affect the profitable operation of the local customer who may not be able to replace those supplies at a comparable price or availability, which may then make that customer uncompetitive in his or her own markets. Projecting such future events are done by analyzing the present and the past and examining each component separately to come to an overall conclusion. The major components of this analysis are (1) economic and (2) political.

ANALYZING THE ECONOMIC COMPONENT

A nation's economy is made up of domestic and international activities. The country's balance of payments "can be broadly described as the record of an economy's international economic transactions, that is, of the goods and services that an economy has received from and provided to the rest of the world and of the changes in the economy's claims on and liabilities to the rest of the world."[2] In essence, it is everything a country does economically with the rest of the world over a stated period of time.

Balance of Payments Preparation

It is important to understand what the balance of payments is—and what it is not. The latter is perhaps less well understood, as many bankers mistakenly look to the balance of payments for information that it was never intended to give.

Each nation assembles its own data for its balance of payments. Obviously, the capability to do so varies considerably among countries. The International Monetary Fund (IMF) (see chapter 16) has standardized the reporting of data to permit comparability between the balance of payments of different countries. The balance of payments is published by the IMF and is available to the public either through subscriptions or at large libraries. The banker should not assume, merely because the information is published under the imprimatur of a respected international financial institution and looks like a balance sheet, that all the numbers are precise in the same sense that the banker expects the bank's balance sheet to be exact and accurate.

"The balance of payments is a record of what has taken place during a given period, in contrast to a statement of the situation on a certain date; it thus refers to changes, i.e., transactions in a comprehensive sense."[3] "Despite its name, the balance of payments is concerned not with 'payments' as that term is generally understood, but with 'transactions' . . . [that] may not involve the payment of money, and some are not paid for in any sense."[4] "The balance of payments should show virtually all economic values provided by the residents of one economy to another economy, including those without a quid pro quo."[5] For the banker trying to understand the balance of payments by relating it to a corporate financial statement, it "can be thought of as analogous to a source and use statement for a firm, with funds in this case defined as external purchasing power or foreign exchange. . . . Unlike the [corporate] income statement, the balance of payments does not provide any information regarding the profitability of the underlying transaction. Unlike a balance sheet, which shows stocks of assets and liabilities at a specific point in time, the balance of payments measures flows of goods, services and capital occurring over a period of time."[6] Adding to the difficulty of such country-company comparisons is that all merchandise imported into a country is counted the same regardless of whether it is for immediate consumption, such as food, or for a long-term capital use, such as machinery. The company financial statement allocates them to different accounts; balance of payments does not.

In addition to these international receipts and payments, domestic transactions also occur and are not directly reflected in the balance of payments, but can be of substantial significance to the economy. For example, a country with a high rate of internal savings can fund the building of new factories to increase exports without having to obtain foreign investment.

Sources of Data

The balance of payments is usually the best information readily available. It is developed from sources that are, however, only as good as each nation's ability to assemble data, and it has been modified when necessary by the most competent people available to make these judgments (see box). Some categories can be precise measures. Foreign trade can be inventoried as it passes through a nation's customs control. Small values, however, are usually exempted, which means that even this category cannot be completely accurate.

Balance of payments practice is to make the entry into the accounts when the merchandise crosses the border. The accounts would show the transaction and then either a claim on or from the buyer or seller, which in turn is offset when the payment is actually made. Thus the balance of payments shows each element of the transaction separately. Recording the merchandise at the F.O.B. (see appendix A, Incoterms) value permits the freight and insurance revenues to be recorded as separate entries.

Data in the service and investment categories can be more difficult to assemble. Tourist expenditures are often determined by asking departing visitors how much they spent during the stay and by making estimates based on hotel revenues. Investment figures likewise depend on a number of sources. For a country with rigorous exchange controls, all foreign investment requires government approval; where there are few exchange controls, authorities rely on surveys and reports from investors. Data about a country's reserves are usually precise. The government itself controls many of the reserve categories or can depend on accurate reports from the country's banks.

Balance of Payments Categories

The balance of payments presentation is divided into three broad categories: current account, capital account, and reserves (see table 3.1, p. 53). Even though comparisons are made between certain accounts, this is only for analytical purposes since income received in one category can be used for payments in any other category.

Current account includes the value of the visible and invisible trade accounts. Visible trade includes imports and exports of merchandise and commodities. An import is a debit; an export is a credit. The same entries are made regardless of whether the trade is paid for in cash, merchandise, credit, or a gift. Invisible trade—in other words, services—includes travel, transportation of merchandise or people, insurance, income or payment on investments, licensing, royalties, immigrant remittances, and other fees for services. Unrequited transfers that can be either public (government) or private (nongovernment) include items given away or for which there is no direct offsetting item such as gifts, dowries, grants, forgiven debt, foreign aid grants, inheritances, and so forth. Each of these can be either a credit or debit to a country's balance of payments, depending on whether the country is paying for the service being provided by another country (a debit) or performing the service (a credit). The debits and credits tend to be independent of each other. For example, a country's earnings from tourists coming into the country will be shown as balance of payments credits while the expenditures of that country's tourists going abroad will be shown as debits. These represent separate activities, independent of each other.

Capital account refers to short-term or long-term investments, which includes bank loans. These can be long-term (over 12 months) direct investments or short-term transactions, such as portfolio investments (stocks), trade credits, and payment agreement balances. They will appear as a debit to the country making the investment and as a credit for the country receiving the investment. The subsequent transfer of interest and dividends is treated as a current account entry.

Obtaining accurate investment data may be difficult. If a country requires government approval for such investments, it may have fairly accurate information. Otherwise it will rely on surveys, reports, and estimates from businesses.

Reserves, which may be considered a subdivision of the capital account, refer specifically to assets "available for use by

---

Balance of Payments Compilation Systems and Methods

Essentially a country's balance of payments account should be a detailed record of all the transactions in a given period between residents of that country and nonresidents. The broad principles and definitions to be employed by all members of the Fund are set forth in the Fund's [International Monetary Fund] *Balance of Payments Manual,* and the Fund's staff regularly collects and publishes national statements and aggregations of national statements based on those principles. . . . Of course, strict conformity with these principles and definitions is not always possible and interpretations differ, leading to some differences in the way countries report the same transaction. However, practical obstacles and difficulties in compiling the comprehensive information

Continued

needed to produce the accounts and the lack of adequate reports from some countries on some types of transactions are far more important sources of actual gaps and discrepancies in the accounts. . . .

Compilers of the international accounts are not in command of a unified and internally consistent set of accounting data, as is the case for any business concern. Instead, compilers use a variety of unrelated sources: for instance, merchandise trade figures banks' balance sheets or from transaction records compiled by banks and others. The main types of collection systems. . . rely on reports based on individual exchange transactions supplied by the banks or the transactors themselves, on reports from transactors that give results over a period of time rather than attempting to identify and measure each transaction, or from some combination of those sources. Such methods must be supplemented in nearly all cases by formulating estimates for missing elements. . . [or] must be supplemented by the imaginative use of es-timates and collateral data from many sources. . . .

Each payment for goods and services by one country should have a counterpart in the receipts of another country, so that when aggregated over all countries, the individual components of the current account, as well as the total, should equal zero. . . .

However, the distinguishing characteristic of the global discrepancies is that they result from inconsistencies in the amounts actually reported by different countries for the same transaction—either party or both parties reporting inaccurately, or one not reporting at all. Consequently, the problem of establishing consistency in reporting across countries is different from, but related to, the problem of compiling consistent accounts for a single country.

Reprinted with permission of the International Monetary Fund, Washington, D.C. *Report on the World Current Account Discrepancy,* pp. 21-23.

an economy's central authorities in meeting balance of payments needs."[7] These include monetary gold, special drawing rights and reserve positions in the International Monetary Fund, and government funds deposited in banks in other countries or owed by other countries. The term refers to assets that actually exist and not to those that could be created under lines of credit, foreign exchange swap agreements, or foreign holdings of residents that could be seized by the government in a national emergency such as war. When money owed by another country is included, it does not indicate whether the loan repayment is being made, is past due, or is rescheduled. The balance of payments shows the changes in the reserves during the period of time. The total amount of the reserves must be determined in other reports.

Once information from all the individual categories is obtained, the country's analyst will discover that the amounts do not balance. This reflects inaccuracies in assembling the raw data or difficulties in obtaining precise amounts. To obtain the balance of debits and credits, an entry will be made to *net errors and omissions.* "That item is intended as an offset to the overstatement or understatement of the record components. Hence, if the balance of those components is a credit, the item for net errors and omissions will be shown as a debit of equal value, and vice-versa. . . . Since some errors and omissions that occur in the course of compilation will almost certainly offset one another, the size of the item does not necessarily provide any indication of the overall accuracy of the statement. . . . An empirical rule of thumb . . . holds that a residual (net errors and omissions) is large enough to create a problem when it exceeds the equivalent of 5 percent of the gross credit and debit entries for merchandise combined."[8]

Achieving a Balance

These three broad categories (current account, capital account, and changes in reserves) tend to offset each other to achieve an overall balance. For example, a developing country (other than the few oil producers) tends to be a net importer: its purchases of industrial machinery and manufactured goods cost more than it earns from its exports of raw materials, expenditures by foreign tourists, and remittances from its workers in other countries. It is therefore normal for it to run a deficit in its current account. To pay for this import gap it needs to be a net borrower of money, attract investment, or receive gifts—all of which are reported as items in the capital account. Thus, the country will show a net credit in this category. Since it is difficult for the current account and investment categories to exactly match in any given year, the balance is achieved by changes in the country's reserves. When the level of capital inflow is less than is needed to cover the current account deficit, the reserves will be drawn down; when it is greater, the reserves will go up.

An industrialized country, on the other hand, is expected to be a net exporter of goods and services. Its manufactured goods will earn more than it spends on raw materials, for its tourists to go abroad, and so forth. Industrialized countries are the sources of the investment, loans, and gifts that the developing countries need. Therefore, as a general rule, the balance of payments of the industrialized countries will show a net inflow in the current account and a net outflow in the capital account. The balancing between these two categories will, as for the developing countries, be reflected in changes in the reserves. The United States in the 1980s, because of its internal domestic policies, was an exception to this generalization (see chapter 12).

Although the current account and the capital account are separate categories in a nation's balance of payments, they are not incompatible with each other. This is particularly evident from the perspective of businesses. There "are numerous ways of competing globally involving choices about where to locate and how to coordinate activities. . . Most global strategies involve an integrated combination of trade and foreign direct investment. Finished products are exported from some nations that import components produced elsewhere, and vice versa. Foreign investment reflects the dispersion of production and marketing activities. Trade and foreign investment are complementary, not necessarily substitutes."[9]

Types of Balances

Within the balance of payments statement there can be a number of levels of "balance." The difference between merchandise imports and exports is the trade balance. The *balance on goods and services* adds the service entries to the trade figures. When the transfer payments are added it creates the *current account balance.* The *basic balance* is made up of goods, services, transfers, and long-term capital accounts. It seeks to assess long-term trends by excluding short-term capital movements, which, because of their potential volatility, are apt to distort the real trends. Finally, there is the balance that comprises "all standard components except reserve assets and, in most cases, certain selected liabilities that may be regarded as being related in some ways to those reserves."[10] This is sometimes called the *official settlements balance.*

Deficit

When its international payments (for imports, outgoing capital, services bought from other countries, and so forth) exceed its income (from exports, incoming capital, services done for others, and so forth), a nation has a balance of payments deficit. Conversely, when the receipts are greater than the payments, the nation has a balance of payments surplus. The long-term threat of a deficit is that, if not corrected, the country will eventually have no means to pay for future imports of food, raw materials, machinery, or needed services, nor will it have the ability to meet its international debt-servicing obligations. For this reason the country risk analyst will be more concerned about a country having a balance of payments deficit than a surplus.

A deficit can be financed by using previously accumulated reserves or by borrowing from the International Monetary Fund or foreign banks. In this sense a country acts much like an individual. When the money going out exceeds the amount coming in, a country draws on its reserves; an individual draws on savings. If the deficit persists, both borrow from a financial institution. If the deficit still continues, then life-style changes must be made.

If the country's currency is widely used, as is the case with the U.S. dollar, a balance of payments deficit can be covered by encouraging other countries to hold more of the country's currency. Thus, the U.S. encourages foreigners who sell goods to the U.S. to invest those dollars in the U.S. If a nation has a persistent balance of payments deficit, it must take further measures. These usually involve immediately reducing payments. Since imports are usually the largest category of international payments, the nation can take steps to reduce imports through tariffs, quotas, or foreign exchange controls. Investments being made in other countries can be held down through capital export restrictions or other administrative measures. The country can restrict payments for invisibles by forbidding its citizens to travel abroad or limiting payments for services. Debt repayment can be renegotiated so that the immediate year's interest and principal amounts may be reduced by permitting a longer time in which to repay. At the same time that it is taking steps to reduce the level of its payments, the nation can also seek to increase its foreign earnings through devaluations, liberalized investment rules, tax reductions, and other measures. A deficit can seldom be met by only one of these methods.

Domestic Policies

Not all of a country's balance of payments problems develop directly from international activities. Domestic economic events will be reflected in the balance of payments. A country running a large governmental budget deficit, for example, will often have a high rate of inflation. This will cause the costs for local goods and services to rise in local currency. If such a country is trying to maintain a fixed exchange rate, either for domestic political purposes or to lessen the apparent impact of inflation, imports become increasingly cheaper and are thereby encouraged. Meanwhile, exports become more expensive, which makes them less attractive to foreign buyers.

When such a country seeks to hold down food prices for its workers living in cities, it may find that it becomes cheaper to import food that was formerly grown domestically. Not only can this increase payments for imports, it also can discourage farmers from continuing to produce, thereby eliminating a source of export income. Many of these farmers will leave farming and move to the cities, thus accelerating the demand for cheap food in those cities and reducing the future capability of the country to change its policy. Eventually the decline in exports and growth in imports causes a payments crisis for the country.

It is interesting to note the different policies that developing and developed countries have for agriculture. The developing country may want cheap food at the expense of the farmer for those who live in the city; the developed countries often have policies to protect the farmers, which often means higher direct food prices or government subsidies paid by the taxpayers.

Fears of possible future economic changes can accelerate outgoing funds transfers as a country's citizens seek safety for themselves or their money. This is what is sometimes called *capital flight*, which can be disguised through many different balance of payments categories. For example, a government imposing controls on imports to reduce a balance of payments deficit may require a permit to get the foreign exchange to pay for an import. An importer gaining such a permit might arrange for the foreign seller to "over invoice," that is, bill at an artificially high price and then when receiving the payment, that seller would put the excess over the real cost into a bank account in the foreign country for the buyer. Human ingenuity demonstrates a record of considerable success when frightened people are desperate to get their money to a safe haven.

Even though it can have a very serious impact on a nation, it is almost impossible to determine the amount of capital flight or to distinguish it "from 'normal' capital outflows—that is, trade credits, working balances, natural portfolio diversification, and the attraction of higher interest rates. The term 'capital flight' implies a further set of factors, such as the fear of inflation, exchange depreciation, political upheaval, tax avoidance, evasion of exchange control laws, etc., but it is statistically impossible to classify capital movements, especially the unrecorded movements, according to motive."[11]

| **ANALYZING THE POLITICAL COMPONENT** | The political outlook for a country is assessed not because of the banker's preference for one political side or another but to evaluate the likelihood of political change and its impact on economic policy or a change in the rules for doing business in that country. Such assessment of future political events is a very difficult task. Bankers have sought to assess political risk as best they can, even hiring political scientists and professed experts. |

Unfortunately, the banker makes loans today, and no one can accurately predict tomorrow. Even though the economic future is not a trend line from the past, "In politics," as a retired British cabinet minister summed up, "the only really useful guide is history."[12] Thus the banker must take the best information available and make an assessment based on the probabilities that such information suggests.

Political Change

Political change in any country can alter the country's economic outlook. Political decisions may result in new taxes, new support for a particular industry, withdrawal of support from other industries, or changes in attractiveness for investors. A government nearing an election might undertake economic policies to maintain its popularity or launch some form of military adventure to distract an unhappy electorate.

It is a fact of politics that in at least 90 percent of the countries some group is plotting to take over the government. The plotting may be, in a democracy, an open plan to win the next election. In other societies it may be a clandestine plan for revolution, either from within or by exiles. Many of these changes will never take place. But some will succeed and, in doing so, will lead to changes that will affect business and the country's economic situation—some for better, some for worse.

The banker, when considering a five-year loan, is concerned with those political events that might change a country's, or business's, ability to repay the loan. In actuality the banker cannot know. All that can be done is to attempt to evaluate the known data to arrive at a degree of probability about a country's political future, recognizing the lessons of history, and expecting that the unexpected will happen.

The banker will consider the country's political tradition. Is it one of regular elections and orderly, nonviolent transfers of power? Is revolution likely? Some countries have a history of dictatorships, either of an individual, family, tribe, or political party. In such countries changes do not come regularly. History has shown that dictatorships, whether benign or repressive, tend to be stable for a while but are almost always followed by violence that has the capacity to tear apart the fabric of society and the economy. In other countries there is a tradition of regular intervention by the military, usually the army. Changes in these situations tend to be decided by a small group of power brokers. In recent years such military control has not been demonstrated to be particularly successful, and there have been a number of instances of the military losing the support of the people and returning government to civilian control.

Other Factors

Other factors that can affect a country's political policies and stability include the existence of a heterogeneous populace or major divisions in the country along religious, language, tribal, or ethnic nationality lines. Countries have seen violent civil disturbances because of such internal divisions. Also to be considered may be the strength of guerrilla forces and their support among the people. In most instances neither the government nor the rebels themselves really know how much it may be.

Corruption is another factor. Every society will accept a certain level of corruption. In some parts of the world petty corruption is more readily accepted than in others. Other countries are completely intolerant of any level. But even in the more relaxed societies the people can suddenly express their anger when the generally accepted level is breached. This can lead to street demonstrations, political unrest, and even a change of government. "Corruption seriously undermines the effectiveness of government. . . . Some corruption is on such a scale that it has major economic consequences: it may stimulate the illegal export of capital or result in large projects being awarded to contractors . . . according to the size of their bribes rather than the quality of their performance."[13]

An important part of the fabric of a nation is the country's history. The identity of a nation is its collective memory, as President Mitterrand of France has pointed out. The banker must understand that history, both the real events and how the people perceived those events. The history (and the historical myths) learned by generations of school children may be a significant catalyst or restraint in a government's selection of policy options. It can quantify "moral geography" and establish what a nation's people accept as standards. The childhood literature of the Dutch, for example, centers on tales of seagoing captains triumphing against shipwrecks and disasters in far-off areas and illustrates "the need for citizen-heroes in a young republic that had repudiated the imperial aura of the Hapsburgs. This was frontier literature, as much as the Wild West stories that fed another young republic's sense of courage, sin and virtue."[14] It may force the government to take actions to satisfy the people's demand for revenge or to inhibit a course of action. In many Eastern European countries the movement from communism reawakened old ethnic divisions that threatened to cripple government plans or disintegrate the nation itself. This may also be evident in examining the country's boundaries. Are they stable, or are there threats from neighbors seeking to reclaim or reestablish old territories lost in previous wars? Political alliances, former colonial and mother-country relationships, and higher education patterns are other factors that can affect future political events.

Colonial relationships have been more than just political. "The trouble with calling all . . . regions 'colonial' economies is that the term . . . suggests that if alien domination of some sort is thrown off, a stunted, narrow economy will no longer remain stunted and narrow, will proceed to become better rounded and capable of producing amply and diversely on its own behalf as well as for others. To be sure, there are often good reasons for throwing off alien domination or influence: reasons that are politically, socially, culturally and emotionally important and sometimes economically important as well. Yet, it should be clear by now, the stultification of . . . regions and the fragility of their economies are not so simply or easily corrected as the epithet 'colonial' suggests. When Fidel Castro disposed of American influence in Cuba he did not throw off Cuba's servitude to sugar."[15]

The residue of the colonial influence can hamper economic growth for decades after independence. In some African cities, costly building codes are maintained that were originally designed for European winters. Workers are forced to live in suburbs. "The idea. . . is to relieve crowding in the capital, to preserve the colonists' spacious city plan. But distant townships strain gasping buses, already hamstrung by a shortage of foreign currency with which to buy spare parts. To nine hours a day in their jobs. . . workers must add another two or three waiting for or travelling on a bus."[16]

Not only can political change affect the way business is conducted, it can so involve a populace that the economy itself becomes a victim. When civil wars or invasions become all-consuming, with everyone struggling merely to survive or fleeing a battle zone, the foreign banker's loans are lost in the melee.

Political Evaluation

Political assessment will likely differ, depending on the bank making it. Banks in two countries may tend to view risk in another country differently. West Germany and France were prepared to extend more credit to the countries in Eastern Europe after the political changes of 1989/90 than were U.S. banks. Similarly, U.S. banks were more committed to Mexico and Latin America than were European banks. Such differing perceptions are not surprising. A country does more business with its neighbor and has perhaps a better, or more comforting, feeling because of proximity.

BANK REGULATION

U.S. bank supervisors assess each bank's country risk exposure as it may have an impact on the overall condition of that bank. The assessment includes a review of "three basic components in every bank's country risk management system: (a) evaluation of economic, political, and social trends in countries where the bank has asset exposure; (b) country exposure limits established by executive bank management; and (c) current, accurate, and complete internal reporting systems to monitor and control country risk."[17]

To coordinate the assessment of country risk between the various regulatory agencies, the Interagency Country Exposure Review Committee (ICERC) was established in 1979 by the Comptroller of the Currency, the Federal Reserve, and the Federal Deposit Insurance Corporation. It meets at least three times a year and assesses information from a number of sources. These include a statistical analysis prepared by the Federal Reserve Bank of New York of the ability of countries to service their external debt, country studies prepared by the Federal Reserve System, U.S. government information, and information and analyses prepared by major U.S. banks for their own country assessments.

"ICERC then categorizes countries on the basis of economic-social-political conditions that may affect the country's flow of foreign exchange necessary to repay U.S. banks' cross-border exposures in that country. ICERC may determine that one category may apply to all U.S. bank loans in a country, or that several categories apply depending on the type of maturities of cross-border exposures U.S. banks have in the country. ICERC distributes its country evaluations to the federal bank

examiners who regularly examine the international activities of
U.S. banks."[18] As a practical matter the regulators tend not to be
concerned with small exposures that a bank might have.

These ICERC categories, in descending order, are strong,
moderately strong, weak, other transfer risk problems, substandard, value impaired, and loss. If a country's debt is categorized
as value impaired or loss, which means that the chances of
repayment are small, then banks with loans to these countries will
be expected either to establish specific loan loss reserves or to
recognize the losses. When a country's debt is put in the less
severe categories of other transfer risk problems or substandard,
banks with loans may not be required to establish reserves. The
examiners will, however, consider such loans when assessing the
quality of the bank's portfolio and the adequacy of its capital.

ASSESSING COUNTRY RISK

Beginning with the foundation of the balance of payments, the
banker tries to determine the bank's risk in making a loan or an
investment in a foreign country. Unfortunately, no one has found
a foolproof formula. This does not mean that the banker must
give up. The assessment is a serious concern. All credit evaluations about a specific borrower will come to naught if the country
where the borrower is located encounters difficulties either from
economic or political causes. When that happens, foreign exchange to repay a loan, to remit a dividend, or to pay for foreign
trade may not be available. Changing economic conditions,
perhaps triggered by political events, may make it no longer
possible for a borrower even to stay in business. Political events
can completely disrupt a market or so completely change the
economy as to make any analysis derived from even recent past
economic data meaningless. For example, the political upheavals
in Eastern Europe suddenly changed centrally planned
economies—that had been conducting most of their international
trade through intrabloc barter—into market-oriented countries
forced to compete in global markets where payments were required in convertible currencies. This led to considerable internal
economic anguish.

Notwithstanding the uncertainties of the future, the banker
must make decisions. Country risk assessment begins with a
study of the most recent balance of payments elements. This must
be more than just a superficial answering of the question "Is it
favorable or unfavorable?" Not all the necessary information to
answer a banker's questions may be detailed in a balance of

Table 3.1 Balance of Payments Transactions Data for Australia

AGGREGATED PRESENTATION: TRANSACTIONS DATA, 1982-89

(In millions of U.S. dollars)

		Code	1982	1983	1984	1985	1986	1987	1988	1989
A.	Current Account, excl. Group F	A . . C A	-8,459	-5,868	-8,577	-8,913	-9,731	-8,401	-10,236	-16,861
	Merchandise: exports f.o.b.	1 A . A 4	20,793	19,501	22,769	22,275	22,189	26,270	32,778	36,173
	Merchandise: imports f.o.b.	1 A . B 4	-23,406	-19,470	-23,653	-23,592	-24,264	-26,749	-33,892	-40,342
	Trade balance	1 A . C 4	-2,612	30	-884	-1,317	-2,076	-480	-1,114	-4,169
	Other goods, services, and income: credit	1 S . A 4	5,617	5,666	6,325	5,724	6,423	8,646	11,185	12,609
	Shipment and other transportation	1 P . A 4	*2,100*	*1,849*	*1,979*	*1,876*	*2,044*	*2,388*	*2,980*	*2,984*
	Travel	1 D . A 4	*1,267*	*1,253*	*1,312*	*1,231*	*1,500*	*2,166*	*3,325*	*3,449*
	Investment income	1 N . A 4	*829*	*1,092*	*1,406*	*1,258*	*1,391*	*2,306*	*2,782*	*3,695*
	Other	1 R . A 4	*1,421*	*1,473*	*1,628*	*1,359*	*1,488*	*1,786*	*2,098*	*2,480*
	Other goods, services, and income: debit	1 S . B 4	-11,268	-11,540	-14,011	-13,745	-14,671	-17,586	-21,781	-27,192
	Shipment and other transportation	1 P . B 4	*-3,712*	*-3,119*	*-3,646*	*-3,521*	*-3,306*	*-3,497*	*-4,363*	*-5,245*
	Travel	1 D . B 4	*-1,941*	*-1,794*	*-2,124*	*-1,891*	*-1,968*	*-2,431*	*-2,923*	*-3,769*
	Investment income	1 N . B 4	*-3,468*	*-4,392*	*-5,699*	*-5,929*	*-6,799*	*-8,687*	*-10,911*	*-14,355*
	Other	1 R . B 4	*-2,147*	*-2,234*	*-2,543*	*-2,405*	*-2,597*	*-2,971*	*-3,584*	*-3,824*
	Total: goods, services, and income	1 T . C 4	-8,263	-5,843	-8,571	-9,337	-10,323	-9,419	-11,709	-18,752
	Private unrequited transfers	1 K . C 4	300	412	451	686	817	1,196	1,706	2,073
	Total, excl. official unrequited transfers	1 U . C 4	-7,963	-5,431	-8,120	-8,651	-9,506	-8,224	-10,003	-16,679
	Official unrequited transfers	1 H . C 4	-496	-437	-458	-262	-225	-178	-232	-182
B.	**Direct Investment and Other Long-Term Capital, excl. Groups F through H**	9 Z 1 X A	**11,994**	**7,497**	**6,397**	**7,463**	**9,712**	**7,438**	**14,817**	**11,428**
	Direct investment	3 . . X A	1,610	2,464	-1,033	397	-2,099	107	1,568	3,762
	In Australia	3 Y . X 4	*2,307*	*2,985*	*375*	*2,052*	*3,140*	*3,383*	*7,303*	*7,543*
	Abroad	3 L . X 4	*-697*	*-521*	*-1,407*	*-1,655*	*-3,033*	*-5,482*	*-5,735*	*-3,781*
	Portfolio investment	6 Z 1 X A	2,399	1,183	610	1,803	977	4,311	4,754	-1,248
	Other long-term capital									
	Resident official sector	4 Z 1 X A	353	30	663	1,270	1,824	1,493	-490	466
	Deposit money banks	5 Z 1 X A	200	167	665	1,378	3,998	1,574	2,872	6,734
	Other sectors	8 Z 1 X A	7,432	3,653	5,491	2,615	2,806	2,160	6,113	1,714
	Total, Groups A plus B	B 1 . X A	**3,535**	**1,629**	**-2,181**	**-1,450**	**-19**	**-963**	**4,582**	**-5,533**
C.	**Other Short-Term Capital, excl. Groups F through H**	9 Z 2 X A	**505**	**224**	**-495**	**-755**	**-682**	**-636**	**-72**	**1,318**
	Resident official sector	4 Z 2 X A	182	-24	-118	-96	109	-196	-439	-450
	Deposit money banks	5 Z 2 X A	249	126	-53	-184	-795	20	265	2,268
	Other sectors	8 Z 2 X A	74	123	-324	-476	4	-460	101	-501
D.	**Net Errors and Omissions**	. A . X A	**863**	**1,178**	**1,369**	**-76**	**1,405**	**1,970**	**741**	**5,743**
	Total, Groups A through D	D 1 . X A	**4,902**	**3,031**	**-1,307**	**-2,282**	**705**	**371**	**5,251**	**628**
E.	**Counterpart Items**	2 . . C 4	**-67**	**-403**	**-227**	**628**	**776**	**1,123**	**-424**	**-419**
	Monetization/demonetization of gold	2 A . M 4	-	-	-	-	-	-	-	-
	Allocation/cancellations of SDRs	2 B . M 4	-	-	-	-	-	-	-	-
	Valuation changes in reserve	2 . . F 4	-67	-403	-227	628	776	1,123	-424	-419
	Total, Groups A through E	E 1 . X A	**4,835**	**2,628**	**-1,533**	**-1,654**	**1,481**	**1,494**	**4,827**	**209**
F.	**Exceptional Financing**	. Y . X B	-	-	-	-	-	-	-	-
	Total Groups A through F	F 1 . X 4	**4,835**	**2,628**	**-1,533**	**-1,654**	**1,481**	**1,494**	**4,827**	**209**
G.	**Liabilities Constituting Foreign Authorities Reserves**	9 W . X 4	**-171**	**-1**	**12**	**-19**	**-2**	**4**	**28**	**-28**
	Total Groups A through G	G 1 . X 4	**4,664**	**2,627**	**-1,521**	**-1,674**	**1,479**	**1,497**	**4,855**	**181**
H.	**Total Change in Reserves**	2 . . R 4	**-4,664**	**-2,627**	**-1,521**	**1,674**	**-1,479**	**-1,497**	**-4,855**	**-181**
	Monetary gold	2 A . R 4	-	-	-	-	-	-	-	-
	SDRs	2 B . R 4	-34	-30	5	-129	-101	-21	-37	35	27
	Reserve position in the Fund	2 C . R 4	294	-114	-69	-24	-24	-37	-7	-47
	Foreign exchange assets	2 D . R 4	-4,960	-2,483	1,719	1,799	-1,434	-1,423	4,882	-161
	Other claims	2 E . R 4	-	-	-	-	-	-	-	-
	Credit from the Fund and Fund administered resources	2 Y . R 4	36	36	-	-	-	-	-	-
	Conversion rates: Australian dollars per U.S. Dollar	. . . F 4	.9859	1.1100	1.1395	1.4319	1.4960	1.4282	1.2799	1.2646

Source: Reprinted with permission of the International Monetary Fund

payments, but may be readily available from other international and national sources.

Certain events in the past can give a hint of the future: heavy incoming investment in past years will almost certainly mean steadily increasing expenses for dividends in the future. A nation that has been dependent on the export of a single commodity in the past is not likely to lessen that dependency in the immediate future. (A country like Australia, however, provides the example of a shift in dependency on export products from wool up to the 1950s, then to beef and then to iron ore and coal.) Ores and minerals are subject to fluctuating demand, competitive sources, and technological changes. Long-term global commodity price trends can suggest future levels of export income. Sudden changes in prices, such as those seen since the 1970s with oil, can have a tremendous impact, both on those countries that have the commodity and on those that do not have it.

Some countries, such as The Bahamas, depend heavily on tourism as a major contributor to their balance of payments. Their ability to import and service their debt is heavily dependent on the continued attractiveness of the country to foreign tourists.

Income from remittances of nationals working in other countries has been a major source of income to some countries. When those nationals are sent home because of reduced jobs in the foreign country, the country's balance of payments can suffer a severe blow from reduced foreign exchange. This was the case with countries such as Bangladesh (described by the World Bank as one of the poorest countries in the world) with the Persian Gulf crisis of 1990 when tens of thousands of workers lost their jobs and had to return home. In 1987 their "workers' remittances from abroad. . . [had] exceeded $700 million, equivalent to about 28 percent of imports"[19] and 60 percent of the country's total foreign earnings from merchandise exports.[20]

Preparing ratios from certain key items in the balance of payments and from other economic sources can be meaningful guides for assessing country risk. Such ratios highlight trends and facilitate comparisons between countries of comparable levels of economic development. Examples of some of these ratios can be seen in the report prepared by the Federal Reserve Bank of New York for the ICERC that ranks countries by their ability to service external obligations. "The rankings are based on five basic ratios: current account deficit to exports; cumulative current account to exports; net external interest payments to exports; net external interest payments to international reserves; and total current debt service requirements to receipts from exports of goods and services."[21] This illustrates the importance of certain categories of data selected to meet a particular analytical need. Another comparison often studied by analysts is the number of months a nation's reserves would finance the country's imports. Good ratio analysis is only the beginning of the evaluation.

Each bank is responsible for making its own evaluation of the risk of doing business in another country. After making the economic and political assessments described, how does a bank come to a conclusion?

There is no one solution. Each bank does its own analysis and comes to its own assessment. Different banks may review the same data and come to different conclusions. Overall, each bank is seeking to answer the question of whether it can expect that any credit extended to a borrower in a country will be repaid. Part of this is the credit assessment of the borrower, whether it be a corporation, a bank, or an entity of the government. Beyond the normal credit assessment process, however, the bank is also concerned that conditions in a country may change. Changes may impair a borrower's ability to obtain foreign exchange to repay the credit or the ability to continue to operate in the same environment as existed when the credit was extended.

Based on its experience, the bank will examine economic trends and project these into the future when the credit is due to be repaid. It will assess political and social trends and the likelihood of changes and their impact, in turn, on the economic environment. Whether the bank does this by relying on the experience of a few key individuals or through a structure of committees, it must arrive at a decision. On the basis of that decision it will develop a business plan for that country, which then must be communicated to all those in the bank responsible for credit, foreign exchange, or investments.

Business Development

Although country risk assessment is usually done to identify, and thereby avoid, risks that may cause a future loss, it can likewise indicate (but not guarantee) those countries that have an outlook for political stability and economic growth. Utilized in this way it becomes a business development tool for the banker in identifying nations and businesses with factors of strength that would lead to their success, precisely those which a bank would want as its customers. "Every nation possesses what economists have termed *factors of production*. Factors of production are nothing more than the inputs necessary to compete in any industry, such as labor, arable land, natural resources, capital, [knowledge], and infrastructure. . . . A nation will export those goods which make intensive use of the factors with which it is relatively well endowed. The United States, for example, has been a substantial exporter of agricultural goods, reflecting in part its unusual abundance of large tracts of arable land. A nation's endowment of factors clearly plays a role in the competitive advantage of a nation's firms, as the rapid growth of manufacturing in low-wage countries such as Hong Kong, Taiwan, and more recently Thailand, attests. . . . The factors most important to competitive advantage in most industries, especially the industries most vital to productive growth in advanced economies, are not inherited but are created within a nation, through processes that differ widely across nations and among industries. Thus, the stock of factors at any particular time is less important than the rate at which they are created, upgraded, and made more specialized to particular industries."[22]

"A nation's competitive industries are not spread evenly through an economy but are connected in . . . *clusters* consisting of industries related by links of various kinds. In Italy, for example, over 40 percent of total exports are due to clusters of industries all connected to food, fashion, or the home. In Sweden, over 50 percent of total exports are industry clusters in transportation, forest products, and metals."[23]

With this type of analysis of a country, the banker can fashion a business-development plan. The information needed for the country profile—that is, the country risk analysis— provides detailed data about the investment sources, the nation's commodity trade, and the countries that are its customary markets. It should be a short step then to match this information with the market in which the bank's present customers deal. This type of application is equally suitable for the small as for the large bank.

ACCOUNTING

When ICERC requires a bank to establish a specific reserve against its outstandings in that country, the bank may do this by either charging off the amount, which may be a percentage of all their outstandings in that country, as any other loan loss, or it may establish a specific reserve account: *allocated transfer risk reserve.* "Such reserves shall be charged against current income and shall not be considered as part of capital and surplus or allowances for possible loan losses for regulatory, supervisory, or disclosure purposes."[24] This means the amount is excluded in calculating the bank's capital adequacy or risk-based capital ratios (see chapter 2).

SUMMARY

Country risk assessment is a vital analysis for a bank doing business in the international market. Proper management of a bank's business as well as the dictates of bank regulators will require attention to the risks of doing business in another country. To do this, the banker needs to understand the balance of payments as a source of economic data and analysis. The banker must also be able to consider and analyze the probabilities of political trends. With these tools the banker can make an assessment as to the level of risks in another country and whether the bank is prepared to accept that level. The country risk decision, credit evaluation of the borrower, analysis of the requested transaction, and the bank's policies are the elements of managing a bank's credit portfolio.

QUESTIONS

1. What is meant by balance of payments?
2. What is country risk?
3. If a country has a deficit balance of payments in one year, how can it correct it?
4. What is the role of ICERC?

PROBLEM

The balance of payments concept can be applied to a city as well as to a nation. Consider your community. This can be a town or a part of a large city, bearing in mind that cities consist of neighborhoods. How would you reflect the following items if you were making up a balance of payments for your community? Each item is either "visible trade," "invisible trade," or "investment." Each item is also either "income" or "expense" to the community unless it takes place completely within the community.

Citrus sold at a local market
New post office building
TV Guide magazine
Your mother flies in for a week's stay
Purchase of shares of IBM stock
Deposit for a hotel reservation in Hawaii
Your salary
Rent paid to a landlord who lives in Florida

Notes

1. Walter Bagehot, "The Danger of Lending to Semi-Civilized Countries" (November 23, 1867), *The Collected Works of Walter Bagehot,* ed. Norman St John-Stevas (London: *The Economist,* vol. 10, 1978), p. 419.

2. International Monetary Fund, *Balance of Payments Manual,* 4th ed. (Washington, D.C., 1977), par. 1.

3. *Ibid.,* par. 30.

4. *Ibid.,* par. 31.

5. *Ibid.,* par. 341.

6. "Balance of Payments," Harvard Business School Case Study 9-384-005, President and Fellows of Harvard College, Boston, 1983, p. 2.

7. International Monetary Fund, *op. cit.,* par. 196.

8. *Ibid.,* pars. 177-178.

9. Michael E. Porter, *The Competitive Advantage of Nations* (New York: The Free Press, 1990), p. 61.

10. International Monetary Fund, *op. cit.,* par. 152.

11. International Monetary Fund, *Report on the World Current Account Discrepancy* (Washington, D.C.: International Monetary Fund, 1987), p. 163.

12. *The New York Times Book Review,* September 23, 1990, p. 9. Quoting from Denis Healey, *The Time of My Life* (New York: W.W. Norton & Co., 1990).

13. The World Bank, *World Development Report 1983* (New York: Oxford University Press, 1983), p. 117.

14. Simon Schama, *The Embarrassment of Riches* (New York: Alfred A. Knopf, 1987), p. 30.

15. Jane Jacobs, *Cities and the Wealth of Nations* (New York: Random House, 1984), pp. 69-70.

16. *The Economist,* "Africa's Cities," September 15, 1990, p. 25.

17. Robert Bench, "International Lending Supervision," *International Banking: U.S. Laws and Regulations* (Washington, D.C.: American Bankers Association, 1984), pp. 4-32.

18. *Ibid.*, Sec. 4, p.27.

19. The World Bank, *Trends in Developing Economies 1989* (Washington, D.C.: The World Bank, 1989), p. 15.

20. International Monetary Fund, *Balance of Payments Statistics Yearbook Volume 39 Part 1* (Washington, D.C.: International Monetary Fund, 1988), p. 52.

21. Bench, *op. cit.*, Sec. 4, p.26.

22. Porter, *op. cit.*, pp. 73-74.

23. Porter, *op. cit.*, pp. 131-132.

24. International Lending Supervision Act of 1983 (97 Stat. 1278) Section 905: (a) (2).

4

International Correspondent Banking Relationships

A key element in international banking is that banks throughout the world are active customers of one another and readily assist each other in various aspects of their business. This *correspondent banking* relationship is the cornerstone for the functioning of international banking. It is the framework for transferring funds, exchanging funds, and financing international trade through the banking system. The role of governments in these activities is slight, usually only to correct occasional imbalances that occur, to conduct their own lending (see chapter 16), or to stabilize foreign exchange markets (see chapter 12). Day-to-day international banking relies on the network of correspondent banking relations.

The objectives of this chapter are to
- explain how correspondent banking relationships begin
- show what types of accounts banks maintain
- compare how these accounts are used
- examine other factors involved in correspondent banking relationships

BACKGROUND

International banking works because banks in different countries are willing to cooperate in doing business with each other. Each bank serves its own national or local market and at the same time is willing to assist the other bank, thereby accommodating each other's customers. This is called correspondent banking.

Major banks become international correspondents of each other to provide their customers with services in each other's markets. Small banks become correspondents of large international banks to obtain services in a major market and also to obtain specialized assistance, including lines of credit to support their operations. Larger banks become correspondents with smaller banks to gain access to regional markets. Small banks in foreign countries particularly need the financial help of major U.S. banks for the banking and financing of foreign trade and for obtaining working capital to enable their customers to borrow for business needs. In providing services and funds to a correspondent bank, the large international bank is putting surplus funds from a developed country to short-term use for development of another country.

A correspondent banking relationship may be initiated by either bank. The large U.S. banks have officers either resident in foreign countries or traveling through them. One of the responsibilities of these officers is to develop new correspondent relationships. A foreign bank will seek out U.S. and other foreign banking relationships. Both sides benefit from a correspondent banking relationship.

Less than 1 percent of U.S. banks have branches in another country, and even the majority of these do not maintain a large global network of branches or subsidiaries. Thus, it is the active foreign correspondent banking relationships that enable a U.S. bank to offer its customers a full range of services in another country. The U.S. bank can request the assistance of its correspondent in the foreign community with trade-related business, money transfers, or introductions for its customers to foreign companies. Such assistance is readily given, thereby enabling a regional U.S. bank to compete in customer service with the largest banks. This use of a correspondent relationship can also assist even the largest banks in areas where they do not have a branch. It enables every bank to help its customers with even an occasional transaction in any country. The cost of a complete global network of branches to do this would be prohibitive.

At the initiation of a relationship, the two banks will exchange information ("terms and conditions") on the services they can perform for each other (collections, payments, letters of credit, foreign exchange, securities, and the like) and the fees for these services. The banks also exchange signature books and confidential telegraphic test keys.

A bank's *signature book* contains facsimiles of the signatures of individuals authorized to commit the bank and states each bank's policy as to whether one or two officers must sign for various transactions. Policies for correspondent banks differ from those for commercial customers. Banks do not require corporate resolutions to open accounts, and signature cards are not used. A unique characteristic of correspondent banking is that both sides exchange signature books. Even though usually only one account is opened, both banks need to have the other's authorized signatures on file. It is always the responsibility of the receiving bank to be certain that signatures on any instructions received from another bank are bona fide. The *telegraphic test keys* are code arrangements that enable banks receiving teletransmissions from other banks to verify that these are authentic in the place of written signatures (see chapter 5).

ACCOUNTS IN AN INTERNATIONAL DEPARTMENT

The basis upon which international banking rests is that banks in one country maintain deposit accounts with banks in other countries to serve the needs of the customers of both banks. When funds are debited or credited in such an account, money is said to "move" from one country to another.

The accounts in a U.S. bank's international department are established by foreign governments, banks in other countries, individuals, and businesses from other countries or in the U.S. who, being actively engaged in international business, require the special expertise of the international banker. These are demand accounts paying no interest. However, in some instances the depositor may establish a time deposit that will earn interest.

Due To Accounts

A demand account maintained by a foreign bank in a U.S. bank is referred to as a *Due To* or vostro account. The account is denominated in U.S. dollars. Such an account may originate at the beginning of a correspondent banking relationship. The major U.S. banks solicit Due To accounts from banks around the world. These accounts are useful for the foreign banks because much of world trade and finance is denominated in U.S. dollars. Having a Due To account enables a foreign bank to make direct payments to other countries, handle foreign collections, and settle drafts under letters of credit. Such accounts are opened routinely at major banks and can be profitable for the bank where they are opened since they provide deposits for the bank.

Due From Accounts

An account maintained by a U.S. bank in a foreign bank is referred to as a *Due From* or nostro account. Such an account is generally denominated in the currency of the foreign country, and the account will be under the control of the foreign exchange trader. The usual procedure in the U.S. bank's international department is to keep the record of the account on its own ledgers in both the foreign currency and its dollar equivalent. By this means the international department can reflect the activity as it will actually be posted in its account in the foreign currency and at the same time have a U.S. dollar equivalent for its own financial statement; thus the Due From account is also called a *Dual Currency* account.

A U.S. bank does not establish a Due From account for each Due To account. A major U.S. bank will have more Due To accounts on its books from foreign banks than Due From accounts it maintains abroad because of the importance of the U.S. dollar in world business, as well as the extensive international correspondent relationships that major U.S. banks have established. A large U.S. bank may maintain one or two Due From accounts in a particular country, while at the same time receiving several hundred Due To accounts in dollars established by banks in that country.

Many factors influence an international department's decision about the location of its Due From account and the size of its balances. Basically, the accounts will be established in countries where a bank's customers need to make payments and in countries whose currencies will be needed for trading activities by the foreign exchange trader. A bank does not want to have more foreign currency Due From accounts than are needed to serve its purposes. "The U.S. bank must maintain adequate balances in its nostro accounts to meet unexpected needs and to avoid overdrawing those accounts for which interest must be paid. However, the bank must not lose income by maintaining excessive idle nostro balances which do not earn interest."[1] Also, holding foreign exchange can be risky as it can devalue relative to the dollar. A bank will therefore tend to establish a Due From account, once it determines it needs such an account, in its best correspondent bank of the country.

Statements on Accounts

The bookkeeping or accounting section of the international department prepares and sends out statements on all of the bank's Due To accounts. These statements usually use a simplified standard descriptive posting supported by explanatory vouchers. The international department also receives statements on its accounts in foreign banks.

These statements must be reconciled with the international department's own entries. Discrepancies often emerge between the statements and the international department's entries, and the correspondence designed to correct such discrepancies may continue for a long time. Thus, the foreign account of a bank (as well as accounts the bank has from other banks) is almost never free from "we debit—you do not credit" or "we credit—you do not debit" items. Regardless of the time needed for such corrections, however, they must be made to prevent losses to the bank.

Using the Accounts

The establishment of only one account between two banks is sufficient for the conduct of all their business, for the transfer of funds from one country to another, for payments to be made in either country in either currency, or to a third country in that country's currency. Usually this account will be the Due To account established by the foreign bank in the U.S. bank. Once the account has been established, the banks use it to conduct international business.

For example, after a foreign bank has purchased a U.S. dollar traveler's check from a tourist paying out the equivalent in local currency, the bank needs to clear the check and get the dollars into usable funds. It does this by sending it to the bank where it has a Due To account and depositing it, just as an individual deposits checks for credit to the individual's checking account. A foreign bank sends *cash letters* containing these traveler's checks, other dollar checks, and money orders that it and its clients receive in payment from U.S. businesses and tourists for deposit to its account in a U.S. bank. A cash letter is a transmittal letter accompanying items for deposit to an account. Occasionally even accumulated cash is shipped. Once these funds are in its account, the foreign bank can send instructions to make payments to individuals in the United States on behalf of one of its clients to the debit of its account or to draw checks against its account for payments. A commercial bank is willing to buy a check or draft drawn in one currency and pay out another because it knows that another customer will need the first currency in another transaction, and in the process it expects to show a profit in the conversion.

This willingness of banks to receive or pay out cash in their country against debits or deposits made to their account in another country is the foundation on which international banking is built.

Conversely, the U.S. bank uses the account established on its books to credit the foreign bank with the proceeds of collections, letters of credit, and payments that it requests the foreign bank to make (see chapter 5). This Due To account can also be used to make payments to third countries. The foreign bank may send instructions for such a payment, and the U.S. bank will debit the Due To account for the equivalent U.S. dollars of the foreign currency amount, which it will instruct a third bank to make by debiting, in turn, the U.S. bank's account in that currency. The fundamental fact is that, once a foreign bank establishes an account with a U.S. bank that has an active international banking department, that foreign bank has global access for all its needs and can provide its customers with worldwide coverage.

The large volume of transfers through a bank's account will occasionally result in a mishandling of a bank's instructions. When this happens the bank that made the error will compensate the other bank for the earnings it lost because the funds were not available for its use.

Domestic Correspondent Banking

International departments of major banks in the United States also make their facilities available to other banks in the United States. Assume that the international business of a small domestic bank is limited to occasional requests from its customers for the remittance of funds to pay for their purchases, subscriptions to publications, and the like. Without facilities for handling such transactions, the small bank would probably resort to the issuance of its own cashier's checks.

The use of a bank's cashier's check is inappropriate for the bank and inconvenient for the payee, primarily because the check is not payable in the payee's own country. A local bank will probably negotiate the check only on a collection basis, which means a delay of weeks and the additional cost of a collection fee. Moreover, charges for the accommodation are shifted from the purchaser of the check, by whom they should be paid, to the payee or the recipient of the funds.

New industry in the service area of a small bank may develop a certain amount of international business, but not enough to justify the bank's establishing a large international department. In such cases, the small bank can turn to its money-center correspondent bank for installation of a drawing plan (for the drawing of drafts through the facilities of the correspondent bank) and a remittance service (facilities for transferring funds by airmail or by cable, depending on the time allowed). When the system is installed, the correspondent bank provides the draft forms, usually consisting of (1) the draft, (2) a receipt for the customer, (3) an advice for the correspondent bank, and (4) a file copy. All these forms are imprinted with the name of the small bank, without mention of the correspondent bank, so the small bank's customer has no knowledge of the involvement of the correspondent bank. The correspondent bank advises the foreign bank on whom the draft is drawn of its issuance and explains the method of reimbursing the drawee bank for its payment, which is usually done by crediting the Due To account of the foreign bank.

A manual outlining the method of handling the sale of both foreign drafts and remittances is provided by the correspondent bank. (Such a manual is also used by branches of large metropolitan banks.) The manual shows the commission to be charged to the purchaser (which the small bank and the correspondent bank usually split), the airmail and cable charges by countries, and the titles and addresses of the banks on which drafts may be drawn. Drafts and remittances may be in U.S. dollars or in foreign currency. The correspondent bank periodically sends the small bank the current selling rates for various currencies in order to facilitate the sale of drafts and remittances in foreign exchange.

Sometimes the manual includes other services that may be extended to the small bank's customers. By having more services at its disposal, the small bank can accommodate its customers at rates similar to those that would have been charged had the customer dealt directly with the correspondent bank.

A large bank benefits by encouraging such business since it provides an opportunity to generate transaction volume from a regional market to which it might not otherwise have access. Increasing volume through such operations may lower the per unit costs for all other business.

**TRANSACTION
ENTRIES**

In the operation of Due To and Due From accounts, each bank in a correspondent relationship views the same account differently. When a foreign bank establishes a U.S. dollar account in a U.S. bank, the U.S. bank considers it a Due To account ("due to foreign bank"), while the foreign bank will consider it to be a Due From account ("due from U.S. bank"). In this example, there is only one account. Conversely, a foreign currency account maintained by a U.S. bank in a foreign bank is a Due From account as far as the U.S. bank is concerned, but a Due To account from the point of view of the foreign bank. Thus, it can often be confusing in bank-to-bank correspondence to use the terms "Due To" and "Due From." Often the accounts are referred to as "your account" or "our account" for clarity.

What happens when a U.S. bank issues a foreign draft or remittance order for $1,000 in U.S. currency on behalf of one of its customers? The entries can be illustrated by using what are generally referred to as T accounts. The left side shows changes (+ increase, - decrease) in the asset accounts of the bank's balance sheet. The right side reflects the changes in the liability accounts:

U.S. Bank		Foreign Bank	
(1) Cash from customer + $1,000	(2) Due to foreign bank account + $1,000	(2) Due from U.S. bank account +$1,000	
		(3) Cash payment to beneficiary - $1,000 (equivalent)	

If the U.S. customer wants the draft or remittance order issued in foreign currency, the two banks' entries will be as follows (assuming that the U.S. bank has an account in the foreign bank):

U.S. Bank		Foreign Bank	
(1) Cash from U.S. customer + $1,000		(3) Cash payment to beneficiary - $1,000 (equivalent)	(2) Due to bank account - $1,000 (equivalent)
(2) Due from foreign bank account - $ 1,000 (equivalent)			

Other Services

On behalf of its international correspondent bank, the U.S. bank will act as the other bank's window into the U.S. market. If a customer of the foreign bank wishes to purchase U.S. stocks or bonds, the foreign bank can request the assistance of the U.S. bank. The latter will forward the order to a registered brokerage firm, arrange for payment to the debit of the foreign bank's Due To account, and receive the actual securities for forwarding or holding on behalf of its correspondent.

The U.S. bank can obtain credit checkings for the foreign bank on U.S. firms that may be buyers from or sellers to the foreign bank's customer. In furthering international trade, the U.S. bank can assist by introducing its customers to foreign businesses or assist the latter, again at the request of the foreign correspondent, in contacting or meeting potential U.S. suppliers or customers. Likewise, the foreign bank may assist by introducing U.S. bankers and their customers to local businesses.

A foreign bank trading in the foreign exchange or Eurodollar markets can use its U.S. dollar account to settle the transaction by arranging to have dollars credited or debited to its Due To account at its U.S. correspondent. In the same manner, a foreign bank can use this account to transfer funds when one of its local customers may be an affiliate, subsidiary, or branch of a U.S. corporation. Many such corporations are very concerned to transfer their cash surpluses into central accounts where the funds may be invested or otherwise quickly used by the company. This practice of *cash mobilization* has become increasingly important to corporate treasurers in order to obtain added earnings from cash balances that otherwise would not be earning anything in a noninterest-bearing demand account. The foreign bank that assists the corporation by the quick transfer of surplus balances through the bank's dollar account will probably obtain other local currency business from that company as compensation.

The use of a correspondent bank is very important in the banking of international trade, as shall be seen in chapters 6 through 9. Likewise, the smaller foreign bank often looks to its U.S. correspondent bank as a source of credit. This is covered in chapter 14.

This relationship can also provide an opportunity for the domestic or international correspondent bank to purchase participations in loans that one of them has made, to be invited into loan syndications, or to provide access for the regional bank's customers into new capital market investment products (see chapter 17).

ACCOUNTING	Due To accounts of foreign banks are listed in the financial statement with other deposits in a bank as Liabilities. The Federal Reserve requires reserves to be held against these deposits in U.S. offices as with all other domestic balances in a U.S. bank. Deposits in overseas branches or IBFs (see chapter 2) do not require maintaining reserve balances at the Federal Reserve Bank.

Due From accounts are listed as Assets. The *Risk-Based Capital Guidelines* risk-weight these accounts, which have a maturity of one year or less, at 20 percent, without differentiation for the country in which they are located. |

SUMMARY

Establishing correspondent banking relationships is vital for banks in foreign countries and in the United States. It allows a small bank to gain assistance from a larger bank in credit and international operations. Banks become correspondents in order to have access to local markets and currencies, to settle trading transactions, and to have a local bank that can provide various services. A U.S. bank with a large correspondent network benefits from the earnings of increased deposit balances, opportunities for foreign exchange and money market trading volume, and fees from many of the noncredit services.

QUESTIONS

1. What is the difference between a Due To and Due From account?
2. What is a correspondent bank?
3. How does a domestic correspondent relationship in the United States with a large bank assist a small bank in conducting its international business?
4. How does a foreign bank deposit dollar checks, such as traveler's checks, that it has cashed from tourists?

Notes

1.   United States Department of the Treasury, *Comptroller's Handbook for National Bank Examiners* (Englewood Cliffs, N.J.: Prentice-Hall, Inc., 1982), Section 202.1, p. 2.

5

Money Transfers

When people need to use the international services of a bank, it is usually for transferring money from one country to another. An individual may want to send money to a relative living abroad, to a child going to school or traveling abroad, or to order something from a store in another country. A business may want to send money to pay for merchandise that is to be shipped when prepaid or to settle a bill for a shipment that was made on open account. Individuals and businesses want to make short- and long-term investments. Businesses and banks also need to transfer money to settle trades in foreign exchange or Eurodollars. Whatever the reason, the mechanisms banks have established as a consequence of being correspondents with other banks enable them easily to meet the needs of all these customers.

The international payments system differs from that in the United States. When a U.S. bank wishes to transfer funds to another U.S. bank or to clear checks drawn in other parts of the country, it may use facilities of the Federal Reserve System, which is the central bank of the United States. Internationally, no such central bank exists. Banks must utilize their correspondent banks to accomplish such services.

Any payment does two things: It sends a message to pay someone and makes the actual transfer of money to settle or reimburse the payment. The distinction between the two things is particularly evident internationally where the U.S. dollar is widely used to make payments to many other countries with their own currencies. The actual settlement of the dollars will be done in the United States where the dollar is legal tender. Similarly, for example, a payment in pounds sterling would be settled over accounts in British banks.

Tourists will usually carry their money with them, and thus they look to their local bank to provide a safe, convenient means to do so. The establishment and acceptability of the traveler's check meets this need.

The objectives of this chapter are to
- show how banks provide this transfer function
- outline the different instruments used to transfer funds
- explain how banks actually accomplish the transfers
- describe the different systems for settlement

BASIC INSTRUMENTS

The basic means by which banks transfer funds upon request of a client is through the network of correspondent bank accounts, both foreign and domestic. Instructions to do this are given through remittance orders or foreign drafts. An essential part of these instructions is *settlement,* the means by which the money is transferred from one bank to the other. The sending bank may credit the account of the receiving bank; the receiving bank may debit the account of the sending bank; or a credit may be made to the receiving bank's account at a third bank. In international payments the selection of settlement will be determined by the currency being used and the existence of accounts between the two banks.

Remittance by Airmail

The simplest way to transfer funds is through an airmail letter from a bank in one country to a bank in another country requesting that bank to pay a specified amount to a named payee. An airmail remittance letter specifies the details of payment: the amount, the name and address of the beneficiary, and the name of the sender. The letter contains the proper number and class of authorized signatures. It indicates how the settlement between the two banks will take place.

When a U.S. customer wants to remit funds to a beneficiary in a foreign country, the U.S. bank receives the money plus its commission and airmail expenses along with the payment instructions. The U.S. bank sends a letter to a foreign bank advising in addition that, in reimbursement, the U.S. bank has credited the money to the account (Due To) of the foreign bank when the remittance is in U.S. dollars or has authorized the foreign bank to debit the account (Due From) when the payment is denominated in that foreign currency. The foreign bank, upon receiving this remittance letter, verifies its authenticity by comparing the signatures on the letter with the facsimiles on file in that bank's signature book. If the signatures compare favorably, then the paying bank knows it is acting on bona fide instructions.

It should be noted that in all remittances or foreign drafts the foreign bank will usually pay the beneficiary in the local currency; if the transfer is stated in U.S. dollars, the foreign bank will convert this amount into the equivalent local currency. There are many reasons for this practice. The laws or regulations of the paying country may require it, but equally important is the fact that the foreign bank will usually not have U.S. dollars on hand, because dollars are not the legal currency of that country. The conversion will be at the rate of exchange as determined by the paying bank.

Remittance by Teletransmission

A remittance by teletransmission is exactly the same as a remittance by airmail, except that the message between banks is sent by means of one of the many telegraphic or electronic communication systems. The expression "cable remittance" is sometimes used; this term originated in the past when the only fast option was through international cable companies. This method of remittance is used when speed is important or the amount is large. Instructions from bank to bank can even be sent by telephone. Since there is no signature to verify the message's authenticity, a code or test key arrangement must be used for verification. These codes are kept under very strict security.

Although test keys vary in format from bank to bank, they generally consist of a group of tables of numbers, perhaps one for the day of the month, another for the month of the year, another for the currency, and another for the amount (omitting decimals) or—if more than one amount is mentioned in the message—the amount of the total. The table for the amount provides numbers for the thousands, hundreds, tens, and digits. This test key may be used by a number of banks. A large bank may use it with all its correspondents. Therefore, to make it a bilateral test key applicable to only one correspondent, a special fixed number is added. The fixed number will be different for each correspondent bank and known only to the two banks. A variable number, based on the number of messages sent on a given day, may also be included. A prefix may be substituted for the variable number. To arrive at a test number, the indicated numbers are totaled; the total usually precedes the text of the message. The receiving bank uses the same procedure, employing its copy of the code, and if it arrives at the same test number, then it can assume that the message originates from the other bank.

Figure 5.1 shows the computation of a test for $1,500 sent on August 31. Additional pages of the test key would cover currency.

Figure 5.1 Telegraphic Test Key

Table 1–Fixed Number

(829)

Table 2–Month

January	86	April	42	July	22	October	36
February	51	May	30	August	(81)	November	58
March	38	June	51	September	18	December	67

Table 3–Date

1st	20	7th	12	13th	53	19th	85	25th	75	31st	(191)
2nd	37	8th	90	14th	62	20th	142	26th	136		
3rd	10	9th	74	15th	19	21st	33	27th	91		
4th	4	10th	77	16th	66	22nd	120	28th	230		
5th	61	11th	83	17th	44	23rd	99	29th	72		
6th	26	12th	17	18th	138	24th	95	30th	93		

Table 4–Amount

100,000	54	10,000	27	1,000	(48)	100	60	10	88	1	79
200,000	29	20,000	110	2,000	14	200	220	20	.52	2	35
300,000	3	30,000	11	3,000	16	300	5	30	9	3	49
400,000	39	40,000	131	4,000	167	400	137	40	81	4	32
500,000	43	50,000	1	5,000	23	500	(171)	50	129	5	13
600,000	87	60,000	56	6,000	59	600	251	60	65	6	205
700,000	15	70,000	89	7,000	68	700	47	70	112	7	96
800,000	6	80,000	161	8,000	156	800	45	80	230	8	92
900,000	2	90,000	97	9,000	71	900	34	90	98	9	7

1,000,000	78	10,000,000	46
2,000,000	25	20,000,000	94
3,000,000	73	30,000,000	40
4,000,000	64	40,000,000	114
5,000,000	24	50,000,000	10
6,000,000	8	60,000,000	84
7,000,000	82	70,000,000	76
8,000,000	28	80,000,000	57
9,000,000	55	90,000,000	70

Note: The test for this message is 1320.

Foreign Draft

A foreign draft (figure 5.2) is a negotiable instrument drawn by a bank on a foreign correspondent bank. It can be issued in any currency and is used when the client wants a negotiable instrument to mail rather than have it done by one bank sending payment instructions to another—that is, a remittance order. A foreign draft must be received by the beneficiary in order for that person to receive payment, whereas a remittance order makes the paying responsibility that of the two intermediary banks.

Figure 5.2 Foreign Draft

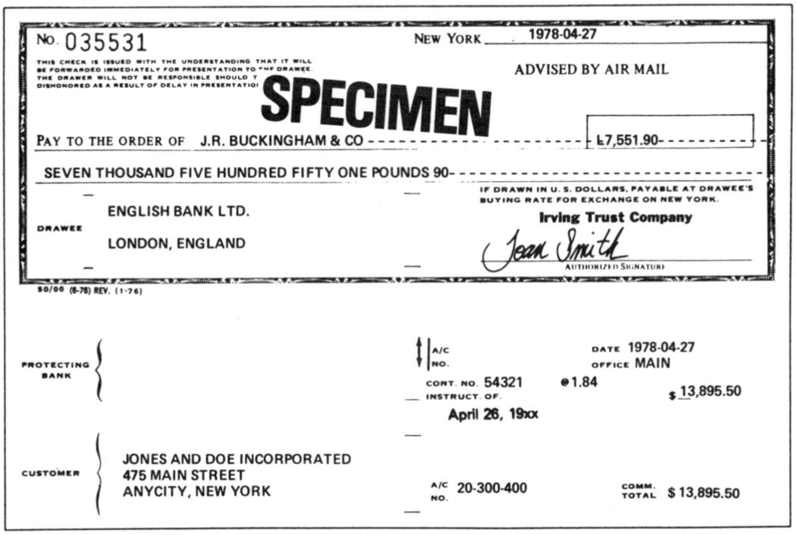
No. 035531
NEW YORK 1978-04-27
THIS CHECK IS ISSUED WITH THE UNDERSTANDING THAT IT WILL BE FORWARDED IMMEDIATELY FOR PRESENTATION TO THE DRAWEE. THE DRAWER WILL NOT BE RESPONSIBLE SHOULD T DISHONORED AS A RESULT OF DELAY IN PRESENTATIOI
ADVISED BY AIR MAIL
SPECIMEN
PAY TO THE ORDER OF J.R. BUCKINGHAM & CO
£7,551.90
SEVEN THOUSAND FIVE HUNDRED FIFTY ONE POUNDS 90
IF DRAWN IN U.S. DOLLARS, PAYABLE AT DRAWEE'S BUYING RATE FOR EXCHANGE ON NEW YORK.
DRAWEE
ENGLISH BANK LTD.
LONDON, ENGLAND
Irving Trust Company
Jean Smith
AUTHORIZED SIGNATURE
50/00 (6-78) REV. (1-76)
PROTECTING BANK
A/C NO.
CONT. NO. 54321
INSTRUCT. OF.
April 26, 19xx
1.84
DATE 1978-04-27
OFFICE MAIN
$ 13,895.50
CUSTOMER
JONES AND DOE INCORPORATED
475 MAIN STREET
ANYCITY, NEW YORK
A/C NO. 20-300-400
COMM. TOTAL $ 13,895.50

A bank's customer may request a foreign draft to attach to an invoice in order to pay a foreign bill. By doing so he or she makes it easier for the recipient to apply the funds to the correct account. When the foreign bank is presented with the foreign draft for payment, it will first verify the authenticity of the draft. This may be done in one of two ways: signature verification or advice. With signature verification the bank will compare the signature on the draft with those in the other bank's book of authorized signatures and with that bank's instructions as to the number of signatures required on foreign drafts. With the advice method, a bank will pay a foreign draft only after receiving a separate advice, that is, a letter from the issuing bank with an authorized signature or a tested teletransmission message. The advice method may be used by a bank with a large number of domestic branches whose officers do not have their signatures on file at the foreign correspondent. The advice method can present problems for the paying correspondent bank since the draft may be presented for payment before the advice is received. The receiving bank must then exercise its own judgment.

A bank with a large international network may place special drawing arrangements at the disposal of its domestic correspondents. This permits them to draw foreign drafts directly on the first bank's foreign correspondents. In this case the foreign bank will usually have to wait for an advice to arrive in order to confirm that the draft has been drawn under the "protection" of its correspondent.

When an original foreign draft is lost, a duplicate may be issued only after a stop payment order has been placed on the original. Some banks insist that the purchaser furnish a bond of indemnity before placing the stop payment. The ability to place the stop payment order will depend on the laws of the country of the paying bank. In some countries there is a minimum elapsed time required before such a stop payment can be placed, which might present problems for the original purchaser.

Operations

A bank with domestic branches or an active number of domestic correspondent banks will set up a system to enable these offices to issue foreign drafts or to take instructions for remittance orders from their customers rather than insisting that the customer go to the foreign department. This system enables the branch or correspondent to serve customers at a location convenient for the customer. It puts the bank's specialized service at the convenience of the user and thereby increases the volume of this business.

The domestic office needs to have a supply of foreign draft and remittance order forms plus an *arrangements book*, also called a *drawing guide*. This is a listing by country of the bank's foreign correspondents in various cities on which the domestic office may draw drafts. It will indicate whether drafts may be drawn on that bank in U.S. dollars or foreign currency. The arrangements book should also provide instructions to the domestic office personnel on how to fill out the draft. Although this may seem obvious to the international banker, it can often be a matter of concern and trepidation to the domestic banker who may infrequently issue foreign drafts.

For remittance orders the foreign department may select the foreign correspondent when it receives the instructions from the domestic office. The customer may wish to know what bank will be making the payment, and, consequently, the selection of the foreign bank may already be made when the instructions arrive at the foreign department.

Drafts and remittances from U.S. banking offices can be issued in either U.S. dollars or in many foreign currencies. If the customer has no preference, it is usually more advantageous for the bank to issue the payment in the foreign currency than in U.S. dollars. The reason is simple: When it is issued in U.S. dollars, the foreign bank sets the exchange rate at which it converts the U.S. dollars into the other currency paid to the payee. When issued in the foreign currency, the U.S. bank sets the exchange rate, thereby making any profit on the conversion (see chapter 11). Drafts drawn on a foreign bank in U.S. dollars usually contain a statement that the draft "Is payable at drawee's rate for bankers' drafts on New York," which means that the foreign bank sets the conversion rate.

After the domestic branch or correspondent bank has sold the foreign draft and given it to the customer or taken the instructions for the remittance order, the information and money must be processed promptly. When settlement is being made by a book entry (see below), the items issued in U.S. dollars will be credited to the Due To account of the foreign bank; those drawn in foreign currency will be posted to the Due From account. Depending on the bank's procedures, an advice may be sent for the foreign draft. For remittances the message will indicate to the foreign bank that in reimbursement "we credit your account" (U.S. dollars) or "charge our account" (foreign currency).

Table 5.1 summarizes the advantages and disadvantages of the three basic ways to transfer funds.

S.W.I.F.T.

Payment orders transmitted by data transmission may use the services provided by a number of independent companies. A widely used system is the *Society for Worldwide Interbank Financial Telecommunications* (S.W.I.F.T.), which began operations in 1977. It provides an automated international communications and information system between member banks. It is organized as a cooperative and is based in Belgium, providing member banks with standardized message formats in place of unstructured messages or incompatible message systems. This

Table 5.1 Summary of Transfer Methods

Method	Advantages	Disadvantages
Foreign draft	a. Can be attached to invoices and bills for ease in paying small amounts.	a. Must be received by beneficiary. Customer is responsible for mailing. b. Stop payments on lost drafts are time-consuming.
Remittance by airmail	a. Bank-to-bank instructions with banks responsible for making payments.	a. Beneficiary must await notification from bank. b. Depends on international airmail service.
Remittance by teletransmission	a. Fastest way to transfer funds. b. Bank-to-bank instructions with banks responsible for making payments.	a. Expensive. b. Beneficiary must await notification from bank.

facilitates processing and transmission. Over 120 message types cover customer and bank funds transfers, foreign exchange, loans, collections, letters of credit, as well as statements. Payment transactions are settled through designated correspondent accounts, since S.W.I.F.T. is only a communications system. S.W.I.F.T. does this through its own communications network, which is linked directly to the member banks. When it began in 1977, "505 users from 15 countries exchanged just 50,000 messages a day. [In 1989] 2,700 users from 67 countries sent more than 1.2 million messages a day."[1]

S.W.I.F.T. is often used instead of other cable systems for sending cable remittance orders because its standard formats have allowed participating banks to link this system directly to automated processing systems in the bank. While its emphasis has been on international transactions, it is used for intracountry transactions in the United States, Japan, and several European and Asian countries. Because S.W.I.F.T. uses a standardized message format, it becomes part of an automated funds transfer system when linked directly to a regional payments system such as CHIPS (described later in this chapter), where 80 percent of the messages are in the S.W.I.F.T. format. Such standardized message formats facilitate translation as well as processing. For example, in a transfer of funds, instead of the statement "by order of," S.W.I.F.T. uses "50:" and then the name. In whatever language they use, both the sending and receiving banks know what this means.

These messages also have various security features that authenticate the sender, the receiver, and verify that the message has not been altered in transmission. While being transmitted through their system, the messages are encrypted. This is separate from the bilateral test keys established between the two banks.

Traveler's Checks

Probably the most widely used negotiable instrument in international banking is the traveler's check (figure 5.3), which is also used domestically. The origins of these checks dates back to the eighteenth century. In the late nineteenth century they began to be regularly issued. Because of its worldwide acceptability, traveler's check in U.S. dollars constitutes the most common deposit to Due To accounts in U.S. banks. (Traveler's checks are also issued by many major foreign and U.S. banks in Japanese yen, Deutsche marks, pounds sterling, and other major currencies.) The traveler's check in the United States is issued by a few large banks and travel organizations in preprinted denominations: $10, $20, $50, $100, $500, and $ 1,000. The issuer commits itself to pay the stated sum to any payee and undertakes to repay the sum to the buyer if the check is lost or stolen before it is negotiated. Travelers thus feel that their money is safe.

The bank or agency that issues traveler's checks in the United States arranges for the design and printing of distinctive traveler's checks, distributes them to banks and travel agencies around the world to be available for sale, maintains comprehensive records of the inventory held by each seller, and is responsible for replenishing that inventory. When the traveler's checks are sold, the money is received by the issuer, who also must maintain a record of the purchaser of each traveler's check. When the check is cashed, the issuer must pay out the amount to the bank where it was deposited and simultaneously record on its records that this numbered check has now been paid. Equally important, the issuer must be prepared to replace lost or stolen checks.

Traveler's checks have become an important part of international banking as well as international travel; they enter into the overall correspondent banking relationships particularly because they generate a steady flow of deposits into Due To accounts in the United States.

Figure 5.3   Traveler's Check

SETTLEMENT

Settlement is the process of actually moving the funds from the sender to the recipient to complete the money transfer. Settlement is accomplished by moving balances in bank accounts; rarely does it involve the shipment of actual currency. It can be as simple as a *book entry*—moving funds from one account to another within the same bank (see chapter 4). For larger transactions, such as foreign exchange trading or money market trading related to Eurodollars (see chapter 15), settlement may generally involve several banks. In such cases settlement will be done through Fedwire or CHIPS.

"In Fedwire, payment orders result in virtually instantaneous debits and credits on the books of the Reserve Banks without any independent action on the part of the sending or receiving bank. Similarly, CHIPS messages are settled virtually automatically at the end of the day. Payment orders sent over S.W.I.F.T., on the other hand, must be settled independently of the S.W.I.F.T. system through correspondent accounts or through Fedwire or CHIPS transfers."[2]

Fedwire

Fedwire is a message and payment system of the Federal Reserve System for transfers within the United States. The network consists of computer systems located in the 12 Federal Reserve District Banks linked together by an automated message switching station. All banks in the United States, including branches of foreign banks, are required to maintain reserves that are a percentage of deposits on their books. These reserves, held in that bank's account at one of the Federal Reserve banks, are then referred to as *federal funds*. The accounts are available for making payments. "Under FedWire, a payment is made as soon as a transaction is completed. For money transferred through the FedWire system (called Fed funds) the transfer is instantaneous and final. When a bank transfers funds over the system to another member bank, the account of the originator bank is immediately debited and the account of the beneficiary credited. Each transaction is independent and there is no 'netting out' of claims."[3]

CHIPS

The *Clearing House Interbank Payments System* (CHIPS) is a private computerized on-line real-time large-dollar network for U.S. dollar transfers that is owned and operated by the New York Clearing House Association. There are 136 participants of which 20 participate in the end-of-day settlement (May 1990). These latter, referred to as settling banks, are those that "have the size and financial strength to handle huge payment volumes."[4] Participants are in New York City and include banks headquartered there, New York branches, and agencies of foreign banks (about two-thirds of the participants), and Edge Acts.

CHIPS enables payments to be made during the day with each transaction considered irrevocable, but with the actual settlement done at the end of the day based on each participant's net position. Thus, a bank sending payment orders of $10 million to various banks during the day and receiving orders for $9 million would make one transfer of dollars at the end of the day to settle its net of $1 million (see box).

CHIPS handles between 100,000 to 200,000 payments on an average day representing approximately $1 trillion some days. It is the "central clearing system in the United States for international transactions, handling over 90 percent of all dollar payments moving between countries around the world."[5]

Daylight Overdrafts

When more money is paid out of an account than is in that account, an *overdraft* is created. This is a form of a loan and, generally, interest will be assessed by a bank when the overdraft exists at the end of a business day. However, to operate the huge volume of daily payments, banks routinely have to temporarily overdraw accounts on their books during the day. They do so with the confident expectation that other covering funds will come in later in the day so that no day-end overdraft will remain.

Settling Through CHIPS

Every participant in CHIPS has a terminal computer, linked by leased telephone lines to the central CHIPS computer, through which it can directly send and receive payment messages. The central CHIPS computer immediately processes all such messages. Then, at 4:30 p.m., it produces for each participating bank item-by-item detailed reports of payments made to and received by it and by institutions holding accounts with it; the printout also indicates the bank's gross position with CHIPS, the gross and net positions of any banks for whom the bank settles, and finally, if the bank is a settling bank, its net net—the dollars it must send out or will receive due to CHIPS settlement. Also, by netting debits and credits, CHIPS figures each participating bank's net position vis-à-vis every other participating bank and the system as a whole....

After CHIPS figures come out at 4:30 participants who are not settling banks settle their accounts at one of the settling banks. Each settling bank that, on a net-net basis, has a debit balance with CHIPS sends over the Fedwire to the [settlement account] that CHIPS maintains at [the Federal Reserve Bank of New York] the sum required for it to settle. After CHIPS has received these monies, it in turn wires out, again over Fedwire, all monies it owes settling banks who have ended the day on a net-net basis with a credit balance at CHIPS. Monies are supposed to flow into CHIPS' account from settling banks with a net-net debit balance by 5:30 p.m. and to go out to settling banks with a net-net credit balance by 6 p.m.; at that time, the balance in CHIPS' account at the Fed should return to zero.

Reprinted with permission, Marcia Stigum, *The Money Market*, 3d ed. (Homewood, Ill.: Business One Irwin, 1990), pp. 894-895.

These are referred to as *daylight overdrafts*. If, however, the crediting funds did not appear, it could present a very serious problem for the paying bank, perhaps causing it to exceed its legal lending limit (see chapter 14) and even impair its capital. To protect intermediaries and ultimately the entire U.S. payments system, banks, CHIPS, and the Federal Reserve System now establish *caps*—predetermined limits on the amount of daylight overdraft they will permit to other banks.[6] A bank, for example, receiving instructions from an overseas correspondent bank to make payments totaling $10 million, but for which it has established a limit of $5 million, will pay out whatever funds are in the account and then $5 million. The remaining payment orders will be held until sufficient funds come into the account during the day.

SUMMARY

Banks provide a variety of means for individuals, businesses, and banks to transfer money from one country to another. The system centers on using the network of accounts that banks have established with each other as part of their overall correspondent relationship. The means include actual negotiable instruments, such as foreign drafts and traveler's checks, as well as bank-to-bank instructions, such as remittances. To transfer large sums rapidly, banks have also developed various computerized systems, which are the forerunners of greater expansion in the future.

QUESTIONS

1. What is the difference between a foreign draft and a remittance order?
2. What is the difference between CHIPS and S.W.I.F.T.?
3. What is the function of a telegraphic test key arrangement?
4. What is a settlement made by book-entry?

Notes

1. "SWIFT and securities: flight or just fancy," *Global Custodian*, March 1990, p. 49.
2. *Federal Reserve Bulletin*, April 1990, p. 214.
3. "A Note on Payment Systems," Harvard Business School Case Study 0-485-030, President and Fellows of Harvard College, Boston, 1984, p. 3.
4. Marcia Stigum, *The Money Market*, 3d ed. (Homewood, Ill.: Business One Irwin, 1990), p. 895.
5. *Clearing House InterBank Payments System* (New York: The New York Clearing House Association), p. 1.
6. For full details on the application of Federal Reserve policies on Net Credit Limits and Net Debit Caps *see:* Board of Governors of the Federal Reserve System, *Payment System Handbook* (Washington, D.C.: 1988-1990) "Risk-Reduction Policy" section 9-1000 and following.

6

The Business of Foreign Trade

Facilitating international trade is one of the most important activities in a bank's international department. While many of a bank's international services can be used by individuals, the international department commits the largest part of its operational staff to servicing the needs of businesses in their international sales and purchases. Bankers have followed business overseas and developed services to meet business needs. As commodities and manufactured merchandise move from country to country in the channels of international trade, they are being financed by either the seller, the buyer, the bank of the buyer, the bank of the seller, or by another bank. This process is sometimes referred to as *trade financing*.

The movement of goods in international trade develops from a business transaction between a buyer in one country and a seller in another country. An integral part of the transaction is the means by which the buyer will pay the seller. Because of the distances involved, as well as differences in legal, political, and business practices, both parties need to evaluate alternative methods of payment in order to select the one most appropriate for their transaction.

Regardless of the option selected for payment, international trade involves documents. Their form, type, and number may vary, depending on the means of payment and the needs of the transaction.

This chapter introduces the various alternatives to financing international trade and then examines the documents of international trade. These documents are common to all trade and, as will be seen in later chapters, provide the basis on which banks enter into the trade financing process.

The objectives of this chapter are to
- outline alternative ways to make payment for international trade
- describe two of these ways in detail
- identify the key documents for foreign trade
- explain the use of trade terms

THE CONTRACT

Trade transactions begin with negotiations between a buyer and a seller. The negotiations can be brief, with the buyer simply ordering from a catalog, or they can be lengthy, as with the ordering of special machinery. The bank is *not* a party to this contract, nor does it participate in its negotiation.

But at some point in the negotiation the buyer and seller must decide how and when the required payment is to be made. In a domestic transaction where they are in the same locality, this is simple; the buyer examines the merchandise; if the buyer likes it, he or she pays for it, puts it in the truck, and drives away.

Because the international buyer and seller are a considerable distance apart, the decision about the means and timing of payment versus delivery of the goods becomes more complex. A number of factors affect this decision: the extent of competition from other sellers, availability of other buyers, payment restrictions between the two countries, reputation of the buyer and seller, and customary practices in the particular industry. Negotiations for the merchandise contract can be concluded only after the buyer and seller agree on a mutually acceptable means of payment.

The general payment options are the following: (1) prepayment by the buyer; (2) open account shipment by the seller; (3) collection; or (4) letter of credit. Within each of these categories are variations, such as progress payments or time drafts within collections and letters of credit. This chapter and the subsequent three chapters examine the alternatives. Even though these alternatives are compartmentalized by the banker, it is a single problem to the customer: How is the payment to be made without jeopardizing the transaction, which both the buyer and seller want to complete because each benefits from it?

Prepayment (Cash in Advance)

In this case, the seller demands that the buyer pay for the merchandise in advance of the shipment. The buyer could agree to this when there is a heavy demand for the seller's merchandise from other buyers, when there is a small buyer and a large seller, or when the buyer has a poor or unknown credit reputation. Prepayment ("cash in advance") by the buyer eliminates all risk to the seller, who is in possession of the full sales payment before shipping the merchandise. Conversely, prepayment is very disadvantageous to the buyer, who runs the risk that the seller will not ship the ordered goods promptly, or perhaps not at all. The buyer bears the cost associated with having neither the use of the money nor the merchandise for the time it takes to make the shipment.

The bank assists in a prepayment transaction by transferring funds on the order of the buyer to the seller through a foreign draft or some other means of money transfer (see chapter 5). The bank may also be involved in obtaining credit information on the buyer, which may induce the seller to insist on prepayment before making the sale, or credit information on the seller, which may encourage the buyer to make the prepayment in the strong expectation that the seller will promptly make the shipment.

Open Account

In this transaction, the buyer insists that the merchandise be shipped and that the seller then send the buyer a bill. The buyer pays this bill after the merchandise is received and found to be satisfactory. A sale on open account would be made when the credit reputation of the buyer is good, so the seller is confident of receiving payment promptly, or when it is a small seller and a large buyer. In some cases the seller would agree to making the shipment on open account where there is a great deal of competition from other sellers, but even in this situation a seller would hesitate to make a shipment on open account to a buyer with a poor credit reputation.

Of all the means of payment, a sale on open account is the most advantageous to the buyer, who does not have to dispense any money until the merchandise has arrived. The risks lie with the seller, who must bear all the costs in giving up the merchandise, making the shipment, and then waiting for payment. If the buyer is slow in paying or completely fails to pay, then the seller's only recourse is through legal action. This can be difficult, since it must take place in another country, with differing legal standards, and it can be expensive. In addition, the seller carries all the risks of foreign exchange restrictions in the buyer's country. An honest buyer may be restricted by his own country from making a payment to another country.

A variation of this type of sales basis is a *consignment* sale. The merchandise is shipped to the foreign buyer, who does not have to pay until he has sold the product and is then able to reimburse the original shipper.

The bank would participate in an open account transaction with exactly the same services listed for prepayment: credit checks and transferring funds on the order of the buyer.

Collection and Letter of Credit

In collection and letter of credit transactions the bank takes a very active role between the buyer and seller. The collection is discussed in detail in chapter 7, the letter of credit in chapters 8 and 9, and the bankers' acceptance, which is used in financing international trade, in chapter 10.

DOCUMENTS

Banks deal only in documents. While foreign trade is concerned with the movement of merchandise from one country to another, it is accompanied by a flow of documents that convey ownership of the merchandise and then record and facilitate its departure from, and arrival in, the respective countries. Foreign trade documents enable each country to compute the impact on its own balance of payments. The documents are also the means by which the banker participates in the trade transaction, either as agent or financier of the buyer or seller. The bank may also extend credit to enable the shipment to be prepared or in anticipation of the payment.

Transport Document

One of the most important documents in international trade is the *transport document,* which is issued by a transportation company when moving the merchandise from the seller to the buyer. Shipment may be by ocean transport (in which the transport document is called a *marine* or *ocean bill of lading*), air (*air waybill*), rail (*rail bill of lading*), truck (*truck bill of lading*), or through the mails (*certificate of posting* or *post receipt*). Each of these has different legal characteristics. The transport document may be a receipt for the goods, a contract for delivery, or a title document.

Transport by ocean vessel is covered by the bill of lading (figure 6.1), which has the means to convey title to the goods shipped. A combined form may be used when the merchandise must move, for example, by truck and then transferred to an ocean vessel. This is referred to as a *combined transport document* or *intermodal bill of lading*. Because most foreign trade moves by ocean vessel, the ocean bill of lading is the most common and will therefore be used in the following discussion. Uniformity of the law on ocean bills of lading was achieved through an inter-

Figure 6.1 Bill of Lading

FORM 1212
J.T.C. 1-66-REV.

States Marine-Isthmian Agency, Inc.

AS AGENT FOR CARRIER INDICATED BELOW

DELIVERING CARRIER TO STEAMER — CAR NUMBER-REFERENCE

FORWARDING AGENT - REFERENCES — EXPORT DEC. NO.

BILL OF LADING

(SHORT FORM INCORPORATING TERMS OF LONG FORM)
(CONTRACT TERMS CONTINUED FROM OVERPAGE)

SHIPPER: Richard Sargeant Design Associates

CONSIGNED TO ORDER OF: Happy Village Toy Shop

ADDRESS ARRIVAL NOTICE TO: Happy Village Toy Shop, 25 Spring Tree Lane, London W.8

ALSO NOTIFY

VESSEL: Garden State — VOYAGE NO. — FLAG — PIER — PORT OF LOADING: New York

PORT OF DISCHARGE (Where goods are to be delivered to consignee or on-carrier): Southampton

PARTICULARS FURNISHED BY SHIPPER

MARKS AND NUMBERS	NO. OF PKGS.	DESCRIPTION OF PACKAGES AND GOODS	MEASURE-MENT	GROSS WEIGHT
A2 180/1-10	10	Boxes toys 2 boxes torn L.S.T	80 cu.ft.	320 lbs.

Received on Board
APR 11, 19xx
STATES MARINE-ISTHMIAN AGENCY, INC
By L.S.T.

SPECIMEN

ALL CHARGES EX SHIP'S TACKLE FOR ACCOUNT OF CARGO

CARRIER: States Marine Lines, Inc. ● — ISTHMIAN LINES, INC. ○ — ○

In witness whereof, the carrier by its Agent has signed three Bills of Lading, all of the same Tenor and date, one of which being accomplished, the others to stand void.

Dated At: NEW YORK, N.Y.

To Be Paid At:

(CHECK ONE OR BOTH)
To Be PREPAID / COLLECT
TOTALS $

BILL OF LADING NUMBER	DATE
3 94678	4-10---

FOR THE MASTER States Marine-Isthmian Agency, Inc.

By: L. S. Tydings

national convention in The Hague in 1921; the resulting document, known as "The Hague Rules," is now accepted by the leading maritime nations.

When the exporter is ready to make the shipment, the merchandise must be packed so that it will arrive in good condition, taking into account the special problems of international shipment:

> There are four problems that must be kept in mind . . . breakage, weight, moisture, and pilferage. Besides the normal handling encountered in domestic transportation, an export order moving by ocean freight will be loaded aboard vessels by a sling, in a net with other items, by conveyor, chute, or other method, putting added strain on the package. In the ship's hold, cargo may be stacked on top of the crate or come into violent contact with it during the course of the voyage. Overseas, handling facilities may not be as sophisticated as in the United States; the cargo may be dragged, pushed, rolled, or dropped during unloading, while moving through customs, or in transit to the final destination. Moisture is a constant problem since cargo is subject to condensation even in the hold of a ship equipped with air conditioning and a dehumidifier. The cargo may also be unloaded in the rain and many foreign ports do not have covered storage facilities. . . . Theft and pilferage are constant threats.[1]

When the merchandise is packed, an exporter delivers it to a shipping company to be conveyed to a foreign buyer. The bill of lading is then prepared based on information given by the exporter (who obtained most of that information during negotiations with the importer), signed by the shipping company and given to the exporter. This document is a receipt that the shipping company has received the goods; it is a contract for the delivery of the goods to the foreign buyer or others; it indicates the shipping company's terms and conditions for performing this service; it specifies both the weight and dimensions of the cargo; it details the charges for the shipment; and it shows the shipping

---

Trade Financing in Renaissance Italy

The businessmen and bankers of northern Italy's Renaissance city-states—particularly Genoa, Florence, and Venice—developed many of the fundamental practices of modern finance. Their innovations included double-entry bookkeeping, and the provision of credit through discounted promissory notes. One of their most important innovations, however, was trade credit.

Suppose that a Florentine textile manufacturer received a potentially profitable order from Barcelona and had the means to fill it. Two things might keep him from accepting the business. First, the importer might not pay until he received the goods—perhaps not even until he had sold them. Meanwhile, the exporter would have to pay for materials, labor, storage, and shipment. Second, having produced

Continued

and shipped his goods, the exporter would have to bear the risk that the importer might simply fail to pay. And there was no court to which the exporter could take the Barcelona merchant.

Commercial banks—that is, banks which specialize in financing commerce—came into being to solve such problems. By providing short-term finance (working capital), commercial banks enabled such merchants to pay for the materials and labor in advance. They solved the second problem by having trusted agents in major cities. For a fee, the bank would pay the exporter as soon as the shipment embarked. The importer would then pay the bank's agent—adding a fee—when the shipment arrived. For an additional fee the same bank might even insure the shipment.

Over time, the Italian banks developed this vital trade-financing function. The leading Florentine banking family, the Medici, acquired agents or correspondents in Europe's trading cities and made itself indispensable in the continent's commerce. Probably in the thirteenth or fourteenth century, the bankers invented a variation that limited the degree to which their own capital was tied up over the course of the transaction. This was the "acceptance," or "four-name paper." The Barcelona agent (name 1) would sign a document "accepting" the liability of the importer (name 2) to the exporter (name 3), and the document would be conveyed to the banker in Florence (name 4). The banker would disburse (after subtracting a discount) to the exporter against this acceptance. The banker could then sell the acceptance at a discount in the Florentine financial market and thus replace most or all of the cash the banker had disbursed. After some weeks the importer would pay the agent, the agent would pay the bank, and the bank would repurchase the acceptance, concluding the operation.

Reprinted with permission of The World Bank, *World Development Report 1989* (New York: Oxford University Press, 1989), p. 43.

marks of the crates. The shipping marks on the crates are usually specified by the buyer to facilitate identification on arrival as well as to help the shipping company identify the cargo for unloading at the proper port. To avoid pilferage en route, these marks should avoid identifying the contents. In some cases, the exporter may hire the services of a specialized freight forwarding agent to arrange many of these details. Exporters today often use various types of *containers*. These are large metal enclosures that are packed, sealed, and delivered to the shipping company.

Ocean bills of lading fall into two general categories: *received for shipment* and *on board* bills of lading. The former is a receipt acknowledging that the shipping company has received the stated merchandise for transit on a specific vessel. The latter means not only that the cargo has been received but also that the goods are actually loaded on board the vessel indicated. The on board bill of lading is usually preferred because it assures that the cargo is on the vessel, eliminating possible oversight by the shipping company.

The bill of lading specifies who is to receive the merchandise when the vessel arrives at the designated foreign port. These instructions are given by the exporter. If he or she directs the shipping company to deliver the shipment ("consigns") directly to the buyer, this is called a *straight bill of lading;* this bill of lading cannot be transferred. This is not usually desirable in a letter of credit or collection, since it would permit the buyer to obtain possession of the merchandise without regard to any bank arrangement for payment. The seller usually instructs the shipping company that the goods are "consigned to the order of the shipper." This is an example of an *order* or *negotiable bill of lading*. In this form it requires that evidence be presented to the shipping company at the port of unloading as to who is to receive the goods. The bill of lading is the required evidence, so that anyone in possession of an order bill of lading can obtain the merchandise. If a letter of credit instructs that the bills of lading, when issued by the shipping company, be "consigned to order of shipper," then the shipper, who is the exporter, can endorse them, just as one would a check. The bill is then in negotiable form and its transfer conveys title to the goods. In these cases title to the goods, in effect, goes with possession of the bill of lading. The shipping agent at the foreign port will release the merchandise to anyone who presents this bill of lading.

Bills of lading may be issued in multiple originals. This is a carryover from the days when sets of documents were split so that a portion went by immediate mail and the other portion by a subsequent mail, or even on board the same ship with the cargo, to ensure that at least one set would get through. Today there is strong trade sentiment to eliminate multiple originals and have only one original bill of lading. When any of these originals is accomplished—that is, presented to the shipping company at the end of the voyage—the others become void. It is important, therefore, that a bank paying or negotiating under a commercial letter of credit or acting as agent in a collection have all the originals (*full set*) issued by the shipping company.

The bill of lading itself indicates the number of originals issued. In addition to the originals, the shipping company may issue any number of nonnegotiable copies of the bill of lading.

Letters of credit usually require "clean" bills of lading. This means that the merchandise was received by the shipping company in apparent good order—that is, the packing crates did not appear to be damaged, leaking, or insecurely fastened. If any of these conditions did exist, the shipping company, to protect itself against a claim for damage in transit, would note the condition on the bill of lading, and such a bill of lading would be called a "foul" bill of lading. It would not be acceptable as a "clean" bill of lading.

The bills of lading described are issued by a shipping company operating on regular routes and accepting cargo from many shippers; such ships are referred to as "liner vessels." In some cases the exporter or other party may rent the use of the entire vessel and then specify the route. This could occur when an exporter is shipping bulk commodities such as petroleum or grain. A bill of lading issued by such a *charter party* must be especially permitted whenever a letter of credit is used, since the seller or buyer is also the issuer of the shipping contract.

Insurance

All merchandise, no matter what means of transport is used, should be covered by insurance. Depending on the terms of the merchandise contract, insurance will be obtained either by the importer or the exporter, many of whom maintain open or floating policies to cover all shipments under which they obtain certificates for specific shipments. Proper insurance coverage provides protection not only to the buyer and the seller of the goods but also to any banks financing the shipment.

Marine insurance covers merchandise transported on an ocean vessel. It is a vast subject and has evolved over a long period of time. Since most international trade moves by ocean transport, the following describes marine insurance in detail. Insurance for other transport means will have different characteristics.

Marine insurance policies (figure 6.2) have described themselves as "covering the adventures and perils of the seas." The most obvious peril is that the ship may sink. This is a recognized risk, and all parties to foreign trade want to purchase protection against total loss of goods in this way.

Even when a vessel does not sink, there are other risks to which the cargo is exposed during an ocean voyage. Maritime law considers the diverse shippers who entrust their cargo to a particular vessel to be joined in a common enterprise. It is the responsibility of the captain of the vessel to serve that common undertaking. For example, if the ship encounters a storm at sea and is in danger of sinking, the captain must do whatever he can to save the vessel and the cargo. If to save the vessel and most of the cargo he has to jettison some of the cargo, he has full authority to do so. When the vessel arrives safely in port, those

Figure 6.2 Marine Insurance Policy

Form 1380

CARGO

$....5,500.00........ **POLICY OF INSURANCE** **No. P** 48029 **F**

FEDERAL INSURANCE COMPANY

INCORPORATED UNDER THE LAWS OF NEW JERSEY

CHUBB & SON INC., *Manager* 90 John Street, New York, N. Y. 10038

NOTE: It is necessary for the assured to give prompt notice to these Assurers when they become aware of an event for which they are "held covered" under this policy and the right to such cover is dependent on compliance with this obligation.

IMPORTANT — IN CASE OF LOSS OR DAMAGE PLEASE FOLLOW INSTRUCTIONS ON THE REVERSE SIDE OF THIS POLICY

BY THIS POLICY OF INSURANCE

In consideration of a premium as agreed
Does insure (lost or not lost) .... Newton Scale Manufacturing Company
to the amount of........ Five thousand five hundred and no/100 - - - - - - - - - - *Dollars,*
on........ 100 precision scales in 5 cases
valued at sum ins. ...*to be shipped on board of the*.... Santa Rosa
at and from........ New York
to .... Barranquilla
and it is hereby understood and agreed, that in the case of loss, such loss is payable to the order of Bank in Colombia ....*on surrender of this Policy.*

Touching the Adventures and Perils which said Assurers are contented to bear, and take upon themselves, in this Voyage, they are of the Seas, Fires, Assailing Thieves, Jettisons, Barratry of the Master and Mariners, and all other like Perils, Losses and Misfortunes that have or shall come to the Hurt, Detriment or Damage of the said Goods and Merchandise, or any Part thereof except as may be otherwise provided for herein or endorsed hereon. AND in case of any Loss or Misfortune, it shall be lawful and necessary to and for the Assured, his or their Factors, Servants and Assigns, to sue, labor and travel for, in and about the Defense, Safeguard and Recovery of the said Goods and Merchandise, or any part thereof, without Prejudice to this Insurance; nor shall the acts of the Assured or Assurers, in recovering, saving and preserving the property insured, in case of disaster, be considered a waiver or an acceptance of an abandonment; to the charges whereof, the said Assurers will contribute according to the rate and quantity of the sum hereby insured.

In case of loss, such loss to be paid in thirty days after proof of loss and proof of interest in the property hereby insured.

In case the interest hereby insured is covered by other insurance (except as hereinafter provided) the loss shall be collected from the several policies in the order of the date of their attachment, insurance attaching on the same date to be deemed simultaneous and to contribute pro rata; provided, however, that where any fire insurance, or any insurance (including fire) taken out by any carrier or bailee is available to the beneficiary of this policy, or would be so available if this insurance did not exist, then this insurance shall be void to the extent that such other insurance is or would have been available. It is agreed, nevertheless, that where these Assurers are thus relieved of liability because of the existence of other insurance, these Assurers shall receive and retain the premium payable under this policy and, in consideration thereof, shall guarantee the solvency of the companies and/or underwriters who issued such other insurance and the prompt collection of the loss thereunder to the same extent (only) as these Assurers shall have been relieved of liability under the terms of this clause, but not exceeding, in any case, the amount which would have been collectible under this policy if such other insurance did not exist.

In all cases of damage caused by perils insured against, the loss shall, as far as practicable, be ascertained by a separation and a sale or appraisement of the damaged portion only of the contents of the packages so damaged and not otherwise.

Losses arising from breakage and/or leakage and/or loss of weight and/or loss of contents are excluded from this insurance unless caused by stranding or collision with another vessel, or unless this insurance has been expressly extended to include such losses.

Warranted free from Particular Average unless the vessel or craft be stranded, sunk or burnt, but notwithstanding this warranty these Assurers are to pay any loss of or damage to the interest insured which may reasonably be attributed to fire, collision or contact of the vessel and/or craft and/or conveyance with any external substance (ice included) other than water, or to discharge of cargo at port of distress. The foregoing warranty, however, shall not apply where broader terms of average are provided for herein or by endorsement hereon.

If the voyage aforesaid shall have been terminated before the date of this policy, then there shall be no return of premium on account of such termination of the voyage.

Wherever the words "ship", "vessel", "seaworthiness", "ship or vessel owner" appear in this Policy, they are deemed to include also the words "aircraft", "airworthiness", "aircraft owner".

THIS INSURANCE IS SUBJECT TO THE AMERICAN INSTITUTE CARGO CLAUSES (FEB. 1949). AND INCLUDING SOUTH AMERICAN 60 DAY CLAUSE WHEN APPLICABLE. ALSO SUBJECT TO THE AMENDED F. C. & S. AND S. R. & C. C. WARRANTIES (OCT. 1959) *(SEE REVERSE)*

Original and Duplicate issued, one of which being accomplished the other to stand null and void.

SPECIAL CONDITIONS	Marks and Numbers
This insurance covers against all risks of physical loss or damage from any external cause irrespective of percentage excepting risks excluded by the F. C. & S. (Free of Capture & Seizure) and Strikes, Riots and Civil Commotions warranties appearing elsewhere hereon. ON DECK—Merchandise and/or goods shipped on deck which must be so specified in this policy are insured.—Free of particular average unless caused by the vessel being stranded, sunk, burnt, on fire, or in collision, but including jettison and/or washing overboard, irrespective of percentage.	CEA X

Where the words "including M. E. C." are typed in the space below at the time the policy is issued, this insurance is subject to the American Institute Marine Extension Clauses.	Where the words "including Strike Risks" are typed in the space below at the time the policy is issued, this insurance is subject to the American Institute S. R. & C. C. Clauses, form 8-A (July, 1961).	Where the words "including War Risk" are typed in the space below at the time the policy is issued, this insurance is subject to the American Institute War Risk Clauses.

NOTICE.—To conform with Revenue Laws of Great Britain in order to collect a claim under this Policy, it must be stamped within thirty days after its receipt in the United Kingdom. In other countries similar laws may obtain. The attention of holders of Policies is particularly drawn to this.

In Witness Whereof, the said FEDERAL INSURANCE COMPANY, has caused this policy to be signed by its Chairman, President and Secretary, but it shall not be valid unless countersigned by a duly authorized Representative of the Company.

Countersigned this 15 *day of* June, 19 --

Authorized Representative. Secretary President Chairman

SPECIMEN

Printed in U. S. A. 00841

shippers whose cargo got through safely must reimburse those whose cargo was sacrificed to save the common venture. This charge is known as *general average* and should be prudently insured against.

The origin of this concept can be traced back to the evolution of the shipping industry. In the twelfth and thirteenth centuries "the merchant vessel originally sailed . . . as a joint venture. It was the property of a small group of users. . . . Each one would have an allotted place on board where he could load his own merchandise.... On board, too, everyone took his turn, whether in navigation, watching, or chores. . . . The actual sailing was handled by three officers ... [who were] paid a wage by the group of proprietors and placed under the command of the master who was chosen from among the co-owners."[2]

Other marine risks include damage to the individual cargo, such as through water dripping on crates from pipes that leak or sweat; damage arising from a strike, riot, or similar civil commotion that could damage part of the vessel and its cargo while the vessel is in port; and cargo damage as a consequence of the vessel colliding with another vessel. Most of these can be covered in a policy against "all risks." A specific protection that will require an added premium payment is coverage for a vessel going into a war zone and for any resulting damage. It is important to the exporter, the importer, and the banker financing the transaction that the insurance be transferable and that it be written by reliable companies.

Invoice

The seller prepares and presents a statement to the buyer describing what has been sold, the price, and other details. This is an *invoice* (figure 6.3), and it is usually prepared on a form printed with the seller's name. It includes the full name and address of the buyer and seller, any contract or order reference numbers, date of order, shipping date, description of the merchandise, price, and other information. Some countries require that invoices be presented to their consular official or some other agency in the area of the seller. The consular official examines them and then stamps and signs them. This is a *visaed* or *consularized* commercial invoice. Some countries require a consular invoice in their language to speed customs clearance at the destination and to provide statistical information.

Other Documents

Depending on the characteristics of the merchandise, the needs of the buyer, or government regulations in either the importing or exporting country, other documents may be prepared. Some of these are as follows:

- A *certificate of origin* establishes where the goods were grown or manufactured. This is particularly necessary if the importing country has different tariffs for different countries and would therefore want to be certain that goods were not being transshipped through another country to qualify for a lower tariff rate.

Figure 6.3 Commercial Invoice

TRIM-MASTER COMPANY

1 Fifth Avenue

New York, N.Y. 10003

Invoice No.   J 3366

Date   July 17,19--

Sold To

Fabrica Helios

Valparaiso

Chile

Quantity	Description	Price	Total
	2 cases: 48" X 31"X 43" each 36.6 cu.ft. 455 #G 255#N Total: 73 cu.ft. 910 # Gross 510 # Net		
2	Trim-Master Deluxe @ $505.00 Serial No. 1023A & 1024A freight to N.Y. Pier	$1010.00 90.00	
			$1100.00 F.A.S.
		Handling Ocean freight Marine insurance	2.00 125.00 20.00
		C.I.F. Valparaiso	$1247.00

• A *weight list* itemizes the weights of individual parcels or bales or, in the case of bulk commodities, covers the entire cargo. This list is usually provided by public companies but may also be provided by shippers. For packaged goods the weight list may show the gross, net, and tare weights along with the measurements of each package. The *gross weight* is the full weight of the loaded package or container; *tare weight* is the weight of the container itself and packing materials; and *net weight* is the weight of the merchandise alone (gross less tare equals net).

- A *packing list* is usually required in circumstances in which merchandise is packed in many containers or cases. It indicates the contents of each container, thereby facilitating an inventory for the buyer. It may also be combined with a weight list giving weight and measurements for each container.
- An *inspection certificate* (or *certificate of analysis*) is usually issued by an independent third party and is required when outside inspection or analysis is agreed upon under the merchandise contract. It confirms that the merchandise shipped is as specified in that contract. A form of this certificate may be required for plants to be certain they are free of pests or plant diseases.

Draft

Although not a document directly related to the movement or protection of merchandise, the draft or *bill of exchange* (figure 6.4) is an important document in letters of credit and collections. "A draft and a bill of exchange do not differ except in the way the terms are applied. In U.S. domestic trade, the instrument is called a draft. In foreign transactions, the same instrument is usually called a bill of exchange."[3] The bill of exchange has a long history, perhaps as far back as the Greeks in the fifth century B.C. One of its uses was as a way around the prohibitions against usury, "reiterated at the Council of Reims in 1049. . . Bills of Exchange. . . were negotiable contracts allowing the holder to

Figure 6.4 Draft

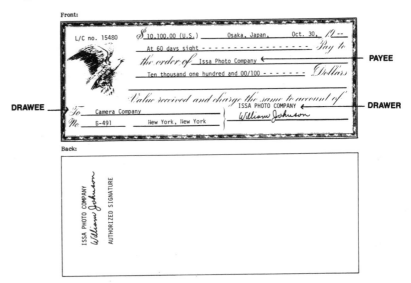

exchange one currency for another at a future date. These flourished during the Renaissance because the central focus of most such bills was an exchange transaction. They were generally considered legal by church scholars, but in their several varieties, a number undoubtedly contained elements of interest compensation built into the future foreign exchange quotation. Such bills therefore could be used as de facto borrowing or credit instruments."[4]

The draft is the document by which the seller demands payment from the buyer, the buyer's bank, or some other bank. In a letter of credit the draft is drawn by the seller, usually on the issuing, confirming, or paying bank, for the amount of money due under the terms of the letter of credit. In a collection, this demand for payment is drawn on the buyer. A draft drawn "at sight" is payable when presented to the drawee. The customary parties to a draft, which is a negotiable instrument, are the *drawer* (usually the exporter), the *drawee* (the importer or a bank), and the *payee* (also usually the exporter), who is also the *endorser*.

TRADE TERMS

Because the buyer and seller are usually quite separated, it is important that both parties understand what is included in the price quoted by the seller. For example, is the price only for the merchandise or does it include transportation? Does it include insurance?

To facilitate this understanding, international rules for the interpretation of trade terms have been agreed on and are stated in the International Chamber of Commerce Publication No. 460, "Incoterms" (appendix A).

The most commonly used Incoterms are, in brief:

- C.I.F. (Cost, Insurance, and Freight)—The seller's price includes the cost of the merchandise, insurance, and freight to deliver the goods to the named place.
- F.O.B. (Free on Board)—The seller's price includes all costs through loading the merchandise on board a vessel at the named port, usually that of the seller. All other costs, such as freight and insurance, are to be paid by the buyer directly to the shipping and insurance companies.

Everyone involved in international trade should become familiar with all the Incoterms, which cover, in addition to these two, such terms as F.A.S. (Free Along Side), C. & F. (Cost and Freight), and others.

In all of those quotations there is a named location. This means that the quoted price of the seller covers the shipment of the merchandise only as far as that location. All shipment or coverage beyond that point is the financial responsibility of the buyer.

SUMMARY

International trade begins with a contract between the buyer and the seller that details the terms and conditions agreed on by the two parties. An essential element of that agreement is the method of payment.

There are four basic options: the buyer prepays before shipment; the seller ships and then sends a bill; collection; and letter of credit. This chapter examined the advantages and disadvantages of the first two options for the two parties. The third and fourth options are examined in succeeding chapters.

No matter which of the four options is selected, the international trade transaction will generate certain standard types of documents to accomplish the transfer and sale. The most important documents are the bill of lading, invoice, and insurance.

QUESTIONS

1. What is the function of the ocean bill of lading and how does it differ from the commercial invoice?
2. If you were buying merchandise from Hong Kong, what would be the difference between a price quotation that was F.O.B., C.I.F., or C. & F.?
3. What is the function of the draft in an international trade transaction?
4. If a shipment is F.O.B., at what specific point, referring to the Incoterms, does the financial responsibility shift from the seller to the buyer?

Notes

1. U.S. Department of Commerce, *A Basic Guide to Exporting* (Washington, D.C., 1981), p. 22.
2. Fernand Braudel, *The Wheels of Commerce* (New York: Harper and Row, 1982), pp. 362-363.
3. Craig W. Smith, *Law and Banking: Applications* (Washington, D.C.: American Bankers Association, 1986), p. 2.
4. Samuel L. Hayes III and Philip M. Hubbard, *Investment Banking: A Tale of Three Cities* (Boston: Harvard Business School Press, 1990), p. 10.

7

Collection

The collection process provides the importer and exporter with an alternative to either prepayment or open-account financing for their international trade transactions. When the two parties cannot agree on either of the two methods, the use of a collection offers a compromise that is generally less costly than a letter of credit, but without the risk protection of the letter of credit. Through correspondent banking relationships, it uses the services of commercial banks as intermediaries so that the seller has to make the shipment before demanding payment from the buyer. At the same time, the seller is afforded protection because the buyer will not get possession of the merchandise before paying or legally committing itself to pay at a future date. Nonetheless, the seller bears certain risks.

The objectives of this chapter are to
- understand the basic principles of collection
- define the different types of collections
- identify the advantages and disadvantages of using collections
- outline the responsibilities of all relevant parties

COLLECTION TYPES

An international collection is basically the same as a domestic collection—it is the process of presenting an item to the maker or drawee for payment.

Every check deposited in a bank is, in a sense, "collected" when it is routed to the bank of the check's writer for payment from money in the writer's account. In the United States, arrangements of the Federal Reserve System and local clearing houses have greatly streamlined this process. A similar system of an international clearing house has not been established. Therefore, checks and other negotiable instruments drawn on a bank in one country and deposited in another country can be collected only by using the correspondent relationships established between commercial banks. In addition to collecting checks, correspondent banks act as agents for exporters in collecting negotiable documents relating to the movement of merchandise, thereby facilitating international trade.

There are basically two types of collections: *clean* (financial document alone) or *documentary* (commercial documents either with a financial document or alone). A financial document is a check, draft, bill of exchange, or promissory note; a commercial document is an invoice, bill of lading, or other shipping document. In international trade, documentary collection is the more frequent type.

The fundamental basis of collections is that banks act only as agents. A bank receives a collection from its customer, who is the principal (in a documentary collection, this will be the exporter), with instructions that must be followed exactly. Normal care must be taken to protect the collection documents from loss or damage. The customer's instructions usually cover presentation of the collection for payment, designation of who will pay the fees, statement of method for transferring payment, and procedures to be followed if the collection is not paid to protect the customer's goods against loss pending receipt of new instructions.

The generally accepted principles for all types of collections are covered in International Chamber of Commerce Publication 322, "Uniform Rules for Collections" (appendix B).

Clean Collections

Checks, traveler's checks, and money orders drawn on banks or agencies in the currency of one country may be received in the course of business by individuals and companies in another country. Tourists, for example, cash traveler's checks or personal checks in the countries they visit. The hotel, restaurant, or business receiving these checks turns them over to its bank for settlement—probably a daily routine for an established business.

The foreign bank collects these financial items by airmailing them to its correspondent bank in the country of origin of the item. Many foreign banks send dollar collections to their

U.S. correspondent to be credited to their account, either for immediate credit, subject to final payment, or as a collection, with the amount of the item to be credited only after payment is made by the check writer's bank. The latter procedure is the safest; however, because of the large volume of items, the comparatively small face amount of many checks, and the certainty that items such as traveler's checks will be paid, many banks eliminate the expense and time of presenting such items as collections and present them for deposit on a cash letter (see chapter 5).

Clean items such as personal checks or promissory notes may be presented as collections in the same manner, either internationally or domestically. The remitting bank sends the item, along with comprehensive instructions, to its correspondent for payment or for presentation to the drawee. The paying bank determines whether the check is in order and whether sufficient funds are in the drawer's account for payment. With these conditions satisfied, the paying bank debits the drawer's account and pays the originating bank either with its draft, by crediting the originating bank's Due To account, or by authorizing a charge to the bank's Due From account either at the drawee's bank or from another correspondent bank in that country. Once the collection is paid, the paying bank credits the account of the foreign depositor with good funds. The foreign bank will apply its buying rate of exchange for the foreign amount. An item not in order may not be paid and is handled according to the originating bank's instructions.

While these illustrations refer to the collection of U.S. dollar checks, the same procedures apply to checks and other non-documentary drafts drawn on any bank in any currency. However, when a U.S. business receives a check drawn on a bank in a country that restricts the conversion of local currency (for example, into U.S. dollars), collecting the check can present problems. Even if the check is in order as far as the writer's account is concerned, there may be difficulties and delays in obtaining permission of that country's foreign exchange control authorities to purchase the equivalent dollar amount to be remitted to the U.S. business.

A bank can process different clean collection items in many ways. The key factor is that the customer must authorize charging an item to his account. When a customer draws a check against his account, the customer's signature on that check is considered to be an order to the bank to take the funds from the customer's account. Thus, when a bank receives such an item on collection, it can pay it immediately after verifying that the signature is in order and that the account has sufficient funds. Other items such as a promissory note may require presentation to the maker for the specific authorization to charge the account.

There will be other instances, particularly in documentary collections, in which the draft drawn is signed by the exporter payable to and endorsed by the exporter. Such items must be presented to the local customer, who, in turn, must separately authorize the bank to pay the draft to the debit of the customer's account.

Documentary Collections

If checks were the only collection business handled by an international department, it would hardly warrant lengthy discussion. Of far greater importance is its other use, by which the bank assists its clients with payment for foreign sales and purchases. In an international trade transaction, the principal—that is, the exporter—may want to use the collection method when prepayment is not acceptable to the buyer and open account is not acceptable to the seller. In such a case (see figure 7.1), the exporter makes the shipment, draws a draft or bill of exchange directly on the importer and presents this draft, with shipping documents attached, to its bank for collection. The draft is, in essence, the demand of the seller for payment by the buyer. Only when the importer pays the draft can it get possession of the merchandise.

Assume, for example, that a U.S. exporter (seller) has a contract order from a European importer (buyer). The U.S. exporter delivers the merchandise to the shipping company and receives a full set of ocean bills of lading consigned to the order of the exporter. The exporter endorses the bills of lading, in blank, and takes them, along with invoices, insurance, a draft drawn by the exporter on the importer, and any other necessary documents, to the bank. The exporter instructs the bank to act as its agent and to present the draft and the documents to the importer through a bank in the latter's country. There will usually be sufficient time to do this while the merchandise is in transit on a ship from the seller to the buyer. The crux of the transaction is that only when the importer pays the draft will the foreign bank allow the importer to take possession of the negotiable bill of lading. The importer's bank notifies the importer when the draft and documents have been received. Upon paying the draft, the importer receives the accompanying documents, one of which is

Figure 7.1 Flow Chart of the Foreign Collection Process Using a Sight Draft

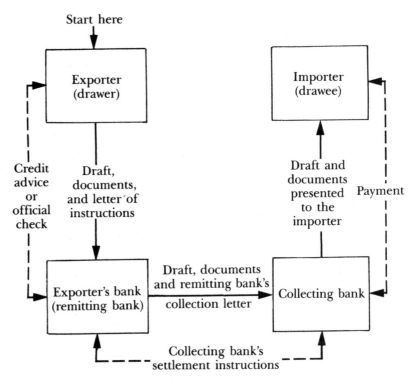

Source: Thomas J. Cusack, "A Small International Department Can Design an 'In-House' Training Program for Its Operations Clerical Staff" (Thesis, Stonier Graduate School of Banking, 1975), p. 22.

the endorsed bill of lading, which enables the importer to obtain the goods on arrival from the shipping company. This procedure is called *documents against payment (D/P)*. The importer's bank is responsible, based on its knowledge and relationship with the importer, to assess that payment has been made in good funds.

Sight Drafts

If the exporter wishes the importer to pay immediately, the exporter draws the draft on the importer at "sight." A sight draft becomes payable when it is first presented to the importer by the collecting bank in the importer's area. In some countries the importer is permitted to wait until the vessel arrives before paying.

To speed up the transaction, many U.S. banks furnish exporters with blank drafts and collection instruction letters; others furnish a combination draft and collection letter in snap-out form with one-time carbons that has additional copies for the exporter and the freight forwarder. These enable the exporter, who has many shipments, to prepare the outgoing collection on behalf of the bank and mail or courier it directly to the foreign bank, thereby saving days in processing at the bank. This is called a *direct collection*. The name of the U.S. bank appears as the payee to assure that the payment is channeled back to that bank. The collection letter serves the dual purpose of reminding the exporter (1) which instructions should be given to the bank and (2) how the instructions should be worded (in banking language) to avoid misinterpretation.

The collection letter (see figure 7.2), whether filled out by the exporter, the exporter's agent, or the bank, includes space for listing documents and instructions for the delivery of the attachments (if any), for protest, for the disposition of charges, and for advice of nonacceptance, nonpayment, or payment. *Protest* is the formal legal process of demanding payment of a draft from the maker or drawee who has refused to pay. This process is often a necessary step before filing a lawsuit. The legal effect of protesting varies between countries. In some countries it may not be recognized or may be of little value. At the other extreme, it may severely damage the importer's business and reputation. The exporter should consider the impact or alternatives in the particular country before automatically requesting protest. Space is also provided for insertion of the name and address of an *in case of need* agent, that is, the exporter's representative. This person is either called upon to help the collecting bank in case of difficulties or is given full authority to act as that individual deems appropriate.

U.S. banks have a more or less standard set of conditions for handling collections. One of these conditions is the right to debit the exporter's account for any charges or out-of-pocket costs; another is the right to waive the requirement that the importer pay the collection fees when the importer refuses to pay such charges. Collection stipulations define the bank's role as a collector; they allow the bank to disclaim responsibility for the selection and actions of the bank's correspondents. Notwithstanding the disclaimer on the part of the exporter's bank, collecting banks are carefully selected because they control the funds given as payment for the collection from time of payment until receipt by the exporter's bank. The exporter, at the behest of the importer, often designates the collecting bank to be used, which is then used, unless the exporter's bank has unfavorable information about that bank. This practice deprives the exporter of the benefit of the

Figure 7.2 Outgoing Collection Letter

CABLE ADDRESS
"BANKAMERICA"

BANK OF AMERICA
WORLD BANKING DIVISION SERVICE CENTER
P.O. BOX 37020
SAN FRANCISCO, CALIF. 94137

ALWAYS QUOTE THIS NUMBER and prefix in advices & statements.
SF 08887

WE ENCLOSE FOR COLLECTION THE ITEM DESCRIBED BELOW.
PLEASE REFER TO REVERSE SIDE FOR STANDING INSTRUCTIONS.

521D

SAN FRANCISCO, CALIF. 94137 March 4, 19XX
DATE

MAIL TO
NATIONAL BANK OF KENYA LIMITED
NATIONAL BANK BUILDING
HARAMBEE AVENUE
P. O. BOX 41862
NAIROBI, KENYA

DETAILS OF DRAFT NO 1250
DRAWN ON EAST AFRICA SUPPLIERS, LTD.
P. O. BOX 60032
NAIROBI, KENYA
Tenor SIGHT | Amount $7,600.00

CUSTOMER
TRANSGLOBE SHIPPERS INC.
333 VAN NESS AVENUE
SAN FRANCISCO, CALIFORNIA 94127

DO NOT PROTEST UNLESS INDICATED
Other Instructions are Marked by "X"

X		Deliver Documents against PAYMENT
		Deliver Documents against ACCEPTANCE
		PROTEST NON-Payment and/or NON-Acceptance
Cable	Air Mail	
X		ADVISE NON-Payment and/or NON-Acceptance
		Advise Acceptance
X		Advise Payment

	Collect Interest from Drawee(s) @ % P.A. from to Approximate Date Proceeds Arrive in
X	Collect Your Charges, Exchanges, Stamps & Our Commission of $15.00 and Postage $1.20 from Drawee(s).

IN CASE OF NEED REFER TO

WHO IS AUTHORIZED to endeavor to obtain honoring of the Draft as drawn without any alteration of our instructions.

SETTLEMENT INSTRUCTIONS ARE MARKED BY "X"

[X] Authorize us by ~~airmail~~ CABLE to charge your account or remit in SAN FRANCISCO PRIME BANK FUNDS to Bank of America · P.O. Box 37020 San Francisco, CA. 94137, QUOTING THE ABOVE SF REFERENCE NUMBER.

[ ] Credit our Account

SPECIAL INSTRUCTIONS: PLEASE REMIT FUNDS BY TESTED CABLE TO THE ATTENTION OF COLLECTION DEPARTMENT QUOTING OUR SF-08887. ALL CHARGES TO BE PAID BY DRAWEE. WAIVE ALL CHARGES IF REFUSED BY THE DRAWEE AND CHARGE THEM TO US.

SPECIMEN

DOCUMENTS	BILL OF LADING	N/N B/L	INSURANCE	INVOICE	CONSULAR INVOICE	CERTIF. ORIGIN	INSPEC. CERTIF.	QUALITY CERTIF	WEIGHT CERTIF.	SANITARY CERTIF.	
ORIGINALS VIA FIRST AIR MAIL	3/3		3	4							
DUPLICATES VIA SECOND AIR MAIL											

COVERING SHIPMENT (S) OF AGRICULTURAL TOOLS
VIA S.S. EVENTIDE B/L No 3767

PLEASE ACKNOWLEDGE THIS COLLECTION DIRECT TO US

ME/lp

BANK OF AMERICA

FX-1435F 7/80 (REV.)

ORIGINAL
BANK OF AMERICA NT & SA

1

bank's experience and deprives the U.S. bank of the opportunity of directing business to its correspondent banks.

When difficulties arise in the presentation and payment of a collection, the reports of the foreign collecting bank are relayed to the exporter for a decision.

Trade Acceptances

In some instances, the only way a buyer may be able to purchase foreign goods is on credit. The buyer wants to get possession of the merchandise before paying and then sell it, thereby generating the money to pay for the goods. The importer has two basic options: seek financing directly from his or her own bank in order to pay the draft, or ask the exporter for credit terms. In some cases, the importer may be unable or unwilling to get the financing from his or her bank and instead asks the exporter for assistance. An exporter, in order to make the sale, may agree to this. Note that the exporter, not the remitting bank, is providing credit to the importer. In agreeing to release the merchandise before receiving payment, the seller wants to have a written promise from the buyer that payment will be made at a specific future date. The exporter draws the draft payable, not at sight, but at a future date, such as "90 days after sight."

The steps taken for the collection of such a time draft parallel those taken for the collection of a sight draft. The difference lies in the conditions under which the documents are delivered to the drawee (the buyer) and in the added operations involved in presenting the draft twice, once for acceptance and once for payment.

When a bank receives time drafts with accompanying documents, the exporter's instructions to the bank are usually to deliver the *documents against acceptance* (D/A) by the buyer. The importer's acceptance of the draft is its promise to pay on the agreed future date. This is a *trade acceptance* (figure 7.3), not to be confused with a bankers' acceptance (see chapter 10). The bank releases the documents, including the bill of lading, and thereby enables the importer to take possession of the goods, presumably for sale. Instructions to the collecting bank are usually "for acceptance and collection," which means that the collecting bank, which is the bank in the importer's area, is to present the draft for acceptance. Upon acceptance by the buyer, the bank releases the bill of lading and other documents and then holds the accepted draft on behalf of the seller until the due date, when it is presented for payment.

On rare occasions and for various reasons, however, the instructions may read "for acceptance and return," which means that the accepted draft is returned to the seller and presented again for collection on the maturity date, with payment to be made at that time by the importer. The exporter bears the cost of the goods

Figure 7.3 Trade Acceptance

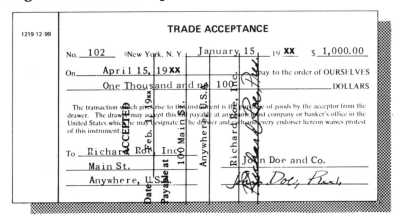

and of shipment until the acceptance matures and the buyer pays. The bank has no obligation or commitment to pay a trade acceptance on maturity should the importer go into bankruptcy or fail to pay debts incurred. The exporter carries all the risk and thus must be confident of the moral character and creditworthiness of the buyer.

Import Collections

While the foregoing examples refer to the use of collections for U.S. exports, the same principles apply for collections covering U.S. imports. Collections for imports are the reverse of those covering exports. From the overseas exporter's point of view, the U.S. bank is the foreign collecting bank. The collections may be in the form of sight or time drafts, in U.S. dollars, or in foreign currency. The collections are usually received from a foreign bank, which conveys all instructions from the seller. Any deviations from the foreign bank's instructions and any action initiated by the collecting bank are at the risk of the collecting bank. When an incoming collection is received from a foreign correspondent bank, the international department may route it to the domestic side of the bank for presentation through the note section to the local customer. The international department may assign a control number and will act as the bank's liaison between the domestic branch, or domestic correspondent bank, and the foreign bank.

Dollar sight drafts are presented to the buyer as soon as they are received. Depending on the instructions, the draft amounts paid by the importer are usually credited to the Due To account of the originating foreign bank. When an account does not exist, the instructions usually request remittance to another U.S. bank for credit to the foreign bank's account. The receipt of a collection from a bank that is not a correspondent may provide an opportunity to establish a new relationship. The international department can use this collection as a logical reason to call on the foreign bank and perhaps encourage it to open a new Due To account.

The handling of an incoming collection with the time draft in U.S. dollars is similar to a sight item. One presentation must be made to obtain acceptance and another to obtain payment.

Foreign Currency Collections

The handling of *foreign currency sight drafts* is similar to the handling of U.S. dollar items. The documents accompanying the draft are presented to the importer. To pay the draft, the U.S. importer will need to purchase the foreign exchange. The bank may quote the U.S. dollar price at which it will sell the foreign exchange. The importer pays the U.S. dollar amount, and the bank remits the foreign currency amount from its Due From account to the bank that sent the collection.

The handling of *foreign currency time drafts* is a combination of the procedures for handling foreign currency sight drafts and U.S. dollar time drafts. The buyer presents the draft initially for acceptance and subsequently for payment. The buyer may also pay the foreign currency amount that is due by purchasing spot foreign exchange at the second presentation or may arrange for a forward contract at the initial presentation (see chapter 11).

Other Collections

Some exporters sell on *cash against documents* terms. This means that the collection consists of the documents alone. This procedure is the same as a sight draft sale, except that the draft does not exist. Instead, the importer's account is debited by the collecting bank. Exporters sometimes sell on such terms to avoid the stamp taxes some countries require on all negotiable instruments, such as drafts.

Edible products entering the United States require the approval of the Food and Drug Administration. When a shipment involves a collection, it is customary for the collecting bank to receive instructions to deliver the documents against trust receipt to the importer for this inspection; after the shipment passes inspection by health authorities, the amount of the collection becomes payable.

An exporter may want to send merchandise to another country in advance of a sale to have it available for prompt delivery as soon as a sale is made. This is particularly important when the foreign product is competing in the local market against a local product. The exporter may ship merchandise by the *consignment* method. In the case of a U.S. importation, the foreign seller, through a foreign bank, may use the services of a U.S. correspondent bank by sending it the shipping documents along with instructions to arrange for customs entry, to pay the duty, to warehouse the goods, and to obtain insurance for the goods. All these expenses are for the account of the exporter. Future delivery of the goods to the buyer or a local agent of the exporter may be authorized either in its entirety or on a piecemeal basis at a given price per unit. Sometimes deliveries against trust receipt are permitted.

The use of a bank for the financing of a consignment has distinct advantages for certain types of imports. For example, foreign car manufacturers have to maintain large, varied inventories in the United States to compete with the quick delivery offered by U.S. manufacturers. They can do this by shipping cars to the U.S. and placing them in a warehouse. As the dealers make sales, the cars can be released against payment. The bank for whose account the customs entry is made should have the importer declared the ultimate consignee. Such a declaration prevents the bank's being held responsible for any additional or increased duty. This procedure also applies to goods entered as nondutiable, because a change in classification might change their status to dutiable.

In some countries or instances, it is not feasible or permissible to use a negotiable bill of lading. The exporter will therefore consign the merchandise directly to a third party, such as a customs-house broker in the importer's country, with a straight bill of lading. The collection then consists of a draft on the buyer plus a *delivery order*. This is a letter written by the seller and addressed to the third party, authorizing release of the merchandise to whomever presents the letter. The collection instructs the bank to release the delivery order when the sight draft is paid or the time draft accepted.

Financing

In collections, if the buyer wants credit, it is usually provided by the seller who agrees to draw the draft payable at a future date rather than at sight—the trade acceptance. The exporter, however, may wish to obtain financing, which can be supplied by the exporter's bank. Typically, the bank advances funds to the seller when the collection is given to the bank for forwarding. In essence, the bank finances the exporter while the collection is being forwarded in the expectation that the importer will pay the draft, either at sight or the specified date, and from that payment the bank will retire the loan it has made to the exporter plus interest. Should the collection not be paid, then the bank will look to the exporter for the repayment.

ADVANTAGES AND DISADVANTAGES	A collection provides more protection for the seller than selling on open account and more protection for the buyer than prepaying the shipment. This is particularly true when using an ocean shipment. In this case, the seller is protected because the buyer cannot obtain possession of the merchandise without paying the sight draft or accepting the time draft. The buyer knows that when funds are paid, the merchandise has been shipped and is in transit or has already arrived. Both parties are willing to bear the slight costs involved in exchange for the advantages offered to each.

The collection, however, has some disadvantages for the seller, who is exposed to nonpayment by the buyer either from the buyer's death, bankruptcy, or refusal to pay. An unscrupulous buyer may refuse to pay, hoping to negotiate better terms. While the seller still owns the goods, they are now en route to a distant point. The return of the goods will mean added shipping costs. To avoid this, the seller may try to find another buyer or even have the merchandise destroyed. An unscrupulous buyer can anticipate this and try to get the goods by offering a lower price. Of course, such a buyer can only do this once. Forever after, the only way the seller will agree to sell goods to this buyer will be by prepayment or with a letter of credit. Before selecting the collection option, the seller must be satisfied with the credit standing of the buyer, particularly in relation to the value and nature of merchandise.

Bank Use

For the bank, too, there are advantages and disadvantages to its customers using collections. The bank's principal advantage is that collections develop business for and from its correspondent banks and are therefore important to its overall correspondent banking business and relationships. The capability to handle foreign collections can facilitate the bank's relationship with domestic customers by both serving existing customers and attracting new ones. The bank does this by acting as an intermediary and agent for its customer, who is the exporter, the exporter's bank, or the exporter's freight forwarder.

The bank must handle each collection with care. In receiving a steady volume of collections from a customer or correspondent bank, the collection personnel must guard against assuming that all collections have the same instructions. Each collection must be considered and processed as an individual item. Mishandling an individual collection can result in financial loss to a bank when, because of its negligence in not following the exact instructions of that collection, the exporter suffers a loss. The bank also needs to remember that, with incoming collections, its customer is the exporter and exporter's bank. The bank cannot take instructions from the importer, even when the importer is a local customer of the bank. The collection is the property of the exporter, and the intermediary banks are the exporter's agent.

The exporter's bank also runs certain risks if a collection is not paid. When the instructions are to protest nonpayment, the exporter's bank may experience in certain countries unfavorable publicity from the local market even when it is merely passing on its customer's instructions. There is also some risk that certain costs, such as for storage, will be charged if the bank cannot collect because the exporter has gone into bankruptcy, out of business, or disappeared. It is important, therefore, for a bank to know its customer.

ACCOUNTING

Outstanding collections do not appear in a bank's financial statement, as the bank is only an agent and has no risks unless it is negligent in following the customer's instructions. Fees and operating expenses are reflected in the bank's income statement.

SUMMARY

In a collection, the bank acts as agent for the seller of goods in presenting the demand for payment to the buyer. Once the payment is made, the bank then gives the buyer the shipping documents needed to take possession of the goods. This resembles a transaction the buyer and seller would manage themselves if they were both in the same neighborhood. For many buyers and sellers the collection affords them sufficient protection for their trading.

QUESTIONS

1. What is a collection?
2. Explain the difference between documentary and clean collection.
3. What is the difference in procedure between documents against payment and documents against acceptance?
4. How does using a collection differ from the buyer prepaying or the seller shipping on open account?

PROBLEM

A manufacturer in your community has received an order from a buyer in Italy for a supply of electrical parts. The total value of the order is $7,500. The manufacturer has heard that the buyer is reputable but beyond that has no information. Discuss the advantages and disadvantages of a collection in terms of cost (use the charges applicable to your bank) and protection.

8

The Basic Letter of Credit

The preceding chapters have examined several ways in which international trade may be arranged. When the related payment is made directly between buyer and seller, either before or after a shipment, the bank's role is basically only to transfer funds. In a collection, the bank acts as the seller's agent in exchanging the shipping documents for immediate or future payment. With the commercial letter of credit, the bank becomes directly involved by committing itself to pay the seller, which enables the trade transaction to take place.

"In its simplest form, a 'commercial letter of credit' involves the payment of a draft in exchange for a document of title. This payment is made through a third party—the issuer."[1] A letter of credit is an instrument issued by a bank by which the bank furnishes its credit, which is both good and well known, in place of the buyer's credit, which may be good but is not so well known. A bank issues a letter of credit on behalf of one of its customers, authorizing an individual or firm to draw drafts on the bank or on one of its correspondents for the bank's account under certain conditions stipulated in the credit.

The commercial letter of credit is widely used and highly regarded as a key bank product that enables an important amount of international trade to take place. It is perceived to be unique to international banking although, in fact, it is equally usable for domestic trade. Providing letter of credit service is central to any bank's commitment to offer international banking services to customers and an understanding of the letter of credit is essential to the banker with customers involved in international trade. This chapter describes the basic import sight letter of credit.

The objectives of this chapter are to
- describe the basic letter of credit transaction
- identify the responsibilities of all parties to the transaction
- compare the letter of credit to collections as a means of financing international trade

---

BACKGROUND

The commercial letter of credit has been described as "the life-blood of international commerce . . . collateral to the underlying rights and obligations between the merchant at either end of the banking chain."[2] Its ancestry can be traced back probably to the twelfth century, although today's commercial letter of credit with its obligations on the bank is no older than the nineteenth century, beginning with the use by Finnish importers for their purchase of Brazilian coffee in 1840.

"The commercial letter of credit was first used in Anglo-American and European trade toward the middle of the nineteenth century and, in less than 100 years, it acquired guiding legal principles which hold true with a remarkable degree of uniformity across the boundaries of nations and legal systems."[3]

All commercial letters of credit are issued at the request and on behalf of the importer, either directly or through a correspondent bank. In discussing the financing of a transaction in which merchandise is imported from one country to another on the basis of a letter of credit, the term *import letter of credit* is often used. In fact, there is no real difference between an import letter of credit and an export letter of credit; the term used depends entirely on where the parties concerned are situated (see chapter 9). To the U.S. buyer of Brazilian coffee, for instance, it is an import letter of credit; to the foreign seller of the coffee, it is an export letter of credit. To the party in whose favor the credit is issued (*beneficiary*), it is an export letter of credit; to the buyer on whose behalf the letter of credit is issued (*account party*), it is an import letter of credit.

Letters of credit can be either *revocable* or *irrevocable*. The overwhelming majority of letters of credit issued are irrevocable, which means they cannot be canceled or changed without the consent of all parties concerned, particularly the beneficiary. The revocable letter of credit, which can be canceled or changed solely at the buyer's request, is rarely used. Unless specifically mentioned, discussions in this book refer to the irrevocable letter of credit. An irrevocable letter of credit adds an element of credit risk for the issuing bank, since it cannot cancel its commitment should the credit standing of its customer change, even before any shipment has taken place.

While the beneficiary (exporter, seller) receives an irrevocable authority of a bank to draw drafts on it, the account party (importer, buyer) must make sure that the exporter is responsible and of good reputation. A letter of credit issued in the beneficiary's favor does not compel the beneficiary to make a shipment. The letter of credit merely provides that if a shipment is made, and if the seller wants to be assured of payment by the bank, the seller must present documents that comply with the terms and conditions of the letter of credit. The buyer relies on the seller to send merchandise of the quality and quantity described in the documents that the buyer will eventually receive under the letter of credit. Irresponsible sellers may ship inferior goods, and the shipping documents will not show this. The bank is concerned only with the documents and cannot be held responsible in such situations. However, if irregularities in the documents presented to the bank exist, the bank will not honor drafts drawn against it until those documents are in order or unless the account party agrees to accept the discrepancy.

"The rules governing letter-of-credit transactions [in the United States] are derived from Article 5 of the Uniform Commercial Code (UCC), entitled 'Letters of Credit', and the 'Uniform Customs and Practice for Documentary Credits'(UCP). In contrast to Article 5, the UCP does not carry the force of law but instead is a compendium of customs and practices developed over the years for letter-of-credit transactions. . . . Frequently, the terms of the UCP are incorporated by reference into the terms of letter-of-credit transactions."[4]

THE MERCHANDISE CONTRACT

A letter of credit transaction customarily begins after a merchandise contract or order between the buyer and seller has been made. The bank is not concerned with the details of the negotiations that led to the merchandise contract, nor is it a party to that contract.

The terms and conditions of a letter of credit should be simple and easily understood. A letter of credit is separate and distinct from the underlying contract between buyer and seller for the purchase of the merchandise. The banks will deal only with the documents and not the merchandise. However, the letter of credit should be drawn in strict compliance with the provisions of that contract. Sundry details of merchandise quality and condition should not be included. The amount of credit, the expiration date, the shipping date, the documents to be presented, the tenor of the draft, and a brief description of the merchandise shipped must be included (see figure 8.1).

For example, a clothing store in California learns of a firm in Scotland that manufactures women's sweaters. The California store asks the Scottish firm to send samples and descriptive literature of its products. The store decides to buy a quantity of sweaters and negotiates a contract with the Scottish seller covering items such as the number of each size, color, and price. Because the two parties have not done business before, the problem discussed in the last two chapters concerning the means of payment occurs. The seller may ask for prepayment; the buyer may ask for open account. The seller wants to be assured it will be paid before surrendering title to the sweaters; the buyer wants to know that the sweaters will be shipped before paying. The seller does not want to wait to be paid until the buyer receives the goods, as it would have to do in a collection or open-account sale, nor to have the risk of the buyer changing its mind. To solve this dilemma, the two parties can include in their merchandise contract an agreement that this shipment will be paid by means of a commercial letter of credit.

Certain protections for both buyer and seller are inherent in all letters of credit. The seller knows it will be paid as soon as it complies with the terms of the letter of credit; the buyer knows no payment will be made until documents are presented showing that the shipment has been made as specified. The next step for the buyer is to approach its bank and apply for the letter of credit required in the merchandise contract.

APPLICATION FOR AN IMPORT LETTER OF CREDIT

A request for a commercial letter of credit is similar to an application for a loan and is treated by the banker in much the same way. The bank will usually insist that the documents be in negotiable form so that it obtains title to the merchandise between the time it makes payment and the time it is reimbursed. Nevertheless, the loan officer, in considering the application, must prudently view it as if it were an application for an unsecured loan. Even though the bank may have control over title documents after making payment, the banker should

Figure 8.1 Irrevocable Letter of Credit

NAME OF ISSUING BANK Bank in Brazil Rio De Janeiro, Brazil Place and date of issue Rio De Janeiro June 15, 19--	IRREVOCABLE DOCUMENTARY CREDIT	Number 7867
	Date and place of expiry August 28, 19-- New York	

Applicant Knitwear, Ltd. Rio De Janeiro	Beneficiary Knitting Machines, Inc. New York, N.Y. SPECIMEN

Advising Bank   Ref. No.
                                  IC 3047
 	
Morgan Guaranty Trust Company of N.Y.
	Amount
	     $ 8,000.00 US Dollars

Credit available with
Morgan Guaranty Trust Company of N.Y. by
☒ sight payment ☐ acceptance ☐ negotiation
☐ deferred payment at

against the documents detailed herein

Partial shipments ☐ allowed ☒ not allowed   Transhipment ☒ allowed ☐ not allowed

☒ and beneficiary's draft at sight

Shipment/dispatch/ taking in charge from/at USA PORT

on
Morgan Guaranty Trust Company of N.Y.

for transportation to Rio De Janeiro

Commercial invoice covering knitting machines FOB vessel, New York

Marine bills of lading issued to order of shipper and endorsed in blank marked "notify Knitwear, Ltd."

All documents should show Import License B1.BG-87/1883

Documents to be presented within 10 days after the date of issuance of the transport document(s) but within the validity of the credit.

We hereby issue this Documentary Credit in your favour. It is subject to the Uniform Customs and Practice for Documentary Credits (1983 Revision, International Chamber of Commerce, Paris, France, Publication No. 400) and engages us in accordance with the terms thereof, and especially in accordance with the terms of Article 10 thereof. The number and date of the credit and the name of our bank must be quoted on all drafts required. If the credit is available by negotiation, each presentation must be noted on the reverse of this advice by the bank where the credit is available.

This document consists of 1 signed page(s).

not consider this to be sufficient security, since the merchandise may have a limited market, the price may change, or difficulties may arise in getting possession of the merchandise.

A letter of credit is considered a self-liquidating extension of credit. This means that the banker expects the transfer of the merchandise from the seller to the buyer, and the subsequent sale by that buyer, to provide cash for the buyer to repay the bank. The bank may consider the collateral value of the merchandise to be shipped, although often this may not be of value to anyone other than the original buyer because many items shipped under letters of credit have a limited market. The banker will usually want evidence that the merchandise is insured as an added protection. The marketability of the goods to be imported, as well as the integrity and financial responsibility of the importer, is important to the bank. Banks deal only in documents in any letter of credit. They do not inspect the goods, although the documents may misrepresent the merchandise, particularly in case of fraud.

From the time it issues the letter of credit until the draft and documents are presented for payment, the bank lends only its credit. It makes no outlay of funds until the draft and documents are presented (see figure 8.2). The bank, however, must be prepared for presentation of the documents and the demand for payment at any time during the life of the letter of credit. The timing of the presentation is completely at the option of the seller, and only in unusual circumstances will the bank have any warning before the actual arrival of the documents.

The application for a commercial letter of credit should identify the precise terms and conditions under which the importer wishes its bank to establish the credit and should describe the documents that the bank will receive in exchange for the payment it will eventually make. The application itself is signed by the importing customer and incorporates a *security agreement* defining the rights of the bank issuing the credit and the obligation of the customer on whose behalf the credit is issued.

The customer's agreement embodies the obligation of the customer to reimburse the bank for payments made under the letter of credit, provided, of course, that such payments are made in accordance with the terms expressed in it. This agreement covers many other eventualities, some of the most important of which follow:

- The customer acknowledges the issuing bank's unqualified right to possess and dispose of all property under the letter of credit as security.
- The customer assumes all risks from the actions of the shippers, or beneficiaries, who use the letter of credit.
- The customer does not hold the issuing bank responsible for the validity, genuineness, or sufficiency of the documents.
- The customer does not hold the issuing bank responsible for the existence, character, quality, quantity, condition, packing, value, or delivery of the property represented by the documents.
- The customer is obligated to pay a specified fee to the issuing bank for issuing the letter of credit. (Although this fee may be called a commission, it is, in fact, a finance charge and may be in addition to a document handling or negotiation fee. Sometimes the two fees are combined into an all-inclusive charge.)

Figure 8.2 Flow Chart of the Letter of Credit Process

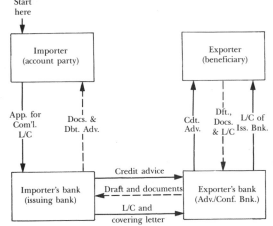

Source: Thomas J. Cusack, "A Small International Department Can Design an 'In-House' Training Program for Its Operations Clerical Staff" (Thesis, Stonier Graduate School of Banking, 1975), p. 29.

In addition to itemizing the documents to be delivered by the exporter, the importer must decide whether it wants all the order to come in one shipment or whether partial shipments will be permitted. The importer must decide whether the merchandise must come on a direct ship from the seller or whether it can be transferred from one ship to another at an intermediate port (*transshipment*). Transshipment can cause delays, or the goods may be overlooked at the intermediate port. The importer must also select the expiration date of the letter of credit so that it can receive its goods in time for their selling season or for its need of them. The banker can advise the buyer on many of these points in preparing the application.

Once the bank is satisfied with the credit responsibility of its customer and the credit risk, it will approve the formal application for a commercial letter of credit. The issuing bank sets up bookkeeping entries on its general ledger. Although no outlay of funds has occurred, the bank has made an extension of credit that is irrevocable, on which it is earning income, and that can be converted into a demand for cash without any further option to the bank.

THE EXPORTER'S RESPONSIBILITIES

Issuing a letter of credit involves more than a bank's statement to honor a beneficiary's drafts and documents upon presentation. The beneficiary is located in a foreign country and consequently wants to be able to negotiate the draft and documents with a bank in its own country. Therefore, a bank issuing a letter of credit must have already established its name and responsibility in the commercially important cities of the world. Many banks are not recognized throughout the world and are not equipped to handle letters of credit; they will use a correspondent bank in opening letters of credit.

A letter of credit is sent either directly to the beneficiary or indirectly through a correspondent bank in the exporter's locale. Upon receiving the credit, the beneficiary examines its terms and conditions to see that they conform to the contract and that the beneficiary is able to perform under the credit. If an *amendment* to the original terms and conditions in the letter of credit is necessary, the beneficiary contacts the buyer directly or through the bank and asks for an amendment covering the changes. Changes may refer to the amount, documentary requirements, expiration date, or shipping date. Any changes must be agreeable to all parties concerned—the beneficiary, the buyer, and the bank opening the credit.

When the beneficiary is satisfied that the terms of the credit agree with the contract with the buyer and can be complied with, the shipment is made. In the case of the Scottish sweaters, the manufacturer packs the sweaters in crates for marine shipment and delivers them to a shipping company in exchange for bills of lading that meet the terms of the letter of credit, as for example when it requires them to be in negotiable form ("to order of shipper, blank endorsed"). Insurance certificates or policies, if required, are obtained to cover the cargo; customs invoices are prepared, as well as any other documents. The beneficiary then prepares its commercial invoice, draws a draft on the specified bank, and presents these documents in the required number of copies with the letter of credit to its local bank for negotiation. The draft can be drawn on the issuing bank or another bank as stated in the letter of credit.

The expiration date on the letter of credit is the final date on which drafts may be presented for negotiation. Unless otherwise stipulated, letters of credit usually expire in the city in which the beneficiary is located. The reason for this provision is that generally a beneficiary can control when it presents documents to its local bank for negotiation. If it needed to have those documents delivered by a stated date to the country of the buyer, however, it would be entirely at the mercy of the mails. If the documents were delivered after the expiration date, the buyer could refuse to authorize payment.

Once the shipment has been made, there is another time limit on the seller—the presentation date. Documents must be presented to the bank not later than 21 days after issuance of the bill of lading, unless otherwise stated in the letter of credit, and before the expiration date. This presentation date allows time for the bills of lading to be processed and delivered into the importer's hands before the arrival of the ship. Bills of lading that reach the importer after the ship has arrived are considered *stale*, which could result in unexpected expenses for the buyer, since the unclaimed merchandise incurs storage charges.

"Frequently, in an international sale of goods, the merchandise arrives at the importer's (buyer's) port before the arrival of correct and complete bills of lading. In such instances, it is customary for the importer (buyer) to obtain immediate possession of the goods by providing the shipping company with a bank guarantee, often called a *shipside bond*,[5] which holds the shipping company blameless of damage resulting from release of the goods without proper or complete documents. Usually the bank's guarantee relies on a counterguarantee issued by the importer to the bank."[6] These transactions are reflected as contingent items in the bank's financial statement.

NEGOTIATION

An important function of a bank issuing a credit arises when it must honor its obligation expressed in the letter of credit. The bank must examine the documents presented to verify that, on their face, they conform to the conditions of the letter of credit.[7] This process of comparing the documents to determine whether they comply with the terms and conditions of the letter of credit is known as *negotiation*.

This process involves checking the documents to make sure that

- the documents have been negotiated or presented on or before the expiration of the credit
- the amount drawn does not exceed the amount available under the credit
- the documents comply with the stated requirements of the letter of credit and all amendments
- the documents conform to each other and are compatible with the Uniform Customs
- each individual document appears to be properly prepared

To determine these, the negotiator takes the bank's record of the letter of credit with all the presented documents and methodically examines them.

If *discrepancies* are noted, they are referred to a discrepancy officer. Some may be minor and can be remedied in the bank, such as an insufficient number of copies of an invoice. The bank cannot alter the documents as presented. Other discrepancies, such as a different description of the merchandise, will be sufficient cause for the bank to refuse payment. Any deviations will be referred to the account party who requested the opening of the letter of credit. This customer has the right to refuse to permit any deviation from the original application. In practice, however, the customer will agree to accept trivial discrepancies in order to receive the goods. The bank will ask for a written concurrence and then will make the payment. However, if the customer refuses to waive the original requirements, the bank will refuse to pay the draft, and it will be up to the seller to correct the discrepancy before payment can be made.

In the sweater transaction, the Scottish beneficiary may present the documents to a local bank. Because the letter of credit represents an irrevocable obligation of a known U.S. bank to honor drafts and documents in conformity with the terms of the credit, the beneficiary's local bank has the assurance it may make its payment. The issuing bank becomes liable to this negotiating bank as a bona fide holder of the beneficiary's draft and documents just as the issuing bank is liable to this beneficiary or drawer of the draft. The negotiating bank, therefore, usually will not hesitate to buy the draft, or advance the funds, and give the shipper its money immediately, making allowance for the time until it can expect to be paid. It then sends the draft and documents to the issuing bank, or possibly to another U.S. bank for presentation to the issuing bank.

Each party in the letter of credit process examines the documents on its own behalf. Even if the first negotiating bank pays the seller, the issuing bank will itself examine the documents to see that they are in accord with the letter of credit they issued. Negotiation of the documents and payment of the draft by the bank do not commit the buyer to pay until it has examined the documents and is satisfied. If the banks have been careless and overlooked discrepancies, the buyer can refuse to pay. This could result in a financial loss for the bank that has made the payment.

The issuing bank pays the sight draft and credits the Due To account of the negotiating bank or transfers the money to it (see chapter 5). The bank then looks to the buyer to pay the bank, either by charging the buyer's account or by refinancing with a line of credit. However, if the buyer is no longer able to repay the bank, the bank's obligation under the letter of credit remains. This is the essence of the letter of credit as a means of financing international trade. In practice, the bank will usually simultaneously pay the seller and debit the account of the buyer. The knowledgeable banker must recognize that these are two distinct and unlinked functions. The bank carries the risk in letters of credit, just as in any other extension of credit, that it will not be repaid. The only difference is in the timing of when it disburses its own funds.

The documents are then delivered to the importer against its receipt, and the letter of credit transaction is complete. The importer arranges with a customs broker for the formal entry and payment of duty on the goods, if necessary. In the sweater example, the California buyer now has the merchandise for subsequent retail sale.

If the importer is unable to pay the bank, the bank has the bills of lading in negotiable form. The bank can take possession of the merchandise and collateralize its loan for whatever value the merchandise represents. This is why the bank requires that bills of lading be in negotiable form and that the goods should not be consigned directly to the buyer.

Besides benefiting the buyer and seller, the letter of credit benefits the banks involved. They collect fees for opening letters of credit, advising the credit, confirming, and for negotiating the documents when presented. The Scottish bank also benefits from an increase in its account balance at the California bank when that bank pays the letter of credit draft. The Scottish bank has the option of purchasing the draft from the seller, thereby earning foreign exchange profit and transit interest from converting the U.S. dollar draft into pounds sterling. Even if it does not purchase the draft in advance of being reimbursed, the Scottish bank can earn the foreign exchange profit when it pays the Scottish seller against the dollars in its account. This illustrates the benefits of correspondent banking through such short-term relationships.

FRAUD

A disturbing problem for banks is fraud, usually by the seller of the merchandise. The *Uniform Customs and Practice for Documentary Credits* (see appendix C) states that "all parties concerned deal in documents and not in goods" (Article 4) and, if there are irregularities, the "bank must determine, on the basis of the documents alone" (Article 16) not to make payment. The dilemma, however, arises when the bank knows or strongly suspects that the documents, when presented, do not describe the actual merchandise or fraudulently misrepresent the facts. In several instances, banks have refused to pay. The resulting court decisions have analyzed the conflicting responsibilities of the banker, including the banker's role in issuing a letter of credit:

> It is well established that a letter of credit is dependent on the primary contract of sale between the buyer and the seller. The issuing bank agrees to pay upon presentation of documents, not goods. This rule is necessary to preserve the efficiency of the letter of credit as an instrument for the financing of trade.... Where the seller's fraud has been called to the bank's attention before the drafts and documents have been presented for payment, the principle of the independence of the bank's obligation under the letter of credit should not be extended to protect the unscrupulous seller.[8]

> That case shows that an exception to the strict rule exists. The bank ought not to pay under the credit if it knows that the documents are forged or that the request for payment is made fraudulently in circumstances when there is no right to payment.[9]

Another case concerned a shipment from the United Kingdom to Peru on the vessel *American Accord* in which the bills of lading were presented showing that the merchandise had been loaded on board on the last permitted shipping date under the letter of credit. The loading, it turned out, had actually been done on the day after and the bills of lading were fraudulently prepared by an agent of the shipping company.

> [The document] is not a genuine or valid document entitling the presenter of it to be paid, and if the banker to which it is presented under a letter of credit knows it to be forged he must not pay. [T]he bank owes no duty to the beneficiary to pay and, I would say, owes a duty to the customer not to pay.[10]

That these court decisions span 40 years makes it obvious that the banker must proceed with caution in selecting a course of action when the issue of possible fraud comes to the bank's attention. Some bankers feel that when fraud is suspected the most appropriate procedure is that the account party, who is usually the first one to uncover it, should apply for a court restraining order rather than put the burden on the bank to decide not to pay.[11] A judge in one case perhaps summed up the continuing dilemma for the banker: "[T]he fewer the cases in which a bank is entitled to hold up payment the better for the smooth running of international trade. But I do not think that the courts have a duty to assist international trade to run smoothly if it is fraudulent."[12]

COLLECTIONS VERSUS LETTERS OF CREDIT

One of the many decisions an exporter must make is whether to insist on having a letter of credit opened in the exporter's favor or to ship on a collection, or sight draft, basis. Such a decision depends on the exporter's past relationship and experience with the buyer as well as on the political and economic circumstances in the importer's country, which may prevent transfer of payment despite the buyer's ability and intent to pay. It is important, therefore, for the exporter and the international banker to review the differences between these two means of effecting payment or financing.

An irrevocable letter of credit is an obligation of the issuing bank. Drafts drawn under a letter of credit are drawn on a bank, either the issuing, confirming, advising, or reimbursing bank, depending on the characteristics of the letter of credit (see chapter 9). Exporters can be certain that if they ship in compliance with the stated terms and conditions, their drafts will be honored, regardless of any calamity or act of the importer. The exporter looks to the bank for payment and knows payment is forthcoming on presentation of the appropriate documents.

In a collection, the exporter must wait until the documents are presented to the buyer to be paid. The exporter's draft is not drawn on a bank; it is drawn on the importer. The bank's role is to present the draft to the importer for payment or acceptance, as the case may be. An importer might not pay an exporter for many reasons. Importers may change their minds or go out of business; the goods shipped may be claimed to be inferior; restrictions on imports may be imposed after the shipment has been made. The danger of nonpayment is particularly great for certain types of perishable commodities for which market price fluctuations can be severe and sudden. If the market price of a shipment should decline sharply, the importer may refuse to pay when the draft is presented. If the exporter has already shipped the commodity and the importer refuses to pay, the exporter may be forced to renegotiate the sale at a lower price to avoid a complete loss on the shipment. The exporter's other options include having the goods returned, storing them until a new buyer is found, or destroying them. Any option, however, incurs substantial expense to the seller.

When a letter of credit calls for drafts to be drawn at, for example, 180 days after sight, the draft is drawn by the exporter on a bank that accepts it (see chapter 10). In the United States, the accepting bank must pay such an acceptance at maturity, regardless of any change in the financial existence or condition of the importer. The active market for bankers' acceptances allows exporters to easily discount the document for cash without consideration of their own credit lines.

In a collection, a draft payable at a future date is drawn on the buyer, not on a bank; the buyer accepts the draft and undertakes to pay it at maturity. But there is always the chance that the buyer may go into bankruptcy or that some other difficulty may arise before maturity. In addition, the exporter is providing the financing during this period, since no active market exists for trade acceptances. Usually the only way exporters can discount a trade acceptance for cash before maturity is by using their own credit lines at their bank on a "with recourse" basis.

When the amount involved is relatively small, the cost to both importer and exporter to use the collection method is generally lower than the cost of opening a letter of credit. The collection method also has the advantage of avoiding the use of bank credit (something the importer may be unable or unwilling to do).

When a shipment involves merchandise that is not subject to sudden market fluctuations, the exporter often considers using the collection method. This ensures a degree of protection, because the exporter obtains payment or at least acceptance of a draft before the buyer can take possession of the merchandise. In the same circumstances, the collection method may also help an exporter make a sale in a competitive market, as the cost to the importer is lower than the cost of obtaining a letter of credit.

If, however, the exporter has once used a collection for a sale to a particular buyer and had difficulty in obtaining payment from the buyer, then the exporter will probably insist on a letter of credit before undertaking further orders.

ACCOUNTING

The amount of the letter of credit appears as a contingent account in the bank's financial statement as soon as it is issued. When the documents are negotiated and the draft is paid or accepted, or if no drawing takes place by the expiration date, the amount is taken out of the contingent account. If financing is provided then the appropriate loan category would be charged.

For the risk-based capital calculation, the amount of the outstanding letter of credit is first multiplied by a credit conversion factor of 20 percent and then assigned to the appropriate risk category of the account party, that is, the bank's customer for whom it is issued. For a business importer, the risk category would be 100 percent. Therefore, this sample calculation would be the amount of the letter of credit x 20% x 100% = the amount against which capital would be required (see appendix D, Section III D).

SUMMARY

The commercial letter of credit is one of the most important instruments in international banking. It is indispensable in banking and financing international trade and a most important activity for most countries.

The letter of credit substitutes a bank's credit for that of a customer and thereby guarantees payment from buyer to seller. The transaction rests on documents that evidence that the shipment, as agreed, has taken place. Buyers are assured that the shipment has been made before they are called on to pay, and sellers know that they will be paid as soon as they ship regardless of any change in the buyer's financial standing.

This instrument in international trade has been a major banking activity for many years. Its continued widespread use after over a century is testimony to its vitality and usefulness in international trade, particularly in times of economic difficulty, when its use has increased. It is an important and unique service that banks provide in international banking.

QUESTIONS

1. What is a letter of credit?
2. What does negotiation mean?
3. What is the responsibility of the importer?
4. What is the difference between a collection and a letter of credit?

PROBLEM

A customer of your bank wishes to purchase toys from a seller in Hong Kong. The seller does not know anything about the credit standing of your customer and is, therefore, willing to make the shipment only if a letter of credit is opened in its favor. What will be your bank's responsibilities and what should you consider in making your decision?

Notes

1. Craig W. Smith, *Law and Banking: Applications* (Washington, D.C.: American Bankers Association, 1986), p. 109.

2. *Harbottle (Mercantile) Ltd. v. National Westminster Bank Ltd.*, (1978) Q.B. 146, 1955.

3. Boris Kozolchyk, "Letter of Credit," *International Encyclopedia of Comparative Law.*

4. Smith, p. 105.

5. Other terms for this include steamship indemnities or steamship release.

6. United States Department of the Treasury, *Comptroller's Handbook for National Bank Examiners* (Englewood Cliffs: Prentice-Hall, Inc.). Section 812.1. National banks are restricted in issuing such guarantees from U. S. offices that differ from foreign branches.

7. The importance of this examination is demonstrated by the landmark decision on November 13, 1942, of the British Court of Appeals in the case of *J. H. Raynor & Company, Ltd. v. Hambros Bank, Ltd.* (Times Law Reports, vol. LIX) that a bank is not bound to honor drafts presented to it under a letter of credit unless those drafts, with the accompanying documents, are exactly as stipulated in the letter of credit.

8.   *Sztejn v. J. Henry Schroder Banking Corporation*, 31 N.Y.S. 2d 631 (1940).

9.   *Edward Owen Engineering v. Barclays Bank International Ltd.*, Q.B. 159 (1978).

10. *United City Merchants (Investments) Ltd. v. Royal Bank of Canada* (1977 V No. 111).

11. Interview with Anthony Ruggiero, *Letter of Credit Update* (Arlington, Va., October 1985), pp. 24-27.

12. *United City Merchants (Investments) Ltd. v. Royal Bank of Canada* (1977 V No. 111).

9

Letter of Credit Variations

One of the great strengths of the letter of credit is its flexibility. The basic sight import letter of credit can be varied to accommodate the particular needs agreed to between buyers and sellers while maintaining the fundamental principles and procedures already discussed.

Letters of credit can provide additional financing for the buyer, advance funds to the seller, or permit a large international bank to provide financial support to smaller banks or to customers. This flexibility is what makes the letter of credit the principal means of bank financing for international trade.

The objectives of this chapter are to
- describe the letter of credit that provides for time drafts
- explain specialized types of clauses
- describe the use of export letters of credit
- identify the special features of standby letters of credit

EXPORT LETTERS OF CREDIT

Because every foreign trade transaction is both an export and an import, every international commercial letter of credit is both an export credit and an import credit. To the beneficiary (the seller) and to the advising, confirming, or negotiating bank, it is an export credit; to the buyer and to the opening bank, it is an import credit.

Regardless of whether the underlying transaction is a U.S. export, a U.S. import, or any trade between two countries, all commercial letters of credit are opened at the request of the importer to its local bank.

Confirmed Letters of Credit

The letters of credit issued by many foreign banks may not be acceptable to a U.S. seller. The ability of some banks to honor their obligations has been affected in the past by foreign government exchange restrictions, local political situations, economic upsets, and wars or the threat of war. In addition, many foreign banks that issue letters of credit on behalf of their customers are small and not known to the U.S. exporter. Even though a U.S. exporter insists on receiving a letter of credit, it may feel that a letter of credit from a small foreign bank does not provide the desired protection.

The U.S. exporter consequently may insist not only that the buyer's local bank issue a letter of credit but also that a U.S. bank add its commitment to pay to that of the foreign bank. This requirement is met by a letter of credit that is an irrevocable obligation of the issuing bank (in this case, the foreign bank), which is *confirmed* by a U.S. bank (see figure 9.1). In other words, the U.S. bank adds its obligation to that of the foreign bank to honor drafts and documents presented in accordance with the terms of the credit.

The U.S. bank "has acted as an intermediate, has assumed the risk of default of the foreign bank, and has assured the draft's holder of payment."[1] The U.S. bank will do this because of the established correspondent relationship with the foreign bank and because the U.S. bank is willing to extend credit to the foreign bank (see chapter 14). By adding its confirmation, the U.S. bank is able to facilitate foreign trade, particularly U.S. exports. The draft in a confirmed letter of credit will usually be drawn on the confirming bank so that it can pay the exporter immediately. The fee collected represents the credit risk the bank is assuming and is similar to interest.[2]

The exporter now has a letter of credit that bears the promise of two banks—the issuing foreign bank and the confirming U.S. bank. The U.S. exporter is thus relieved of any concern about whether the foreign bank will be able to obtain dollars to pay; this risk is borne by the confirming U.S. bank.

If an exporter receives a letter of credit that has not been confirmed and wants it to be confirmed, it cannot directly request a U.S. bank to add its confirmation. The exporter must request the importer to have the importer's bank ask the U.S. bank to confirm. This may seem cumbersome, but the U.S. bank is looking for reimbursement from the foreign bank that is its customer. No one else can ask the U.S. bank to provide credit to

Figure 9.1 Confirmed Letter of Credit

ComericA Bank
International Banking Department
Post Office Box 64858
Detroit, Michigan 48264

SPECIMEN

Telex: 23-6383
Swift: DBTDUS33

CONFIRMED IRREVOCABLE CREDIT

February 11, 19--

Terrance Tool Company
13 Avenue F
Detroit, Michigan

Our Confirmed Advice No.: JA 908
Correspondent's No.: JT 1089

Gentlemen

We are instructed by Bank in London, London, England, that they have issued their irrevocable credit in your favor for account of L.K. Leroy Associates Ltd., London, England up to the aggregate amount of U.S. $925.00 (Nine Hundred Twenty Five and 00/100 Dollars).

Credit is available with Comerica Bank, Detroit against the documents detailed herein and beneficiary's draft at sight on Comerica Bank, Detroit.

Commercial invoice in triplicate, stating that it covers: "Lathe" C&F Southampton.

Ocean bills of lading consigned to order of Bank in London, London England marked "Freight Prepaid," evidencing shipment from New York to Southampton.

Drafts must clearly specify the number of this credit, and be presented at this office on or before April 10, 19--.

At the request of our correspondent we confirm their irrevocable credit and thereby undertake that all drafts drawn under and in compliance with the terms of this credit will be duly honored by us.

This credit is subject to Uniform Customs and Practice for Documentary Credits (1984 Revision), International Chamber of Commerce Publication 400

Sincerely,

(Authorized Signature)

Note:
If you are unable to comply with the terms of this credit, please contact your customer and/or us promptly in order to effect the necessary changes.

bj

Source: *Letters of Credit* (Washington, D.C.: American Bankers Association, 1985), p. 89.

the foreign bank. The U.S. bank must be careful to distinguish between its responsibilities to its customers in such a transaction. Although the exporter may be a bank's customer for many types of business, the foreign bank is the party to whom the bank is extending credit when it confirms a letter of credit. The U.S. bank should not get into a situation where it is attempting to respond to the demands of both parties.

Although this illustration has referred to a U.S. exporter, the procedure is the same when the trade transaction takes place between two foreign countries. A U.S. bank will add its confirmation at the request of a bank issuing a letter of credit in favor of a beneficiary anywhere in the world. Likewise, the confirmed letter of credit can be in U.S. dollars or another currency. Confirmation does not indicate what type of letter of credit is being issued.

When a U.S. bank adds its confirmation to a letter of credit issued by a foreign bank, it charges a fee to the foreign bank that is ultimately passed on to the foreign buyer. This fee, which may be called a commission, represents the bank's charge for extending credit. In some instances, the exporter may agree to pay this confirmation commission.

Advised Credits

As foreign exchange conditions in many countries have become normal and as business competition has become greater, many exporters have been willing to forgo the confirmation of letters of credit by U.S. banks. Many of the larger foreign banks have become well known; consequently, exporters have been willing to accept their letters of credit directly. As a result, banks are frequently not asked to confirm a foreign bank's letter of credit but merely to *advise* it. This is sometimes called an *unconfirmed* letter of credit. The U.S. bank states that this "is solely an advice of a credit opened by the mentioned correspondent and conveys no engagement by us." In the example of a U.S. export, the U.S. bank, after verifying that the signatures on the foreign letter of credit are bona fide, advises the beneficiary of this fact and volunteers its services in general. Because they are often in U.S. dollars, such letters of credit usually provide that drafts can be drawn on the advising U.S. bank. When such drafts are negotiated, the U.S. bank earns a commission as well as activity through the Due To account of its correspondent.

LETTERS OF CREDIT AVAILABLE BY TIME DRAFTS

In addition to letters of credit available by drafts payable at sight, a frequently used letter of credit is the time or usance letter of credit.* This letter of credit specifies that drafts are drawn on the

---

* The *Oxford English Dictionary* traces the origin of usance to the seventeenth century: "the time or period (varying in respect of different countries) allowed by commercial usage or law for the payment of a bill of exchange, etc., especially as drawn in a foreign or distant land."

issuing or other designated bank, depending on the currency or other conditions, and that payment is to be made at some future time. When the draft is in dollars, this means up to six months after sight. In such a letter of credit, the seller draws the draft and presents it with all the shipping documents to the designated bank, which "accepts" the draft. This means that the bank promises to pay the full face amount of the draft, not when the documents are presented but on a specified future date. The accepted draft is returned to the seller, who holds it to maturity and presents it to the bank on the future date to receive the full amount, regardless of whether the buyer has paid the bank or not. Such time drafts may be drawn, for example, "X days after sight," "after date," or "date of bill of bill of lading," and in such cases the specific maturity date must be indicated when the draft is drawn. The accepted draft is a bankers' acceptance; these are examined in detail in chapter 10.

The procedure for using the time letter of credit is similar to that for the sight letter of credit. The importing customer submits an application to the bank for the letter of credit that identifies the documents to be presented, the amount of the credit, expiration date, and other information. The bank establishes the letter of credit, following the procedure previously outlined. The shipper provides the documents stipulated and the draft to the issuing bank for examination, honor, and eventual release of the documents to the importer. But the similarity between sight and time letters of credit ends with the routine of issuance and negotiation. A sight letter of credit is payable upon presentation of documents to the issuing bank, as long as those documents conform to the terms of the letter of credit. The bank is obligated to make such payment regardless of the ability of the importer to pay. Subsequently, the bank will release the documents when payment is made to it by the importing customer. A time letter of credit, on the other hand, implies an extension of credit by the issuing bank beyond the date on which the documents are presented. The seller has to agree to a letter of credit providing for a time rather than a sight draft. In essence, the seller agrees to wait the period of time, 90 days in this example, before receiving full payment. The reasons why the seller is willing to wait are varied: a highly competitive market in which other sellers of similar goods are offering buyers 90 days before having to pay, or the need for a delay because otherwise this particular buyer would be unable to complete a purchase contract at all. In any event, the seller surrenders title to the merchandise in return for a promise of the issuing bank to pay for it at a future date. The seller might quote a slightly higher price for the goods for a 90-day delay in payment, even though a bank is obligated to pay at that time.

An importer's primary reason for requesting a time letter of credit is to have time to obtain and sell the goods in order to pay the draft. But the bank issuing the time letter of credit has a different credit consideration than exists with a sight letter of credit. The bank must release the goods to the importer immediately, thereby losing possession of the title documents to the goods, but will not receive payment from the importer until the end of the 90 days. At the same time, the bank must honor the obligation whether the customer pays or not. The banker, therefore, considers to what extent the bank is willing to fulfill the customer's request in such a situation, because the banker will be releasing the bank's collateral in trust to the customer. In other words, how much of a credit line will the bank give its customer on *trust receipt*? "This is an arrangement in which the lender retains title to the goods that are held by the borrower. The borrower holds the goods in 'trust' for the lender."[3] (Factors to be evaluated in extending a credit line are covered in chapter 13.)

Note that the seller has a bank commitment to pay throughout the transaction, whether the letter of credit provides for a sight or time draft. The seller ships, in either case, against a bank's commitment to pay upon presentation of specified documents under certain stated conditions. With a sight draft, the seller surrenders title to the merchandise for a cash payment. With a time draft, the seller surrenders title against the bank's unconditional commitment to pay on a stated future date. Once the shipment is made in accordance with the letter of credit, the seller never loses the protection of the bank's credit standing and is never exposed to the buyer's credit capabilities. The bank stands in place of the buyer in both sight and time letters of credit until the drafts are paid in cash.

A trust receipt is a document signed by a buyer in which a bank retains a security interest in the goods while the buyer has possession of them. It is intended to be used for short periods of time. The buyer is obligated to maintain the identity of the goods or the proceeds from the sale of those goods distinct from other assets and subject to repossession by the bank. Depending on the law in a state, the U.S. bank may wish to have greater protection by taking a lien on the inventory or some other form of collateral.

In spite of these legal obligations, the bank does not have possession of the goods and may not be able to find them to repossess. In fact, the goods may have been sold to a third party without the bank's immediate knowledge. The bank must consider these realities when making its decision.

In most cases when the bank issues a time letter of credit, it presupposes that the merchandise will be released on trust receipt at the time the draft is presented for acceptance. However, a bank may elect not to release the shipping documents to its customer. In such circumstances the issuing bank itself, holding documents giving title to the goods, may decide to store these goods in a public warehouse and hold the warehouse receipt as collateral. Releases may then be made against payment or as otherwise determined by the bank. This, however, will not be the usual case. Thus, the essential differences between a sight letter of credit and a time letter of credit are (1) the added credit risk assumed by the issuing bank and (2) the technical procedure of creating an acceptance liability.

Deferred Payment Letters of Credit

Time letters of credit may provide for drafts drawn more than six months after sight or date. Under the Federal Reserve Act, this is the maximum term permitted for eligible U.S. dollar bankers' acceptances, which is what the letter of credit draft becomes when the documents are presented and the draft accepted. The seller of the goods may be willing, however, to extend credit to the buyer for longer than six months. This *deferred payment* may be particularly suitable in sales of heavy equipment. To do this the letter of credit may specify that sight drafts are to be presented not at the time of shipment but, for example, one year later. The shipping documents and all other documents will be presented at the time the shipment takes place. The bank acknowledges their correctness to the seller and forwards them to the buyer. A year later the shipper presents the sight draft to the bank; the bank pays it and looks to the buyer for reimbursement at that time.

The bank's direct commitment to pay at the end of the deferred payment period is assumed at the time the bank receives the documents in order and acknowledges their receipt to the beneficiary. Therefore, issuance or confirmation of such a letter of credit must take place only after full evaluation of a credit exposure for this longer time and after the merchandise has been delivered to the buyer (at the time of presentation of the documents to the bank, which is before the time of payment). The actual financing is made by the seller, who, in this example, is willing to wait a year before payment. Deferred payment letters of credit may also provide for a series of payments over a number of years.

OTHER LETTERS OF CREDIT	The letter of credit is a flexible document. Clauses may be added to the basic letter of credit or may be changed to meet the special needs of a bank's customers and thereby broaden the uses of this document.

Red Clause Letters of Credit

The buyer of goods may be willing to make cash advances to the seller before shipment. The need for advances can arise when the seller is an agent of the buyer and needs cash to buy a crop from farmers in the interior of the country. For example, a letter of credit for the shipment of copra from the Philippines to the United States might contain a *red clause* to permit advance payments that will enable the seller to buy the commodity from planters who insist on cash. When the crop moves to the port and is shipped, the shipping and allied documents are presented to the negotiating bank; the payment to the seller would be the difference between the invoice amount and the amount already advanced.

The term red clause derives from the red ink in which such clauses were originally written. A typical red clause would read as follows:

> The negotiating bank is hereby authorized to make advances to the beneficiary up to the aggregate amount of X dollars or the remaining unused balance against the beneficiary's receipt stating that the advances are to be used to pay for the purchase and shipment of the merchandise covered by this credit and the beneficiary's undertaking to deliver to the negotiating bank the documents stipulated in the credit. The advances with interest are to be deducted from the proceeds of the drafts drawn under this credit. We hereby undertake the payment of such advances with interest should they not be repaid by the beneficiary prior to the expiration of this credit.

The buyer assumes the risk that the seller might draw the advance and not ship the goods. The bank will issue a letter of credit with such a red clause only when it knows that it can obtain reimbursement from the buyer if the shipment is not made. The buyer, in requesting a red clause, should be aware of the exposure on the interest cost. The rate of interest varies substantially in various parts of the world. A drawing in U.S. dollars can be converted into the local currency and re-lent by the beneficiary at many times the interest rate in the United States. If the foreign bank honors a drawing, it can immediately negotiate the draft under the letter of credit and the amount will subsequently be charged to the account of the buyer. An unscrupulous seller can thus profit at the expense of the U.S. buyer.

A *green clause* letter of credit is a variation of the red clause. It is used in a few countries, such as Australia for the wool trade. It permits advances to the seller but requires that the merchandise be stored under the bank's control until it is shipped.

Transferable Letters of Credit

A letter of credit may be used only by the addressed party, normally the seller of the merchandise. In some cases, however, this party may be an agent who wants to transfer the letter of credit to the actual seller. At the request of its customer, the issuing bank addresses the letter of credit to the beneficiary as before, but either states in the letter of credit that it is *transferable* or adds to the addressee "and/or transferee (or transferees)," depending on whether the letter of credit may be transferred in its entirety to another seller or in part to a number of sellers. In either case, the credit may be transferred only once, and the new beneficiary cannot transfer it again. The original beneficiary must give the issuing bank the name of the new beneficiary, from whom documents will then be accepted.

Such letters of credit are also useful for a business representative making a buying trip. The representative can carry a letter of credit and transfer portions of it from time to time as purchases are made from manufacturers.

Assignment of Proceeds

A beneficiary of a letter of credit may seek financing from another supplier or third party in order to prepare the shipment. As collateral the beneficiary may agree to pledge to the supplier the proceeds of the draft drawn under the letter of credit. This is done by instructing the bank to pay a portion or all of the letter of credit payments to the third party. Called an *assignment of proceeds*, it is of value only if the beneficiary presents documents in compliance with the letter of credit. If no draft is drawn under the letter of credit, then the bank has no obligation to honor the assignment of proceeds.

A bank can also advance funds to the beneficiary and take the assignment of proceeds as repayment, called *discounting a letter of credit.* If the letter of credit's beneficiary does not make the shipment and present the documents, the bank that discounted the letter of credit cannot make the shipment or present documents to recover the money it has advanced. To permit anyone other than the beneficiary to do so would make the letter of credit transferable, which cannot be done unless the letter of credit so states.

Back-to-Back Letters of Credit

Back-to-back letters of credit are two letters of credit with identical documentary requirements[4] except for a difference in the price of the merchandise and, possibly, curtailed expiration dates. This is appropriate when an agent acts between buyer and seller and uses the creditworthiness of the ultimate buyer as the agent's own. The agent agrees to purchase the goods against a letter of credit. The agent then asks the buyer to open a letter of credit at the buyer's bank in favor of the agent with identical documentary requirements except for the draft amount . This credit is deposited with the agent's bank, which issues a new credit for account of the agent in favor of the seller.

The documents differ only in the amount of the draft and the invoices, providing profit for the agent. The agent's invoices and the draft for the higher amount are given to the agent's bank when it issues its credit. When documents are presented under credit opened by the agent's bank, that bank can pay the seller and can present to and collect from the bank that issued the credit for the ultimate buyer in favor of the agent.

If the agent dies, the presigned draft and invoices may not be usable. Of greater concern is the possibility of discrepancies in the documents. The second bank might find the documents to be in order; the first bank may not. As a consequence, any bank issuing the second letter of credit in a back-to-back transaction must carefully evaluate the transaction and all the involved parties.

The agent may prefer to use a back-to-back letter of credit instead of a transferable letter of credit because this may prevent the buyer from knowing the identity of the seller. A buyer who had this information might elect to deal directly with the seller instead of using the agent.

Revolving Letters of Credit

When a series of identical shipments for the same amount with the same parties involved are to be made over a period of time and the total value is greater than the amount the bank or the buyer is willing to have outstanding at any time, a letter of credit may be issued for a smaller amount, with the provision that after a shipment takes place and an amount is drawn, the credit will be amended to reinstate that amount. This is a *revolving* letter of credit. It has the advantage of using one letter of credit instead of issuing a new letter of credit each time, which may be less costly for the customer. After each shipment is made, received by and paid for by the buyer, the bank notifies the beneficiary that the letter of credit has been reinstated with a new expiration date.

Revolving letters of credit provide some means of control over the bank's credit exposure and ease administration tasks. A letter of credit may be established with a fixed amount and a provision that only a certain amount of merchandise may be shipped each month. This provision restricts the exposure of buyers so that they cannot be faced with a larger shipment than expected. Such revolving credits may be cumulative or non-cumulative; that is, any amount not drawn in one month may or may not be added to the shipment made in the following month. The revolving letter of credit usually requires notification to the seller that it has been reinstated for the next shipment, or it may be automatically reinstated at specified periods. It can be issued for the amount of each transaction or for the full amount of all of the shipments but be available only in specified increments.

Straight and Negotiation Credits

When the exporter is in the same vicinity as the confirming bank, it is convenient to have the letter of credit expire at the office of the confirming bank. The credit will contain the statement that documents must be presented "at this office on or before" a given date. When the exporter is in a different area or even in a different country from the confirming U.S. bank, the varying reliability of mail service may make it difficult for a shipper to get the docu-

ments to the confirming bank before the expiration date. Therefore, confirming banks will have these letters of credit (*negotiation credits*) expire in the area in which the shipper is located.
The exporter can then present the documents to the local bank or
any other bank at any time up to the expiration date. By doing
so, the exporter has complied with the letter of credit, even though
the documents do not reach the office of the confirming bank until
later.

Straight credits require that documents be presented to the
confirming bank, which agrees to honor the draft and documents
only to the beneficiary. If some other bank negotiates the documents, there is no legal commitment to that bank. A negotiation
credit provides for negotiation of the beneficiary's drafts and
documents at banks other than the confirming bank. The engagement runs to drawers, endorsers, and bona fide holders of such
drafts and documents. This, however, should not be confused
with a transferable letter of credit. The choice of which type to
use depends on the ability of the beneficiary to present the draft
and documents directly to the confirming bank. A straight credit
is appropriate if the beneficiary is in the same city; if the
beneficiary is in another area and will need to negotiate the draft
through another bank, then the negotiation type is used.

Revocable Letter of Credit

A letter of credit that can be canceled by the buyer or the opening
bank without the concurrence of the seller is a *revocable letter of
credit*. Because such a letter of credit negates one of the main
advantages of a letter of credit for the seller, it is rarely used. The
only protection for the seller is that, if the documents are
presented and the seller is paid before cancellation by the buyer,
the issuing bank will honor the draft and documents if they are in
order.

Authority to Pay

A similar but less frequently used type of letter of credit is the
authority to pay. This document is really not a letter of credit but
merely an advice of a place of payment, carrying neither the U.S.
bank's nor the foreign bank's obligation to make such payment.
In effect, it is only as good as the foreign buyer and provides
payment in advance of arrival of the documents in the foreign
country, provided that revocation does not take place before

presentation. It therefore acts merely as a guide to the shipper in the preparation of shipping documents.

Authority to Purchase

An *authority to purchase*, used primarily in Asia, is similar to a letter of credit except that the draft is drawn on the foreign buyer. It can be either irrevocable or revocable. In revocable form, it should call for drafts drawn with recourse on the beneficiary, meaning that the beneficiary must return the funds if payment is not made by the buyer. Irrevocable drafts are without recourse to the beneficiary. The use of authorities to purchase has decreased in recent years.

Reimbursement Arrangements

In some instances, a bank will issue its letter of credit in favor of a beneficiary in a country where it does not have a correspondent bank. For the letter of credit to be payable at a bank near the beneficiary, the paying bank will be authorized to draw on another bank to reimburse itself for the payments it makes. Usually this third bank (reimbursing bank) will be a correspondent of both the other two banks. This is a *reimbursement arrangement*, which is basically a paying mechanism. The reimbursing bank will receive a letter or telecommunication from the issuing bank with information about the letter of credit and authorization from the issuing bank to honor the request for payment by the paying bank. All shipping documents go directly from the paying bank to the issuing bank. The arrangement can also provide for usance drafts. The letter of credit will provide for the seller to draw a usance draft on the reimbursing bank, which accepts it for the account of the issuing bank. The negotiating bank has to supply the necessary details of the transaction so that the reimbursing bank can complete the acceptance.

Letters of Credit Payable in Foreign Currency

Letters of credit issued by U.S. banks may be expressed not only in U.S. dollars, but also in the currency of the seller or in a third currency. An example would be a letter of credit expressed in pounds sterling under which drafts are drawn on the London correspondent of the U.S. bank issuing the credit. (A U.S. bank that has a branch in London would, of course, use that branch instead of a correspondent.)

An importer may request a letter of credit be denominated in a non-U.S. currency to meet the demand by the seller for payment in the seller's currency, thereby eliminating their foreign exchange risk (see chapter 11). After negotiating the documents, the bank makes payment through its Due From account and charges the importer the U.S. dollar equivalent. When the letter of credit provides for a time draft, the U.S. bank will make arrangements for a bank in the country where that currency is legal tender to accept the draft under the credit responsibility of the U.S. bank.

Government-Sponsored Letters of Credit

International development agencies, such as the World Bank, and U.S. government agencies, such as the Commodity Credit Corporation and foreign-aid servicing entities, often use the commercial letter of credit as the vehicle for disbursing funds.

Once the government agency has approved a loan, it will issue a letter of commitment to a commercial bank. This permits the foreign borrower to send applications to a commercial bank to open letters of credit in favor of suppliers of specific items authorized as part of a multimillion-dollar loan. The individual letters of credit may be for only a few thousand dollars or for a very much larger amount. The commercial bank issues the letter of credit. The required documents will include some specialized ones demanded by the government entity. When the shipment is made, documents and draft are presented to the bank as in any other trade transaction. When the documents are in order, the bank pays the seller. However, instead of then looking to the importer for payment, the bank requests reimbursement from the government entity under its letter of commitment. In this way the government entity can disburse its large loan without becoming involved in the technical trade requirements that are routinely handled in any major bank's letter of credit section.

Traveler's Letter of Credit

Before worldwide use of traveler's checks, banks issued a special document for travelers. This was the *traveler's* or *circular letter of credit*. Its purpose was to enable a traveler to draw money at any of a bank's correspondents anywhere in the world. The letter of credit was issued with a separate letter that contained the specimen signature of the traveler. When the two documents were presented, the correspondent bank would advance cash up to an overall stated limit. Each drawing was noted on the letter of credit so that subsequent correspondent banks could know how much was still available to the traveler.

The use of the traveler's letter of credit has almost disappeared. It is a cumbersome document requiring safeguarding by the traveler, and it is inconvenient because it could only be used at a bank during banking hours.

DOMESTIC LETTERS OF CREDIT

Use of a U.S. bank's commercial letter of credit is not confined to financing the importation or exportation of merchandise. Whether it is available at sight or at any number of days up to six months, the letter of credit is applicable in the financing of merchandise transactions within the United States and within the Uniform Commercial Code. Time can be saved and many troublesome credit problems eliminated by the use of the letter of credit domestically.

A seller of goods, for instance, may request such a letter of credit and thereby eliminate much credit investigation, knowing that it will receive a bank's irrevocable obligation to pay against stipulated documents. The seller need not worry about payment or extension of credit; rather, it should be concerned with its own ability to perform under the terms of the credit and within the time limit stipulated in that credit. The seller, furthermore, is protected against cancellation of an order by a buyer because the bank cannot cancel its irrevocable obligation without the seller's consent. The financial position of a seller with its own bank is strengthened when it can show that its sales are made against commercial letters of credit.

Use of the letter of credit also has many advantages for the buyer of goods. When there is a heavy demand for a particular commodity, a buyer offering its bank's obligation to pay in the form of a letter of credit may receive more favorable consideration from possible suppliers because those suppliers are, in effect, selling on a cash basis. At the same time, the buyer does not necessarily have to pay cash until delivery of documents to its bank. Furthermore, a buyer may fix an expiration date on a letter of credit to assure that seasonal merchandise is received on time. The cost of such letters of credit is nominal.

Standby Letters Of Credit

In recent years, requests to banks to provide credit backing to support a borrower's commitment to pay a third party or to perform certain contractual obligations have substantially increased. This can be done with a *standby letter of credit* . For example, a bank's client may request a letter of credit that is available only if another business transaction is not performed. It is customary in construction projects for the contractor to put up a financial guarantee as support, so that if it wins the contract it can demonstrate that it has the financial capability to perform and complete the project within the specified terms of the contract. One way of doing this is by furnishing a bond from an insurance company; an alternative is to use a standby letter of credit. Such a letter of credit can be drawn against by means of a sight draft and a statement from the beneficiary stating that the contractor had not performed as agreed under the contract.

The beneficiary of a standby letter of credit looks first to the account party for payment before seeking payment from the bank. In contrast, in a commercial letter of credit the beneficiary "obtains payment from the issuing bank without looking to the buyer for payment even in the first instance."[5]

Standby letters of credit have also been used on behalf of bank clients to enable them to borrow from private and institutional lenders at lower rates or more favorable terms than they could obtain from their own bank. If the issuing bank has a strong credit rating in the bond or commercial paper market, the customer can gain access to that rating with its lower interest rate through a standby letter of credit. Such standbys extend the bank's credit judgment of its client, which induces an investor or other source of private money to grant a loan to that client. The private lender relies on the bank's letter of credit, knowing that the lender may draw on the bank for repayment if the borrower does not directly repay the loan. Although a bank issuing a standby letter of credit may not expect it will ever have a drawing, the credit risk is very real and begins as soon as the standby letter of credit is issued. The bank credit officer must recognize this and not be deluded into assuming that somehow by issuing a standby letter of credit the bank has less exposure to a loan loss than by making a loan (see chapter 14). Even for standby letters of credit issued on behalf of reliable contractors, a sensitivity to financial exposure both for the bank and its customer has developed. The standby requires only the beneficiary's statement that the work was not completed properly in order to draw on the bank. If the work is being done for a foreign government and a change of government occurs, the standby can be arbitrarily drawn against if the new government disavows its predecessor's obligations, regardless of whether the work was done properly or not. Attempts to require a third-party inspection before a drawing have been rebuffed by many foreign governments.

Unfortunately, standby letters of credit have also been abused when used in favor of foreign institutions to induce them to lend local currency or Eurodollars to a local subsidiary of a U.S. corporation. In one much-publicized case, the parent company went into bankruptcy and was unable to pay for such standby letters of credit. The bank that had issued the standby letters of credit consequently failed because of the resultant worldwide claims under the standby letters of credit. As a consequence, U.S. regulatory agencies now require U.S. banks to count all standby letters of credit with other direct lending to any one borrower when calculating the legal lending limit of each bank to a single borrower (see chapter 14). As with commercial letters of credit, standby letters of credit are covered under the Uniform Customs and Practice for Documentary Credits.

USING THE SERVICES OF A CORRESPONDENT BANK

The procedure involved in successfully completing a letter of credit transaction requires a trained staff thoroughly familiar with all the ramifications of the letter of credit instrument. In addition, the procedure presupposes that a bank with an established reputation has placed its authorized signatures on record with banks located in commercially important centers throughout the world.

Relatively few U.S. banks are equipped to handle letters of credit. Nevertheless, the lack of trained personnel and of an international reputation need not deter a bank when it is asked to assist a customer in opening a letter of credit. The facilities of a domestic U.S. correspondent bank capable of handling all phases of letters of credit are available. For a bank without a full international department to operate effectively, however, an official in the bank should have at least a rudimentary knowledge of the subject to discuss intelligently the various phases of the business. The actual mechanics of the procedure can be turned over to the correspondent bank maintaining an international department.

An active correspondent bank is eager to cooperate with its correspondents in other cities. It solicits letter of credit business and will split the fees thereby making it attractive for both banks. The correspondents are supplied with the necessary forms, including the application blank. This application differs from the form the larger bank receives from its own commercial customers in two respects:

- Addressed to the correspondent bank in the form of a request, it asks the correspondent bank to act as agent for the small bank.
- It bears the signatures of both the bank without the international department and its customers.

Otherwise, the forms of the commercial letter of credit agreement are substantially similar. The customer's agreement included in the form is, under appropriate circumstances, a protection for both banks involved. Banks operating without an international department do not necessarily have to prepare complicated forms to bind their customers.

The smaller bank using the facilities of a correspondent bank assumes the credit risks involved in accommodating its customer. This emphasizes the importance of bank officers having at least a basic understanding of what is needed to appraise the risks properly.

When it receives an application for a commercial letter of credit from one of its correspondents, the larger bank looks to that correspondent for payment. All details involved in establishing the credit, handling documents, handling foreign exchange operations, advising of payment, and preparing forms and trust receipts are taken care of by the correspondent bank in most cases.

ACCOUNTING

The letters of credit that have been described in the chapter are reflected in a bank's financial statement as contingent accounts in the same manner as described in chapter 8.

The risk-based capital calculations for standby letters of credit differ from those for other letters of credit. Standby letters of credit that back "repayment of financial obligations such as: commercial paper. . . commercial or individual loans or debt obligations" are called financial standby letters of credit. These have a credit conversion factor of 100 percent (see chapter 8). Standby letters of credit that back "the performance of nonfinancial commercial contracts or undertakings . . . [such as] construction bids" are called performance standby letters of credit. These have a credit conversion factor of 50 percent.[6]

SUMMARY

The great strength of the commercial letter of credit is its flexibility. This perhaps is why it is used so widely and for so long. To meet special needs, clauses may be added or items changed.

A particularly important characteristic of the letter of credit is that it makes it easy for major international banks to back the transactions of smaller banks around the world, thus facilitating the movement of international trade. This occurs when a letter of credit is confirmed.

While most commercial letters of credit require that someone do something (usually ship goods) in order to obtain funds, the standby letter of credit is drawn against the failure of someone to do something. This has become important for construction bids, performance guarantees, obtaining local market financing for a corporate subsidiary, or supplying a credit backing for outside funding.

QUESTIONS

1. What is the difference between an import letter of credit and an export letter of credit?
2. What is the difference between a usance and a sight letter of credit?
3. What is the difference between a confirmed letter of credit and an advised letter of credit?
4. How does a standby letter of credit differ from a commercial letter of credit?

PROBLEM

Your bank's customer has an order to sell machinery to a company in Singapore. He has received a letter of credit from a bank in Singapore to which a major California bank has added its confirmation. Explain to your customer what he must do in order to be paid for his shipment.

Notes

1.   *Bank of America v. United States*, 680 F.2d 142 (Ct. Cl. 1982).

2.   *Ibid.*

3.   Jay M. McDonald and John E. McKinley, *Corporate Banking: A Practical Approach to Lending* (Washington, D.C.: American Bankers Association, 1981), p. 228.

4.   Henry Harfield, *Bank Credits and Acceptances*, 5th ed. (New York: Ronald Press, 1974, p. 193.

5.   *Federal Deposit Insurance Corporation v. Philadelphia Gear Corp.* U.S. Supreme Court 84-1972, May 27, 1986. In this opinion the Court held that a standby letter of credit was not considered a deposit covered by FDIC.

6.   Board of Governors of the Federal Reserve System, Press Release, January 19, 1989, pp. 57-59. See also appendix D, Section III D.

10

Bankers' Acceptances

In the United States, a bankers' acceptance is a means of providing financing, primarily associated with international trade, by creating a unique financial instrument that is attractive to money market investors. It facilitates and expands the sources of credit funds beyond what is available directly from a commercial bank.

The bankers' acceptance is separate and distinct from the letter of credit, although many arise from it. A bankers' acceptance is a time draft drawn by one party (the drawer) on a bank (the drawee) and accepted by the bank as the bank's commitment to pay a third party (the payee) a stated sum on a specified future date. The bank's acceptance of this draft is a formal acknowledgment of the bank's irrevocable unconditional promise to pay the draft at maturity.

Section 13 of the Federal Reserve Act permits banks to discount such an acceptance at a Federal Reserve bank when the acceptance finances specified types of commercial transactions, mostly relating to foreign trade. Through the bankers' acceptance, banks can provide credit to their customers without requiring the use of the bank's own funds. This is done by creating a negotiable instrument with a specified maturity date that is attractive to investors seeking a short-term, noninterest-bearing note sold at a discount that will be redeemed by the accepting bank at maturity for the full face amount. The bank creating an acceptance thus becomes primarily liable for the payment on the maturity date.

While bankers' acceptances exist in varying forms in other countries and currencies, this chapter is concerned only with what is permitted to banks in the United States and in U.S. dollars. The expression "prime bankers' acceptance" is often used and refers to the stature of the accepting bank. What constitutes a "prime" U.S. bank is a matter of investor judgment.

The objectives of this chapter are to
- explain how the bankers' acceptance is used
- outline what a bankers' acceptance can finance
- describe the role of the various parties in the transaction
- examine typical transactions using the bankers' acceptance

BACKGROUND

The bankers' acceptance or bill of exchange is a financing instrument with origins as far back as the twelfth century as a means of financing international trade.

"When in the second half of the eighteenth century, the entrepôt trade of Amsterdam deteriorated. . .[it] brought new prominence to another 'branch' of Dutch commercial activity, the so-called acceptance trade. . . . Thus Amsterdam remained the 'cash box' and the Dutch 'the bankers of Europe'. . . . The acceptance trade related to the countless bills of exchange which had long been the vehicle of credit throughout Europe. . . . Transfers, endorsements, discounting, drafts and deposits made the bill of exchange an indefatigable traveller from one centre to another, one merchant to another,. . .from a businessman to his correspondent or to a discounter (as he was known in Holland)."[1] It was essential then because of the time it took from production to sale to final payment.

For the two centuries before the creation of the Fed, world trade was denominated and financed primarily in sterling, and a market in sterling bankers' acceptances flourished in London. The founders of the Federal Reserve System, created in 1913, felt that a domestic bankers' acceptance market patterned after the London market should be developed to enhance New York's role as a center of international trade and finance, to promote U.S. foreign trade, and to improve the competitive position of domestic banks. The Fed's founders thus empowered national banks to accept time drafts, which these banks were previously unauthorized to do. They also took other actions to support the growth of this infant market, including permitting the Federal Reserve to rediscount and purchase eligible acceptances.[2]

So far as the legal incidents are concerned, one acceptance is like another. The distinctions. . .between trade and bankers' acceptances. . .have no legal significance that is related to the form or the effect of the instrument. A 'bankers' acceptance' is a draft or bill of exchange that is drawn on a bank or banker and has been accepted by the drawee. If the drawee-acceptor is not a bank or banker, the instrument is called a 'trade acceptance'[3] (see chapter 7).

Its principal purpose is to provide current financing. . . . The principal use of an acceptance is to permit one person to use the credit of another person to facilitate the acquisition of money. Historically, the credit of a bank or banker has been preferred to that of merchants, with the consequence that the market for bankers' acceptance has developed virtually independently from the market in which mercantile obligations are traded and entirely distinct from the securities market.[4]

Figure 10.1 Bankers' Acceptance

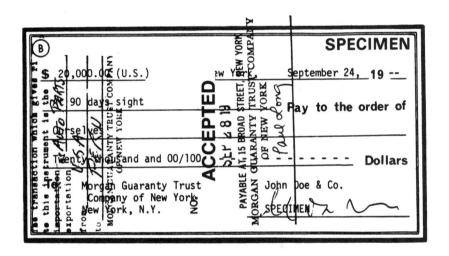

FOREIGN TRADE

In a typical foreign trade transaction a U.S. bank issues its letter of credit on behalf of its customer, the importer. As seen in chapters 8 and 9, the letter of credit may provide for drafts to be drawn on the bank payable at sight, at a specified number of days after sight, or on a specific future date. The latter are time letters of credit. When the importer knows at the time of negotiating the merchandise contract that it cannot pay for the merchandise when it is shipped, it must arrange for credit.

The importer may ask the exporter to agree to wait for payment until the importer can take possession of the merchandise and sell it. If the exporter agrees—in order to make the sale—it will make the shipment against a time letter of credit. The exporter agrees to give up the title documents to the goods (for example, the bill of lading) in exchange for a continuation of the bank's promise to pay. To enable importers to possess and sell the merchandise before paying for it, the letter of credit will provide for the exporter to draw a draft on the bank payable at a future date. This draft is formally accepted in writing by the bank as its obligation to pay. The exporter may hold this bankers' acceptance to maturity and then present it to the accepting bank for payment of the full amount.

If, however, the exporter wishes to receive cash immediately, the accepted draft may be sold prior to maturity to an investor at a discounted amount. The investor then presents it to the bank for payment at maturity. It is the bank's commitment to pay that enables intermediaries to hold or trade the draft so that the bank's customer may have the needed financing. In periods of tight money, this feature becomes vitally important, since it is a means by which banks can obtain funds for their customers from outside the bank's own resources by selling it to an investor.

The following example of a foreign trade transaction illustrates the parties involved in using bankers' acceptances and demonstrates options each may have.

- *The Borrower.* The importer needs financing to make a purchase. The importer may obtain a loan from the bank, pay the seller in full, and then repay the bank upon selling the goods. Using the bankers' acceptance, the importer still obtains credit from the bank and is likewise still obligated to pay the bank cash at maturity. What differentiates the bankers' acceptance from a direct bank loan or other financing options the buyer may have, such as commercial paper or various types of Eurodollar financing, is the type of instrument used to obtain financing and the manner in which the financing costs may be paid.

- *The Seller.* To make the sale, the exporter agrees to ship merchandise against a letter of credit that stipulates that the draft will be payable at a future date. The exporter required a letter of credit initially because of unwillingness to make the shipment relying solely on the buyer's credit. The exporter is willing to wait now for payment provided it retains the bank's commitment to pay. The exporter therefore surrenders title to its merchandise in exchange for agreeing to the time letter of credit. If the exporter insisted instead on a sight letter of credit that would require payment at the time of presentation of documents, the burden would be on the importer to get a loan from its bank. Once the exporter receives the bankers' acceptance, it may opt to hold it until maturity and then present it to the accepting bank for payment in full. In essence, the exporter has invested its manufacturing and other costs in the merchandise until the date of payment. The other option is to sell the bankers' acceptance before maturity and receive a lesser amount of cash now as opposed to the full draft amount on the future date. When the exporter does this, it remains secondarily liable to the investor should the bank default when the bankers' acceptance matures and payment is due.

- *The Bank.* The bank's customer, the importer, requests credit. The bank must evaluate that request. Once it has determined that its customer is creditworthy for the requested amount, it then must determine how to fund the request. The bank may use its own money and make a direct loan. Or it may decide that it wishes to carry only the credit risk but let some other party provide the funding. In this case, it structures the credit to use the bankers' acceptance.

The creation of a bankers' acceptance is an extension of credit by the bank to its customer. "The use of the bankers' acceptance . . . cannot mask their essence. The essence of the transactions, like that of a direct loan, is the use of [the bank's] credit."[5] The bank is committing itself to pay the obligation at a stated future date, thereby inducing a seller of goods to surrender the goods to the buyer in exchange for the bank's commitment. The bank does this by stamping "accepted" across the draft, indicating on the draft the underlying purpose that is being financed, signing it with authorized signatures, and indicating the date the acceptance begins or matures. Because the bank has committed itself in writing to pay, investors are willing to furnish their funds during the interim period. The bank is irrevocably committed to pay the acceptance when it is presented on the maturity date, regardless of whether the bank has been paid by its customer.

A bank's decision to extend credit to any customer is based on its judgment of the conditions and risks involved (see chapter 13). The fact that a bank is lending its credit and not its funds cannot exempt the proposed financing from a thorough credit analysis. However, the bankers' acceptance is used basically to finance transactions that are self-liquidating, an important feature in the decision to extend credit. The expected source of repayment will be from the sale of the financed merchandise to another party or parties. However, if the bank were to cease payment of its obligations, the holder of the acceptance would become a general creditor and not be reimbursed from the sale of the merchandise. The holder could seek reimbursement from the drawer of the draft or prior endorsers.

- *The Broker.* The function of a broker is to act as a centralized distributor who puts people wishing to sell bankers' acceptances in contact with people wishing to buy them. The broker may be a company specializing in this function or a commercial or investment bank providing the service as part of its overall money market activities. Because of the large size of the U.S. money market, the broker will usually quote a price to the seller of the acceptance, buy the instrument, and then find an investor who would be interested in buying the acceptance. The broker sells the acceptance at a slightly higher price than was paid for it and thereby earns a profit. This is the broker's spread.

- *The Investor.* Corporations, banks, municipalities, money market funds, foreign central banks, domestic and international institutions, and individuals have temporary surplus funds on which they wish to earn a return. In the United States, they can select from a wide range of money market instruments. The safest such investments are the obligations of the U.S. government. However, the investor may determine that short-term obligations of a U.S. bank are almost as safe as government obligations; the investor may be attracted to purchase bankers' acceptances because they offer a higher rate of return. The investor may perceive that the bankers' acceptance offers greater security than a bank's certificate of deposit, since there is an underlying commercial transaction that should generate the source of repayment to the bank. The investor also may have recourse to endorsers of the bankers' acceptance if the bank should default. On the other hand, the certificate of deposit may qualify for FDIC insurance.

ELIGIBLE BANKERS' ACCEPTANCES

Bankers' acceptances drawn in accordance with Section 13 of the Federal Reserve Act are eligible for discount or purchase by a Federal Reserve member bank at any of the Federal Reserve banks. Although seldom necessary as long as an active private trading market exists, it does protect the bank. (In fact, the Federal Reserve has not discounted bankers' acceptances for a number of years.) Nonetheless, the criteria for Federal Reserve discounting or purchasing define the instruments the market will readily trade. The following are the permitted underlying purposes for which a bank may create a bankers' acceptance that can be discounted at a Federal Reserve bank:

- importation or exportation of goods
- domestic shipment of goods
- storage of readily marketable staples

Member banks are also permitted to accept drafts for the creation of dollar exchange, although this is not widely used.

Bankers' acceptances may be created for a maximum term of six months. This term is calculated on the basis of the underlying transaction. In the case of a foreign trade shipment, the acceptance term will begin to be calculated, in general, from the time the shipment takes place. If the bankers' acceptance will be used for the creation of dollar exchange, the maximum permitted term is three months.

Section 13 of the Federal Reserve Act permits the creation of bankers' acceptances for a maximum of six months. Any acceptances created for a longer term and discounted are interpreted under Regulation D to be a "deposit" for which a bank is subject to the usual reserve requirements. The Federal Reserve banks are permitted to discount only acceptances "which have a maturity at the time of discount of not more than 90 days' sight," or six months in the case of acceptances drawn for agricultural purposes.[6]

Drafts may be accepted by banks in the United States, including the U.S. agencies and branches of foreign banks, or by overseas branches of member banks, provided that the acceptance is payable at the bank's head office. Bankers' acceptances that meet the requirements of the Federal Reserve Act to be *eligible for discount* are exempt from reserve requirements. Acceptances are also not subject to assessment for deposit insurance.

State and private banks had been allowed to engage in acceptance financing before enactment of the Federal Reserve Act, but such financing was not extensive. Although the impetus for the development of a discount market and banking system that would be similar in many respects to that in England was strong, the enactment of the Federal Reserve Act was in keeping with the existing U.S. banking structure.

The Federal Reserve Act governs only member banks. State banks may have broader acceptance powers under their respective state laws. Notwithstanding, practically all bankers' acceptances follow the Federal Reserve guidelines in order to be readily marketable.

A national bank may have bankers' acceptances outstanding up to 150 percent of the bank's capital and unimpaired surplus unless it receives permission from the Board of Governors of the Federal Reserve System to go up to 200 percent. The limitations on lending to any one customer apply.

International and Domestic Trade

The shipment of goods categories include the financing of goods being imported into the United States, exported from the United States, shipped between two foreign countries, or shipped within the United States. Neither the importer nor the exporter need be in the United States. At the time that the bank is asked to accept a draft, it must have evidence that the shipment has, in fact, taken place, when the shipment was made, and what the merchandise was. The bank usually has a copy of the bill of lading or invoice for this purpose. The bankers' acceptance may also extend over the preshipment period needed to assemble the merchandise; however, this cannot include any manufacturing, processing, or growing. The bankers' acceptance should cover a current shipment, which generally means it has taken place within 30 days of the creation of the bankers' acceptance. Exceptions to this occur when a reasonable explanation exists, such as the acceptance financing beginning after the use of normal trade credit.[7]

Although most bankers' acceptances evolve from letters of credit, they need not necessarily do so. A collection can be refinanced by a bankers' acceptance, as can a sight letter of credit or even a shipment made on open account or prepaid. In such cases, the importer pays the exporter and then draws a time draft on the bank, which it accepts and discounts in the market, giving the importer the net amount. On maturity, the importer repays the bank just as if it were a direct loan.

The creation of bankers' acceptances under letters of credit is considered in chapter 9. In instances where the client has already signed a letter of credit agreement, that agreement usually suffices. For transactions not covered by such a letter of credit agreement, the bank may ask the customer to sign an acceptance agreement.

An acceptance covering shipments between two foreign points is similar to acceptances financing both U.S. imports and exports. The acceptance may be made under either a letter of credit or an acceptance financing arrangement. If the transaction is executed on behalf of a commercial customer, the documents may have been released against trust receipts, but if the drawer of the bill is a foreign bank, the accepting bank is unlikely to have received the controlling shipping documents. The bank creating the acceptance must retain evidence showing the nature of the underlying transaction.

Although domestic U.S. shipments can be adapted easily to acceptance financing, buyers and sellers alike generally resort to the more usual forms of financing because they are not familiar with acceptance financing.

Storage

Merchandise that has been put into storage may be financed by means of bankers' acceptances. This practice is widely used, particularly in the agricultural areas of the United States. A wheat farmer, for example, may deliver wheat to a public warehouse, which will issue its *warehouse receipt* to the farmer. The warehouse receipt is a title document and, in essence, states that the warehouse company is holding a certain quantity of a stated commodity and that the company will continue to hold these goods until the warehouse receipt is presented. At such time, the merchandise is returned in exchange for the warehouse receipt. The wheat farmer can endorse the warehouse receipt and deliver it to the bank, thereby providing security for the bank's creation of the bankers' acceptance. If the farmer fails to repay, the bank can take possession of the wheat and sell it to repay the acceptance. Since there is no seller to draw a draft on the bank, the acceptance is created by the wheat farmer drawing a draft on the bank to pay him- or herself the stated sum at the future date and endorsing the draft. The bank accepts this draft, sells it to an investor, and gives the farmer the discounted proceeds. On the maturity date, the farmer repays the full draft amount.

Public warehouses are private companies that maintain buildings for the storage of goods for third parties. Such buildings are referred to as *terminal warehouses*. In addition, private companies set up *field warehouses* on the premises of a farmer or manufacturer. In a field warehouse, the warehouse company takes possession of the customer's warehouse building or part of a building, puts its own locks on the doors, and puts its own warehouseman in charge. The warehouse receives the merchandise and issues warehouse receipts just as though the building were owned by the company. In this way farmers and manufacturers have the benefits of a public warehouse on their own premises, without having to go to a distant terminal warehouse. Banks insist that warehouse companies obtain insurance against various types of calamities, including fraud by the warehouse companies' employees.

Banks may create acceptances to cover the storage of goods in the United States or to cover storage in other countries, provided a valid warehouse receipt comparable to those in the United States can be obtained that will secure the bank during the life of the transaction. This is possible in relatively few foreign countries.

The reason for such financing is to enable the farmer or manufacturer to store goods pending their sale. There are costs associated with the manufacturing, growing, or processing for which interim financing is needed and which are expected to be recovered when the final sale is made. In general, such stored goods eligible to be financed by bankers' acceptances are commodities (wheat, sugar, corn, coffee, copper, silver) and processed goods that have a ready market. However, if the goods have been processed to such a degree that only one company can buy them, then the bank is not secured because if that company does not buy the goods they cannot otherwise be sold.

Regardless of whether the bankers' acceptance has covered preshipment, shipment, storage, or any combination of these, the maximum term for the financing is six months. An acceptance for a longer term "which was ineligible for discount at the time of its creation becomes eligible once its maturity reaches the minimum specified level."[8] The maturity of the bankers' acceptance should match the completion of the transaction being financed.[9]

It is important to note the difference between acceptances arising from a time letter of credit and those created for other purposes. When establishing letters of credit calling for a beneficiary's draft to be accepted by the bank, the bank expects the customer for whom it opened the letter of credit to reimburse the bank at maturity. When creating acceptances for other types of financing, the bank looks to the drawer of the draft for reimbursement at maturity.

Dollar Exchange

Although bankers' acceptances for the purpose of creating dollar exchange are now rarely requested, they were a way for foreign countries to raise dollars needed for purposes of trade. The procedure was cumbersome, since it required the foreign government, in essence, to request eligibility for these acceptances. Once this was done and the country was on the Fed's list of approved countries (the last list was published in the Federal Reserve Bulletin in 1922)[10] designated foreign banks could request acceptance financing for no stated purpose other than to obtain dollars for a short term for the needs of trade. Such countries generally had a single crop to export and this financing was to advance foreign exchange to the country pending the sale of its crop, which would then provide the export earnings to repay the bankers' acceptance.

The Market for Acceptances

A money market is a center where the demand for short-term funds meets the supply. The leading international money market has been established in New York City. The facilities there attract and redistribute funds from all over the nation and the world. This general market comprises many different clearly defined markets, each of which deals in a different type of credit.

"The U.S. money market is a huge and significant part of the nation's financial system in which banks and other participants trade hundreds of billions of dollars every working day. . . . *The money market is a wholesale market for low-risk, highly liquid, short-term IOUs.* It is a market for various sorts of debt securities rather than equities. The stock in trade of the market includes a large chunk of the U.S. Treasury's debt and billions of dollars worth of federal agency securities, negotiable bank certificates of deposit, bank deposit notes, bankers' acceptances, short-term participations in bank loans, municipal notes, and commercial paper. . . . The money market. . .provides a means by which the surplus funds of cash-rich corporations and other institutions can be funneled to banks, corporations, and other institutions that need short-term money."[11]

The market trades in "eligible" acceptances and is therefore limited to specific transactions. The skills needed for marketing bankers' acceptances are the same as those needed for marketing other short-term obligations. Dealers who handle bankers' acceptances generally are part of the active market in a wide range of government paper—federal, state, and municipal.

The bankers' acceptance is an attractive short-term investment since its rates, while usually moving in concert with those of U.S. Treasury bills, offer a slightly higher yield. In normal circumstances, most investors will find that the higher yield compensates for what is not, in many judgments, a significantly higher risk. Table 10.1 shows 1990 figures for numbers of bankers' acceptances in existence according to the nature of the transaction.

Table 10.1 U.S. Dollar Bankers' Acceptances in Existence, October 31, 1990 (in '000 US $)

According to nature of transaction:

Imports	12,407,850
Exports	13,238,263
Goods stored in or shipped between foreign countries	21,006,536
Domestic shipment and storage	5,440,644
Dollar exchange	-0-
Total	52,093,293

Source: Federal Reserve Bank of New York

Mechanics

There are generally two charges for an acceptance: the accepting bank's commission for creating the acceptance and the market price for discounting the bankers' acceptance if it is traded. The bank's commission for accepting the draft is determined by the bank's credit relationship with its client and is analogous to a portion of the interest rate on a loan. The acceptance commission is collected at the time the draft is accepted and is paid by the bank's customer. For example, a U.S. importer for whose account the letter of credit was opened pays the acceptance commission. The foreign exporter can ask that the acceptance be returned to it so it can be held until maturity. At maturity, the exporter presents the acceptance either through its bank or directly to the accepting bank for full payment. In essence, the exporter invests its costs for the period from the time of exportation until the maturity date of the acceptance. Though an acceptance has been created, it does not mean that it has to be sold in the market.

In practice, most exporters want funds as soon as the draft becomes a bankers' acceptance and will instruct the accepting bank to discount the acceptance immediately at the prevailing rate of other short-term money market instruments. Exporters are willing to receive less than face value immediately rather than the full face amount in the future. The discount charge, therefore, is generally borne by the exporter, which may have adjusted its selling price to anticipate this charge. For the buyer to have acceptance financing, the seller may require that the buyer pay for this discount. This is referred to as "discount for buyer's account."

Since the bankers' acceptance has no provision for any interest payment, the investor receives a rate of return by buying the bankers' acceptance at a discount. The dollar price and yield are calculated as follows:[12]

$$\text{Dollar price (\% of face amount)} = 100 - \frac{\text{Discount rate x Days to maturity}}{360}$$

To convert a discount rate on a bankers' acceptance to the equivalent simple interest basis, the formula is[13]

$$\text{Interest rate} = \frac{\text{Discount x 360}}{360 - (\text{discount x days})}$$

Having created an acceptance, the bank can, on instructions of the holder, sell it to a dealer at the dealer's discount rate. The proceeds are credited to the account of the holder of the acceptance—the exporter, in the previous example. The exporter has now completed the transaction; the importer will not be called on to pay until the acceptance matures. The dealer, in turn, recovers the funds by selling the acceptance to an investor, usually taking a small spread. Upon maturity of the acceptance, the holder presents it to the accepting bank for payment. The bank pays, and then its customer pays the bank. The failure or inability of the customer to pay does not relieve the accepting bank of its commitment to pay. Likewise, if the investor delays in presenting the acceptance after the maturity date, no further interest will be paid. The bank is obligated to pay the face amount only.

Bankers' acceptances may be created for other types of transactions, such as storage of commodities, in which the entire purpose of creating the acceptance is to obtain funds immediately; thus the discount is automatic. The customer receives the net amount after deduction of the acceptance commission and the discount. When the purpose is to finance goods in storage, the bank's customer is the only other party. The customer draws the draft on the bank, which accepts it and then discounts it with a dealer. The net proceeds go to the bank's customer, who is obligated to repay the full face amount of the acceptance on maturity.

Since the acceptance is a short-term prime obligation of a U.S. bank, it is very attractive to many investors. As more corporations, foreign banks, and individuals have become familiar with bankers' acceptances, the market has broadened, and dealers are able to establish a highly liquid market for acceptances. Established dealers quote rates at which they will buy and sell acceptances. These rates change in accordance with the supply and demand for short-term investments and the investor's perception of the creditworthiness of the accepting bank.

Between the original discounting and the final maturity, the original investor may no longer wish to hold the acceptance. Because of the liquidity of the market, the investor can readily sell the acceptance to a dealer at the prevailing discount rate, having earned a rate of return for the number of days the bill was actually held. Thus an acceptance can pass through many hands without the knowledge of any of the original parties.

Because the bankers' acceptance is a liquid and competitive investment, an accepting bank may want to hold some of its own acceptances, or a bank may hold other banks' acceptances as part of its own portfolio. The bank uses its investment funds to purchase the acceptance from the holder at the prevailing market discount rate and at maturity realizes the investment income itself. Within the bank, the acceptance goes from the books of the international department to those of the investment department rather than to the dealer. None of the bank's clients are aware of this, since the same discount rates apply.

Advantages of Acceptance Financing

The U.S. bankers' acceptance has become established in the financial market as an instrument by which banking institutions lend their name as part of the process of granting credit to their customers. Its great advantage to commercial banks comes in periods of tight money. At those times, banks have great demands made on them for the use of their loanable funds, often greater than their ability to make loans. If certain customers can be financed with bankers' acceptances, a bank will be eager to do so, since the funding is obtained when the bankers' acceptance is sold to an investor. In essence, the bank uses someone else's money to make loans to its customers.

Another advantage has developed in recent years when banks have held their prime interest rates well above the price at which short-term obligations are traded in the money market. A customer with a transaction that can be financed by bankers' acceptances may find that the overall cost of the acceptance commission plus market discount is less than borrowing on a promissory note at a bank's prime interest rate.

The bankers' acceptance competes with other money market instruments both for the customer seeking financing and for the investor. The borrower will consider the available financing options. It may be cheaper or more convenient to borrow directly from the bank with a loan, arrange with the seller for delayed payments, issue commercial paper that is placed with investors, or utilize a Eurodollar short-term borrowing. "Bank loans become an attractive alternative to [bankers' acceptance] financing when spreads are reasonable and the borrower is unsure how long he will need financing. If a borrower repays a [bankers' acceptance] early (as Fed regulations require him to do if the underlying transaction is terminated early), no proportion of the bank commission on the [bankers' acceptance] is repaid to him. He does get a pro-rata rebate on the discount fee, but minus 1/4 or so."[14] The investor likewise has options about where to place funds to obtain the most favorable rate of return commensurate with personal standards of safety. Banks creating bankers' acceptances need to be mindful of these alternatives.

INELIGIBLE ACCEPTANCES

The foregoing discussion has dealt with bankers' acceptances created in compliance with Section 13 of the Federal Reserve Act and therefore eligible for discount at the Federal Reserve bank. These acceptances can be discounted without making the bank liable for the creation of any reserves.

Banks, however, may create bankers' acceptances for any underlying purpose or for terms longer than six months, but such acceptances are not eligible for discounting at a Federal Reserve bank. A bank may choose to use this instead of a promissory note as a financing instrument. As long as the bank retains such ineligible acceptances, it has merely made its customer a loan, using bank funds to do so, just as if it had made the loan against the customer's promissory note. If the bank wishes, it may use this as a means of making a loan at a financing rate lower than the bank's prime rate. It does this by charging the borrower an acceptance commission and a market discount rate as if it were an eligible acceptance.

Banks sometimes find this useful when their prime rate is maintained at a higher level for competitive reasons. In some cases, the bank may be able to sell such ineligible acceptances to investors. Such sales are usually based on direct negotiations between the bank and the investor. Sometimes a broker may be involved. However, discounting ineligible acceptances incurs a reserve requirement to the creating bank. "Thus a borrower who requires ineligible as opposed to eligible [bankers' acceptances] financing pays a higher rate."[15]

SYNDICATED ACCEPTANCES AND PARTICIPATION

In recent years, a number of banks have formed syndicates to meet the credit needs of some large borrowers, often foreign governments. Sometimes these borrowers wish to use bankers' acceptances. The pattern of operating such a syndicate is the same as for loans (see chapter 13). The mechanics of drawdown require the borrower to supply, either in advance or at the time of drawdown, a quantity of signed drafts. The agent bank advises each bank of its prorated drawdown. Each participating bank then fills in the draft, accepts it, discounts it at an agreed common rate, and remits the net proceeds after deducting its acceptance commission to the borrower through the agent bank.

To preserve the short-term character of the bankers' acceptance, with its limited exposure of exchange and country risks in syndicated facilities that are basically created for long-term financing needs, the Federal Reserve applies a two-year maximum on syndicated commitments. "The 2-year limit on bankers' acceptance syndicates is complied with if each syndicate bank has the right to withdraw from the syndicate, without restriction, every 2 years. . . . The Federal Reserve Bank of New York maintains that syndicated bankers' acceptances should be liquidated at maturity from sources of funds independent of the creation of new acceptances."[16]

A variation occurs when a bank sells a participation in a bankers' acceptance to another bank. This occurs when a bank creates a bankers' acceptance and then decides to sell part of its liability to another bank. The creating bank may need to stay within its legal lending limit to the borrower or reduce its total outstanding acceptances. A legal document is signed by both banks, and the second bank thereby commits itself for a portion of the liability to pay the acceptance on maturity and receives a proportionate share of the acceptance commission. The borrower's commitment is unchanged. When the borrower repays the bank that accepted the draft, that bank will pay a portion to the participating bank.

For the accepting bank to reduce its liability, documentation between the participating and accepting banks must clearly transfer the liability to the participant in the event the borrower does not pay and thereby give the participant the right to take legal action directly against the borrower. The participating bank must also satisfy itself of the creditworthiness of that borrower.[17]

ACCOUNTING

Once the bankers' acceptance has been created it appears on the bank's financial statement. The outstanding acceptance is listed as a liability ["Acceptances Outstanding"]; the customer's liability to pay the bank at its maturity is shown as an asset ["Customer's Acceptance Liability"]. If these result from a time letter of credit, the contingent balance for the letter of credit is reduced when the negotiation takes place and the acceptance entries are made.

SUMMARY

The bankers' acceptance in the United States is a means of financing certain transactions, generally related to international trade. It is a negotiable credit instrument that readily attracts short-term investors. Because of this, the bankers' acceptance provides an alternative source of funds to a bank and its customers that can be important in periods of tight money. In addition, its rates reflect yields in the money markets and, at times, offer the banks' customers a preferential rate of return.

QUESTIONS

1. What is a bankers' acceptance?
2. How is a bankers' acceptance different from a trade acceptance?
3. What is the role of the Federal Reserve in bankers' acceptances?
4. For what underlying purposes can a bankers' acceptance be created?

PROBLEM

A processor of foodstuffs in your area, who is a good customer of your bank, must purchase wheat when it is harvested in Canada and the Midwest of the United States in order to have a supply during the year. Explain how he or she can use the bankers' acceptance to finance and store the wheat purchases.

Notes

1. Fernand Braudel, *The Wheels of Commerce* (New York: Harper and Row, 1982), pp. 243-44.

2. Marcia Stigum, T*he Money Market*, 3d edition (Homewood, Illinois: Dow Jones-Irwin, 1990), p. 995.

3. Henry Harfield, *Bank Credits and Acceptances*, 5th ed. (New York: Ronald Press, 1974), p. 118.

4. Ibid., p. 119.

5. *Bank of America v. United States*, 680 F.2d 142 (Ct. Cl. 1982).

6. Federal Reserve Act, sec. 13, par. 6.

7. Walker F. Todd, "An Introduction to Bankers' Acceptance in the 1980's." *International Banking: U.S. Laws and Regulations* (Washington, D.C.: American Bankers Association, 1984).

8. Edwin M. Truman, Staff Director, Division of International Finance, Board of Governors of the Federal Reserve System, letter January 7, 1991, to the author.

9. Todd, *op. cit.*

10. *Published Interpretations of the Board of Governors of the Federal Reserve System*, paragraph 1500, p. 80B (6-78). The approved countries are "Australia, New Zealand, and other Australasian dependencies, Argentina, Bolivia, Brazil, British Guiana, British Honduras, Chile Colombia, Costa Rica, Cuba, Dutch East Indies, Dutch Guiana, Ecuador, French Guiana, French West Indies, Guatemala, Honduras, Nicaragua, Panama, Paraguay,

Peru, Puerto Rico, Salvador, Dominican Republic, Trinidad, Uruguay, and Venezuela."

11. Stigum, *op. cit.*, pp. 1-3.

12. Marcia Stigum, *The Money Market: Myth, Reality and Practice* (Homewood, Illinois: Dow Jones-Irwin, 1978), p. 542.

13. *Ibid.*, p. 474.

14. Marcia Stigum, *The Money Market*, 3d edition, p. 1,009.

15. Marcia Stigum, *The Money Market: Myth, Reality and Practice*, p. 467.

16. Todd, *op. cit.*, pp. 1-23.

17. *Ibid.*, pp. 1-21.

11

Principles of Foreign Exchange

Both the currency of a foreign country and the process of exchanging it for the currency of another country are referred to as *foreign exchange*. Foreign exchange conveys an aura of mystery that has been encouraged by foreign exchange traders and writers of fiction.

One attribute of sovereignty is a nation's power to have its own money, named or renamed as it wishes.[1] From at least the time of the Greek and Roman Empires, the names of coins have reflected their value—usually determined by the weight of the gold or silver content. Pound sterling, peso, peseta, drachma, lira, kyat, baht, ouguiya, mark—refer to weights; guilder, birr, zloty, rupee, rupiah—refer to gold or silver. Dollar takes its name from a sixteenth century German silver mine. Other currency names reflect national heroes: bolivar, sucre, lempira, colon, balboa. Some countries call their currency after the name used by another country; dollar, for example, is used by 18 countries other than the United States, each of which is a distinct currency. A few countries use another country's money or have joint currencies. Regardless of the name, each currency is legal tender, which means it can legally be used for payments in that country. Foreign exchange trading, as a consequence, is the acquisition of purchasing power in one country with the money of another.

Trading one currency for another arises from the elements that make up a nation's balance of payments: movement of international trade, short- or long-term investments made and redeemed, dividends on previous investments, loans, interest, the payment for services, and tourist and immigrant movement. Whenever any international transaction takes place, eventually one currency is exchanged for another. The trading of foreign exchange is similar to trading any other commodity, such as wheat or cotton, and also attracts speculators and hedgers. Many of the major challenges in international business begin with first establishing a value for one currency in terms of another (for example, how many deutsche marks will one dollar buy?) and, second, obtaining sufficient quantities of each. Within a commercial bank, these activities are focused in the foreign exchange trading section.

The objectives of this chapter are to

- show how banks trade in foreign exchange
- explain how the foreign exchange market operates
- demonstrate how the bank's foreign exchange trader participates in this market
- identify participants in the market and discuss their needs

BACKGROUND

Foreign exchange trading originally was considerably simpler than it is today. Countries used gold or silver coins or had paper money that was payable on demand in gold. To determine the value of one country's currency for another, one assessed the gold weight of the coins. If gold could buy more wheat, for example, in one country than in another, people brought their gold to that country and exchanged it for wheat to take home. This increase in demand and reduction in supply would cause the price of wheat to go up in the cheaper country as well as increase the amount of money in circulation. As the wheat price rose, people no longer came to buy the wheat since it was no longer cheaper. Thus the international monetary system tended to balance itself.

This is a much-simplified example of what was the *gold standard.* "To be on the gold standard a country needed to maintain the convertibility between [bank]notes and gold and to allow gold to flow freely across its borders."[2] The system was probably destroyed by World War I, although an attempt in the 1920s was made to restore it. By the 1930s, the gold standard was gone, victim of industrial protectionism, depression, a shortage of gold, and national politics that required internal control and manipulation of the money supply that was incompatible with the freedom of the gold standard. In retrospect, one can question whether the gold standard ever really worked well since only a few countries, principally Great Britain and the United States, ever allowed the free movement of gold out of their countries[3] and even imposed severe restrictions at times, particularly after World War I. However real it may have been, the gold standard has left its legacy in a nostalgic yearning for a simpler world monetary system (even prompting the appointment of a government commission in 1981 to consider returning the United States to the gold standard) and, more important, in the establishment of an international monetary system after World War II for setting the value of each nation's currency in terms of gold. The ratio between these stated gold values gave the rate of exchange beween any two currencies.

THE FOREIGN EXCHANGE RATE

A foreign exchange rate is a numerical expression of the value of the currency of one country in terms of that of another country. The rate of exchange between any two currencies may be stated in terms of one unit of either currency. For example, a rate between U.S. dollars and Japanese yen may be stated as follows:

> 1 U.S. dollar = 200 Japanese yen (European terms)
> 1 Japanese yen = U.S. dollar 0.005 (U.S. terms)

Each rate is merely the reciprocal of the other. The trader must be careful in quoting rates because when the rate changes, each number moves in the opposite direction:

> 1 U.S. dollar = 100 Japanese yen
> 1 Japanese yen = U.S. dollar 0.01

At any given moment, a wide range of rates exists depending on the underlying transactions. There is a rate for buying the currency and a rate for selling. The difference between the buying and selling price is called the *spread*. Large transactions have a different rate from small ones. There are different rates for trading paper money. The trading of bank balances constitutes what is primarily referred to as foreign exchange trading. At a given moment, traders at different banks may quote differing rates for the same transaction. The establishment of a rate for a particular transaction depends on many factors.

The principal countries of the free world are members of the International Monetary Fund (IMF), and after World War II each country established a *par value* for its currency. This "became fully operational only at the end of 1958, when most foreign currencies became convertible for the private sector into dollars for current account transactions. . . . Par values were established for the currencies of IMF member countries in terms of gold or the 'U.S. dollar of specified gold content.' Foreign monetary authorities were obligated to intervene in foreign exchange markets to maintain the value of their currencies within 1 percent of their dollar parities. Monetary authorities in major foreign countries undertook this intervention in dollars."[4] In the case of Great Britain, for example, when the par value of the pound sterling equated to $2.40, the British maintained the price between $2.38 and $2.42. Whenever the price in the market dropped to $2.38, the Bank of England bought pounds with dollars; when the price rose to $2.42, it sold pounds for dollars.

This system descends from the gold standard, even though the convertibility into gold no longer exists. The idea of maintaining the value within a 1 percent band owes something to the old "gold points":

> The currencies of those countries that adhered to the gold standard could fluctuate in price among themselves only by minor variations—the so-called gold points. . . [which was] the cost of shipping gold from one country to another, plus insurance charges and loss of interest for the duration of the shipment.[5]

Whenever a country in the postwar period changed its rate of exchange by an amount greater than this 1 percent band, it was required to restate its par value. Changing the par value downward (in terms of gold) is *devaluation*; changing the par value upward is *revaluation*. Such a drastic step is not taken lightly and would be the result of many factors, such as a higher rate of inflation in one country compared with that of another or loss of confidence in a government.

The par value is, however, only a reference point for actual business and is not a price at which a bank will actually trade. A bank will quote one rate of exchange for large cable transfers and a different rate for the purchase of a few dollars' worth of foreign bank notes. A bank will quote one price at which it will sell a foreign draft for 100 pounds sterling to a customer and a different rate at which it will buy a British bank check for the same amount from a customer. Different banks may quote differing rates at the same time, depending on their immediate supply of or need for a particular currency. A bank with a large inventory of pounds in its account and no immediate need would have less incentive to buy more pounds than would a bank with a shortage of pounds.

By 1973, the maintenance of a country's official exchange rate within a fixed range of a par value was abandoned. The structure had become too rigid and protected speculators when the market rate moved close to the range limits. The speculator knew that the government had to support the rate. Although still officially obligated to return to par values, most industrialized countries now allow the exchange rate of their currency to *float*. "A dollar was still a dollar, but its international value would fluctuate daily, depending on the judgments by millions of economic players on what a dollar was really worth compared with other kinds of money."[6]

From time to time central banks enter the market to support a rate, but this is solely their own decision. When a central bank allows the currency rate to float, that country's reserves suffer no

---

The Gold Standard: Descriptions and Definitions

Fixing the value of a country's monetary unit in terms of a specific weight of gold constituted the essence of the gold standard. For example, the United States went back on the gold standard in 1879 by defining a dollar to equal 23.22 fine grains of gold or, equivalently, by setting a price of $20.67 for one troy ounce of gold. Before the First World War, most countries were on a form of the gold coin standard. These countries minted gold coins that circulated, along with notes that were fractionally backed by gold reserves, in the payments system as legal tender. To economize on gold reserves after the war, many countries, including Britain but not the United States, stopped circulating gold coins. Instead, these countries instituted a gold bullion standard, under which notes could be exchanged for gold bars.

Under the international gold standard, currencies that were fixed in terms of gold were, necessarily, tied together by a system of fixed exchange rates. The fixed relative quantity of gold between two currencies in the system was known as the parity. The prewar parity between the dollar and the pound sterling was $4.8665 to 1 pound, but the dollar-pound exchange rate could move in either direction away from the parity benchmark by a small amount to the gold export point, where it became profitable to ship gold to the country with the stronger currency. Before the First World War, many central banks held pounds as a reserve asset, and the pound usually served in lieu of gold in international transactions; this system was known as the sterling exchange standard. At the Genoa Conference of 1922, all European governments declared the reestablishment of the international gold standard to be their ultimate and common financial objective and, to economize further on gold reserves, resolved to adopt a gold exchange standard under which gold-based assets would serve as reserve assets. This goal was achieved by the mid-1920s.

Continued

However, the extensive holdings of foreign exchange reserves (primarily dollar- and pound-denominated deposit balances) under the gold exchange standard went beyond what the participants at the conference had envisioned. In the 10 years before World War I, total foreign exchange reserves ·in European central banks fluctuated between $250 million and $400 million. In contrast, at the end of 1924, foreign exchange holdings totaled $844 million; at the end of 1928, they were $2.513 billion.

Source:

Federal Reserve Bulletin, "The International Gold Standard and U.S. Monetary Policy from World War I to the New Deal," June 1989, p. 425.

direct impact whenever the rate changes. It is only when the central bank attempts to manage the float that the nation's reserves can be affected, and those reserves can be seriously depleted if the country tries to maintain an exchange rate that the rest of the world deems to be unrealistic.

Many smaller trading countries of the world still maintain a fixed par value for their currency, but to keep in line with the major currencies of the world they change the par value (usually by devaluation) frequently, in some cases even monthly. Many countries have linked their currency to a major currency solely to determine its value for international transactions. In 1990, for example, 29 countries linked the value of their currency to the U.S. dollar.

A market exists between currencies when there is sufficient supply of and demand for each currency (table 11.1). Between the major European currencies, for example, enough buyers and sellers exist to enable rates to be quoted in terms of marks to francs. For many others, however, demand is insufficient, and trading one for the other necessitates going through a third currency, usually dollars. For example, between Greece and Brazil there would be a very small demand for each currency. To make such a trade when a need arose, the foreign exchange trader would sell drachmas for dollars and then dollars for cruzeiros. The resulting exchange rate for cruzeiros expressed in drachmas is a *cross rate*.

With floating exchange rates, one of the factors influencing the price of a country's exchange rate is the trend of its balance of payments, which is influenced, in turn, by many factors and events. Despite this trend, temporary influences may be the most important consideration in making a pricing decision. For example, supply and demand, seasonal factors, political considerations, international events, or the timing of large payments may

Table 11.1 Foreign Exchange Rates for Trades of $1 Million Minimum, New York Prices, Ending Friday, December 14, 1990

Foreign Exchange
WEEK ENDING FRIDAY,
DECEMBER 14,1990
NEW YORK (AP) - Foreign Exchange, New York prices.
Rates for trades of $1-million minimum.

	Fgn. currency In dollars Fri.	Dollar In fgn. currency Fri.
f-Argent (Austral)	.000203	4924.5
Australia (Dollar)	.7645	1.3080
Austria (Schilling)	.0960	10.42
c-Belgium (Franc)	.0326	30.69
Brazil (Cruzeiro)	.0069	145.02
Britain (Pound)	1.9332	.5173
30-day fwd	1.9228	.5201
60-day fwd	1.9128	.5228
90-day fwd	1.9054	.5248
Canada (Dollar)	.8624	1.1595
30-day fwd	.8595	1.1634
60-day fwd	.8565	1.1676
90 day fwd	.8540	1.1710
y-Chile (Peso)	.003078	324.92
Colombia (Peso)	.001912	523.00
Denmark (Krone)	.1754	5.7010
z-Ecudr (Sucre)	.001142	876.00
ECU	1.3799	.7247
d-Egypt (Pound)	.3529	2.8335
Finland (Mark)	.2796	3.5770
France (Franc)	.1990	5.0250
Germany (Mark)	.6729	1.4861
30-day fwd	.6737	1.4843
60-day fwd	.6747	1.4821
90-day fwd	.6757	1.4800
Greece (Drachma)	.006462	154.75
Hong Kong (Dollar)	.1282	7.8010
y-India (Rupee)	.0553	18.083
Indnsia (Ruplah)	.000529	1889.00
Ireland (Punt)	1.7910	.5583
Israel (Shekel)	.5031	1.9877
Italy (Lira)	.000895	1117.00
Japan (Yen)	.007506	132.23
30-day fwd	.007507	133.21
60-day fwd	.007508	133.19
90-day fwd	.007508	133.19
Jordan (Dinar)	1.5603	.64090
Lebanon (Pound)	.001356	737.50
Malaysia (Ringgit)	.3713	2.6935
z-Mexico (Peso)	.000340	2940.00
Nethrlnds (Guilder)	.5986	1.6706
N. Zealand (Dollar)	.5980	1.6720
Norway (Krone)	.1721	5.8100
Pakistan (Rupee)	.0460	21.72
Y-Peru (Inti)	.0000020	493722.
z-Philpns (Peso)	.0360	27.80
Por tugal (Escudo)	.007625	131.15
Saudi Arab (Riyal)	.2667	3.7500
Singapore (Dollar)	.5841	1.7120
So. Korea (Won)	.001395	716.80
So. Africa (Rand)	.3992	2.5050
Spain (Peseta)	.010610	94.25
Sweden (Krona)	.1793	5.5775
Switzerland (Franc)	.7837	1.2760
30-day fwd	.7844	1.2748
60-day fwd	.7852	1.2736
90 day fwd	.7859	1.2724
Taiwan (NT S)	.0375	26.66
Thailand (Baht)	.03994	25.04
Turkey (Lira)	.000356	2812.00
U.A.E. (Dirham)	.2723	3.6727
f-Uruguay (Peso)	.000647	1546.00
z-Venezuela (Bolivar)	.0198	50.3900
Yugoslav (Dinar)	.09624	10.39

ECU: European Currency Unit, a basket of European currencies. The Federal Reserve Board's Index the value of the dollar against 10 other currencies weighted on the basis of trade was 82.85 Friday, up 0.48 points or 0.59 percent from Thursday's 82.37. A year ago the index was 94.93

Late closing prices as of 3:00 pm Eastern Time from Telerate Systems and other sources.

c-commercial rate, d-free market rate, f-financial rate, y-official rate, z-floating rate, r-revised.

be reflected in the quoted price. "Foreign currency decisions are crucially dependent upon expectations . . .and exchange rate expectations are influenced by every conceivable economic, political, social, or psychological factor, not just balance of payments trends."[7] For the major currencies, exchange rates can also be affected by the comparative levels of short-term interest rates in the domestic markets. Governments can make decisions for purely internal money-management reasons, which can lead to large movements of internationally held funds with a resulting impact on exchange rates.

MARKET PARTICIPANTS

The foreign exchange trading day is 24 hours. It starts when a calendar business day opens in Tokyo, Hong Kong, and Singapore and then moves to the Middle East, to Western Europe, to New York, to the West Coast of the United States, and back to Asia, with each market active as the earth rotates through a 24-hour cycle. In many countries, such as the United States and Western European nations, foreign exchange trading has few restrictions. At the other extreme are countries that severely restrict trading by anyone other than the government.

The principal foreign exchange market in the United States is in New York City and is considered very informal. It has no central marketplace or "bourse," no official setting of rates, no fixed hours or rules of trading except the acceptance of an unwritten order of financial and moral conduct that has evolved over time. It exists as a means whereby buyers and sellers of foreign exchange are brought together. Its tangible framework is the system of direct rapid communications equipment that links participating institutions: domestic banks, U.S. branches and agencies of foreign banks, brokers, businesses, and even individuals whose commercial pursuits require participation in the market.

United States banks that make and maintain the market—because of their size, historical position in the international banking community, or management attitude toward exchange trading—engage in foreign exchange business with sufficient regularity and quantity that they can handle it without undue risk. They balance their positions when required to by the volume and direction of business. In fact, as the frequency and volume of their transactions increase, the risks inherent in exchange trading are minimized and the opportunity for trading profits increases.

Foreign exchange trading risk occurs when a bank buys an amount of foreign currency and the price in dollars drops before the bank can sell it, thus exposing the bank to loss.

New York agencies and branches of the many foreign banks that are in constant contact with their head offices add to the breadth and depth of the market, particularly in their respective currencies. Occasionally, some investment-banking firms participate in the market because of their special interests and overseas connections. Other active participants include a number of nonbank foreign exchange dealers.

Foreign Exchange Traders

Each bank's foreign exchange trading is the responsibility of a designated trader or dealer. Large banks may employ many traders working under a chief trader. The trader is responsible for meeting the needs of the bank's customers. To do this properly, the trader must keep informed about market activities, since the bank's larger customers will often seek advice about the present market and about expectations for the future. For larger banks, this requires continuous participation in buying and selling of currencies. Active traders constantly monitor a number of video screens displaying rates quoted by major banks, along with immediate news information.

The trader is a competitive person who enjoys the activity of trading, the tension, and the mental struggle. "Most traders, including many experienced ones, are under 35 years old. In a rapidly fluctuating market, experience is compressed and those who don't learn quickly go on to other pursuits."[8]

A trader's activity contributes directly to the improvement of the bank-customer relationship. A variety of factors have a bearing on the pricing decision and must be resolved in a matter of seconds during a conversation with a customer before a quotation is given. This unending process of gathering facts, evaluation, and reappraisal makes the work of a foreign exchange trader challenging and stimulating.

Foreign Exchange Brokers

Providing breadth to the functioning of the market are the foreign exchange brokers. They do not trade for their own account nor deal directly with the public, but they specialize in locating bank and business buyers and sellers and bring them together. In 1989, they arranged about 44 percent of foreign exchange turnover in the United States, which was the same percentage as three years before.[9] In London, brokers accounted for a third of the business.[10]

Having limited capital resources, the broker does not act as a principal in an exchange transaction. A regional bank, for example, that only occasionally has foreign exchange transactions, can use the broker to locate the needed buyer or seller. When there are a number of buyers or sellers, the broker can assist the regional bank in finding the best price without the bank having to make numerous calls to gauge the market. When many such banks communicate their needs, the broker has the opportunity to match these up or use the market-making capabilities of the larger banks' foreign exchange traders. When two parties with offsetting needs are located, the broker will work between them to agree upon a rate. Only then will the identities of the two parties be revealed to each other. If they are willing to trade with each other, the deal is closed between them and the broker is paid a modest commission.

Businesses and Individuals

In terms of number, the many individuals and businesses whose activities require international payments or receipts of funds represent an important group participating in the foreign exchange market. Banks have developed facilities for handling foreign exchange transactions because of their customers' needs. Without this underlying foundation of customer business, a bank would have less justification for a foreign exchange department. These participants—importers, exporters, investors—use the market because they require the means to effect the payment for their business.

Regional Banks

While many of the U.S. participants are in New York, the foreign exchange market is basically conducted over the telephone. The physical location of traders is therefore of little consequence. This enables bankers in other cities to make important contributions to the overall functioning of the foreign exchange market since they recognize and serve the needs of their respective customers. Many small regional banks, as they buy or sell foreign exchange, immediately arrange an offsetting transaction with a domestic or foreign correspondent bank or through a broker in New York. They may even have a policy of dealing in foreign exchange with their customers only after they have already obtained or disposed of the counterpart. Although these banks perform relatively few daily transactions individually, they play an important role collectively as they channel the nation's exchange business through the market.

For example, a customer contacts a local bank and wishes to sell 10 million Japanese yen just received in payment for an export sale. The local bank may not wish to quote a price in U.S. dollars until it has found someone who will buy the yen. It can contact its correspondent bank in a money center, obtain a price, and then quote a slightly lower price to its customer. If the customer agrees, the local bank closes its deal with its correspondent bank and makes a small profit without incurring any exposure to loss.

If, on the other hand, the local bank has a regular flow of foreign exchange business, it might be willing to buy the 10 million yen for its own account. The bank would expect to sell the yen later to another customer who needed the money for payment of a purchase.

OPERATIONS IN THE FOREIGN EXCHANGE MARKET

All activities that make up a nation's balance of payments will influence trading in that country's currency. Regardless of whether the currency used is one's own currency or a foreign currency, almost every international transaction involves one of the party's exposure to exchange risk.

Payments for Imports and Exports

If all the United States's international trade were priced in U.S. dollars, the U.S. would have no need for a foreign exchange market. There would, of course, be a lively supply of, and demand for, dollars in foreign exchange markets abroad. The demand would be reflected on the ledgers of U.S. banks by transfers of dollars among foreign accounts. Dollars earned by foreign exporters, for example, would flow into the accounts of their banks, and dollars paid by foreign importers of U.S. products would flow out of the bank accounts of foreigners here and into the bank accounts of U.S. exporters. The U.S. exporter, quoting a price in U.S. dollars, is merely putting the exchange risk on the importer.

Foreign Exchange Trading Rising, Central Banks Say

The world's foreign exchange market is growing rapidly, according to reports released by central banks yesterday. London is still the largest foreign exchange market in the world, but the United States and Japan are catching up.

The worldwide market is nearing $500 billion in total transactions. And as foreign exchange trading grows, it is playing a larger role in reflecting worldwide reaction to economic news and to American economic policy.

Far more than just several years ago, the movement of the dollar on any day now tends to influence the moods of the bond and stock markets.

The foreign exchange market in the United States, which is No. 2, grew by 120 percent over the last three years, the reports said. At $128.9 billion, it now rivals the size of the government securities market, where daily trading is at $125 billion to $150 billion.

In London, trading volume was $187 billion, up by 107 percent from $90 billion in March 1986.

The trading figures are from reports by the central banks, including the Federal Reserve Bank of New York. The last survey was conducted three years ago. The reports are the broadest and most coordinated effort to measure foreign exchange activity.

The market has grown as world economies have become more interrelated and capital markets more integrated, said Gretchen Greene, the senior vice president in charge of foreign exchange at the New York Fed, which did the American survey. This internationalization of the economy has led to easier capital flows and has opened the opportunity for people and companies to invest abroad, which has increased the need for swapping currencies.

Looking to Hedge Risk

The volume of trading has also risen, she said, because more commercial banks and investment banks are getting into the business, partly because it is seen as a new avenue for profits. And more companies are using the market to hedge their risk in doing business in other countries.

The Federal Reserve report does not detail the specific nature of the trading—that is, whether it is mostly by speculators. But Ms. Greene said the survey showed that only about 12 percent of the trades reported were with customers not involved in regular foreign exchange trading.

The New York Fed said that average daily trading in April totaled $128.9 billion, up from $58.5 billion in March 1986 and from $18 billion in 1980. This combines the trading completed by banks and other institutions, mostly investment banks based in the United States. Of the total, 40 percent was done by subsidiaries of foreign banks.

The figures are adjusted to remove double counting of trades between institutions in the United States. But the totals reported for each country are

Continued

not adjusted for this double counting, so adding the individual figures do not give a precise amount for worldwide volume.

Plenty of Movement

The Fed's report does not disclose the volume of trading by institution, but it does show that it is a volatile business and that a lot of movement exists among the leaders. Ms. Greene said that four of the top five institutions in 1986 fell to the bottom of the Top 10 list this year and that two institutions fell off the list this year.

The West German mark is still the leading currency traded against the dollar, but the Japanese yen is gaining. This year, 32.1 percent of the volume was in marks, down from 33.7 percent in 1986, while the volume

of yen trades was 26.4 percent, up from 23.7 percent in 1986.

Almost two-thirds of the trading is direct, or spot-currency trades, the same proportion as in 1986. But currency options, a tool used to limit risk, have grown to 4.3 percent of the volume this year, from nine-tenths of 1 percent in 1986.

Other countries reporting yesterday included France, Canada and the Netherlands, where the trading volume was much lower. It was $26 billion in France, $16 billion in the Netherlands—with the double counting of trades—and $15 billion in Canada.

By Jonathan Fuerbringer. Reprinted with permission of *The New York Times*, Sept. 14, 1989.

In practice, many U.S. firms and individuals receive foreign exchange in payment of goods and services sold abroad. Others make payments to foreigners in their currency rather than in U.S. dollars. A U.S. firm selling in Great Britain, for example, may invoice its sales in pounds sterling. International business is highly competitive, and to make a foreign sale many U.S. firms prefer to quote prices in the local currency and then undertake the problem of conversion into U.S. currency. If the U.S. business only deals in dollars, it will discover that many other sellers are eager to make a sale and willing to quote prices in the buyer's currency. The years after World War II when the U.S. business attitude was "dollars or nothing" are gone, probably for good.

Although some large international firms are able to use foreign exchange acquired in previous transactions to meet current needs, in practice it is difficult to balance these needs exactly. Similarly, it is extremely difficult for other importers or exporters to find exact counterparts with the proper amount of foreign exchange to complete a trade transaction. As a result, the foreign exchange market, like other financial and commodity markets, has developed as a means through which these needs can be easily met.[11]

A country's balance of payments is reflected in the value of its currency against other currencies. A country with a balance of payments deficit will have an increasing supply of its currency in the market as importers, investors, and individuals pay their foreign counterparts; thus the value of the country's currency will decline as supply exceeds demand. A balance of payments surplus usually brings a rising value for that country's currency as more foreigners seek it to pay in that country, and demand for the currency exceeds supply.

Trading in Foreign Currencies

To satisfy the needs of their customers, commercial banks hold foreign exchange inventories in the form of working balances with foreign banks or have access to such balances through their major correspondent banks. In U.S. banks, such accounts are Due From accounts (see chapter 4). These inventories are maintained by the purchase and sale of balances owned by firms, individuals, and other banks—domestic and foreign—and by the purchase of bills of exchange, traveler's checks, dividend warrants, and so forth that are denominated in foreign currencies. A bank's foreign exchange traders, within the operating principles of the bank, must manage these balances and make every important trading decision themselves, usually in a matter of seconds. Once a trade has been completed, operations personnel will handle the posting, confirming, and settling of the transaction. The size and number of these Due From accounts reflect to some extent the amount of activity the bank experiences in a given currency.

The Due From account is also referred to as a *dual currency account* because it is kept simultaneously in two currencies. The ledger reflects the balance in the foreign currency and shows debits and credits by the foreign bank. The ledger is also kept in U.S. dollars, since that is the currency in which the U.S. bank maintains its records. As the bank reports its balance sheet, it will show the U.S. dollar equivalent of the foreign currency in its account abroad.

Fundamental to any foreign exchange transaction is the transfer of ownership of a given amount of foreign exchange from one person to another. Chapter 5 described the methods of transferring funds: foreign drafts and remittances. These are equally applicable whether transferring foreign exchange or U.S. dollars.

As a bank's customers need foreign exchange for their business needs, they communicate with the bank's foreign exchange trader to learn the price at which the bank is willing to sell the foreign currency for the local currency. This is the *foreign exchange rate*. Conversely, a customer who has received foreign currency from a business transaction will seek the price at which the bank will buy it. In each transaction, between a bank and a commercial customer or between two banks, one party is buying while the other party is selling. It is necessary that both parties must clearly understand which currency they are buying or selling. In U.S. banks, many traders find it convenient to quote all transactions as buying or selling dollars. This facilitates the operations of a trading room, since the bank will report its daily balance sheet in terms of dollars.

Once a trade has been completed, *settlement* (delivery of the currencies on the designated *value date*) must now be done. For example, Bank A has purchased 1 million pounds sterling from Bank B as a *spot transaction* on June 1, which means delivery two business days later. Bank A has sold dollars and bought pounds; Bank B has bought dollars and sold pounds. The price is $1.51/pound. As soon as the trade has been agreed, both traders notify their operations units. Bank B sends a tested cable, generally using the S.W.I.F.T. format (see chapter 5), to its correspondent bank in London to "charge our account 1 million pounds and pay to X London Bank for credit to the account of Bank A value June 3." Bank A will send a message to its London correspondent telling it "you will receive" the amount. If the funds do not arrive, the London correspondent bank will notify Bank A. While sending the instructions to London, Bank A arranges to pay $1,510,000 in the United States to Bank B, also on June 3, generally through Fedwire or CHIPS. A spot trade is settled two business days hence to provide time for these messages to be sent and for the London banks to have time to pass their necessary entries, taking into account the difference in time zones.

Events elsewhere in the market have a critical bearing on an exchange rate the trader will quote for a given transaction. The trader often attempts to anticipate what the market's position will be in the immediate future in order to trade more favorably. The bank's own position in a given currency has a direct bearing on this decision, as does the cost involved in carrying or *covering* a position. Covering a position means protecting against possible loss from a change in the rate by an offsetting transaction.

Forward Trading

Settlement of a spot transaction generally takes place two business days after the trade. A *forward exchange contract* between two parties calls for delivery at a future date of a specified amount of one currency against payment of another, with the exchange rate fixed at the time the contract is made. When the contract falls due, the spot rate for the currency may be above, below, or the same as the rate specified for the transaction; this fact has no effect on the contracted rate. Settlement occurs on the maturity date of the contract. Forward rates can be obtained for many of the major currencies that have a substantial number of businesses needing to either buy or sell for delivery in the future.

While forward contracts are often written for periods of time such as one, three, or six months, contracts can be for any number of days. One-year forward quotations can often be obtained, and contracts covering several years may sometimes be successfully negotiated in the market for some actively traded currencies. Contracts may also be written that allow the customer to take delivery any day between certain specified dates (*option contracts*). The bank is exposed to more risk with a customer involved in a forward transaction than in a spot transaction because of the future date of settlement. As a result, the creditworthiness of a customer is an important element in forward exchange operations.

"There has always been a desire to avoid the risk associated with trade and economic activity across currency boundaries. . . Forward exchange markets reduce the risk associated with foreign trade to the extent that importers' demand for and exporters' supply of foreign currency are matched in the market at a given exchange rate, or the risk is shifted to . . .speculators who are willing to assume it."[12]

For example, a U.S. company bidding on a contract to sell equipment to a buyer in Great Britain will need 90 days to assemble the order. To meet competition from European suppliers, the company wants to quote its price in pounds sterling. The problem is how to quote a sterling price to be paid on delivery of the equipment in 90 days, then convert the foreign exchange into dollars and show a profit, when the company has no idea what the spot rate will be in 90 days. The company's interest is in the business deal, not in currency speculation. Enter the U.S. bank, which can arrange a forward contract with the company setting a U.S. dollar price today at which it will buy the pounds sterling when the company is paid in London in 90 days. Regardless of what happens to the exchange rate, the conversion rate is fixed. Such protection is referred to as *hedging*.

Similarly, an importer may buy forward foreign exchange needed to fix the U.S. dollar cost of imports. For example, a U.S. business may be deliberating between a machine made in the United States and a similar one made in Canada. Based on today's exchange rate, they may be nearly equally priced. However, it will take three months before the machine will be ready, at which time payment will be made. By checking with its bank, the importer may discover that the forward Canadian dollar rate is lower than the spot rate. By arranging a forward contract, the Canadian machine becomes cheaper than the machine made in the United States. The U.S. business would therefore be likely to buy the Canadian-made machine. Some firms leave their exchange risks uncovered except in times of uncertainty over the future of the exchange rate.

In cases in which capital transfers are involved, an investor may wish to buy or sell forward the amounts expected to be paid or received in order to take advantage of prevailing *premiums* or *discounts* in the forward market. A forward is at a discount when the forward rate is lower than the spot rate; at a premium when the forward rate is higher than the spot. Thus a U.S. investor due to receive 1 milllion deutsche marks in three months may wish to sell these forward if the DM spot rate is $0.40 and the forward rate $0.405, If the investor waits until the deutsche marks are in hand ("uncovered"), then the spot rate might be higher or lower, and the investor benefits or loses accordingly. However, with a forward contract entered into now, the investor will receive $405,000 in three months. If the spot rate in three months is unchanged, or lower, the investor has profited by the forward contract; if the spot rate turns out to be higher, he has still benefited by having replaced risk with certainty for the period.

Forward transactions do not usually replace foreign exchange transactions that would otherwise take place in the spot market to cover exports, imports, or capital transfers; forward transactions simply shift the timing of such exchanges. Importers, exporters, and capital remitters and recipients often cover their activities in response to changes in expectations concerning the movement of exchange rates. These shifts can have material effects on the exchange market.

The use of the forward market to *hedge* is widely practiced by investors making short-term investments. A corporate treasurer with surplus funds wants to invest them until they are needed for the company's operations and is seeking the highest return for comparable safety. Because of the relative freedom now for money to move from country to country, the treasurer will evaluate the rates in different markets for short-term investments. To calculate the true yield on any investment, the treasurer considers not only the rate on the investment itself but also the cost of converting currency to make the money market investment, as well as the cost of converting back into the original currency upon maturity (see chapter 12).

Another activity in the foreign exchange market is *speculation*. Speculation is the purchase or sale of foreign exchange, usually on a forward basis, for the sole purpose—or at least with the fervent hope—of subsequently being able to cover the open position at a profit. The defensive operator, or hedger, buys or sells exchange—again usually on a forward basis—as a means of avoiding an exchange risk or of insuring against loss from an exchange rate change. The speculator hopes to profit from a rate change; the hedger tries to avoid the consequences of a change.

Speculators in foreign exchange generally have no underlying commercial transaction relating to their trading activities. They are betting against the market and hoping to realize a profit. Their actions can have a beneficial effect on the market. A speculator who expects a rate to go up may be readily attracted by a declining forward rate, while one who expects the rate to go down may be attracted by a rising rate. In this way, speculators can give the market more breadth and flexibility. Insofar as speculators may drive forward rates out of line with interest rate levels, they become the arbitrageur's best friend. Recent experience has demonstrated, however, that purely speculative influences have tended to have an unstabilizing effect. When the exchange markets become seriously unsettled by uncertainties, normally beneficial speculation may have quite the opposite effect.

A form of speculation can occur when market participants anticipate that a country with fixed exchange rates is going to change the par value, or a country with floating exchange rates is going to support the rate in the market. If the expectation is that the rate will go down, anyone with payments to make for commercial transactions in that currency will delay payment as long as possible to benefit from the new lower rate. Conversely, anyone in that country with payments to make in a foreign currency will prepay to make the conversion at today's more favorable rate. This is known as *lags* and *leads*, respectively. These speculative maneuvers tend to aggravate the situation and, in effect, become a self-fulfilling prophecy forcing government action. The government suffers heavy outflows of reserves as its citizens prepay foreign debt, while facing delayed income to its reserves as foreigners wait before paying their local debts.

"The positive effects of forward markets on trade and capital transactions in particular are clearly appreciated by the authorities of many countries. Industrial countries have, therefore, generally kept their forward markets functioning effectively with a minimum of regulation, at least for cover of commercial transactions and debt service payments. When such markets have not existed, forward cover facilities have generally been made available by the authorities."[13]

Maintaining the Position

The foreign exchange trader buys and sells for the bank's clients on a continuing basis. It is not necessary, nor is it often desirable, for traders at major banks to offset each transaction immediately. These banks maintain active foreign exchange trading departments that operate within general guidelines established by bank management. These guidelines set the maximum *position* the trader can have in any one currency at the end of the day, which is the net balance of purchases and sales. While the trader may want to keep the bank's position as balanced as possible and thus be protected against major rate changes, the trader may nevertheless let the position be unbalanced, expecting that other clients will bring in new transactions that may restore the balance. This decision depends on the trader's opinion of what the future trend of that currency will be.

As trades are made, they are taken into the position and recorded by the clerk who maintains this record and reflects all changes. At the beginning of a day, the bank's pound sterling position may be as shown in table 11.2.

Table 11.2 Example of Opening Balance Position

Opening balance with correspondents		£200,000
Purchases not yet credited to account		
Cable transfers	£350,000	
Sight drafts	65,000	
Forward contracts	100,000	515,000
Total balance and purchases		£715,000
Sales not yet charged to account		
Cable transfers	£400,000	
Sight drafts	40,000	
Forward contracts	350,000	
Total Sales		£790,000
Overall position		−£ 75,000

The trader may have an overall position limit of £100,000. The bank's overall position is short £75,000, even though it has £200,000 in its account. The trader can estimate how many days will elapse before the sight drafts purchased and sold will be reflected in the account balance. Knowing that the cable transfers will be put through the account on the value day, the trader today has ample cash in the account to cover immediate sales. If no further transactions take place, the trader will have ample cash in the account to meet maturing forward sales for 60 days.

The maturity dates of various forward contracts are shown in table 11.3.

Table 11.3 Example of Forward Contract Maturity Dates

	30 Days	*60 Days*	*90 Days*	*180 Days*
Sales	−£ 50,000	−£100,000	−£100,000	−£100,000
Purchases		+ 50,000		+ 50,000
Cash balance in account today: £175,000[a]				
Cash position	+£125,000	+£ 75,000	−£ 25,000	−£ 75,000

[a]From Table 11.2, opening balance plus cable and sight draft purchases less cable and sight draft sales.

The position clerk must keep a record of the delivery dates of all forward transactions so that they will be reflected in the spot position at maturity. To balance the overall position, the trader could buy £75,000, but this would only increase the cash supply. Since the forward contracts do not mature immediately, the trader may decide to reduce the large cash position because it is not earning any interest by means of a *swap*.

"A swap transaction is a simultaneous purchase and sale of a certain amount of foreign currency for different value dates. The key aspect is that the bank arranges the swap as a single transaction with a single counterparty, either another bank or a nonbank customer. This means that, unlike outright spot or forward transactions, a trader does not incur any foreign exchange rate risk, since the bank contracts both to pay and to receive the same amount of currency at specified rates."[14]

In this case, the trader could sell spot and buy for forward delivery on a date that is close to the delivery date of the other forward sales contracts. Although this would not change the overall position, it would reduce the cash position. Swaps can be made between any two dates: one month against three months, two months against six months, or between spot and a future date. Applicable rates are quoted for these various dates. Thus the trader would sell the sterling spot, receiving the rate for a spot sale, and buy forward at the rate for that future date.

In this way, the trader has flexibility in adjusting maturities to coincide with the needs of clients, while at the same time remaining within the limits established by the bank's management.

Department Controls

A foreign exchange trading department must have effective controls to limit a bank's exposure to loss. The first control is proper evaluation of customer risk. A spot transaction where settlement with the customer will take place within two days of the trade has little risk exposure for the bank. However, in entering into a forward contract with a customer, the bank is involved with a credit evaluation. If the customer is unable to deliver his or her part of the transaction at the future date, the bank may suffer a loss, since it has committed itself to another party for the offsetting transaction or has taken the contract into its position for other

operations. The bank may have even delivered the funds. Because of time differences, the bank may have instructed the
foreign bank to pay out before debiting the customer's account.
The bank must therefore make a credit evaluation of its customer
before entering into a foreign exchange contract. The basic
question is whether the customer has the financial resources to
meet his or her contractual obligations and will indeed do so.

The second control is the potential exposure with other
traders. Each bank will make its own determination of the
maximum amount in outstanding forward contracts it wishes to
have at any time with a particular bank or corporate customer,
either domestic or foreign. Banks can fail, so there is a risk in
entering into foreign exchange trades. If a bank goes bankrupt,
other banks will be unable to realize contracts with that bank and
will have to replace the amounts, perhaps at a considerable loss.
Bank managements will also limit the amount of exposure on
settlement from a correspondent or customer in any one day,
which would guard against a customer being overcommitted to
come up with cash at any one time.

Internally, the operation of a foreign exchange trading section
requires management direction and subsequent supervision. At
the outset, limits are established for each currency. Management
will determine the maximum exposure it is willing to have in a
currency. The trader may enter into any number of trades, spot
and forward, but at the end of each day the difference, if any,
between total sales and purchases must be within the limit, either
long (more purchases than sales) or short (more sales than purchases).

Strong internal controls and audit are very important. Foreign
exchange traders are not infallible and they may not always judge
the direction of the market accurately. In the heat of trading
activity, mistakes will be made. Bank management must expect
that this will happen. It is important that the trader recognizes
such mistakes or misjudgments and cuts losses quickly. The
skilled trader must do this and go on to the next transaction. There
have been instances in which traders remained convinced that a
situation would turn around and, to recover the loss, took greater
and greater risks. The results were staggering losses to the banks.
In a few cases the bank failed as a consequence. Strong, independent in-bank auditing of daily positions is vital for a foreign
exchange section. It is also important that the back-office operation and the audit function report to separate offices outside the

trading activity. Thus there is a measure of immediate control against manipulation of the banks.[15]

Local Correspondent Services

Banks with extensive Due From accounts frequently make these accounts available to their domestic correspondent banks for drawings. In addition, regular foreign exchange rate sheets or computer information services will be made available, giving the U.S. dollar price at which the correspondent can issue foreign payments in any of several foreign currencies. Correspondents authorized to use such facilities are thus able to arrange foreign exchange transfers for their own customers without incurring the expense of their own network of foreign currency accounts and, in most cases, without the necessity of first having to communicate with their principal foreign exchange correspondents. Banks with a large branch system will use the same system so that their branches can easily issue drafts and remittances for their customers in foreign currency without having to contact the foreign exchange trader for small amounts.

If a branch or correspondent bank's customer has no preference, the foreign exchange trader will always prefer to have foreign drafts and remittances issued in a foreign currency rather than in U.S. dollars. When payments are denominated in U.S. dollars, the receiving bank will make the conversion to local currency at its rate of exchange and make a profit on the conversion. However, if the foreign draft or remittance is issued in foreign currency, then the U.S. bank will have that conversion profit.

Bank Notes

A service performed principally for travelers by the foreign exchange trader is that of buying and selling foreign bank notes and coins. The price spread between buying and selling for this type of trading is always wide because the market is small and moving this type of exchange from one market to another poses certain problems, since it is cash. If a bank buys a larger quantity of bank notes from returning travelers than it can expect to sell, it can sell the surplus to specialized brokers or, in some cases, mail the bank notes to a correspondent in the country of origin for deposit in its account. The expense of registered insured mail plus the handling costs of maintaining a current inventory must be taken into account in determining the rates of exchange.

Buying and selling bank notes is basically a service a bank provides to individual customers. Tourists are often well advised to have a small amount of local currency in their possession when they arrive in the foreign country to facilitate getting to their hotel. Only a few countries prohibit tourists from bringing in a small supply of local currency.

NONBANK MARKETS

In addition to the foreign exchange markets established by banks, foreign exchange is bought and sold in some specialized markets as a commodity for future delivery in the same manner as for corn, wheat, copper, pork bellies, and so forth. This involves contracts for a prefixed standard amount of delivery only on specified dates. In foreign exchange, for example, a standard contract may be for DM125,000 maturing on the third Wednesday of March, June, September, or December. There is an important distinction between forward transactions and *futures* contracts. "The former are individual agreements between two parties, say, a bank and a customer. The latter is a contract traded on an organized market of a standard size and settlement date, which is resalable at the market price up to the close of trading in the contract."[16] Contracts are available in only certain major currencies. It is also possible to trade foreign exchange options.

SUMMARY

Converting the money of one country into that of another country is a service banks provide for their customers through foreign exchange trading. In essence this is a continuation of the concept outlined in chapter 5 in which money was able to move from one country to another through accounts maintained by banks with each other.

The need for the foreign exchange service arises from international trade, investments, invisible trade, and other payments between countries. In each transaction, one of the parties needs to convert the money to that of another country. A designated trader knowledgeable about the spot market and the forward market provides this service to the bank's customers. The foreign exchange trader is supported by an operational staff and must operate within guidelines established by the bank's management that will limit the bank's exposure in the volatile exchange markets. The foreign exchange trader is dealing in a very complex market and can provide advice to the bank's customers to guide them through the foreign exchange marketplace.

QUESTIONS

1. How is the foreign exchange rate determined?
2. Who are the major participants in the foreign exchange market?
3. What is the difference between a spot trade and a forward trade? Why would a business use one or the other?
4. Why does foreign exchange trading exist?

PROBLEM

Your customer, a wholesaler of electronic equipment, has committed to purchasing in Japanese yen 100 million worth of merchandise. The equipment will be ready in three months, at which time the payment will have to be made. Should the customer buy the yen spot or for forward delivery? Using the prices quoted in a current newspaper, make the calculations for the cost to the customer of either approach.

Notes

1. For a full discussion of the meaning of money names, see: Peter K. Oppenheim, "Money of the Realm," *Verbatim, The Language Quarterly*, Spring 1989, pp. 7-9.

2. *Federal Reserve Bulletin*, June 1989, p. 426.

3. Allan M. Loosigian, *Foreign Exchange Futures* (Homewood, Illinois: Dow Jones-Irwin, 1981), p. 10.

4. B. Dianne Pauls, "U.S. Exchange Rate Policy: Bretton Woods to Present." *Federal Reserve Bulletin*, November 1990, p. 891.

5. Loosigian, *op. cit.* p. 9.

6. William Greider, *Secrets of the Temple* (New York: Simon and Schuster, 1987), p. 338.

7. Roger M. Kubarych, *Foreign Exchange Markets in the United States,* Federal Reserve Bank of New York, 1978, p. 40.

8. *Ibid.*, p. 28.

9. Federal Reserve Bank of New York, press release, Sept. 13, 1989, p. 1.

10. Bank of England, press notice, Sept. 13, 1989, p. 2.

11. Alan R. Holmes and Francis H. Scott, *The New York Foreign Exchange Market,* Federal Reserve Bank of New York, 1965.

12.   Peter J. Quirk, Graham Hacche, Viktor Schoofs, and Lothar Weniger, *Policies for Developing Forward Foreign Exchange Markets.* Occasional Paper No. 60 (Washington, D.C.: International Monetary Fund, 1988), p. 3.

13.   Quirk, et al., *op. cit.*, p. 4.

14.   Kubarych, *op. cit.* p. 10.

15   For a full description of the operation of such a control system, see *Foreign Exchange Trading Techniques and Controls* (Washington, D.C.: American Bankers Association, 1977).

16.   K. Alec Chrystal, "A Guide to Foreign Exchange Markets," *Federal Reserve Bank of St. Louis Review,* March 1984, p. 8.

12

Foreign Exchange Applications

Every user of the foreign exchange market affects other users. This chapter examines how businesses and governments use the foreign exchange markets to achieve their objectives. The present markets provide the opportunity for payments for international trade transactions, for investments, or for speculation. The existence of active markets enables businesses to place surplus funds in another country to earn a higher rate of return than might be available in their own country. As a consequence of thousands of individual transactions, money flows have become massive, volatile, and unrestrained, with rates often moving in wider swings than in previous decades. Governments are seeking to restrain the fluctuations and protect the competitiveness of their industries. They are facing balance of payments deficits and trying to conserve the value of their national currency.

The objectives of this chapter are to
- examine how businesses and governments use the foreign exchange market
- demonstrate the use of interest-rate arbitrage
- examine how governments attempt to influence foreign exchange rates
- illustrate some of the problems and options facing businesses and governments

MARKET CHARACTERISTICS

The needs of buyers and sellers of other nations' currencies are funneled through one global foreign exchange market. Individual traders in specific geographic locations, in constant telephone or electronic contact with each other, react to the cumulative total of specific trades. Traders generally do not need to know why a customer is buying or selling a currency, they are concerned only with the transfer of payments. Payments for imports, short-term investment, and speculation are intermingled and indistinguishable as they move through the market. Each, however, is affected by the existence of the others in establishing a rate of exchange. This describes the markets for currencies of the major industrial countries who have floating exchange rates.

In addition to these relatively free markets, many countries restrict the use of their currencies in order to solve balance of payments problems, to ration limited foreign exchange earnings for essential imports, and so forth. Many countries limit access to foreign exchange and maintain fixed exchange rates under the direct control of that government.

TRANSACTIONS

A characteristic of foreign exchange is that the same commodity—money—is traded in different markets at the same time. And the possibility exists that the prices quoted may be different. Trading to take advantage of this difference in price is called arbitrage.

Trading Arbitrage

A foreign exchange dealer receives and gives quotations during the trading day. The dealer may discover that dealers in different markets are quoting rates that make it possible to buy a currency in one market and sell it immediately in another and show a profit. For example, if pounds sterling are cheaper in London than in New York, a dealer may buy them in London and sell them in New York and make a profit. This is referred to as *space arbitrage*.

In another example, called *triangular arbitrage*, the dealer may see that rates quoted in three markets would make it possible to execute a series of trades and end up with a profit. Dealer A may have a quantity of deutsche marks in an account in Frankfurt. Checking the rates offered by others, dealer A discovers that he or she can sell the deutsche marks in London and obtain Italian lire, sell the lire in Zurich for dollars, which can then be sold to a trader in New York for deutsche marks, which will net more deutsche marks than in the beginning, even after deducting telephone and telex expenses.

When this can be done, it must be done very quickly, often in a matter of minutes, since the rates are constantly changing and other traders will have also seen this disparity in the cross rates. Realistically, however, in recent years, such possibilities have become rare as a consequence of the development of sophisticated communication systems and the growing number of active participants in the market.

Interest-Rate Arbitrage

One of the characteristics of international finance today is the relative freedom of money to move from one industrialized country to another for short- or long-term investment. Each currency remains a domestic currency whose market interest rates are basically determined by conditions within that country, such as rate of inflation, monetary policy, government expenditures, taxation policy, and enforcement. The term *international capital markets* or *international money markets* does not refer to some supranational financial market, but rather to the link of these domestic markets, which allow money to move across national boundaries. The difference between the terms capital markets and money markets is that the latter usually refers only to short-term debt instruments.

Money will tend to be attracted by the higher rate of interest in comparable risk, just as metal filings are attracted to a magnet. As a consequence, funds flow through the foreign exchange market as funds in one currency are converted to that of another to be invested in higher-yielding instruments. This is the meaning of *interest-rate arbitrage*. This can best be understood by looking at an example.

Consider a situation in which two corporate treasurers of manufacturing companies find they have surplus funds that their companies will not need for 90 days. At the end of that time, they must have the money in their account to meet contracted purchases of equipment. One of these corporate treasurers is in the United States and has $10 million; the other is in Great Britain and has £10 million. They want to put these funds to work to obtain interest income during the 90 days with the maximum safety. They are not interested in losing these funds in a high-risk investment since investing is not the principal business of their company; manufacturing is. Thus, each decides to consider purchasing only a government money market IOU. Governments cannot go bankrupt in their own currency since they have the power to tax or to print more money, although either of these has political and economic consequences.

The objective: Invest the funds for 90 days for the highest yield with maximum safety. At the end of 90 days, each must be converted back into its own currency.

The situation: Three-month Treasury bills issued by the British government in pounds sterling yield 14 percent per annum; three-month Treasury bills issued by the United States government in dollars yield 7.5 percent per annum.

The options: Each corporate treasurer can invest in the Treasury bills of their own government, obtain the stated return, and have no foreign exchange risk; or, they can purchase the Treasury bills of the other country, receive that rate of return, but have a foreign exchange risk.

The problem: Which will yield the higher rate of return? If the corporate officer decides to purchase the Treasury bill of the other country, he must convert his local currency into the foreign exchange, invest it, and at the end of the 90 days convert the foreign exchange back into his local currency. This means having a foreign exchange exposure for the 90 days. The exchange rates are:

Spot: £= $1.8241
90-day forward: £= $1.7938

The analysis: The U.S. corporate treasurer might be more attracted to the British Treasury bill since a 14 percent annual return appears obviously higher than 7.5 percent. To invest in the British Treasury bill, the U.S. treasurer must sell his dollars spot for pounds, buy the British Treasury bill; at the end of the 90 days receive principal plus interest in pounds and sell the pounds for dollars. If he wishes to be fully protected, he will hedge this by entering into a swap: sell dollars spot, buy dollars back 90 days forward. To buy a pound today he must pay $1.8241; however, when he sells the pounds in 90 days he will get only $1.7938. The treasurer is thus going to lose money on the foreign exchange swap, but is earning a higher rate of interest on the investment.

How much is the loss versus the gain? To convert the foreign exchange swap into a percent figure, the formula is

$$\frac{\text{Forward rate} - \text{Spot rate}}{\text{Spot rate}} \quad \text{x} \quad \frac{360}{\text{days to maturity}} \quad \text{x } 100 \ = \ \% \text{ p.a.}$$

or

$$\frac{1.7938 - 1.8241}{1.8241} \quad \text{x} \quad \frac{360}{90} \text{ x } 100 \ = \ -6.6\% \text{ p.a.}$$

For the U.S. treasurer this would mean earning 14 percent p.a. on the British Treasury bill and losing 6.6 percent p.a. on the swap, resulting in a net rate of return of only 7.4 percent p.a. (14% - 6.6%). This is lower than he would earn by buying the U.S. Treasury bill at 7.5 percent. Should he decide not to hedge the foreign exchange fluctuation risks, then he would make only the spot trade, buy the British bill, and hope that during the 90 days the exchange rate would move up.

For the British corporate treasurer, the same basic calculations apply, except that there would be a gain on the swap. He would receive $1.8241 spot for each pound and at the end of the 90 days have to give up only $1.7938 to get back one pound. Thus, if he decided to buy the U.S. Treasury bill, he would earn 7.5 percent p.a. plus 6.6 percent p.a. on the swap, for a total rate of return of 14.1 percent—a 0.1 percent increase over buying his own Treasury's bill. Bank handling or custody charges or other incidental expenses might reduce the profit, but these are predictable and are generally small enough to be unimportant.

Effect on Foreign Trade

Such flows of money from one country to another to take advantage of higher interest rates will affect the balance of trade.

To illustrate, consider two competing manufacturers of machinery who have equivalent selling prices. One is in Germany quoting a price of DM1.5 million; the other is in the United States with a selling price of $1 million. If the exchange rate is $1 = DM1.5 then the price to both a buyer in Germany and the United States is the same. When the demand for dollars rises in Germany because investors are attracted by higher U.S. interest rates, then German investors compete and offer more deutsche marks to obtain dollars. The exchange rate moves to $1 = DM1.6. The effect of this on the two sellers of machinery is that *both a German and a U.S. buyer will find the German-made machine cheaper.* For a U.S. buyer, the cost in dollars becomes $937,500 (DM1,500,000 ÷ 1.6); for a German buyer the U.S.-made machine would now cost DM1,600,000 ($1,000,000 x 1.6). As a consequence, the U.S. manufacturer would be unable to compete, losing potential export sales. German exports would rise and U.S. imports would rise.

Another illustration of this dilemma was seen in the early 1980s in Germany. That country must import energy, and it exports 40 percent of the manufactured goods it produces. The oil imports must be paid for in dollars.

> Normally, if the dollar rises, the West German mark falls, and vice versa.... The German Government is constantly faced with a dilemma: If the German mark rises in value its oil-import bill goes down but German goods become less competitive in the international marketplace, the balance of trade worsens, and unemployment eventually rises. . . . On the other hand, if the mark loses its value relative to the dollar. . .then the cost of imported oil rises.[1]

CORPORATE PROBLEMS

In addition to the comparative interest rates in different markets, other factors can influence short-term investment decisions. National accounting practices, for example, may impose a cost on a company with long-term investments in another country when there are changes in foreign exchange rates. Corporations consolidate the balance sheet of a foreign subsidiary with that of the parent. Some countries require that this be based on the current exchange rate rather than on the historical rate at which an investment may have been made.

Thus, for example, if a U.S. corporation made a $1 million investment in its French subsidiary when the rate was $1 = 4 francs, the subsidiary would show the investment as Fr 4 million. At a subsequent balance sheet date, the rate had changed to $1 = 5 francs. The French subsidiary still had the investment as Fr 4 million. To the U.S. parent, however, this was now on paper worth only $800,000 (F 4,000,000 ÷ 5), a loss of $200,000 that would have to be reflected in the parent company's balance sheet. The investment was unchanged, but a *translation loss* had occurred. Likewise, an accounting gain could occur if the rate had changed instead to $1 = 3 francs. To avoid having such gains or losses distort the parent company's balance sheet, the parent may want to borrow French francs, thereby having both an asset and a liability in the foreign currency that would offset each other in a consolidated statement.

When the Mexican peso dropped so sharply in value after 1982, many U.S. corporations had to absorb translation losses in consolidating their Mexican subsidiaries into their U.S. financial statements. For example, if a U.S. company had invested $1 million in its subsidiary in 1982 when the rate was 50 pesos per dollar, it would have shown in the Mexican company as Pesos 50 million. By 1990, the exchange rate was over $1 = Pesos 2,500, which—had nothing been done in the interim—effectively reduced the value of that peso investment to $20,000. At the same time, many of the Mexican subsidiaries' borrowings were in dollars. A $1 million debt that had to be restated in pesos would have gone from Pesos 50 million to Pesos 2.5 billion on the Mexican company's balance sheet, resulting in an accounting loss. A few subsidiaries, however, had borrowed exclusively in pesos. They did not have an accounting loss, regardless of the devaluation, since their debt was in pesos.

U.S. companies in the past have been attracted to the low loan interest rates in European countries, such as Switzerland. Companies borrowed Swiss francs for five years without hedging, only to discover in that time that the value of the Swiss franc rose in relation to the dollar. After five years of interest and amortization payments, they still owed almost as many dollars as at the outset. They had reduced the Swiss francs balance, but each franc was now worth more in terms of dollars, so that the true cost of paying off the loan in terms of dollars far exceeded what they would have paid a U.S. bank.

The internationalization of production and markets combined with floating exchange rates and the explosion in foreign exchange trading activity has left corporations with a number of other problems. When a company produces goods in country A for sale in country B, movement in the exchange rate can suddenly make that product more expensive than a similar product produced locally. Or a movement in exchange rates in the other direction can mean that the company producing in country B finds imported goods are coming into that market at a cheaper price. The true production cost in each case has not changed.

The problem also exists when a manufacturer is dependent on imported raw materials or parts to manufacture its product. Exchange rate fluctuations can raise its costs, which it may not be able to recover through higher prices for its finished product. This movement in exchange rates can affect long-term investment decisions, short-term operating earnings, market share, corporate competitive advantages, and even the survival of the company.[2]

Investment Arbitrage

The growth of foreign stock and bond markets has attracted increasing worldwide interest. Sophisticated investors do not confine themselves to their own national markets but consider long-range expectations for differing currencies as part of their investment strategy. Thus, the comparative merits of particular stocks or bonds can be magnified by the foreign exchange outlook.

The rate of return for the same investment can be dramatically different for the local investor and the foreign investor. A Swiss government bond, for example, denominated in Swiss francs yielded a considerably different total return in the first half of 1990 for the Swiss investor and the U.S. investor (see figure 12.1). The latter would have converted dollars into francs for the investment and then at the end of the six months, sold the bond, and converted the principal and interest in francs back into dollars. During the period, the Swiss franc rose 8 percent against the dollar. The total return to the U.S. investor would have been 7.3 percent, while the Swiss investor had a negative return of 1.6 percent.[3]

Foreign Exchange and Global Financial Flows

Foreign exchange rates do not exist in a vacuum but are intertwined with the other elements of a nation's economy and political conditions. As seen in the example of interest rate arbitrage, any slight change in the interest or exchange rates in either country would have changed the business decisions of each of the corporate treasurers. Experiences of the United States in the last years of the 1980s demonstrate the effect of such interconnections.

Since the foreign exchange market has so many participants and so many different forces around the globe, changes can be sudden and far reaching. "Wednesday, October 14 [1987]. . . . At 8:30 a.m. the government announced that the merchandise trade deficit for August was $15.7 billion, approximately $1.5 billion above the figure expected by the financial markets. Within seconds, traders in the foreign

Figure 12.1 Long-Term Government Bonds

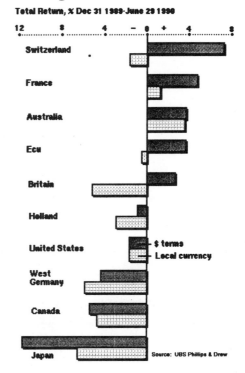

Total Return, % Dec 31 1989-June 29 1990

Reprinted with permission. *The Economist Newspaper Ltd.*, July 28, 1990.

exchange markets sold dollars in the belief that the value of
the dollar would have to fall further before the deficit could
narrow. The German deutsche mark and the Japanese yen rose
dramatically in value. Treasury bond traders, fearing that a
weakening dollar could both discourage international investment in U.S. securities and stimulate domestic inflation, sold
on the London market and on the U.S. bond market, when it
opened. The Treasury's bellwether 30-year bond began to
trade above a 10 percent yield for the first time in two years."[4]

During these years, the "globalization of financial flows
was evident to Americans in the increased purchases by foreigners of U.S. securities (both bonds and equities). That trend
has been underway for a number of years. It began picking up
in 1985, more so in 1986, and reached unprecedented levels
in 1987. On the fixed income side it had become very apparent
that foreign, particularly Japanese, investors played a vital role
in purchasing increasingly large portions of the U.S. Treasury
Bond auctions and consequently were crucial to financing the
U.S. government budget deficit."[5]

"The increased demand for funds to finance both the gaping budget deficit and growing private investment in the face of a declining private savings rate put substantial upward pressure on U.S. interest rates. Higher interest rates made investment in the United States more attractive to foreigners, increased demand for dollars to implement such investments, and thereby, pushed up the foreign exchange value of the dollar. The higher dollar, in turn, reduced U.S. international price competitiveness and contributed to the widening of the external deficit. The fiscal stimulus and downtrend in private savings also led to strong growth in U.S. domestic demand, which raised demand for imports and contributed further to the external deficit."[6]

GOVERNMENTS AND THE MARKET

Normal day-to-day trading of foreign exchange, particularly among the major industrialized countries, is generally a free market, with banks, corporations, individuals, and brokers participating. Rates are determined by the market forces of supply and demand. When the demand to buy a currency is greater than the supply of those offering to sell it, the price goes up; when there are more sellers than buyers, the rate goes down. But governments are also involved in this market, and they exert considerable influence that can drastically shape, direct, and alter the free market.

Exchange Controls

As the issuer of the national currency, the government, acting usually through the nation's central bank or treasury, will prescribe rules for the use of the national currency by both its residents and nonresidents. The objective is to execute national policies and, in periods of economic difficulty, protect the nation's foreign exchange reserves. Each country establishes rules that are generally referred to as *foreign exchange controls* or *regulations*. Foreign exchange controls are often accompanied by trade restrictions, such as tariffs or quotas.

Although often extremely complex, the function of these controls is to restrict or prevent a resident of the country from acquiring the currency of another country or to limit the use of the nation's currency when it is owned by a nonresident. For example, when a country is experiencing balance of payments difficulties, it will want to preserve the earnings from exports to be used for essential imports, such as food or raw materials. The government does this by issuing regulations, such as those listed below:

- restraining banks in the country (both national banks and branches of foreign banks) from selling foreign drafts without a government permit
- restricting banks from opening import letters of credit unless the buyer has obtained a government permit
- prohibiting local investors from investing in other countries
- limiting the amount of money a traveler may take out of the country
- requiring exporters to sell the foreign exchange they earn to the central bank rather than being able to sell it in a free market

The government can set the rate for its purchase of export proceeds and may, in fact, have multiple rates, depending on the underlying commodity. By paying a higher rate for foreign currency earned by the sale of one type of commodity over another, the government tries to diversify a country's economy from a heavy concentration on a single export, such as coffee, copper, or sugar.

Exchange controls can be imposed for political objectives to prevent a nation's businesses from doing business with certain countries or to force them to do business with political allies.

The operation of exchange controls has an administrative cost requiring a bureaucracy to administer and to police. Bankers and businesses must divert staff and time to learn and comply with the regulations. The government also has to be prepared to enforce the regulations by imposing fines or even prison sentences for violations. In some extreme situations, violations have been considered capital crimes.

Market Operations

Only some national currencies are internationally traded, when foreigners are willing, and are permitted, to hold other currencies and invoice trade transactions in them, and when they are accepted by other foreigners in payment for goods and services.

Under the post-1973 international agreements, most of those currencies do not maintain a fixed rate of exchange to other currencies, but rather their rates float. From time to time, governments may feel that the market rates are too high or too low because of temporary factors, speculations, or fears. This is not unusual in active and intense trading. The central bank will then enter the market and seek to influence the rate as a market participant, buying or selling. Because it can be the biggest participant in the market, it usually affects exchange rates, although for how long depends on whether the factors unsettling the rates are merely temporary or reflect a fundamental change in the value of a currency.

For example, if the Bank of England felt that a rate of $1.20 per pound was too low, it could enter the market as a buyer of pounds and a seller of dollars. There would then be fewer pounds, and the dollar rate would go up. Conversely, if the rate rose to $2.10 and the Bank of England decided it was too high, it could sell pounds, which would increase the supply and push the rate down.

To stabilize a market, a government central bank or treasury needs to have foreign exchange available. The United States has the Exchange Stabilization Fund for this purpose. Maintained by the Treasury, this fund was established with $2 billion of the profit created when the U.S. gold holdings were revalued from $20.67 per ounce to $35 per ounce on February 1, 1934,[7] thereby devaluing the dollar. (The U.S. quota subscription to the IMF of $1.8 billion was paid from this Fund. It has been increased over the years from subsequent revaluations of gold, interest, and net profits from government foreign exchange operations.)

Since the government is the issuer of the nation's currency, it has an unlimited supply of its own money. To obtain foreign exchange, it can use the nation's reserves of gold and other currencies. Since 1962, many governments have established standby reciprocal currency arrangements, sometimes referred to as "swap" arrangements. The Federal Reserve has 15 such arrangements (table 12.1) in addition to the Exchange Stabilization Fund. Either the Federal Reserve or the foreign central bank can request a drawing under these swap lines. The United States then credits the account of the foreign central bank with dollars and receives a credit of the foreign currency in the foreign country. Furthermore, the foreign country can draw under its subscription in the International Monetary Fund and can even borrow from foreign and domestic commercial banks. It can call on other central banks for assistance in stabilizing the foreign exchange rates. The central bank will repay the swap as soon as the markets have stabilized. If, however, a currency is perceived to be overvalued, that is, it has an exchange rate higher than its purchasing power warrants, then speculative market forces can, and will, eventually overwhelm any effort of a central bank.

Table 12.1 Federal Reserve Reciprocal Currency Arrangements (millions of dollars)

Institution	*Amount of facility* *January 31, 1990*
Austrian National Bank	250
National Bank of Belgium	1,000
Bank of Canada	2,000
National Bank of Denmark	250
Bank of England	3,000
Bank of France	2,000
German Federal Bank	6,000
Bank of Italy	3,000
Bank of Japan	5,000
Bank of Mexico	700
Netherlands Bank	500
Bank of Norway	250
Bank of Sweden	300
Swiss National Bank	4,000
Bank for International Settlements:	
Dollars against Swiss francs	600
Dollars against other authorized	
European currencies	1,250
Total	30,100

Source: *Federal Reserve Bulletin*, April 1990, p. 205.

To strengthen the ability to counter disorderly market conditions, in recent years certain central banks and finance ministers have held regular meetings and coordinated their efforts by joint interventions and policy statements that indicate what they expect the rate range to be. These joint policy statements have been attempts to influence the decisions of traders that rates should stay within certain limits, since the rapid growth of the amount of foreign exchange being traded in recent years has made it more difficult for central banks to manage rates through intervention in the market.

In 1989, "U.S. monetary authorities intervened in the exchange markets on 97 of the year's 260 business days. All of the interventions involved selling U.S. dollars against foreign currencies. Total purchases of foreign currencies amounted to $22,056 million equivalent, of which $10,926 million equivalent was Japanese yen and $11,131 million equivalent was German marks. . . . [It] recorded a net translation gain of $1,272 million on its foreign currency position as the gain on marks far exceeded a small loss on yen. At year-end, the value of the [Federal Reserve] System's gross foreign currency balances, including those warehouses for the [Exchange Stabilization Fund] was $31,333 million equivalent, predominately marks and yen."[8] Such interventions in the foreign exchange markets also affect the balance of payments. "Net official dollar purchases by [the major foreign] central banks effectively financed more than two-thirds of the $144 billion U.S. current account deficit in 1987."[9]

The central bank always has the option of allowing the free market to set the rates of exchange. The country's reserves then would not be directly involved unless other countries became unwilling to hold that currency and lost confidence in it.

For countries whose currency does not float, the government's options are limited. They tend to rely on exchange controls rather than intervention in market trading. If the currency is not freely traded, such intervention is not feasible. When governments maintain unrealistic fixed exchange rates, the economy can be severely damaged. Imports become very cheap; exports are overpriced for sale externally. Governments, such as some oil producers, can maintain this situation as long as they are willing to use the nation's reserves. In the interim, foreign-produced agriculture, for example, can be sold in the country cheaper than domestically grown agriculture—a situation that will destroy a country's ability to feed itself.

ARTIFICIAL CURRENCIES

Individual currencies fluctuate in value for many reasons, as has been seen. To reduce the impact of such changes, nations have found it advantageous to create artificial currencies for certain specific uses. These take two main forms: *baskets of currencies and clearing arrangements.*

A basket of currencies is a group of national currencies weighted in some formula. These may provide greater stability than basing transactions on just one of the national currencies.

To keep the national currencies of the countries of the European Economic Community aligned with each other to facilitate trade and payments, these countries created the *European currency unit (ECU)* in 1979. "One European currency unit (ECU) equals a pocketful of the EEC currencies. Its value is determined by taking a weighted average of the currencies of the European Monetary System (EMS). This weighting is based on each country's share of Community trade and GNP and is usually reviewed every five years."[10] (See figure 12.2.) "Central banks participating in the EMS received at the outset of the system an initial supply of ECUs against deposit of 20 percent of their gold and gross U.S. dollar reserves."[11]

The ECU is used as an official currency between the member governments to settle accounts and is part of the

Figure 12.2 Composition of the ECU

September 20, 1989

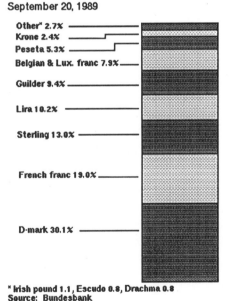

Other* 2.7%
Krone 2.4%
Peseta 5.3%
Belgian & Lux. franc 7.9%
Guilder 9.4%
Lira 10.2%
Sterling 13.0%
French franc 19.0%
D-mark 30.1%

* Irish pound 1.1, Escudo 0.8, Drachma 0.8
Source: Bundesbank

Reprinted with permission: *The Economist Newspaper, Ltd.*, September 9, 1989.

reserves of member countries. The private sector uses it to denominate Eurobonds, syndicated bank loans, and other interest-bearing financial assets, and it is traded like other currencies in spot and forward foreign exchange markets. "A private ECU deposit, for example, can be created by a bank accepting currency and recording the value of the deposit in ECUs. The bank will generally wish to cover its newly created

ECU liability by exchanging the currency deposited in a way that establishes an asset of the same value in terms of the ECU [or] the bank may exchange the currency deposited for the [individual] currencies in the ECU valuation basket in the same proportion (a process referred to as 'unbundling')."[12]

"For many market participants, it has apparently proved convenient to use the ECU to hedge against exchange rate fluctuations because the exchange rate risk of the ECU is smaller than that of any of the component currencies."[13] One of the features of S.W.I.F.T. (see chapter 5) has been to provide a daily reporting means to net ECU payments between a group of European banks. The Bank for International Settlements (see chapter 16) has established a multilateral banking clearing system in ECUs.[14]

Special Drawing Rights (SDRs) were established in 1967 by the International Monetary Fund (IMF) to alleviate what was then perceived to be a problem of inadequate international reserves. Member countries as well as some multinational official organizations agree to accept SDRs as payments and to count them in their reserves. The growth of international capital markets has reduced many of the original purposes, with SDRs now primarily used as the unit of account for all IMF transactions. The value of an SDR "is determined by the Fund each day by summing the values in U.S. dollars based on market exchange rates, of a basket of five specific currencies. The Fund's procedures require that the SDR valuation basket be revised each five years, and provide that the basket is to include the currencies of the members having the largest exports of goods and services during the five-year period." [15] The five currencies that make up the SDR (amount of each) are the U.S. dollar (.452), the Deutsche mark (.527), the French franc (1.02), the Japanese yen (33.4), and the pound sterling (.0893). The total amount of SDRs allocated by the IMF in 1989 were 21.4 billion, unchanged since 1981.

The ECU and the SDR differ in two main ways. "(i) the SDR basket contains the U.S. dollar and the Japanese yen, while the ECU basket does not but includes other currencies that are not in the SDR basket; and (ii) most of the currencies in the ECU basket are part of a mechanism designed specifically to stabilize exchange rates among the participating currencies, while the currencies in the SDR basket are generally not related by such a mechanism."[16] The German mark, French franc, and British pound sterling are in both baskets.

In addition to the needs of countries for such artificial currencies, companies with worldwide operations also have the problem of settling accounts between subsidiaries. Since many intracompany payments net out, it is usually impractical to settle each transaction by market trading. The companies or subsidiaries "could agree to trade in the dollar, the D-mark or yen, or for intracompany trade in an invented currency. Intraflora, for example, an international say-it-with-flowers company, has an internal currency, the fleurin (based on the Swiss franc and made up of 100 petals)." Other companies use the ECU. "This cuts conversion costs, since for internal trade each subsidiary is only dealing with two currencies, its own and the ECU."[17]

In an effort to keep their trade in relative balance with each other, often in conjunction with barter agreements, some countries have established clearing arrangements. Essentially these require that all trade transactions between the two countries are to be paid through special accounts in the central banks. The agreement will specify the maximum credit that can build up in each account.

For example, country A can buy goods from country B up to a certain amount. When that is reached, country A cannot buy any more until country B buys something from it. This effectively binds the two countries to trade with each other, and the trade is paid for through special accounts, not with a major currency like dollars. If country B bought goods from country A and had to pay in dollars, country A would be free to spend the dollars on purchases from country C. Country B would not be exporting and soon could run out of dollars and be unable to buy from anyone. The clearing arrangement solves this problem.

The use of such bilateral payment arrangements has been declining. One of the largest, the *Council for Mutual Economic Assistance (COMECON)*, was begun in 1949 as a multilateral trading and payment settlement group between the USSR, Bulgaria, Czechoslovakia, East Germany, Hungary, Poland, Rumania, Cuba, Mongolia, and Vietnam. The currencies of these countries were not traded outside of this sphere and all had artificial values arbitrarily assigned to them. Trade between these countries was conducted only through this system. COMECON was virtually dead by 1990 as Eastern European countries sought to trade directly with Western Europe and had to convert to realistic market payments systems. The artificial valuation of currencies in such clearing arrangements was evident in the experience of East Germany. While officially the ostmark was at parity with the deutsche mark, it was trading in the free market in late 1989 at 6:1. Upon the monetary union with West Germany, literally overnight on July 1, 1990, an arbitrary conversion value was set supported by the economic strength of West Germany, which agreed to accept East German marks in exchange for deutsche marks at 2:1, except for the first 2,000-6,000, which converted at 1:1. This was as much a politically determined exchange rate as an economic one. For the other countries of Eastern Europe, the only way they could obtain western currencies was through exports, loans, or investments.

ACCOUNTING

Foreign exchange contracts are reflected in a bank's balance sheet as contingent accounts. The risk-based guidelines specify that outstanding contracts be included in calculating the capital ratio. Contracts of less than 14 days are excluded. The remaining ones are then revalued based on the current market price. This is added to a factor for potential credit exposure increases by multiplying the total notional value of the contracts by one of the following credit conversion factors: remaining maturity of one year or less, 1 percent; over one year, 5 percent. Contracts with the same party can be netted out under certain conditions.

SUMMARY

Because the volume of money flows has expanded in recent years, and rates have been allowed to float, exchange rates have been volatile. Although both would be reluctant to admit it, governments and businesses have an important stake in stabilized rates. For businesses, the need for stability naturally leads to hedging foreign exchange exposure. Even though it usually has a cost, hedging is the best option for a business to know what its exposure and return is going to be. Governments likewise need stable rates to discourage the unsettling effect that speculation can have on a currency.

QUESTIONS

1. What is the impact of exchange rate changes on exporters?
2. What are exchange controls and why are they used?
3. What is an ECU?
4. Why does interest rate arbitrage occur?

PROBLEM

You are a U.S. corporate treasurer. You have $10 million to invest for the next 90 days, after which you will need the dollars to pay the quarterly dividend. Examine the foreign exchange and U.S. Treasury bill rates in the newspaper or the *Wall Street Journal.* Consider the Japanese yen and the German deutsche mark. If you were to invest in a 90-day government bill in each of these countries on a hedged basis

1) how much would you gain or lose in the swap?
2) what would the yield on the foreign government bill need to be to make it more attractive to you than investing in a U.S. T-bill?

Your objective is the highest rate of return fully hedged between these government-backed investments.

Notes

1. Thibaut de Saint Phalle, *Trade, Inflation, and the Dollar* (New York: Oxford University Press, 1981), p. 131.

2. See Donald R. Lessard and John B. Lighstone, "Volative Exchange Rates Can Put Operations at Risk," *Harvard Business Review,* July-August 1986, pp. 107-114.

3. *The Economist,* July 28, 1990, p. 84.

4. Report of The Presidential Task Force on Market Mechanisms ("The Brady Commission"), January 1988, p. 15.

5. *Ibid.,* Study I, p. 1.

6. Federal Reserve Bulletin, March 1990, p. 126. Statement by Federal Reserve Board Chairman Greenspan to U. S. House of Representatives, January 25, 1990.

7. Milton Friedman and Anna Jacobson Schwartz, *A Monetary History of the United States, 1867-1960* (Princeton, N.J.: Princeton University Press, 1963), p. 471.

8. Board of Governors of the Federal Reserve System, *Annual Report* 1989, p. 25.

9. B. Dianne Pauls, "U.S. Exchange Rate Policy: Bretton Woods to Present." *Federal Reserve Bulletin*, November 1990, p. 907.

10. *The Economist.* September 9, 1989, p. 120.

11. David Folkerts-Landau and Donald J. Mathieson, "The European Monetary System in the context of the Integration of European Financial Markets." Occasional Paper No. 66 (Washington, D.C.: International Monetary Fund, 1989), p. 3.

12. International Monetary Fund, "The Role of the SDR in the International Monetary System." Occasional Paper No. 51 (Washington, D.C: International Monetary Fund, 1987), p. 36.

13. Folkerts-Landau, *op. cit.*, p. 18.

14. *Ibid.*

15. *Annual Report*, International Monetary Fund 1989, p. 119.

16. International Monetary Fund, *op. cit.*, pp. 30-31.

17. *The Economist*, January 13, 1990, p. 76.

13

Principles of International Credit

"If we don't take risks, then we're not real bankers."
—*The Money Lenders*

Banks' main source of profit comes from extending credit. Few other activities of the international department produce substantial net income after expenses. The bank engaging in international finance extends credit as an adjunct to international banking and to service local customers and correspondent banks. The United States makes its greatest contribution to international finance by providing credit facilities to stimulate worldwide trade and development.

The principles of international and domestic credit are the same; however, the international banker's customers are quite different: importers or exporters who need to finance international trade; correspondent banks that need to finance their customers in international trade and for local economic development; multinational businesses that want to build manufacturing plants, open mines, and control interest and foreign exchange rate exposures; and foreign governments that need to facilitate all of these.

A bank may extend credit by furnishing funds to a borrower using deposits placed with the bank, borrowed funds, or its capital; depositing funds with a correspondent bank; entering into a contract on behalf of its customer to supply funds at a future date; or committing to repay another lender if the customer does not. In all cases, the bank has a *credit risk* and will incur a financial loss if the borrower cannot or does not repay when expected to do so.

This chapter examines how banks extend credit internationally. The objectives of this chapter are to
- examine the fundamentals of international credit analysis
- detail the types of credit
- outline the special factors in making international loans
- examine the application of the risk-based capital guidelines to international credit

---

FUNDAMENTALS OF CREDIT

When a bank extends credit, it contemplates the riskless rental of money. But few bank loans are completely without risk. Thus, bank lending officers must assess the degree of risk in each application and, exercising prudence, should not make any loan if repayment seems unlikely. Bank lending officers must constantly remember they are lending depositors' and stockholders' money. A banker lending money differs from an investor who uses his or her own funds. If the business fails, both will lose their money. However, if a business succeeds, the investor can expect great profit from dividends and appreciation in the equity value. The bank, on the other hand, can only expect repayment of the loan and a stated amount of interest earned. Thus, credit risk and equity risk offer different rewards.

Arriving at a credit judgment involves gathering and analyzing certain facts and making a decision based on those facts. The first step in considering an application from a customer for credit, then, is to determine answers to four basic questions:

1. *How much money do you want?*

   This question sets the framework for the entire credit consideration. The lending officer can begin to determine how much thought potential borrowers have given to their proposal. Surprisingly, many applicants do not have a clear idea of exactly how much money they need. Vagueness on this point is often a prelude to more confusion as the loan discussion continues.

2. *What do you want the money for?*

   A bank will provide credit for worthwhile or productive purposes, such as financing imports and exports, the production or growing of goods that will enter into international trade, or the development of foreign economies to increase the market for imports and exports through establishment of new manufacturing plants.

3. *How long do you want the money for?*

The term of the requested financing should bear a relationship to the purpose of the loan. For example, an importer of toys for the Christmas season should expect to repay the loan quickly. The importer needs financing to cover the time of shipment from the foreign manufacturer, time to sell it, and time to give customary credit terms to the store buyer through the Christmas selling period. This calls for a letter of credit and financing to last up to six months. A request for financing to build a new manufacturing plant, however, would normally require an extension of credit lasting several years. Generally, the international department does not engage in foreign mortgage financing. In recent years, banks have been willing to make international loans for as long as 10 years, but the general preference is up to 7 years.

4. *How will you pay the money back?*

The source of repayment for the imported toys would come from their sale. This illustrates self-liquidating financing, an important characteristic of letters of credit. The financing for the movement of goods that will ultimately be sold to another party is repaid from the proceeds of the sale. The financing is *short term* (less than one year). Repayment for *long-term* loans (more than one year) for purposes such as factory expansion is often based on the increased production capacity of the enlarged plant. This increased production is expected to lead to increased sales, and hence larger profits. The revenue from these sales represents a part of the company's cash flow.

Financial Risk

Once these basic questions have been answered, the international lending officer will ask for additional information to clarify the loan request. The international lending officer, like the domestic lending officer, analyzes and evaluates the factors commonly known in the United States as the three Cs of credit: character, capacity, and capital. In other words, the lending officer evaluates the integrity of the borrower, the borrower's ability to repay, and the soundness of the borrower's financial position.

In developing information about a borrower's character, the lending officer is seeking to determine whether the applicant is a serious individual or company that will recognize debts as obligations and make every effort to honor these obligations despite possible adverse developments; whether the borrower is experienced in the business; and whether there is a demonstrated capability to run the business profitably. The basis for character evaluation includes the lending bank's own experience with the borrower, other banks' experiences, and the borrower's business reputation. When the borrower is a company, the character of management is evaluated. Companies such as Dun and Bradstreet in the United States provide some data on businesses.

The international department, however, deals not only with local importers and exporters, about whom it is relatively easy to obtain such information, but also with foreign borrowers, including banks, corporations, and individuals. It is often more difficult to obtain detailed credit checks from foreign sources. However, banks around the world customarily share with other banks their lending experiences with particular customers on a confidential basis.

A bank establishes a credit file for each borrower. This file contains a complete history of its credit experiences with that customer. By studying this file, the loan officer can assess the bank's past relationship with the borrower, have a record of the financial statements and previous borrowings, and determine how well the customer has adhered to the terms and conditions of previous loans, including repaying on time. The international department maintains credit files primarily for its own use, but these files can also furnish clients with credit information about prospective purchasers abroad. This information in summary form is available only in accordance with certain well-established customs and on a confidential basis.

To evaluate capacity and capital, the banker asks for the customer's financial statement, which is "a written record of a firm's financial position at a point in time, as well as that firm's performance over a period of time. Financial statements include an income statement, balance sheet, and statements of cash flow."[1] The balance sheet is a snapshot showing the financial position of the company on a given day; the income, or profit-and-loss, statement is a history showing the earnings for the year or over some other period. Ideally, these documents should be prepared and signed by independent auditors. The banker wants to see these statements for the past three years and for the same day of the year in order to analyze the financial trends. Although such statements are usually easily obtainable from U.S. clients, they are often not so readily available from foreign clients; their format varies from country to country, and they are often not audited. Customarily, the financial statement reflects the company's situation as of the end of its business year. This year-end statement may be December 31 or whatever date the company designates as its fiscal year. Some industries—for example, department stores—find that December 31 is not a suitable date as they have not yet concluded their major selling season. For department stores, a date such as the end of February is usually better, since by that time they have received payment for the Christmas purchases. Whatever the date, the banker wants to see the condition of the company at the same time each year.

By comparing various items on the balance sheet, the banker can make certain conclusions about the operation of the firm. Comparison of the balance sheet over several years may reveal a trend. In the United States, comparison of these figures on an industrywide basis may be possible, as specialized firms summarize such figures from time to time. Comparable figures are less available outside the United States.

The banker must also be aware of the way this information has been prepared. The company keeps its financial accounts on a daily basis during the year. At regular intervals, perhaps monthly, it will prepare a summary, which is called a statement. For the year-end, the company may hire an independent firm of auditors to verify the company-prepared statement. These auditors or accountants will examine the records, verify parts of them by making certain tests, and compare the company's procedures and allocations with what are known as generally accepted practices. Such practices vary from country to country. In the United States, this may mean the interpretations and practices as set forth by accounting industry groups. At the end of the audit, the accountants state in writing what they have looked at and give an opinion of the accuracy of the company's financial statement. The banker should read this opinion very carefully to know how much the independent auditor agrees or disagrees with the company's numbers.[2]

For international businesses with subsidiaries in many countries, the banker wants to have financial statements from all subsidiaries as of the same date in order to interpret the global operations. This may be difficult when accounting practices in different countries have different annual close-off dates. Sometimes the company may deliberately attempt to confuse the banker about intersubsidiary transactions.

Figure 13.1 Balance Sheet

NEW FRONTIER MANUFACTURING COMPANY
Balance Sheet
December 31, 19XX

Cash	$ 525
Accounts receivable	2,625
Raw materials	1,920
Finished goods	4,260
Total current assets	$ 9,330
Fixed assets	$ 8,240
Accumulated depreciation	(3,490)
Net fixed assets	$ 4,750
Other assets	1,280
Total assets	$15,360
Accounts payable	$ 700
Notes payable	3,030
Accrued liabilities	1,490
Accrued taxes	250
Total current liabilities	$ 5,470
Long-term debt	3,500
Preferred stock	1,000
Common stock	3,500
Earned surplus	1,890
Total liabilities and net worth	$15,360

Currency Risk

Although the fundamentals of credit are the same, an international loan is different from a domestic one. The international loan officer must also evaluate the risks of lending in other countries before making a decision. In all international lending, someone has a currency conversion exposure.

U.S. commercial banks usually prefer to grant loans to foreign borrowers in U.S. dollars. The bank wants to be repaid in dollars, thereby avoiding exposure to changes in the rate of exchange. If the proceeds of the loan are used in the borrower's own country or in a third country, the borrower will convert the loan money into local or some other currency. Even when financing imports from the United States, the borrower sells these goods in another country and receives payment in the currency of that country. While the borrower may be successful in selling the imported goods and have the local currency to pay the U.S. bank, the country may not have the dollars available to sell. Thus, a borrower is at the mercy of the central bank of the country and may be unable to repay in dollars.

When considering a loan, the bank not only must assess the current position of the borrower's country with regard to international liquidity but also must anticipate what this position may be when the loan matures. The possibilities of devaluation in times of financial and political stress must be considered. The impact of devaluation can be severe. For example, since the mid-1970s borrowers in Mexico have regularly obtained loans from U.S. banks and converted the U.S. dollars into Mexican pesos at the prevailing rate of exchange. If they obtained the loan at the rate of 50 pesos for each dollar, when the Mexican government devalued the peso to 2,500 pesos to a dollar, the Mexican borrower had to have 2,500 pesos to buy one dollar to repay the debt. In late 1982, the Mexican government virtually ran out of dollars, and for some periods Mexican borrowers were unable to obtain dollars from their bank, even though they had the pesos to repay.

In some countries, the borrower must obtain approval from local foreign exchange control authorities to borrow abroad and also obtain permission to pay interest on the loan and repay the principal at maturity. Such requirements arise from that nation's effort to control foreign expenditures as part of a program to improve its balance of payments.

Country Risk

Country risk is an expression that endeavors to cover all the risks other than credit that a bank has in making loans to a borrower in another country. Such risks include the currency risk just mentioned and also the risk that economic or political conditions in the borrower's country might change to such an extent that it would jeopardize the borrower's ability to repay the loan or even to survive as a business.

Some European countries, such as Great Britain, Sweden, and Switzerland, have had stable governments and political systems for centuries. Other countries have governments that rest on the tenuous support of the electorate. Numerous new countries in Africa and Asia have no national history or political tradition at all. Hence the international loan officer, although satisfied with the credit risk and the currency risk, must examine many other factors that affect the prospective borrower's ability to repay the loan. Will the customer be in business if the foreign government changes? What are the prospects of nationalization or expropriation of the customer's business? Is the borrower's country likely to find itself at war with one of its neighbors?

Even if the political situation remains stable, governments may change laws or taxation procedures that could seriously affect the borrower's ability to repay. It is obviously impossible for the banker to predict the future, but a thorough understanding of the borrower's country can alert the banker to potential risks. For further consideration of country risk, see chapter 3.

STRUCTURING OF CREDIT

Thus far, the terms *credit* and *loan* have been used interchangeably. The lending officer must be careful to evaluate the credit risk separately from the means of funding the loan. Credit is credit; funding is funding—and the experienced loan officer does not mix up the two. Whether an extension of credit is to be funded by the use of domestic dollars (that is, from the bank's own pool of deposits), Eurodollars, a standby letter of credit, bankers' acceptance, foreign currency, or any other means, the bank has the same credit risk. If the bank's borrower does not pay, the bank may suffer an actual loss of money. The rate or fee must compensate the bank for its risk.

Interest Rate

A loan made in dollars can be funded with either domestic dollars or Eurodollars. For loans that will be funded domestically, each bank establishes its own *prime rate*. The prime rate is a commonly used reference rate established by the bank for pricing loans. Each bank's prime rate is set at a level that covers the bank's cost of funds, its operating expenses, and a margin of profit. The cost of funds recognizes that interest is paid to depositors on time deposits; commercial accounts have certain maintenance costs seldom fully recoverable through service charges. Banks must hold minimum reserves against deposits in the form of interest-free deposits at their Federal Reserve bank for their domestic office deposits. Banks also pay an insurance premium for those deposits at domestic offices that are insured by the Federal Deposit Insurance Corporation.

The degree of risk assumed by the bank must be reflected and compensated for in the rate of interest: the higher the risk, the higher the rate. A longer-term loan will add to the risk. To attempt to compensate for added risks, the bank will add a margin over its prime rate. No precise mathematical computation determines how these elements can be evaluated and an interest rate charged. Rather, the rate is established by the judgment and experience of the lending officer and the bank. They must also be aware of rates offered by competing lenders in the market. An interest rate for a loan will be quoted as "our prime rate + x percent p.a." When the bank changes its prime rate and the interest rate on the loan also changes, it is known as a *floating rate*. Or banks may quote a *fixed interest* rate, which does not change during the life of the loan regardless of any change in the bank's prime. Because of the volatility of the cost of funds to the bank in recent years, the trend has been to quote floating rates on most international loans.

The second means of funding a dollar loan is with Eurodollars (see chapter 15). Such loans are traditionally quoted as "LIBOR + x percent p.a." *LIBOR*, the acronym for London interbank offered rate, is the interest cost to the bank to obtain a deposit in this market. The bank borrows Eurodollars, pays the LIBOR rate, and then lends these dollars to its customer. Eurodollars are time deposits; thus, for a term loan the bank will usually borrow Eurodollars for six months at a time at LIBOR and then replace it with another deposit for successive six-month increments. The borrower's interest rate is fixed for each six months and will change according to what LIBOR is at each renewal of the deposit.

It is important to note the substantial difference in earnings to the bank in an interest rate quoted as "prime + x percent p.a." and "LIBOR + x percent p.a." A prime rate has built into it the cost of funds to the bank plus something to cover the bank's overhead plus something to provide the bank with a return on its equity. LIBOR is solely the cost of funds. Thus, the increment charged over LIBOR, usually referred to as the *spread*, provides the only source of earnings to the bank. From this, the bank must pay its expenses, earn a profit, and be compensated for the credit risk.

Bankers may price loans as a spread above the interest rate paid on certificates of deposit (CDs) in the United States. This reflects the current domestic money market rates with greater sensitivity than a bank's prime rate. It is often used to compete with the rate a multinational company can obtain by issuing commercial paper.

When the means of extending credit is a letter of credit or bankers' acceptance, the bank quotes a rate, often inaccurately referred to as a commission, to compensate the bank for the credit risk in the transaction. The bank may make other charges, such as commitment fees, structuring fees, and so forth as part of its overall compensation.

Secured and Unsecured Financing

A loan may be either *secured* or *unsecured*. In granting an unsecured loan, the bank relies solely on the financial strength and reputation of the borrower. The financing is based on the signing of a note or other debt instrument. In secured financing, the bank requires not only the financial and moral integrity of the borrower and the signing of the note, but also possession of, or title to, outside value as protection. For example, the borrower may have marketable securities in negotiable form pledged to the bank. The bank could sell these if repayment for the financing does not come from the transaction itself. Internationally, the title to marketable goods in warehouses, and the title to goods moving in trade under a letter of credit are examples of collateral or security (sometimes referred to as the fourth C of credit).

Such collateral provides additional protection for the bank and reduces its risk in the transaction, which may result in it being willing to charge a lower interest rate. In marginal cases, a bank will lend only if collateral is pledged, but a bank should never lend solely on the basis of collateral. Collateral values—other than cash deposits in the currency of the loan—change. The values of securities and commodities change, based on the supply and demand expressed in the market price. The value of fixed assets (like buildings) and capital goods (such as airplanes and ships) may change as a result of the demand for their use. The cost of building a vessel, for example, may not be the price that a buyer would pay. The value of the vessel is based on the amount of cash flow its use will bring. In recent years, the substantial oversupply of ships, which resulted in low shipping rates, also resulted in declining collateral value of the ships. Buyers were willing to purchase them only at a price that would enable owners to earn profits at prevailing shipping rates.

To illustrate, in 1986 a second-hand bulk cargo carrier of 26,000 dwt could be bought for $1.4 million. "If the owner can play the spot market well, at a charter rate of about $3,250 a day and operating costs of just over $2,000 a day, he should be able to pay off interest and principal over a three-year period and have the scrap value ... for his profit."[3] Regardless of what the original cost of the vessel was, or what the book value was, or what value the banker had originally put on the vessel, this reality will determine what the vessel now should be worth as collateral for the banker.

The amount that can be realized by the sale of collateral will be affected by many factors, such as its location. A paper mill, for example, is not easily moved. Its value to buyers in another country will be restricted to those who wish to own a mill in that particular location. The value of such fixed-asset collateral is also affected by the political stability of the country in which it is located, availability of raw materials supply, proximity of competitors, and general business outlook for the product. If the borrower was unable to make a profit operating a manufacturing plant in a particular location, the banker has to consider whether it was due to other problems of the borrower or inherent problems in the plant itself. If the latter, then the realized value can be adversely affected. Poorly located oil refineries, for example, have attracted little interest even in times of high demand.

Guarantor

In some instances, the banker may not consider it prudent to lend to a potential borrower solely on the basis of that borrower's financial strength, which may be inadequate, and the borrower may not have any collateral to pledge. Another person or corporation, however, may be willing to guarantee repayment to the bank in the event of the borrower's nonpayment. This other party serves as *guarantor*, and the banker makes the credit decision by evaluating the capacity, character, and capital of the guarantor. Requiring a guarantor is common in new businesses, because the owners or parent companies may be willing to provide a guarantee to enable the new company to obtain the bank financing it needs. International lenders may ask a foreign government to guarantee the borrowings of the government's development agencies or a parent company to guarantee the debt of an overseas subsidiary.

Depending on the laws of the country, this guarantee may be evidenced by a separate document, an endorsement, or *aval*. The aval is accepted in some countries (not the United States) and by signatories to the Geneva Convention on Negotiable Instruments. It permits the guarantor to sign on the promissory note with the statement *por aval* or *bon pour aval* and be legally bound as the guarantor of that document.

In international transactions, the country risk of the guarantor must be specifically considered. If the guarantor is in the same country as the borrower, then the same country risks associated with the borrower will apply to the guarantor. However, if the guarantor is in another country, as when a parent company in an industrialized country guarantees the bank's credit to a subsidiary in a developing country, then the bank will base its decision on the country risk of the guarantor. This may change an otherwise unfavorable assessment of the borrowing request. The bank must always consider how it could enforce any guarantee in the laws of the guarantor's country. It is not an automatic process, and a guarantor may have many legal means of delaying its obligation if called upon to pay.

Lines of Credit

Many customers of an international department have a series of transactions to be financed over a period of time. For these customers, the establishment of a *line of credit* is more suitable than a one-time loan. Importers, for example, need to have letters of credit established regularly as they make purchases; foreign banks need lines of credit for confirmation of letters of credit and other short-term financing of international trade. The bank determines the maximum amount of credit outstanding at any one time it will allow that customer. Then it grants a revolving line of credit that permits the importer to request any number of individual transactions within the credit limit. As transactions mature and are paid, the cycle may recur. Such an arrangement enables the bank to serve the customer more quickly and easily.

Term Loan

A loan with a maturity greater than one year is generally referred to as a *term loan*. A term loan may be for construction of a new plant when the borrower is not expected to begin repayment until after a long period of construction. In term loans, the bank establishes a schedule of *drawdowns* (disbursements) and a definite schedule of repayment. The preferred system of repayment is by installments, as the new stream of income is generated, rather than by a large single payment at the end of the term. Multinational corporations and governments typically request term loans.

The lending bank often expects to receive a fee between the time the bank has committed itself to provide the financing and when the actual drawdowns are made, at which time the bank begins to earn interest. This is a *commitment fee*. Interest accrues from the time each drawdown takes place. In some cases, the customer will request that the schedule for repayment of principal begin upon completion of construction, for example. A delay of this kind is referred to as a *grace period*.

TYPES OF FINANCING

The lending officer may extend credit in several ways. The purpose and the type of transaction often govern the method of financing. Some of the techniques are also used in domestic banking, but others are special to the international department. The nature of the transaction usually determines the selection of the debt instrument. If several means exist, the customer may indicate the choice.

Direct Loan

A promissory note is the most commonly used borrowing instrument in banking. The borrower signs a note, acknowledging receipt of the money and making a commitment to repay this money with interest. The note may provide for interest to be paid at stated intervals—for example, quarterly between the time of disbursement and the date of maturity. Similarly, repayment of principal may be due in installments or in full on a stated date. Generally, banks allow full repayment in one installment at the end of a specific period only for loans of a year or less.

When a borrower is in a foreign country, the bank must be certain that the promissory note is in a form enforceable not only in U.S. courts but also in a court in the borrower's country. Sometimes the promissory note must be bilingual, and a bank active in such types of financing should have legal counsel. Some banks assume that, because such financing occurs in the United States, they can use basic domestic note forms. If the foreign borrower has no U.S. assets, however, a judgment obtained in a U.S. court may not be enforceable.

Trade Financing

An exporter's objective is to be paid promptly in cash for the full amount of its sale. In many instances, an importer is unable to do this because of constraints on its own cash flow or conditions in its country, or it may be offered delayed payment terms by other sellers that are competing to make the sale. The exporter then must decide what alternatives it is prepared to accept to make the sale. If there is a large demand for its product, the exporter may be able to find other buyers that can pay cash, or it may be able to insist that the buyer obtain bank financing and pay the exporter promptly. Otherwise, the exporter will examine the means of payment the buyer can offer and then decide whether to accept them. The following are some of the alternatives.

The importer wants to pay at a future date. It expects to generate the cash by selling the merchandise before paying the exporter.

For example, a U.S. seller shipping on a collection draws a draft on the foreign importer due 90 days after sight. The documents are released upon acceptance of the draft by the importer, who commits to pay 90 days from the date of acceptance. (The draft has become a trade acceptance for which the exporter expects to receive the full amount at its maturity in 90 days.) If the exporter wants funds before then, the bank can assist by discounting the trade acceptance with recourse to the exporter. The exporter receives less than the full face amount, and the bank will present the trade acceptance to the importer for full payment in 90 days. The differential is the bank's income for the financing. If the trade acceptance is not paid by the importer, the exporter will be expected to pay the bank and then seek repayment from the importer. The bank's decision to discount will depend on its analysis of the credit capacity of the exporter. If the bank will rely solely on the credit capacity of the importer, the bank may discount the trade acceptance *without recourse*. In this case, if the importer does not pay, the exporter has no obligation to repay the bank.

If the importer can obtain a guarantee from a government export agency or commercial bank on this trade acceptance or similar obligation to pay, the exporter can then sell the debt a *forfait* (a French commercial term meaning "outright" or "by contract," which has become anglicized to "forfaiting"). This is a means of financing that grew up in Europe originally for financing East-West trade and is available in the United States by means of specialized finance companies and banks that buy trade obligations of importers at a discount without recourse to the exporter. The financing entity is relying on the credit strength and country risk of the guarantor. The guarantor is usually better known and financially stronger than the importer, which makes financing easier to obtain than relying only on the credit strength of the importer. This guarantee is often evidenced by endorsing the note by aval. "Although it may be used for all export transactions, in practice it has been applied mainly to exports of capital goods with credit terms of five to seven years maturity."[4]

When the importer opens a U. S. dollar usance letter of credit, the exporter will receive a bankers' acceptance (chapter 10) after presenting the specified documents evidencing shipment. The exporter can discount this immediately and be paid. The importer normally will not have to pay the bank until the bankers' acceptance matures. If it is a deferred payment letter of credit, the exporter will be paid by the issuing bank at specified future dates when the buyer also pays the bank, although in some circumstances arrangements can be made by the seller to discount these payments before the due date with a third party.

The importer cannot pay in money. There are many situations today in which an importer cannot obtain any, or can obtain only a part, of the foreign exchange from its government in order to pay for the purchase. This usually occurs when a country has a balance of payments problem, but it may also develop when a government wishes to force the sale of some of its country's goods that might otherwise not be easily sold internationally.

The exporter will be told that the sale can be made only if it agrees to accept merchandise as payment or if it commits to purchase merchandise at a future date. These compensatory trade arrangements are referred to as *countertrade.* The exporter will receive merchandise in payment, which he or she must then sell in some other country for cash. This may not be simple and can result in delays. The price ultimately received will, in effect, be the payment for the original sale.

Some countries require that trade between themselves or within a bloc of countries be balanced. An exporter may find that its ability to make an export sale will depend on the other country having made sales in the exporter's country. These are referred to as *clearing agreements.* The exporter is paid in its own currency from a "clearing account" by its own government.

The exporter may need to obtain the financing itself. This can be done by utilizing the programs offered by its country through a government export agency (chapter 16). Many countries have these agencies to encourage and promote exports that provide employment and income to the nation. In addition, the exporter may ask its bank to provide financing to the buyer. When the bank does this, it will then consider the buyer as its borrower and make its credit decision based on the creditworthiness of the buyer. If this is not sufficient, then the bank may require a partial or full guarantee from the exporter.

Financing by overdrawing a commercial account is a customary means of extending credit to a customer in many foreign banks. Both custom and law make this method unacceptable in the United States. Therefore, to provide flexibility of financing in a manner comparable to that provided abroad, a bank may enter into an agreement with a customer that, from time to time when the customer requests funds for certain purposes, the bank will make the disbursement without any promissory note. The client's obligation to repay is contained in the agreement. In this way each disbursement retains its identity without the customer's having to prepare a promissory note each time.

Chapers 8 and 9 explain the use of letters of credit, while chapter 10 deals with the use of bankers' acceptances. An experienced bank lending officer knows that there is virtually no substitute for either.

Syndicate Loans

When a borrower seeks a large loan, a single bank may be unwilling or unable, because of its lending limits, to make the entire loan itself, even though the proposal is sound. To make the loan, a bank may seek to attract other banks to make the loan jointly as a *syndicate* (figure 13.2). Each bank determines whether the proposal is creditworthy and how much it is willing to lend.

The basic principle behind syndicating loans is diversification of the loan portfolio—spreading the risks. As one banker has described it, "There's never anything so good. . . that we want to have a hundred percent of it."[5] The size of a single transaction or the total number of transactions from the same borrower may have grown so large that banks feel it is almost a necessity to syndicate most large loan requests considering their impact on each bank's legal lending limit.

One bank or a small group of banks is given the mandate by the borrower to raise the funds and serves as the syndicate manager to locate enough banks to make the loan. This lead bank may bring in other banks to be co-managers. This is partly in recognition of their willingness to take a large portion of the loan and partly to gain expert help in the long, sometimes tedious, process of convincing a number of banks to join the syndicate, negotiating the details, and providing the documentation. The lead bank will be paid a fee by the borrower, and the bank may offer a portion of the managing fee to other banks to become co-managers. Syndicates are composed of both U.S. and foreign

Figure 13.2 Loan Syndication Tombstone

This announcement appears as a matter of record only. September 1982.

Bougainville Copper Limited
Papua New Guinea

US$225,000,000
Revolving Credit Facility

Managed by
· ·

BA Asia Limited
Commonwealth Trading Bank of Australia

Provided by
· ·

Bank of America NT&SA
Commonwealth Trading Bank of Australia
The Chase Manhattan Bank, N.A.
Dresdner (South East Asia) Limited
International Westminster Bank PLC
Amsterdam-Rotterdam Bank N.V.
Australia and New Zealand Banking Group Limited
     Singapore
Bank of New South Wales (PNG) Ltd.
     Port Moresby Papua New Guinea
Bank of New South Wales Singapore Branch
Barclays Bank International Limited
The Hongkong and Shanghai Banking Corporation
The Mitsubishi Bank, Limited
Mellon Bank N.A. Hong Kong Branch
SFE Banking Corporation Limited SFE Group
Australian European Finance Corporation NV
MAIBL Bermuda (Far East) Limited
Mitsui Finance Asia Limited
Papua New Guinea Banking Corporation
Toronto Dominion Bank
Union Bank of Switzerland

Agent
BA ASIA LIMITED

banks. Since many foreign banks do not have a source of U. S.-based dollars, syndicates are usually funded in Eurodollars. The borrower and all participating banks write and sign the loan agreement. One of the managing banks is the *agent* and assumes the responsibility for coordinating disbursements, repayments, and dissemination of other documents such as financial statements and progress reports. The syndicate manager has many responsibilities to the participating banks. Basically the manager must represent the borrower to the group of lenders and represent the lenders to the borrower.

Many smaller banks have come into syndicated loans. These banks provide an added source of funds and broaden many syndicates. In exchange they earn the interest, have a chance to diversify their loan portfolio, have an opportunity to meet the senior officers of the borrower, or in the case of a foreign government as borrower, to meet the senior financial ministers. This is usually done at athe loan closing, which customarily is an elaborate event and banquet. The participating banks will all be listed in the ads in the financial press announcing the loan (usually referred to as *tombstones*). Thus, even the smallest participating bank will be identified as being an international bank, which may attract new business for that bank. The smallest bank in a syndicate must, however, recognize that it has to evaluate the credit risk for itself, since a foreign government borrower seeking to reschedule its repayment in times of trouble presents the same problem to the small bank as to the large bank.

Leasing

Leasing is a common method of financing in the United States, but has limited use in many other countries. In a typical leasing transaction, the bank, either directly or through a special subsidiary, purchases a piece of equipment, such as a machine. The borrower enters into an agreement with the bank to lease this machine for a stated number of months and to pay the bank a certain sum each month as rent. At the end of the term the customer may have the option of buying the machine for the remaining depreciated value.

An advantage of leasing for a customer in some countries is that the entire monthly payment may be treated as an expense for tax purposes. If the customer had purchased the machinery directly or had obtained a bank loan, only a portion of each monthly payment would be a taxable expense. The bank's advantage in a lease is that, as the owner of the equipment, it is entitled to all the depreciation and investment tax credits in computing its overall taxes. These are *direct leases*. A *leveraged lease* is basically the same, except that the bank locates other investors to become joint owners of the equipment and receives, in turn, a pro rata share of the tax benefits.

Documentation

The bank protects itself by having the borrower sign certain bank legal documents. In these documents, the borrower acknowledges receipt of the funds and makes a commitment to repay them. In addition, the borrower provides the bank with the means of recourse if repayment does not occur. When the loan is large and other lenders are involved, such documentation may be extensive and include controls on the borrower while the debt is owed as a means of protecting the bank.

For syndicate loans the principal legal document is a loan agreement. This document may be very long and detailed. It must be legally enforceable in the borrower's country, and this may require special knowledge of the laws of different countries. Besides serving to commit the borrower to repay, the loan agreement should remove any confusion between the borrower and the lender or among the lenders about the procedures of disbursement and repayment. The document provides definition of relevant procedures and terms. Most loan agreements now provide details of what violations of the agreement constitute a *default* by the borrower as well as cross-default provisions. A *cross-default* provision means that if the borrower defaults on any other loan, this loan becomes immediately due and payable. This protects the bank by giving it equal standing with any other lenders. The loan agreement also requires the borrower to submit interim financial and operating reports. Thus, the lender can detect any adverse development at an early stage.

Although loan agreements in international syndicate loans greatly depend on work by lawyers, the banker must ensure that the document reflects banking needs. The banker, not the lawyer, makes credit or business decisions.

Managing the Credit

The decision to extend credit is only half of the banker's task. Equally important is to see that the credit is repaid. The banker's responsibility does not end until final repayment has been made. This means that the banker must stay involved with the customer during the disbursement of the credit, in the course of its utilization, and as the borrower's business is conducted.

During the actual disbursement of the loan, the banker will monitor that the funds are being delivered to the borrower in accordance with the agreed use. In the case of a term loan, the funds may be released as certain stages in the construction are reached. In a trade financing, the credit may go through a series of transactions as the goods move. It is the banker's responsibility to know what is happening.

The banker needs to stay informed about the financial condition of the borrower and to be alert to warning signs that the borrower may be encountering unanticipated difficulties. These can show up in such things as late payments of interest or principal installments, information from trade sources of other slow payments, or further unexpected requests for short-term financing. The experienced banker knows that it is important to be aware of developing problems and to discuss these with the borrower as soon as possible, since early attention can often prevent major problems that could later lead to a loan loss.

When a borrower is unable to repay, the banker can anticipate spending considerable time and effort to assess what has caused the borrower's difficulties, what can be done to correct these problems, and what must be done to protect the bank's commitment and avoid a loss. This is equally true whether the borrower is a company or a country. Often this must be done in conjunction with other banks that have also lent money to the borrower as part of a creditors' committee. Working out problem loans is not an easy task, and it requires all the skills and experience of the banker.

ACCOUNTING

Loans are assets in the bank's balance sheet regardless of how they are funded. Loan commitments are contingent accounts until a drawdown occurs, then the amount of the drawdown is reduced from the contingent account and becomes a loan asset.

Before the effective date of risk-based capital guidelines, all international loans are given the same weight in calculating the primary capital-to-asset ratio. However, the risk-based capital guidelines change this and different risk weightings are applied depending on the borrower, guarantor, or collateral as follows:

1. A distinction is drawn in the risk percentage for a bank's loans to borrowers in differing groups of countries.

Loans to central and local governments in Australia, Austria, Belgium, Canada, Denmark, Germany, Finland, France, Greece, Iceland, Ireland, Italy, Japan, Luxembourg, Netherlands, New Zealand, Norway, Portugal, Spain, Sweden, Switzerland, Turkey, United Kingdom, and Saudi Arabia[6] are assigned the same risk percentage as comparable U.S. government entities. For the central government this is 0 percent, for local governments it is 20 percent. Loans to the governments in all other countries are risk weighted at 100 percent. In effect this means that loans to national and local governments in Latin America, Africa, and most of Asia will require banks to use more capital than for financings to governments in Western Europe, North America, and certain industrialized countries of Asia.

2. Loan commitments with an original maturity date of less than a year are excluded. Loan commitments over a year require that 50 percent of that commitment be counted and then given the risk weighting of the borrower or guarantor.

3. The collateral securing a credit can alter the risk weighting. For example, a loan to a foreign corporation would be weighted 100 percent in calculating the risk-weighting formula. However, if that loan is collateralized by a government bond issued by the United States or any of the above countries, then the loan instead will be risk weighted based on the percentage applicable to that foreign government, which may be 0 percent for central governments or 20 percent for state or municipal governments.

SUMMARY

This chapter has examined the many facets of international credit. These have included the facts the lending officer needs to know about the transaction, how to evaluate the information, and how to apply all this to creating the proper blend to meet the borrower's needs as well as to protect the bank.

The loan officer has to evaluate all the information obtainable, apply the bank's standards and policies, and then make a decision. Most loan decisions, however, are not obvious and thus require intelligence and expertise to decide. But this is the job of the loan officer, one that is learned from experience. In the next chapter we shall examine that process of decision making.

QUESTIONS

1. Why do U.S. banks lend abroad?
2. What are the three Cs of credit?
3. What is collateral?
4. What are financial statements and how are they used by a credit officer?

Notes

1. American Bankers Association, *Banking Terminology*, 3d ed. (Washington, D.C., 1989), p. 153.

2. For a more detailed discussion of financial statement analysis, see Jay M. McDonald and John E. McKinley, *Corporate Banking: A Practical Approach to Lending* (Washington, D.C.: American Bankers Association, 1981), chapter 4.

3. *Asiabanking*, "The Left-overs," April 1986, p. 101.

4. International Monetary Fund, *Exchange Arrangements and Exchange Restrictions*, Annual Report 1986, p. 33.

5. Anthony Sampson, *The Money Lenders* (New York: Viking Press, 1981), p. 19.

6. These countries are members of the Organization for Economic Cooperation and Development (OECD) (see chapter 16) and those that have concluded special lending arrangements with the IMF associated with the Fund's General Arrangements to Borrow.

14

The International Credit Decision

Having assembled the information described in the previous chapter, the banker must now make a decision. For the past several decades, and particularly since the onset of what has been called the international debt crisis in mid-1982, it has been assumed that a credit decision for an international purpose was vastly different than one for a domestic purpose. What distinguishes these two types of credit decisions is that for the international purpose, the banker must assess country risk (see chapter 3). In fact, limiting a bank's exposure in any one country is similar to what banks do in controlling their exposure to a particular domestic industry.

Examination of an international transaction begins with the same considerations as for a domestic one. The decision must be founded on the bank's lending policies and objectives, the constraints established by law, and the dispassionate assessment of the risks involved. The fundamental question the banker is seeking to answer is, "If I make this credit available to this customer, will I get paid back?" The banker knows that the funds being used are primarily those of the bank's depositors and therefore the credit must be viewed differently than if the banker was an investor using exclusively his or her own funds. To approach an answer, the banker filters the available information through the Cs of credit:

- Character—"Am I dealing with an honest, responsible, experienced borrower?"
- Cash flow—"Will the borrower have a stream of income sufficient to meet the interest and principal repayment schedule?"

- Capital—"Does the borrower have other assets that could be used to pay interest and principal if its cash flow falls below expectations and is not enough?"
- Collateral—"If the cash flow and capital are not enough, are there other assets that I can convert to cash?" These are common questions asked of all transactions. But for international credit, the banker must add the following query:
- Country risk—"Will there be political or economic events in the borrower's country that could affect the ability to repay?"

The banker has traditionally relied heavily on the borrower's financial statement as the source for most of these answers. Most loans are structured so that the "full faith and credit" of the borrower are behind the loan. This means that the banker expects that any borrower will use, if necessary, all their available cash flow from all sources to meet the interest and principal repayments of a particular loan. Some loans, such as for developing mineral resources, however, have been structured so that only that particular project is the source of repayment. This involves a comprehensive evaluation of the financial and economic factors.

An international credit decision involves all of these factors plus the awareness that the bank's customer is functioning in the global business community with its unique considerations. These basically focus on the characteristics of an international borrower as well as assessing the risks for a domestic borrower with an international transaction. The customer expects to have a banker who is able to understand and evaluate these. The banker cannot become panic-stricken by international risk. By carefully detailing and assessing the risks of global business, the domestic credit officer can comfortably make a credit decision for an international transaction utilizing the skills and experience from having made domestic credit decisions. This chapter will examine these factors and look at the risks to be considered in international credit.

The objectives of this chapter are to

- describe the types of borrowers that seek international credit and the risks each represents
- evaluate the elements in making an international credit decision
- outline an approach to establishing a policy for international lending
- establish a transitional approach between domestic and global credit

BASIC CONSIDERATIONS

Having assembled and analyzed the basic Cs of credit (character, capital, capacity/cash flow, collateral, and the international C of country risk), the banker must now apply what could be called the banker's Cs of credit--*competence*, to evaluate the information, and *courage* to make a decision. The banker has a responsibility not only to the bank but equally to the customer. To the bank there is more than just the obvious responsibility to avoid the loss from a bad loan, but equally to earn the profits that a successful loan can bring. To the customer the banker has the responsibility to make available the resources that can develop a business to the benefit of a community. Internationally this can also include the opportunity to raise the standard of living in other countries, increase the food supply, and encourage economic and environmental development. Balancing these responsibilities is neither easy nor automatic. This is where the banker's courage must enter the picture.

In the early twentieth century, bankers lent only to the rich, the successful, and the powerful. They made loans based on collateral, which gave rise to the complaint that bankers extended credit only to those who did not need it. For most banks today this pattern has changed. Every community has stories of the business that was saved or an idea that developed into an industry because a banker had the courage to stand by a customer when the need was great. This has been the foundation for many long-term profitable relationships.

While a primary function of a bank is to make loans, it is not easy to make a credit decision, particularly so today when considering international credit. The needs of the customer and of the bank require that such decisions be made. Further, the reality is that business today is global and all countries, including the United States, depend on international economic growth. The courageous banker will assess the risks and seek to find a way to make a loan; the timorous banker, too often hiding behind an imagined reputation for high credit standards, will seek to rationalize turning down that same loan request. Whatever the banker's decision is after evaluating the facts and risks, the customer is entitled to a prompt reply. Such promptness is especially important if the banker intends to decline the request, since clients often consider a long delay a favorable omen. A delayed negative response may create difficulties for them in later seeking alternative sources of financing.

Facts, common sense, and experience form the basis of a credit decision. Notwithstanding the many books and courses available on the various facets of banking, most credit officers learn how to make credit decisions primarily through on-the-job experience.

Lending Policy

An international credit decision begins with the bank's written lending policies. These are senior management's instructions to loan officers on the types of credit the bank wants to make, its terms and requirements, geographic and industry distribution, and generally includes a statement of the bank's overall objectives in extending credit.

After deciding to grant a loan, a lending officer must obtain internal approval within the bank. Each bank establishes its own procedures to be followed before committing the bank. U.S. banking regulations limit the aggregate amount a national bank may extend to any single borrower to a percentage of the bank's unimpaired capital and surplus. This is the bank's *legal lending limit*. "The general rule is that a bank may lend no more than 15 percent of its capital and surplus to any one borrower on an unsecured basis; if the loan is secured, the limit becomes 25 percent. In this way, banks are forced to diversify their loans, avoiding the problem of 'too many eggs in one basket.'"[1]

Lending to foreign government entities can pose a particular problem in defining what constitutes a single borrower. "Generally speaking an agency of a foreign government that can be demonstrated to stand alone, having its own assets and revenue base, may be regarded as an entity apart from the government itself for lending limit purposes while agencies that derive their current funds from general tax revenues will be counted as part of the government."[2] Thus, a bank's unsecured lending to all of the latter would be *aggregated*, that is, counted together and limited as though it were one borrower.

Within the bank each lending officer may be given a lending limit based on that officer's experience. For large amounts the bank's senior credit officers or directors may become involved; it is the responsibility of the lending officer who has direct contact with the customer to make the necessary presentations within the bank to obtain approval of the application. Once a loan is approved, the customer must be informed, in writing, of the terms and conditions of the bank's willingness to extend credit.

BORROWERS

The international banker has four general categories of borrowers: governments, banks, businesses, and individuals. Sometimes it is difficult to classify a particular borrower—the government-owned corporation (business or government?) or the sole proprietorship (individual or business?). It is difficult to analyze all borrowers against the same basic criteria. The banker is influenced by the characteristics and capabilities of each in making a credit decision based on their particular needs as well as the goals of the bank. For some classes of borrowers—the business and the individual—the international credit officer may take a different perspective than for a domestic transaction.

Governments

A foreign government normally represents the best credit risk in that country. The borrower may be a government bank that needs the same type of facilities as correspondent banks; government corporations, which seek financing for specific projects as do private corporations; or the government itself for the financing of infrastructure development (roads, ports, electricity distribution, and so forth) or balance of payments deficits. Regardless of the actual borrower, the banker considers that this is lending to a foreign government, often referred to as *sovereign risk* lending. This group of borrowers usually represents the bank's largest credit exposure in that country.

Sovereign risk lending may be the safest loan in a foreign country because the government is the strongest financial entity in its country and has certain unique characteristics as a borrower. One prominent banker observed that even "LDCs don't go bankrupt. . . the infrastructure doesn't go away, the productivity of the people doesn't go away, the natural resources don't go away. And so their assets always exceed their liabilities, which is the technical reason for bankruptcy."[3] A government has the power to tax, it has access to substantial financial resources by its membership in the International Monetary Fund and various international development banks, and it has the capacity to set the rules by which all business in a country is conducted.

It can also be a risky borrower precisely because it is a sovereign entity; history is replete with rulers who decided not to repay their loans, suffering little or no penalty as a consequence. Even the modern banker may find it difficult to force a sovereign borrower to adhere to repayment schedules, particularly when the country encounters financial problems (see chapter 17). While the statement that a country cannot go bankrupt because its assets always exceed its liabilities is technically true, it may not be helpful in the immediate repayment of a loan since the assets may not be saleable. The power to tax is a unique power, but it will produce revenue in the local currency and not necessarily in the foreign currency needed to repay foreign borrowings.

In dealing with a foreign country, a banker may be interacting with a *state-owned enterprise* (SOE), sometimes called a *parastatal.* This term "covers all state-owned industrial and commercial firms, mines, utilities, and transport companies as well as financial intermediaries."[4] These are prevalent either because a country lacks a private sector capable of running or developing an essential industry or because the political environment dictates public ownership of certain activities. The quality of management varies widely, may be subservient to government policies and interference, or may even be civil servants with no competitive business experience. The SOE is sometimes used for internal political purposes to the detriment of its financial success. The record of the SOE has been mixed and when they are unprofitable they look to the government for financing, which adds to the internal national budget deficit. The foreign banker evaluates each one separately and determines whether to treat it as a borrower that can be expected to meet its loan obligations from

---

Creeping Capitalism

For decades in Latin America, military dictators and populists alike had considered an omnipotent and benevolent state as the ideal engineer of development for their economies. The state filled a blessed position: to crash through their economic bottlenecks, to invest where no mere entrepreneur would dare, to persist where no capitalist could afford to. Today, however, the wheezing, bloated and resource-burning state sector is widely viewed as a tool of entrenched interests and an impediment to progress due to its awesome inefficiency and unresponsiveness. In the 1980s too many Latin American nations chose to consider their industries above the hurly-burly of the marketplace, and they paid for it with shrinking economies, swelling fiscal deficits and raging inflation.

For the seventeen countries, mostly Latin American, classified by the World Bank as middle income and highly indebted, a decline in the role of the state looms not simply as an ideological nicety but a matter of economic necessity. Relative to the size of their economies, the public-sector deficits of Brazil, Argentina, Peru, Venezuela and thirteen other nations are nearly twice the average of the developing world as a whole. They cannot afford to run those kinds of deficits ad infinitum.

Whether or not diminishing the state's role will produce new economic miracles in the 1990s is open to debate. Contrary to much of today's political rhetoric, it is hardly a foregone conclusion. "We do not have the answer," says Rudiger Dornbusch, professor of economics at the Massachusetts Institute of Technology. China has led the world in growth this decade, but it also ranks very high in the size of its state apparatus, he notes. In fact, the lack of correlation between the bulk of the state and its success in the marketplace is seen in the four fast-rising economies of East Asia. Singapore has heavy state control and ownership in its industrial sector, while Hong Kong thrives with negligible state interference.

Continued

"The size of the government is irrevelant," insists Dornbusch.

Indeed, what matters is what the state does with its bulk, not how much it has. While the state in the economies of Singapore, Korea and even Japan may be large and may wield significant power, it is both highly flexible and responsive to changing conditions. It also shows a commendable willingness to take politically hazardous actions for the sake of longer-term economic efficiency. Witness early in the 1980s the forced consolidation of shipyards in South Korea, and the actual closing of shipyards in Japan, in response to a decline in worldwide demand for their output. In Latin America—or Europe, for that matter—the response would far more likely have been to preserve jobs (and votes) by subsidizing weak industries.

In Mexico the market has now been brought closer to many boardrooms. About 500 companies have been privatized in the past four years, but the hardships and complications are numerous. A good many companies entered the public sector not via any grand design but were nationalized only after they had failed. For example, Mexico found itself in the perfume business after it seized one enterprise for back taxes.

its own resources and activities or whether to finance it only with a guarantee of that government.

Correspondent Banks

As was seen in previous chapters, the foreign correspondent bank is important to the U.S. bank's capability to conduct many international banking functions. Likewise, the U.S. bank is important to many foreign correspondent banks, particularly in developing countries, as a source of credit that enables the foreign bank, in turn, to provide credit to its own customers. For example, an importer needs a letter of credit to make a foreign purchase of tools, but its local bank is not well enough known to have its letter of credit accepted by the foreign seller. The foreign bank needs to have its letter of credit confirmed by a U.S. bank. This confirmation, which is an extension of credit to the foreign bank, permits the transaction to be done and the foreign bank is thereby able to provide credit to its local customer.

Having opened an account with a U.S. bank does not automatically mean a foreign bank will be given credit. The U.S. bank provides financing to a correspondent bank based on an assessment of the foreign bank and the transaction being financed. Usually the U.S. bank does not know who the foreign bank may be relending to nor the financial capability of that customer. The U.S. bank may be asked to provide financing on a seasonal basis to enable the foreign correspondent bank to finance its local farmers. The farmers can then buy the seed, fertilizer, and tools to grow and export a crop that otherwise might not have been possible because of a shortage of capital in that country. The U.S. bank thereby facilitates international trade through financing the production of a crop that will move through the channels of world trade. This same type of financing can provide working capital through the correspondent bank to the foreign manufacturer to produce goods for export. In some cases, these exports may be to the bank's local customer.

The U.S. bank may provide financing to the foreign correspondent bank by opening an account (Due From) with it and keeping a certain balance in that account. The foreign bank thereby has deposits that are the source of funds for its loans. The risk to the U.S. bank, in the event of difficulties, is that its legal relationship to the foreign bank is now as a depositor rather than a lender. Each has a legal position that can be significantly different when a bank is facing liquidation.

The banker analyzes several risk factors in deciding to extend credit to a foreign correspondent bank. The transaction is expected to be not only self-liquidating (the goods being financed provide the ultimate source of repayment), but also short term, which limits the time during which something can go wrong. The primary source of repayment is the commodity or product being financed as it moves through the international trade cycle. The secondary source of repayment is the financial capacity of the correspondent bank—its balance sheet. Additionally, the banker must be knowledgeable about the legal or implied backing from the government to banks in their country, the degree of examination, and any controls on loan concentration to one borrower or to the owners. Few countries have deposit insurance, so depositor panics can result in sudden withdrawals and the collapse of the bank. In some countries, on the other hand, the government has a policy of not permitting local banks to fail, but instead will take them over. As with any international borrower, the banker will evaluate the quality of the bank's management, its capital strength, and the country risk.

In the years of the debt crisis, lines to correspondent banks have been given special consideration because of their importance to the developing countries' economy. Letters of credit for imports of raw materials, food, and manufactured components provide essential items to keep the economy functioning. Even when a country is unable to repay its long-term borrowings, it has usually made prompt payments for its trade finance lines. International banks have likewise kept these lines of credit available.

Businesses

The types of businesses that the international banker finances vary from the small importing and exporting company to the large multinational corporation having manufacturing plants and operations in many countries. Business often demands the greatest sophistication in structuring financial solutions to their needs. These may include traditional trade financing, term loans for building a new plant, risk management programs through foreign exchange and interest rate hedging, complex financings for developing mineral resources, and a variety of capital market products (see p. 256).

To analyze the business credit risk, the international banker examines the financial condition of the company, the cash flow projections of the future sources of repayment, collateral, quality of management, and other factors much as the domestic banker will. Additionally, the business's future operations may be particularly vulnerable to country risk changes. As with other types of borrowers, the bank expects the company's cash flow to be the primary source of repayment and its capital and other assets to be a secondary source of repayment.

A global business that manufactures in different countries for assembling in another country may adjust the *transfer pricing* between subsidiaries. This refers to the setting of a price at which one subsidiary sells to another. Each subsidiary's price, for example, can be set so as to accumulate profits in a particular country, usually one with low taxes. Individual countries are usually alert to this as it can affect their tax revenues. The banker should be, too, particularly when lending to just one subsidiary. The multinational corporation may find it to their overall advantage to have some subsidiaries operate at a low, or even nil, profit. A banker therefore must be certain that the bank will have access to a profitable subsidiary in the chain either by direct lending or through a guarantee.

Individuals

The individual is the smallest of the four categories of borrowers, both in numbers and in monetary amount. Generally, the international department does not make loans for retail purposes (for example, buying a car), except through a branch in that country.

Lending to individuals may be part of a *private banking* relationship. "In the 1980s private banking means specialist banking for the rich,"[5] sometimes referred to as high-net-worth or upscale individuals. These individuals have different backgrounds and financial objectives. Those with inherited wealth are often most concerned with preserving the value of their capital. Successful entrepreneurs seek lines of credit for new ventures and investments. And capital flight is another source of activity.

Private banking internationally views capital and money markets on a worldwide scale. The private banking individual customer is comfortable investing in different currencies and domestic capital markets in a variety of countries. The banking products vary from investment management to unsecured lending; often these individuals will be handled by specialized account officers.

A PLAN FOR THE DECISION	A banker making a decision for international lending needs to develop a plan that recognizes the customer's and the bank's objectives and is consistent with the economic and business realities of today's world. The need for financing is as great today as it has ever been while the means of doing it has become ever more complex. Financial statement and cash flow analysis are not enough any more; not all government projects are qualified for bank borrowing. The capacity of countries to service foreign debt and the expanding interdependence of individual country money and capital markets are realities that the banker must incorporate into the credit decision.

What, therefore, are elements of an international credit decision plan?

1. *The bank determines the risks it is comfortable with and makes its commitments accordingly.*

The management of each bank must honestly assess what it wants to do in the international arena and establish its lending policy guidelines for its account officers accordingly. The bank may decide that it does not want to incur any foreign country risk exposure. In that case, it will provide its local customers with operational facilities for them to conduct international transactions, but the bank will lend only on the credit strength of the local customer. For example, it can issue letters of credit for imports since this involves the risk only of the ability of the local importer to pay when the required documents are presented. It can provide financing for export transactions when the local customer is the beneficiary of a confirmed letter of credit. It can finance outgoing collections or trade acceptances, but only on the basis that the bank has recourse to the local customer in the event the foreign buyer does not pay. On a longer-term basis the bank could provide financing to a local company for their construction of a manufacturing plant in another country considering this solely as a credit risk of the local company, but the banker must analyze the potential financial drain on the local borrower if that foreign plant fails to be profitable.

A step beyond this would be the bank being willing to carry *some* country risk. This would enable the bank to assist a local exporter by providing financing directly to the foreign importer or to a bank so that it can finance the buyer. To do this the bank would carry both the credit risk of the foreign buyer or bank and the country risk of that country. Such a policy can be selective, limited to specific countries with a risk level acceptable to the bank. International lending does not obligate a bank to be lender to the world.

By incremental steps a bank could move into greater country risk exposure, longer term. A bank may determine that it wants to have the business of larger corporations and be a lender to foreign governments in order to attract their deposits, earn the fees from the larger transactions, and have the opportunity to service their high-volume payments and other operational needs.

Once each bank has determined what part of the market it wants to serve and what risks it is willing to take to generate the resulting rewards, then the bank must develop the expertise in its personnel to conduct that business. A bank that finances local businesses would want its domestic account officers to understand the risks of trade financing and for them to have access to trade financing skills either through the bank's own specialists or from domestic correspondent banks. It will concentrate its expertise on those foreign countries where its local customers are doing business.

The bank determined to obtain larger corporate and foreign government business would need to develop the capacity and technical expertise to lend in multiple currencies and be willing to undertake the greater risks.

2. *What is being financed generates its own source of repayment.*

The successful extension of credit injects funds directly into the business activity cycle of the borrower. The funds are used as a catalyst to generate the cash flow that will ultimately provide for the repayment of the credit.

It is a common characteristic of trade financing that it is expected to be self-liquidating. When a bank issues a letter of credit for an importing customer, the underlying merchandise will move from one country to another, where it will be sold. That sale provides the funds from which the bank's customer repays the credit extended by the bank.

The same principle can be applied to term lending to a business or a government. The purpose of a term loan for a business can be to build a new manufacturing plant. The output from this new plant should provide the cash flow to repay the loan after all the direct labor, materials, and financing costs of production have been covered. The term loan will be repaid from this production cycle over a number of years. This moves the banker from just the analysis of the corporation's financial statement into a more direct involvement with the economics and operation of the new plant. The banker needs to understand the assumptions that underlie the cash flow projections and the capacity of the expected global market to absorb a product. The banker would ask who else is producing the product now and who else will be producing it when the new plant's production will be available. This question needs to be considered not only for a loan to build a plant in another country, but even for one domestically, since competition is now global and foreign competitors are in domestic markets.

While the prudent banker will usually insist that the full faith and credit of the corporation is behind a credit for a specific project, the banker recognizes the reality that most corporate balance sheets have many demands on them, and therefore the banker can rarely rely on a corporation's general cash flow to service a new financing should the new venture be unsuccessful.

For loans to foreign governments, this principle would mean that bank loans would be for specific projects that have the capability to generate their own source of repayment in foreign exchange. Lending to foreign governments to meet a deficit in their balance of payments is a function often best left to international institutions and other governments. Several hundred years of history of private bankers lending to kings and princes is a reading of the tombstones of defunct banks. The events of recent years have proved no exception to this history.

3. *The credit decision is independent of the funding.*

Credit is credit; funding is funding, and the two decisions should not be mixed up.

When committing itself to extend credit to a borrower, the bank has exactly the same risks whether it disburses its funds immediately, borrows funds to disburse, or merely commits itself to provide funds at some future date should some event occur by issuing a standby letter of credit, for example. Making credit available internationally with its wider range of products and means to do so has often resulted in more confusion about the distinction between credit and funding decisions than does domestic business.

The prompt disbursement of a loan means providing funds immediately to the borrower. From then on the banker's risk of nonrepayment is very evident. If these funds were already in the bank from many depositors, the banker knows that if the loan is not repaid, the bank must still return the deposits, which can mean utilizing some part of the bank's capital. Funding a loan with Eurodollars is no different a risk. If the borrower is unable to repay, the bank must likewise return the Eurodollars to the depositor on the deposit's maturity date. The same consideration exists if the funding is in a currency other than dollars.

The use of a standby letter of credit means that the bank does not disburse funds immediately, but may have to at some future date. For example, a standby letter of credit to back a customer's borrowing from a third party would mean that the supplier of the funds can draw on the bank if the borrower fails to repay. The bank's credit decision was based on the existing financial condition of the borrower. If at some future time the borrower cannot repay that money, the third party will draw under the letter of credit and the bank will then be required to disburse funds. This is probably going to be at a time when the borrower's financial condition has deteriorated and the bank's disbursement is now likely immediately to be a loan in trouble. The bank may be in a worse situation than if it had disbursed the funds at the outset since there may be a tendency by an account officer not to watch such a borrower as much as if the bank had disbursed the loan.

It is important for the banker to treat a standby letter of credit with the same care as a loan. The bank is at risk as soon as it is issued. The borrower should be monitored in the same way as with any loan.

4. *The borrower does not exist in a vacuum.*

The borrower is part of an industry and has local and global competition. In extending credit the bank must analyze not only the borrower's past record (the financial statement), but also what factors will affect the borrower in the future, which is when the credit is to be repaid. This is as true for a domestic credit arrangement as with an international one. The banker needs to look at the borrower within the context of that global competition: How does the borrower succeed against its competitors, what position does the borrower have in its industry, who is in the industry, who is likely to come into the industry, what are the characteristics of the industry that will affect the borrower?[6] Put another way: How does the borrower make money and what actions by its competitors could change that?

Such competitive analysis can be a problem when lending to a foreign government or one of its state-owned enterprises. The repayment by such a borrower should depend on its ability to compete successfully in its industry. A government, however, may go into an industry not because it expects it can compete successfully, but because it is available. A country, for example, that has reserves of copper may decide to borrow to develop that copper, which can be sold internationally, thereby generating foreign exchange even if the company will operate at a loss. Since part of the production costs and loss is in local currency, but the income is in foreign exchange, the government may continue to produce even when it is uneconomical to do so. The industry can also provide local employment, which is important to that government.

The international banker faced with a loan request for such a project will view such a credit not as one that will stand on its own but as one that will require resources from the government. It is essentially a sovereign risk loan dependent on the country's ability to generate foreign exchange from this and other transactions to repay the loan.

Similarly, on short-term trade transactions a government may import food or raw materials and sell them below cost in order to maintain the supply of cheap food for political advantage. The accumulation of such actions can increase a government's deficit thereby generating internal inflation, unrealistic exchange rates, and other economic distortions.

Thus, in making a credit decision the international banker must see such transactions in their total environment and realistically assess the risks and real sources of repayment.

5. *The banker is competing against the borrower's financing alternatives.*

The commercial bank is not the only source of credit. Capital is now global among the industrialized countries of Europe, North America, and Japan. As a consequence, borrowers may seek to structure their transactions to attract these global sources of funds, which may offer a lower cost than the direct bank loan or other structural features of greater flexibility.

With the decline in lending to governments and corporations in the developing countries combined with the freedom of access to many national money and capital markets, attention has shifted to meeting the more sophisticated needs of corporations and governments in industrialized countries with specially structured credit that takes advantage of these opportunities.

"A sharp acceleration in the pace of innovation, deregulation and structural change . . . transformed the international financial system in important ways. Major new financial instruments—mostly taking the form of off-balance sheet [bank] commitments—have either been created or have dramatically increased their role in the financial structure; international credit flows have shifted away from loans through large international banks into direct credit markets; the volume of daily transactions have multiplied; financial markets have become far more closely integrated worldwide; capital has become more mobile."[7]

These activities are referred to as *capital market* products. "The common thread is that the bank does not provide its own funds but acts as intermediary to bring the borrower and lenders together."[8] While some activities, such as stock underwriting, are still prohibited to commercial banks in the United States, there are many other services and products in which the commercial banker can compete with the investment banker, particularly internationally. Global sources of capital are available to borrowers who deal in a single domestic market just as readily as to those with business interests in many parts of the globe.

Certain factors about this shift bear noting. First, the borrowers are not developing countries but are corporations and government entities, which are comparatively stronger financially. This now includes not only the largest international corporations, but smaller ones with sound financial elements. Second, capital market products often separate credit risk from *market risk*. The latter refers to the cost or expected rate of return for the use of the money or the ability to sell the transaction to another investor before it matures. Third, the profit for banks is from the fees they collect for putting together a transaction between a borrower and investors. When the banks carry a credit risk, there is also a charge for that risk.

Some capital markets products have developed from traditional investment activities that are prevalent in a national market and have been combined with skills from international banking, such as international loan syndications, foreign exchange trading, Eurodollar dealings, and the experience from working in diverse money markets. Innovation creating new products and structures is ongoing as needs of borrowers and sources of funds dictate.

In recent years capital market products have included the following:

Eurobond. A bond "generally offered outside the borrower's country of residence, denominated in an international currency (often not the currency of the borrower), and placed by a multinational underwriting syndicate of financial institutions."[9] These are usually long term.

Euro CP. The extension of the U.S. commercial paper market internationally with funding usually in Eurodollars. Commercial paper provides for short-term borrowing by one corporation directly from another.

Financial Future. Purchase or sale of financial instruments effective at a future date at a price agreed upon now.

Floating Rate Notes (FRN). Negotiable promissory notes for long-term borrowing with the interest rate reset every three or six months based on some formula to reflect short-term money market rates, such as LIBOR. The lender considers this a short-term loan and expects to be able to sell the note if he desires to another lender or market maker any time before maturity.

Forward Rate Agreement. A contract agreeing on an interest rate to be paid on a deposit of specified maturity at a specified future time.

Interest Rate Options. The right, but not the obligation, to buy or sell a specified financial instrument at a fixed price by a certain future date.

Interest Rate Swap. Agreement between two borrowers to exchange the commitment to pay interest on their individual borrowings. This enables them to take advantage of the difference that each has to borrow favorably in a particular market (see box).

Note Issuance Facility (NIF) and *Revolving Underwriting Facility* (RUF). Variation on FRN with a bank giving a formal commitment to buy the note from the lender before maturity if no other lenders are available.

An international credit decision may now involve the skill at mixing and matching various products in order to produce the maximum benefit for the borrower as well as the lender of the funds. It may be difficult to assess the credit risk in some transactions; the banker should not become so bedazzled by the complexity of the transaction that he or she loses sight of this. Generally, if the banker is providing a standby letter of credit or some other specific undertaking as in NIF or RUF to provide funds directly to the borrower or to repay some investor on behalf of the borrower, then the bank is carrying a credit risk.

There are some activities, such as a *private placement*, in which the bank brings the borrower and investor together and

---

Interest Rate Swap

To illustrate the mechanics of an interest rate swap, suppose a highly rated firm, A, can borrow in the Eurobond market at 10 1/2 percent or at a variable rate of LIBOR plus 1/2 percent. Another firm, B, could borrow in the bond market at 12 percent or at LIBOR plus 1 percent. Thus, firm A can issue debt more cheaply than firm B in both markets, but its advantage is 1 percentage point greater in the fixed-rate market. If the firms issue debt in the markets where they have a relative advantage and enter into a swap agreement with each other, they can lower their total cost of debt, in effect splitting the 1 point difference between them. That is, firm A could issue the Eurobond and agree to pay firm B a variable rate equal to LIBOR applied to a notional principal equal to the amount of its debt. Firm B in turn would borrow at a variable rate and agree to pay A a fixed rate of 10 1/2 percent of the notional principal. In effect, firm A transforms its fixed-rate debt into a variable-rate obligation and firm B converts its variable rate debt into a fixed-rate obligation. In the process, firm A lowers its cost of variable rate funding 1/2 percent, in this case to LIBOR. And firm B also saves 1/2 percent on its fixed rate financing at an all-in cost of 11 1/2 percent— the 10 1/2 percent it pays firm A plus the 1 percent differential between its cost of variable rate funds and the rate it receives from firm A.

Source: *Federal Reserve Bulletin*, November 1986, p. 753.

---

helps to structure a transaction directly between them. The bank would have no credit risk unless it provides some commitments to support the borrower. One of the problems that the Floating Rate Note market had in past years arose because of a confusion between the parties. Investors, who wanted short-term exposure, believed they had an implied commitment by some banks to make a market in these long-term notes so that the investor could always sell the FRN before maturity. Many banks believed their commitment was only to do so on a best-efforts basis.

Swaps and market risk transactions have credit risks, just as foreign exchange and other trading activities do. That risk is the possibility that the other party will fail to pay its side of the arrangement. When the bank is between two parties in order to structure a swap, the bank has such a risk.

ACCOUNTING

When the bank is carrying any risks in a transaction that may require disbursement of funds in the future, this will be reflected in the bank's financial statement, usually as a contingent account.

Capital market products that are reported in a bank's contingent accounts are included in the calculation for risk-based capital "by multiplying [the face amount] by a credit conversion factor. The resultant credit equivalent amount is assigned to the appropriate risk category."[10] The credit conversion factor for forward agreements is 100 percent, NIFs and RUFs are 50 percent. For interest rate contracts, such as swaps, the procedure is similar to foreign exchange contracts: the contract is first adjusted to reflect the current market value then an estimate is made of the future credit exposure by using a credit conversion factor, and the resulting number is assigned to the risk category appropriate to the bank's customer. When a bank has a series of offsetting contracts with the same party, the exposure may be netted out under certain conditions.

SUMMARY

A decision to extend credit to a borrower in another country or for a local borrower to conduct global business begins, as does one for a domestic purpose, with the same analysis of the financial condition of the borrower, the cash flow, and the quality of management.

To make the international credit decision the banker must consider the risks associated with the borrower's country and then the characteristics of the borrower, whether it be a government, bank, business, or individual. The transition to the international credit decision can be done by an orderly plan for such lending. In a changing international world, the banker needs to apply the lending procedures that will meet the needs of the customer as well as provide the bank with protection and earnings. That is the banker's responsibility in making the international credit decision.

QUESTIONS

1. Why may a corporate borrower be more interested in borrowing through capital market products than directly from a bank?
2. Describe an interest rate swap.
3. How does a bank's risk differ in lending to a foreign government corporation than to a U.S. state government?
4. What is private banking?

Notes

1.   Eric N. Compton, *Principles of Banking* (Washington, D.C.: American Bankers Association, 1988), p. 192.

2.   William H. Baughn and Donald R. Mandich, *The International Banking Handbook* (Homewood, Illinois: Dow Jones-Irwin, 1983), p. 730.

3.   *Institutional Investor, The Way it Was: An Oral History of Finance: 1967-1987* (New York: William Morrow and Co. Inc, 1988), p. 25.

4.   World Bank, *World Development Report 1983* (New York: Oxford University Press, 1983, p. 75.

5.   *The Economist*, Survey of Private Banking, June 24, 1989, p. 3.

6.   For a detailed presentation of the impact of global competition on a company see, Michael E. Porter, *Competitive Strategy* (New York: The Free Press, 1980), particularly Part I and chapter 13. Also Michael E. Porter, *The Competitive Advantage of Nations* (New York: The Free Press, 1990).

7.   Bank for International Settlements, *Recent Innovations in International Banking*, 1986, p. 1.

8.   *Euromoney Trade Finance Report*, February 1986, p. 32.

9.   Samuel L. Hayes III and Philip M. Hubbard, *Investment Banking: A Tale of Three Cities* (Boston: Harvard Business School Press, 1990), p. 34.

10. Press Release. Board of Governors of the Federal Reserve System, January 19, 1989, p. 57.

15

The Eurodollar Market

The Eurodollar is a phenomenon of the post-World War II financial world. It is unique in having become a major world currency without existing in either bank note or coin and without a central bank to regulate it. It has spawned smaller extranational markets in other major currencies. Its development advanced as financial markets sought growth between national regulations. Each attempt at regulation, particularly in the United States, led to another expansion of the market, so that today Eurodollars exist and thrive for reasons that are very different from those that led to their creation.

The objectives of this chapter are to examine the Eurodollar to see

- what led to its creation
- how it operates
- how it is used by different segments of the market
- how the accounting is handled

BACKGROUND

A Eurodollar is a U.S. dollar deposited in a banking office outside the United States. The bank does not have to be a foreign bank; it may be an overseas branch of a U.S. bank. It may also be an International Banking Facility (see chapter 2). Eurodollars constitute basically a wholesale market.

In the 1950s and 1960s the U.S. dollar was the major world currency; the dollar was the strongest currency and the one in most demand. However, in the early 1950s several communist countries feared that, in the event of increased political hostility between the United States and the USSR, the U.S. government might block their working balance deposits in U.S. commercial banks. (Such actions are a feature of wars. The United States blocked German, Italian, and Japanese bank balances in 1941. In recent years the United States blocked Iraqi accounts and the British blocked Argentine accounts.) Before the creation of the Eurodollar, a national currency generally would only be deposited in banks in that country where the currency was legal tender. As a consequence of USSR concern about working balance deposits, several European banks, principally in London, offered to accept the deposits and to maintain them in U.S. dollars instead of converting them to the local currency. Continued worry about a "dollar shortage" provided a strong incentive for banks to obtain and hold U.S. dollars.

The next step in the Eurodollar evolution was the willingness of these European banks not only to maintain deposits in their offices in U.S. dollars but also to pay interest on the deposits for periods of less than 30 days, even periods as brief as overnight. U.S. banking regulations at that time prohibited banks in the United States from paying interest on such short-term deposits. A Federal Reserve regulation then in effect also limited the maximum amount of interest a U.S. bank could pay on time deposits.

Having attracted a supply of dollars, generally for a short term and for which they were paying interest, the European banks sought ways to use these dollars. Traditionally, banks put deposits to work by making loans. U.S. banks at that time were unwilling to make short-term loans at less than their stated prime rate. There were, however, major international firms that borrowed short-term dollars from their U.S. bankers. The European banks offered these large firms short-term dollar loans at an interest rate below the prime rate of U.S. banks. Thus, by working within the range of what U.S. banks could pay on deposits and the minimum rate at which the U.S. banks were willing to lend, the European banks were able to develop what has become known as the Eurodollar market. Both the deposits and the loans were carried on the books of the European banks in dollars. Thus, the bank had no currency conversion risk because both its assets and its liabilities were in the same currency.

In 1965 the U.S. government imposed both the Voluntary Foreign Credit Restraint program on U.S. commercial banks and the Foreign Direct Investment program on U.S. corporations. The reason for their enactment was to limit the outflow of dollars from the United States as part of an overall program to reduce the balance of payments deficit of the United States. The program severely restricted U.S. bank loans made with U.S.-based funds and U.S. corporations' investments with dollars sent from this country. The previous year the United States had imposed an Interest Equalization Tax to discourage foreigners from raising money by issuing bonds in the United States. Indirectly, these programs encouraged the expansion of the Eurodollar market and the growth of U.S. bank branches overseas.

The only dollars available for many U.S. banking and business activities were Eurodollars. Both banks and corporations turned to the Eurodollar market. The banks were primarily interested in loans, whereas the corporations needed both loans and longer-term funds. Such needs gave rise to Eurodollar-denominated bonds.

When U.S. banks could not continue to meet the credit needs of good international customers with loans in U.S.-based funds, they made these loans with Eurodollars, which had no deficit impact on the U.S. balance of payments. By the time the U.S. government eliminated these balance of payments measures at the beginning of 1974, the Eurodollar market had become, for all apparent purposes, a permanent part of the international financial scene.

In the mid-1970s when the price of petroleum rose sharply as a consequence of the actions of the Organization of Petroleum Exporting Countries (OPEC), the Eurodollar market had a greatly increased supply of funds as the oil producers placed their rapidly expanding holdings of dollars in this Eurodollar market. The major banks, through both the Eurodollar market and the domestic U.S. dollar market, took on the task of "recycling" the money from the oil producers to the other nations, which were in need of dollars both to meet their now much larger oil bills and for their developmental needs. The banks were performing the classic role of intermediation—taking deposits from those with temporary surpluses and lending to those with temporary needs. "Recycling" is a term that basically "came to be applied increasingly to the re-lending of OPEC deposits."[1] While no separate reporting of the Eurodollar volume is made, it is estimated that the size of the market is about $2 trillion dollars.

EURODOLLAR TRANSACTIONS

Today, the Eurodollar is traded in financial centers around the world. The business day begins in Singapore, the center of the Asian market, moves to the Middle East, then to London, the center of the European market, and then to New York, the center of the North American market. Trading is done in many locations

within each market; however, the major focus is in London and
New York. Like foreign exchange, the Eurodollar market is
conducted by telephone and telecommunications rather than in a
central physical location.

A number of names have been used for Eurodollars to denote
special ownership. When the expansion of the price for
petroleum occurred, the oil-producing countries began to acquire
large amounts of Eurodollars from their sales; these dollars were
often referred to as Petrodollars. In fact these were simply
Eurodollars owned by oil producers and indistinguishable from
any other Eurodollars. Asian dollars are another form of
Eurodollars, which are Eurodollars traded in Asian money centers
such as Singapore.

Operations

All Eurodollar transactions are time deposits for a stated fixed
term, even if that is just one business day or requires only one
business day's notice to cancel (*call money*). The interest rate
quoted depends on the term of the deposit.

A Eurodollar may be created in many ways. When a U.S.
business pays for an import, the U.S. dollars move from the
importer's account to the account of a foreign exporter, either by
draft or by a credit to the exporter's dollar account in a bank in
the United States. The exporter may choose to sell the dollars in
exchange for the local currency or to keep the dollars and put
them on deposit in a bank or banking office outside of the United
States for a fixed term, thereby earning interest. Such a deposit
represents what is referred to as Eurodollars. The exporter who
keeps the dollars may then approach any foreign bank and offer
to put these dollars on deposit in that bank for a fixed term and
receive interest. Upon deposit, the U.S. dollars become Eurodollars.

It is important to recognize that, even though the money has
now become Eurodollars, *the money has never left the United
States*.

For simplicity of illustration, assume that the foreign exporter
received payment from the U.S. importer by having the funds
deposited in a U.S. dollar checking account that the foreign
exporter maintains in a U.S. bank. To make the deposit in the
foreign bank, the exporter instructs the U.S. bank to charge its
account and pay the money to another U.S. bank for credit to the
Due To account of the foreign bank. It is now a Eurodollar.

The foreign bank now has accepted a Eurodollar deposit, on which it pays interest, and the bank has the money in its demand account in a U.S. bank, on which it receives no interest. It may invest the dollars in a Treasury bill, bankers' acceptances, or other forms of short-term money market investments to receive a return on these funds. Alternatively, it may make a deposit in another bank or make a Eurodollar loan. To do the latter, the bank transfers the dollars from its U.S. account to a U.S.-dollar account of the borrower. Although the dollars have now been paid out of its U.S. bank Due To account, the foreign bank has, on its own ledgers, a Eurodollar deposit and a Eurodollar loan (see table 15.1).

While most Eurodollar deposits are represented as transfers between accounts, some are in the form of certificates of deposit (CDs). The principal advantage of CDs is that they are a means whereby a depositor may, essentially, sell the deposit prior to its maturity. This is done in the Eurodollar market, as in the similar domestic money market, by selling the CD to another investor at a price that gives the holder the current market yield.

As the Eurodollar has developed into its present role as a worldwide monetary unit, it is closely linked to changes in the U.S. money market and the rates for domestic money transactions. Holders of dollars have the options to place them in the United States or in Eurodollar instruments and will make such decisions based on yield, safety perceptions, and possible tax consequences.

There are several fundamental differences between a Eurodollar and a "domestic" dollar. All Eurodollar deposits are for a fixed term, anywhere from one day to as long as five years. In the domestic dollar market, there are demand accounts. All Eurodollar deposits earn interest. The rate of interest varies, depending on the supply and demand for any given maturity. Federal Reserve regulations formerly did not permit paying interest on demand accounts in the U.S. market. Eurodollar deposits are free of any reserve requirement, and therefore all the funds deposited are available for use. In the domestic market, reserves must be held for all deposits. Federal Reserve Regulation D may require a U.S. bank to hold reserves against its net borrowing of Eurodollars, regardless of whether this is done through a branch or a foreign bank, and when it lends Eurodollars to a domestic borrower for domestic use.

A Eurodollar is indistinguishable from a "domestic" U.S. dollar and, consequently, it is easy to move from one market to another. As in foreign exchange, money will move to the higher

Table 15.1 Eurodollar Accounting for Transactions

Bank Transaction	Outstanding deposit liabilities of banks in New York	Outstanding Eurodollar deposit liabilities of banks located abroad
(1) Swiss bank holds deposit with New York bank	$1	—
(2) Swiss bank deposits balance in Eurodollar market with merchant bank in London	1	$1
(3) Merchant bank in London places Eurodollar deposit with French bank	1	2
(4) French bank places Eurodollar deposit with Italian bank	1	3
(5) Italian bank makes Eurodollar loan to Italian trader	1	3
(6) Italian trader pays dollars to commodity dealer	1	3
(7) Italian trader repays Eurodollar loan to Italian bank	1	3
(8) Italian bank repays Eurodollar deposit to French bank	1	2
(9) French bank repays Eurodollar deposit to merchant bank in London	1	1
(10) Merchant bank in London repays Eurodollar deposit to Swiss bank	1	—

Source: Bankers Trust Company, *The Eurodollar Market*, New York.

Table 15. 1 (continued)

The transactions would be reflected in the T accounts of the banks as follows (D/T = Due To account; D/F = Due From account [TD = Time Deposit; DD = Demand Deposit]):

New York or Other U.S. Banks		Foreign Banks	

(1)

Assets	Liabilities	Assets	Liabilities
	D/T Swiss Bank DD	D/F U.S. Bank DD	

(2)

U.S. Bank A		Swiss Bank	
	− D/T Swiss Bank	− D/F U.S. Bank + D/F Merchant Bank TD	

U.S. Bank B		Merchant Bank	
	+ D/T Merchant Bank DD	+ D/F U.S. Bank B DD	+ D/T Swiss Bank TD

(3)

U.S. Bank B		Merchant Bank	
	− D/T Merchant Bank	− D/F U.S. Bank B + D/F French Bank TD	D/T Swiss Bank

U.S. Bank C		French Bank	
	+ D/T French Bank DD	+ D/F U.S. Bank C DD	+ D/T Merchant Bank TD

(4)

U.S. Bank C		French Bank	
	− D/T French Bank	− D/F U.S. Bank C + D/F Italian Bank TD	D/T Merchant Bank

Table 15. 1 (continued)

U.S. Bank D		Italian Bank	
	+ D/T Italian Bank DD	+ D/F U.S. Bank DD	D/T French Bank TD

(5)

U.S. Bank D		Italian Bank	
	− D/T Italian Bank	− D/F U.S. Bank DD + Loan Italian Trader	D/T French Bank

U.S. Bank E		Italian Trader	
	+ D/T Italian Trader DD	+ D/F U.S. Bank E DD	+ Loan from Italian Bank

(6)

U.S. Bank E		Italian Trader	
	− D/T Italian Trader	− D/F U.S. Bank E + Merchandise from Com modity Dealer	Loan from Italian Bank

U.S. Bank F		Commodity Dealer	
	+ D/T Com- modity Dealer DD	+ Cash − Inventory	

Steps 7–10 merely reverse the entries between Italian Trader and the European Banks on one side and the flow of offsetting deposits from U.S. Bank E to U.S. Bank A. As of step 6, adding up the balance sheets of the Foreign Banks, there is expansion of asset and liability totals; on the U.S. Banks there has been no expansion.

interest rate, and when rates for short-term investments are higher in the United States, money is attracted there. The Eurodollar rates, as a consequence, must likewise increase. The historical pattern has been that both markets tend to move up or down in tandem. The main impetus comes from changes in the U.S. domestic market simply because it is the larger market.

Interbank Trading

A bank has two basic sources of Eurodollars—its customers and the interbank market. As the Eurodollar market grew, fewer instances arose in which a participating bank would have a deposit offered to it for precisely the same amount it had a borrower seeking a loan. A bank would often find itself paying interest on a Eurodollar deposit from one of its customers but with no borrowers seeking loans. To put these deposits to work and receive interest income to offset the interest expense, an interbank trading market developed. Banks redeposit Eurodollars with another bank that might be seeking the money to fund a loan. Because of the size of the market, interbank trading now encompasses most Eurodollar activity. The depositing of Eurodollars with another bank is referred to "as a *placement* of funds and to the receipt of Eurodollar deposits from another bank as a *taking* of funds. Other people in the U.S. money market are likely to use the jargon of the Fed funds market, referring to placements of Euros as *sales* of funds and to takings of Euros as *purchases* of funds."[2]

A substantial amount of interbank trading is done through brokers. As with the foreign exchange market, the broker performs an important role in bringing buyers and sellers together. The process can be more efficient for the participants in the market if they tell the broker what their objectives are (buying, selling, and in what quantities) and then have the broker coordinate deals, rather than for the participants to try to find a counterpart on their own. The broker, once having found a match, will work with both parties to settle on the exact price.

Only then will the broker reveal the identity of the taker of the deposit to the lender. Each lender will have internal bank limits on the total amounts of deposits the bank is willing to have with any given bank. If the amount of this transaction is within the bank's limit, then the deal will be done, with each side paying the broker a small fee. All of this can take just a few minutes because of the heavy volume of trading activity. Another advantage of using the broker is that it provides anonymity, which enables a taker or placer to make a large transaction without disrupting the market. Notwithstanding the wide use of brokers, many active banks will conduct a large amount of their business directly with customers and other banks.

As in any money market, Eurodollar rates fluctuate with supply and demand. In the course of a business day, a bank's trader is offered deposits by brokers or other banks and offers to place deposits with another bank. For example, a bank trader may have a $1 million Eurodollar deposit for which the bank is paying 6 percent annual interest that is committed to remain with the bank for a period of six months. The trader may have an opportunity to redeposit that money with another bank for 30 days for 6-1/16 percent annual interest. Anticipating higher rates at the end of the 30 days, when another short-term placement of the deposit will be sought, the trader may be able to obtain a greater spread (profit) on the $1 million on deposit. The renewing of a deposit or a loan is called a *rollover*.

As Eurodollars are traded between banks, they will show up on the balance sheets of each bank. When Bank A takes the original deposit from the foreign exporter, it has a deposit liability. When it in turn places this deposit with another foreign bank (Bank B), the first bank adds an asset, "Due From" Bank B. Bank B acquires a deposit liability, and when it in turn places the deposit with another foreign bank, the cycle is repeated. Thus, the combined balance sheets of all these foreign banks show a pyramiding of Eurodollars.

While the foreign banks are trading the Eurodollars and adding assets and liabilities to their balance sheets, there has been no corresponding increase in the supply of U.S. dollars. As each foreign bank places and accepts these Eurodollars, for fixed periods of time, the U.S. dollars are moving from the Due To account of one bank to that of another. Thus, the original payment from the U.S. importer can move from one Due To account that is a demand account to another while, at the same time, it is showing up as deposits and Due From accounts in a seemingly endless number of foreign banks. In the foreign banking offices they are time deposits, while the money in the U.S. banking system retains its demand deposit character.

Table 15.1 illustrates how this redepositing has a pyramid effect on the foreign bank deposit liabilities while having no corresponding multiplication effect in the U.S. system. The accounting becomes considerably more complicated when a redeposit is taken by the overseas branch of a U.S. bank for the sole purpose of adding to the loanable funds available domestically for the parent bank. Essentially the branch becomes a depositor in its own head office bank.

As each transaction is made, settlement instructions are sent to a U.S. bank to debit the Due To account of the seller and credit the Due To account of the buyer. Most of this is done through accounts maintained in New York City banks. To facilitate the prompt processing of this enormous volume of daily payments, a computerized communications network was established by the member banks of the New York Clearing House and certain other active Edge Acts located in New York City. This is the Clearing House Interbank Payments System (CHIPS). Since the fall of 1981, the settlement between the members of their net position is done at the end of each day. The CHIPS system and S.W.I.F.T. (see chapter 5) have been designed to provide a computerized interface, thereby eliminating clerical handling.

Lending

A loan in Eurodollars will be made at a banking office outside the United States. For the purposes of Eurodollar lending, an International Banking Facility is considered to be outside of the United States. Most Eurodollar lending is to borrowers outside of the United States.

A Eurodollar loan requires exactly the same credit criteria as any other loan. It differs only in the means by which the loan is funded. In essence, a Eurodollar loan is being made with borrowed funds. If a Eurodollar loan is not repaid, a bank suffers the same loss it would from a loan made in the United States funded with depositors' money. This fact has been overlooked by too many bank credit officers in recent years.

A foreign borrower applies for a loan to a U.S. bank in the same manner, whether the loan is to be funded in Eurodollars or U.S. dollars. The terms "on-shore dollars" or "U.S.-based dollars" informally distinguish a loan made from the funds in a bank within the United States from a loan made in Eurodollars, or "off-shore dollars." After completing all the steps outlined in chapter 13 and making the decision to extend the loan, the bank officer selects the means to fund the loan. It may be funded by the deposits that a bank's customers have placed with it, or the loan may be funded by Eurodollars. The determination is based on the other loan demands on the bank, its liquidity, cost of funds, customer's preference, and the comparative interest rates.

If the bank decides to use Eurodollars, then it must take several additional steps:

1. *The bank must domicile the Eurodollar loan outside the United States.* Regardless of whether the foreign borrower made the loan request to an overseas branch of the U.S. bank or to the head office in the United States, the bank must select an overseas location for making the loan. It may be a foreign branch of the U.S. bank, one of the off-shore financial centers, such as The Bahamas or Cayman Islands, or an IBF. The selection depends on the management policy of the U.S. bank.

2. *The interest rate must be fixed for a given period.* A Eurodollar loan is quoted to the borrower at an interest rate of a stated percentage over the cost of obtaining the Eurodollars. When the actual disbursement is made, the bank obtains a Eurodollar deposit for the stated amount. This deposit may be obtained directly from a depositor. It is unlikely, however, for a depositor to offer funds to the bank on exactly the day the bank needs the funds for the loan. Therefore, the bank usually bids for a deposit from another bank in the interbank trading market. The rate at which these funds are obtained are the bank's cost, to which is added the additional stated percentage to determine the exact interest cost to the borrower.

    Eurodollar deposits are placed for a stated period of time, usually six months. If the loan is for a longer period, such as a term loan of five years, then the bank takes the deposit—borrows the funds—for six months at a time. At the end of each six months, the bank must pay back the deposit and obtain another one. The loan interest rate for the borrower thus changes each six months.

    The cost to the bank of the deposit is referred to as the London Interbank Offered Rate (LIBOR). Because the Eurodollar interbank trading has been concentrated in London, London rates have become the usual base quotation. The use of LIBOR does not mean that the loan must be domiciled in London, only that the price for the funds is that at which a bank obtains a deposit in the London Eurodollar interbank market. The funds may be obtained in another market—Asia, New York—and the interest rate can be stated based on any of these interbank markets rather than London. In legal documents, many banks refer to the rate simply as the Interbank Offered Rate.

3. *Advance notice must be given for a disbursement.* The Eurodollar market has the characteristics of the foreign exchange market. Settlement on a trade will occur two

business days in the future. In order to make a disbursement on a Eurodollar loan, the bank must buy a deposit in the market. The money will be available only in two days, at which time the loan can be disbursed. The bank must also take into account that the two days are needed in a foreign market. Considering international time differences, a borrower in Latin America, for example, may have to give three days' notice.

Syndicates

Many large loans are syndicated by the managing banks (see chapter 13). Most such loans are made in Eurodollars in order to attract a large number of potential participating banks, particularly non-U.S. banks that do not have a source of domestic dollars. The syndicate loan made in Eurodollars requires that the base cost of funds be set by the managing banks. This cost is usually determined by taking the average cost of a Eurodollar deposit as quoted by three or more major banks as of the agreed-on time three or more days prior to disbursement.

Bonds

In addition to borrowing from banks and bank syndicates, some major corporations and governments have raised money by issuing long-term bonds. Such a bond has a stated interest rate for the entire term, usually payable upon presentation of a coupon. The success of selling such bonds depends on the willingness of holders of Eurodollars to commit their funds for the long term at the fixed interest rate. The volume of outstanding Eurobonds in comparison to outstanding Eurodollar loans is quite small.

PROBLEMS AND RISKS

The Eurodollar market is unique in that it employs a currency that really belongs to no country. It is therefore periodically exposed to exceptional problems and dangers. Usually these arise because there is no "lender of last resort." That is, there is no central bank directly responsible for the maintenance of an orderly and adequate flow of money.

Every major country has its own national currency and a central bank responsible for the control and supply of that currency. In the United States the Board of Governors of the Federal Reserve System performs this role; in Great Britain, the Bank of England; in France, the Bank of France. Each central bank has the power to print and create its nation's money. It is therefore impossible for a country to run out of its own money. In the sophisticated economies of the United States, Europe, Japan, and other advanced nations, the central bank is committed to the concept of maintaining sufficient money in the banking system so that the national economic system will function. This commitment includes standing in support of the national banking system. In the United States, for example, commercial banks use most of the money left on deposit to make loans. If, at any given moment, all of a bank's depositors want their money, no commercial bank would have enough cash in its vault to meet all withdrawals. But a sound commercial national bank could look to the Federal Reserve Bank to lend it the cash to meet such a crisis. Thus, it can be said that in the United States the Federal Reserve System, as the central bank, is the "lender of last resort."

No such situation exists for Eurodollars because it is a non-national money. During some of the periodic liquidity crises in the Eurodollar market, some national central banks have made dollars available from their own reserves. Such action has usually succeeded in alleviating the short-term problem.

The Eurodollar market experienced a major crisis in the summer of 1974 when, on June 26, the German banking regulatory authorities closed Bankhaus I.D. Herstatt, a small Cologne bank, because of large losses that left it insolvent. Notwithstanding its comparatively small size in the German banking sector, Herstatt had been active in Eurodollar trading. With its collapse, it was unable to meet any of its obligations to repay the Eurodollar deposits it had taken, mostly in the interbank trading market. As the deposits came due, Herstatt could not repay them; this inability to pay had a multiplying effect. The banks that had placed funds with Herstatt were still obligated to repay the funds to those banks or others that had deposited the Eurodollars with them. The banks could repay only by employing their own capital. Thus, Herstatt's collapse resulted in losses for all the other banks. The Herstatt collapse involved over $500 million in Eurodollar transactions.

This incident illustrates the credit risks inherent in trading activities. The focus too often is on rates and market activity, with little attention to the financial soundness of the takers of the deposits. If the institution accepting the deposit fails before the maturity of that deposit, then the depositor will lose the entire amount. Deposit insurance, even to the limited extent provided by the FDIC for most deposits in the United States, does not exist in the Eurodollar market. The depositor in a failed bank can only expect to recover a small fraction of the funds at some future date when the bank is liquidated. To protect against these risks, banks placing funds establish internal control limits on the amount that may be placed with any other bank. These limits are determined as a credit judgment.

The central banks now find themselves linked to supporting liquidity in the European market during a crisis. This was implied in the Basle Concordate, a broad policy statement issued by the major central banks after the Herstatt failure.

EUROCURRENCIES	In addition to dollars, a smaller international market exists for certain other major currencies, including Deutsche marks, Swiss francs, and Japanese yen. When these currencies are held by nonresidents and deposited in banks outside the respective countries, they have the characteristics of Eurodollars. In fact, they are referred to as Eurocurrencies. "The conventional definition of the Eurocurrency market includes deposits and loans booked outside the country in whose currency they are denominated."[3]
LIABILITY MANAGEMENT	Banks manage their liabilities to ensure that they have liquidity (that is, funds available to disburse loans, invest in securities, meet deposit withdrawals) and an interest rate spread between the cost of such funds and the earnings of their assets (loans, securities). The Eurodollar market offers bank treasurers an added source of funds and different interest rate opportunities than would be available solely in the U.S. money market. This is done either through foreign branches or an IBF.

Although Eurodollar deposits are free of reserve requirements when taken in an overseas branch or IBF, Federal Reserve Regulation D can require reserves when a bank, in essence, is a net taker of Eurodollar deposits to use for the bank's domestic funding. Nonetheless, the level of interest rates and the availability of fixed-term deposits may make Eurodollar liability management operations advantageous for a bank.

"On every Eurodollar loan a bank makes and funds, it has three potential sources of profit. First, there is the spread the bank gets over LIBOR, which compensates it for operating expenses and the credit risk it is assuming. Second, there is the extra 1/16 or 1/8 percent that the bank may be able to make if its dealers can pick up the needed funds a little below LIBOR, for example, through astute timing of the purchase. A third way a bank can profit from a loan is through mismatching its book."[4] Mismatching means, as an example, charging interest on a loan based on the rate for a six-month LIBOR deposit, but actually only taking a one-month deposit that has a lower interest rate payment and then rolling that deposit over for each of the six months. As long as the one-month rate stays below the initial six-month rate, the bank will have an extra profit. The borrowing customer does not know this, and is not concerned, since the loan rate is set assuming the bank took a six-month deposit.

Many strategies and techniques are available to a bank when it runs a single global book.[5]

ACCOUNTING

Eurodollar deposits that a bank takes are carried on the bank's financial statement as liabilities; Eurodollar placements are assets. In the risk-based capital guidelines, short-term Eurodollar placements generally have a 20 percent risk weighting.

SUMMARY

The Eurodollar has become an integral part of the international financial world. It began as a way to meet a perceived political need but now has become a free, global currency that enables the U.S. dollar to remain the principal currency for international trade and finance.

A nonresident business that acquires dollars can deposit them in this market and in turn be financed. Although essentially the same as any other U.S. dollar, it functions as an unregulated world currency, with its price a true function of supply and demand.

QUESTIONS

1. What is a Eurodollar?
2. What is LIBOR?
3. What is the difference between a loan in Eurodollars or in domestic U.S. dollars?
4. How does a Eurodollar deposit differ from a demand deposit in a U.S. bank?

PROBLEM

Taking the figures in the newspaper, make a list of the rates quoted for the following: 90-day Eurodollar deposit, 90-day U.S. T-bill, and 90-day certificate of deposit. Why do you think there is a difference?

Notes

1. Anthony Sampson, *The Money Lenders* (New York: Viking Press, 1981), p. 122.

2. Marcia Stigum, *The Money Market*, 3d edition (Homewood: Ill.: Business One Irwin, 1990), p. 205.

3. *Federal Reserve Bulletin*, October 1982, p. 565.

4. Marcia Stigum, *op. cit.*, p. 246.

5. See Stigum, *ibid.*, chapter 7: The Banks: Euro Operations. Also Marcia Stigum and Rene O. Branch Jr., *Managing Bank Assets and Liabilities* (Homewood, Ill.: Dow Jones-Irwin, 1982).

16

Government Agencies

Commercial banks are not alone in financing world trade and economic development. Governments participate in these activities, both directly through their own national entities and indirectly through their membership in a variety of international economic organizations. When using its own national entities, a country's primary objective is to support and expand exports to benefit its balance of payments, which creates jobs domestically. This is done through programs that offer foreign buyers a subsidized preferential rate of interest for loans, guarantee commercial banks in export lending, insure national exporters against commercial and country risks, and make aid grants as an inducement to purchase national goods. Through these means, a country hopes to encourage domestic exporters and foreign importers to expand that country's foreign trade. Because so many countries today have these objectives, national entities continue to be active, allowing each country to remain competitive in certain types of international business.

Multinational organizations have also been established jointly by countries whose goals are to maintain orderly financial conditions globally or to provide long-term development capital in amounts and at rates that could not be supplied by the commercial banking system. These organizations became increasingly important in the 1980s as many borrowing countries and creditors became enmeshed in debt-servicing problems, which reduced the availability of private-sector financial resources. For several years, particularly from 1985 on, such organizations were the only net lenders to many developing areas.[1]

The specific programs of each organization, as well as their requirements, undergo constant modification. For the current policies, the banker working with domestic and international clients needs to be in regular contact with the organization and to be on its announcement mailing list. Some of these organizations directly affect U.S. business, whereas others influence conditions in other countries. U.S. business, for example, is affected not only by the programs of the U.S. government entities but also by those of international organizations and the programs of other governments.

The objectives of this chapter are to

- describe the types of government support used to further national exports
- describe the major multinational organizations
- discuss how these affect the commercial bank and its customers

NATIONAL EXPORT AGENCIES

Many countries have established programs to encourage the export of their products. The competition between manufacturers, particularly of capital goods (for example, large machines, aircraft) is very intense. As a consequence, a manufacturer's success in making a sale often depends as much on the conditions of financing that a foreign buyer can obtain (rates, terms, down payment) as it does on the competitive quality of the product. Because a successful sale can mean jobs in a country, governments are actively involved in providing attractive terms to foreign buyers as an inducement to purchase their country's product instead of another country's. This competition between nations has become so intense that governments have periodically attempted to agree on limits both as a floor on interest rates and a ceiling on maximum terms. But international agreements to limit export credit terms have been difficult to maintain, particularly when economic activity in a country slows and unemployment rises.

Governments often feel that the cost of the subsidy that they are giving for the export is offset by the internal employment created. In addition to offering attractive interest rates and repayment terms on financing, governments may combine the financing with a *grant*, which is a nonrepayable gift of funds as part of a foreign-aid program. These tied aid-credit export subsidies, more commonly referred to as *mixed credits*, have the overall effect of lowering the total financing cost to the buyer.

Exact terms and conditions of national export agencies change, and the banker will need to have the current rates, policies, and programs, which can be obtained from the agencies themselves. Some changes may be made on short notice as a result of internal political and budgetary considerations. The existence of these programs enables the bank's customers—exporters, investors—to remain competitive with businesses from other countries. Importers likewise may find that they can benefit from the programs of other countries.

The programs are generally one of two types: *supplier credit*, in which the exporter permits the buyer to pay over a period of time up to as much as five years, or *buyer credit*, in which the foreign importer arranges financing with a bank and pays the exporter immediately. The export agency provides financing to either the exporter for supplier credit or the importer for buyer credit.

Organizations wholly owned by the U.S. government follow policies established by Congress and the executive branch. The government provides financial support through the provision of initial capital, annual appropriations, or the organization's authority to draw on the government, if needed, to meet its guarantees. The organizations' operations are subject to periodic review, and many have undergone changes from time to time in their authorized activities. Some of the programs may be conducted in conjunction with private business and state government programs. The features of programs offered by other countries will have many similarities. To illustrate the mechanics and impact of these programs, the next sections examine U.S.-offered programs.

Export-Import Bank of the United States

The principal U.S. government agency in this field is the *Export-Import Bank of the United States* (Eximbank). Its basic mandate is to assist in financing U.S. exports of goods and services by providing credit support for those transactions that cannot be made in the private sector. It does this through direct credit, insurance, loan guarantees, working capital guarantees and other programs for hundreds of U.S. exporters, both large and small. It supplements rather than competes with private financing. In spite of its name, it does not provide support for imports into the United States.

In general, Eximbank has interpreted its legal mandate "to mean that private capital should play the leading role in financing U.S. exports, and Eximbank's programs should not be used unless private financing is not available on competitive terms.

Eximbank has viewed its role as encouraging greater participation by private financing, but not displacing private capital that is available to provide the necessary financing."[2] Eximbank does not cover the full 100 percent exposure. It covers political and commercial risk. In past years Eximbank's total authorizations for all programs represented only about 5 percent of total estimated U.S. exports.

Eximbank was established in 1934, originally to finance trade between the United States and the Soviet Union. The volume of the bank's operations was already large before World War II, but after the end of hostilities, the bank's activities expanded rapidly. In 1945 the bank was reorganized to concentrate on its present activities. It is an independent agency wholly owned by the U.S. Treasury and has capital along with the right to borrow from the U.S. Treasury up to $6 billion. Its liabilities are considered to be "general obligations of the United States backed by its full faith and credit."[3] Its charter must be regularly renewed by Congress, and its programs are affected by U.S. global policies, as, for example, it examined business in Eastern Europe following the events of 1989-90. Operating funds come from borrowing from the U.S. government, repayments on outstanding loans, and net income. It does not receive an annual appropriation from Congress, although its activities are included in the consolidated budget.

Loans are made to governments or private borrowers with or without the guarantee of private banks, substantial stockholders, or governments, depending on the nature and size of the transaction. Eximbank is required by law to make loans that "shall generally be for specific purposes, and, in the judgment of the Board of Directors, offer reasonable assurance of repayment."[4] Its variety of programs include direct domestic loans and international loans through banks, generally in U.S. dollars, for a percentage of the contract value to overseas buyers of U.S. exports, U.S. exporters themselves, and banks, with maturities generally from 5 to 10 years; commercial guarantees and insurance, also from 5 to 10 years; medium-term credits to exporters, up to 5 years; and a working capital guarantee program to assist exporters.[5]

Eximbank performs its own credit analysis based on the information supplied by the banks. Collateralization is done in a manner similar to the procedures used by commercial banks. Applications for assistance come directly from customers or banks.

"Many of the bank's transactions involve high technology and specialty goods and services from smaller companies. The products include CAT scanners, telecommunication ground stations, air navigation equipment, computer software, wood products and even soft-shell crabs now being shipped daily by plane to Tokyo from the Chesapeake Bay. Nearly 30 percent of Export-Import Bank transactions help small and medium sized companies. . . . Ten years ago, bank figures show, the comparable number was 5 to 6 percent."[6]

Foreign Credit Insurance Association

Under the auspices of Eximbank, the *Foreign Credit Insurance Association* (FCIA) was created in 1961. It is a private association of about 10 major U.S. insurance companies providing insurance against commercial and political risks that will result in nonpayment to U.S. exporters of their foreign sales. Commercial risk is that the buyer will be unable to pay because of insolvency or other business problems; political risk is that the buyer will be unable to pay because of expropriation, revolution, lack of foreign exchange, or other country-risk problems. The objective of FCIA's insurance programs is to remove these risks for the exporters and thereby encourage them to do business that they otherwise might not attempt. FCIA reinsures commercial risk with Eximbank and acts as agent for Eximbank, which carries all of the political risks. It offers short-term policies (up to 180 days) and medium-term policies (up to five to seven years).[7]

FCIA works in concert with Eximbank in providing assistance to U.S. exporters. "The basic support for supplier credits is furnished by Eximbank through the commercial bank guarantee program and export credit insurance of the Foreign Credit Insurance Association. . . . Under both programs, financing is provided by the private sector, with Eximbank or FCIA protection against defined commercial or political risks. Although neither program furnishes any direct assistance with interest charges on the financing . . . it is expected that shifting most of the risks to Eximbank or FCIA will lower the cost of financing to the U.S. exporter and his foreign customer."[8] Eximbank and FCIA programs can also be combined with state programs that may provide for state guarantees.

Agency for International Development

Beginning with the Marshall Plan after World War II, the U.S. government established a series of programs with the objective of making funds available to other countries for economic development. These funds were generally given as nonrepayable grants or on concessionary terms to be used to alleviate disease and famine or to help countries that could not do so on their own to raise the standard of living of their people. The *Agency for International Development* (AID) is the present government agency that administers these programs. It is funded by annual appropriations from Congress. When these grants are used in conjunction with Eximbank programs, they are mixed credits.

In the decades that these programs have been in existence, their focus has shifted as economic and political conditions changed. The goal has been "not simply to keep people alive for the next 12 months. Rather, it is to give people the tools to be self-sufficient economically and to pursue more advanced levels of economic growth in an atmosphere of political stability."[9]

Directory

The following is a list of some other export-related organizations established by the U.S. and other governments for their own country's purposes or private groups that assist governments:

Berne Union— Founded in 1934, an association of 36 export credit agencies to work for sound principles of export credit insurance.

Commodity Credit Corporation (CCC)— U.S. government agency, part of the Department of Agriculture, responsible for term financing of export sales of U.S. surplus grains and commodities.

Compagnie Française d'Assurance pour le Commerce Extérieur (CoFACE)— French government agency for insuring exports from France.

Compania Espanola de Seguros de Creditos (CESCE)— Spanish entity, majority-owned by government, for export credit insurance and guarantees.

Eksportkreditradet (EKR)— Danish government agency providing export guarantees and insurance.

Export-Import Bank of India— Autonomous government institution for financing international trade.

Export-Import Bank of Japan— Japanese agency for encouraging and financing exports from Japan.

Export Credits Guarantee Department (ECGD)— United Kingdom agency for encouraging and financing British exports.

Export Development Corporation (EDC)— Canadian government entity for encouraging and financing of Canadian exports.

Export Finance and Insurance Corporation (EFIC)— Australian entity for providing export finance guarantees and insurance.

Export Import Bank of Turkey— Institution for providing medium- and long-term credits and insurance to Turkish exporters and overseas contractors.

Exportkreditnamden (EKN)— Sweden's government agency for export credit, insurance, and guarantees.

Garanti-Instituttet for Exksportkredit (GIEK)— Norwegian government agency for export credit, insurance, and guarantees.

Hermes— German private company that operates official credit insurance program for financing exports from the Federal Republic of Germany.

Nederlandsche Credietverzekering Maatschappij (NCM)— Private Dutch entity for export credit insurance that reinsures transactions over one year maturity with the Dutch government.

New Zealand Export Guarantee Office (EXGO)— Government export insurance entity of New Zealand.

Oesterreichische Kontrollbank (OKB)— Austrian government agency for export credits.

Office National du Ducroire (OND)— Belgian government export credit insurance and guarantee agency.

Overseas Private Investment Corporation (OPIC)— U.S. government entity to insure private investments in other countries.

Private Export Funding Corporation (PEFCO)— U.S. private corporation formed by 62 banks and corporations to work with Eximbank in raising private capital for financing U.S. exports.

Sezione speciale per l'Assuricazione del Credito all'-Esportazione (SACE)— Italian agency for providing export insurance and guarantees.

INTERNATIONAL ORGANIZATIONS

Other organizations have been established by governments working together whose purpose is to maintain orderly international financial conditions and to provide capital and advice for economic development, particularly in those countries that lack the resources to do it themselves. The U.S. government is a participant in these, providing a minority portion of the capital and exercising a share of the management and policy guidance. The U.S. contribution is authorized by congressional appropriation.

The majority of these organizations were created toward the end of World War II as part of an overall spirit of international cooperation. The Allied countries emerging from the war were determined to avoid the economic conflicts that many believed had contributed to the outbreak of that war. On July 22, 1944, Articles of Agreement were signed by delegates from 16 nations at a conference at Bretton Woods, New Hampshire, to create two major international organizations: *International Monetary Fund* (IMF) and *International Bank for Reconstruction and Development* (IBRD), commonly known as the *World Bank.* They came into existence on December 27, 1945. In subsequent years, other organizations were formed principally to meet regional needs.

These international organizations obtain funds for their lending activities from two basic sources. The first is the contribution of capital that each nation makes when it becomes a member. The amount of this contribution varies with the financial capacity of the country; from time to time member countries have been asked to contribute additional capital. The second source of funds is through borrowing.

Although the IMF and the IBRD were created at the same time, their purposes are different. In general, they operate independently of each other, although a degree of informal cooperation and information sharing occurs. Each has its own organizational structure, with management direction from representatives of all the member countries. They are both headquartered in Washington, D.C.

World Bank Group

The World Bank Group encompasses the International Bank for Reconstruction and Development (World Bank) and three subsidiary organizations: *International Development Agency* (IDA), *International Finance Corporation* (IFC), and *Multilateral Investment Guarantee Agency* (MIGA). Each of these has a specific mission within a common objective "to help raise standards of living in developing countries by channeling financial resources from developed countries to the developing world."[10]

The World Bank began in 1946 with 38 member countries. By 1990 it had grown to 152 members, ranging in size from the Seychelles (population 67,000) to the People's Republic of China (population 1 billion). Notwithstanding being headquartered in Washington, D.C., its staff is international and represents over 100 nationalities. Voting is based on a formula that is periodically reviewed and is related to the amount of capital subscribed. For example, in 1990 the United States had about 15.37 percent of the votes.[11] The total subscribed capital at that time was $125 billion.

The World Bank obtains its funds from the capital subscribed by its members, from issuing bonds in world capital markets, retained earnings, and repayments on previously made loans. Loans "generally have a grace period of five years and are repayable over fifteen years or fewer. They are directed toward developing countries at more advanced stages of economic and social growth. . . . It must lend only for productive purposes and must stimulate economic growth in the developing countries in which it lends."[12] These loans are made at market rates of interest to governments or are guaranteed by governments. It has also supported programs for easing the debt crisis by making loans for the purposes of principal reduction, interest support, or to enable a country to buy back its commercial bank debt at a discount (see chapter 17).

Such economic development is a complex problem, much like a wheel—each part needs another and is closely interrelated with other parts. For example, a country may aim to raise the standard of living of its people by creating the industrial capacity to process a natural resource rather than by merely exporting the raw material, a situation that many countries view as exploitive. To develop industry requires electric power. This means hydroelectric dams or coal-burning power stations. The power must be transported from its source to its users, and this requires a power transmission system. To get people to work in industry they must be encouraged to leave agriculture, with the result that those who remain in farming must become more efficient to feed those in the cities. This requires all-weather roads to markets, fertilizer, and increased irrigation. The health of the populace must be improved to reduce infant mortality, conquer disease, and increase longevity, which means improving the water supply, more efficient sewer systems, and public health programs. To export its product, the country may need efficient transportation and port systems.

Obviously all of these goals cannot be accomplished at one time. The role of the World Bank has been to advise and help a country finance the individual components. Since 1948 the World Bank has done this through project loans. A project is a separate "package of investments, policy measures, and institutional and other actions designed to achieve a specific development objective . . . within a designated period."[13] The Bank is involved from the identification stage through the construction and completion phase, not only with financing but also by providing technical advice and supervision.

Beginning in the 1980s the Bank began to shift toward policy-based loans, "which differ from standard project loans in being disbursed in as little as one year rather than the customary five to eight; they are also targeted not at building another highway or housing complex but at fostering far-reaching structural reforms, such as an end to import restrictions or the establishment of market prices for agricultural goods."[14] These are of two types: structural adjustment loans, for economic policy changes such as covering a balance of payments shortfall caused by a structural economic shock (for example, the collapse of commodity prices); or sector adjustment loans, for a specific economic category such as agricultural (for example, to allow a government to meet the foreign exchange costs of reducing an import tariff).[15] "Sector adjustment loans address an issue specific to one part of the economy. . . Structural adjustment loans aim to support economy-wide policy changes."[16] As such loans have increased, project loans have declined to about half of the new commitments.

In 1990, the IBRD made new loan commitments of $15.1 billion represented by 121 loans to 38 borrowing countries. The gross disbursements in that year were $13.8 billion and after repayments from previous loans, the net disbursement was $5.7 billion. Loans are made in major world currencies and are to be repaid in such currencies.[17]

A number of countries, however, are unable to meet the repayment criteria of a World Bank loan. Countries that have an annual per capita gross national product of $650 or less (in 1988 dollars) receive development funds from IDA. These are called credits to distinguish them from the loans made by the IBRD. Credits "are made only to governments, are with ten-year grace periods, thirty-five to forty-year maturities, and no interest."[18] Such loans are often called *soft loans*, which refers to the repayment terms. The projects themselves meet the same criteria as the IBRD loans and are managed by the same staff. In fiscal year 1990 IDA approved credits to 47 member countries for a total of $5.5 billion.[19] These credits are made in major world currencies, but may be repaid in the currency of the borrower.

Another part of the World Bank Group is IFC (135 member countries), which was established in 1956. Its function is to make equity investments and loans to the private sector of developing countries as well as serving as an adviser. By so doing, the IFC assists these private companies by acting as a catalyst to attract more capital from domestic and foreign sources. In 1990 they made new investments of $1.5 billion in 38 countries in 122 private sector projects, bringing the total number of companies IFC holds loan or equity investments in to nearly 500. As of mid-1990, its net worth was $1.9 billion.[20]

Recent IFC projects have been for the development of private companies in industries such as food processing, fishing, textiles, wire drawing, tourism, dry-cell battery production, paper products, and so forth.

MIGA was established in 1988 with the specialized mandate of encouraging the flow of direct foreign investments to developing countries by reducing the risks to the investor through issuing guarantees for noncommercial risks, primarily political risks. In addition, it offers advisory services. In the decade prior to its establishment, direct foreign investment in the developing world was less then 15 percent of the total worldwide flow of such direct investment.

The World Bank Group also assists the flow of foreign investment with the *International Centre for Settlement of Investment Disputes* (ICSID), established in 1966 to provide "facilities for the conciliation and arbitration of disputes between governments and foreign investors."[21]

International Monetary Fund

The basic purpose of the International Monetary Fund is to "oversee the international monetary system in order to ensure its effective operation."[22] It does this by providing interim financing to member countries experiencing balance of payments difficulties and to assist them in correcting the conditions that brought it about. Its origins date back to the Bretton Woods conference in 1944. Its founding countries believed that many of the financial difficulties experienced between the first and second world wars could have been alleviated with the help of an agency capable of providing financing, which would help a country survive an economic crisis, and then to supply technical analysis and guidance in plotting a return to economic stability.

In addition to overseeing the operation of the international monetary system, the IMF also exercises surveillance over the exchange rate policies of member countries, monitors developments in the field of international liquidity, manages the Special Drawing Rights (SDR) system (see chapter 12), and provides guidance for the standardized presentation of national balance of payments data.

The International Monetary Fund has grown from the original 44 member countries to over 150 members in 1990. Each country subscribes capital, which is used as the primary means to fund the lending activities of the IMF. "When countries join the Fund, they are assigned a quota that fits into the structure of existing quotas considered in the light of the member's economic characteristics relative to those of other members of comparable size. The size of the member's quota determines, among other things, the member's voting power, the size of its potential access to Fund resources, and its share in allocations of SDRs. . . . Subscriptions are equal to quotas. Initial subscriptions, and normally subscriptions associated with increases in quotas, are paid mainly in the members' own currencies, and a smaller portion, not exceeding 25 percent, in reserve assets (SDRs or currencies of other members acceptable to the Fund)."[23] As of mid-1990 the total member-country quotas were SDR 135.2 billion. The United States has the largest quota, followed by Japan and Germany, who share second place and the United Kingdom and France with equal quotas for third place.[24]

"The principal way in which the Fund makes its resources available to members is by selling to them the currencies of other members or SDRs in exchange for their own currency."[25] Depending on the severity of the problem, the Fund's assistance may be up to 440 percent of the country's quota and provides for repayment up to 10 years.

The lending activities of the IMF have evolved to reflect changing world conditions. In the immediate postwar period the need was to move toward free convertibility of currencies. This meant dismantling each country's exchange controls, which could only be done slowly in concert with their growing economies. The sharp rise in petroleum prices in the 1970s strained many economies, which looked to the Fund for short-term financing.

The Fund has also established facilities to meet specialized needs of some member countries. *Structural Adjustment Facility* (SAF) and *Enhanced Structural Adjustment Facility* (ESAF) provide "concessional financial assistance to low-income members facing serious balance of payments problems and needing to undertake programs of structural adjustment." The *Compen-*

satory and Contingency Financing Facility (CCFF) is to "help stabilize the earnings of countries exporting primary commodities. . . [including] receipts from tourism and worker remittances in calculating the export shortfall. . . [and provides] compensation for countries experiencing an excessive rise in the cost of specific cereal imports."[26]

Throughout its existence the Fund has provided assistance to countries experiencing balance of payments difficulties. The general pattern has been for a country to request assistance, then the Fund sends a team of experts to that country to examine the magnitude of the problem and to determine its cause. These may be internal inflation, unrealistic exchange rates, or high government deficits. The Fund will make recommendations on correcting these. The government will then sign an agreement with the Fund to put these recommendations into effect, and the Fund makes a short-term loan (usually two to three years) to assist during the transition period. While this procedure may seem simple, it has led to great strains and political turmoil in some countries with severe international debt problems, as we shall see in chapter 17. As of mid-1990 the total amount of Fund credit outstanding was SDR 24.4 billion to 88 debtor countries (of which SDR 3.25 billion from 11 countries was in arrears), down from a peak of SDR 37.6 billion outstanding in mid-1985.[27]

Directory

The following are some other international financial organizations:

African Development Bank— Multilateral development bank specializing in development loans to African countries along the pattern of the World Bank.

Asian Development Bank— Multilateral development bank specializing in development loans to Asian countries along the pattern of the World Bank.

Bank for International Settlements (BIS)— Originally established to handle payments of German World War I reparations, now functions to provide cooperation between central banks, primarily of industrial countries.

European Bank for Reconstruction and Development— Development bank specializing in loans for economic revival of Eastern Europe. Brainchild of French President Mitterrand following political events of 1989.

General Agreement on Tariffs and Trade (GATT)— Organization established in 1947 to reduce world trade barriers.

Presently consisting of over 100 member countries, who account for almost 90 percent of world trade, it is committed to "the principle of non-discrimination in trade. Members must provide the best trade terms available, by treating all others as they treat the 'most favoured nation'."[28] Conducts multilateral bargaining rounds to progressively lower tariffs. Also provides rules for the settlement of trade disputes.

Inter-American Development Bank— Multilateral development bank specializing in development loans to Latin American countries along the pattern of the World Bank.

Organization for Economic Cooperation and Development (OECD)— International organization of industrial countries established in 1960 to stimulate economic progress and world trade.

Paris Club— Informal term for facilities provided by the French Treasury where officials of a debtor country requesting to reschedule its foreign debt can meet with governmental creditors, generally from industrial countries. "The debt to be rescheduled is limited to officially guaranteed export credits and straight government loans."[29]

ROLE OF U.S. COMMERCIAL BANKS	U.S. commercial banks actively cooperate with the various national government and international lending agencies by participating in loans (usually the shorter maturities), interim financing, or co-financing. Disbursement procedures for the loans of these agencies frequently provide for establishment of commercial letters of credit, which are processed by banks since the government entities are not equipped to provide the technical operational support needed. Basically the lending agency approves a loan for a development project. The borrowing country and its agencies then issue individual contracts and purchase orders to suppliers. To pay these suppliers the foreign country requests banks to issue letters of credit. After shipment is made and documents are presented to the commercial bank, letter of credit negotiation is done and payment is made to the supplier. The U.S. bank then receives reimbursement from the international lending agency.

When commercial banks provide financing to exporters using any of the guarantee or insurance programs offered by national agencies, the bank has a credit with the added backing of the government entity. Because of this strength, the bank can often offer credit to its customers on better terms than if it had to rely solely on the company.

SUMMARY

Governments actively compete to expand their own country's exports. The major industrial countries and a number of developing countries have created government agencies to provide preferential financing rates and terms for loans to foreigners who buy from that country's exporters. In the United States this is done principally through the Export-Import Bank of the United States.

International agencies such as the World Bank and International Monetary Fund were created to provide financial assistance and advice to member countries in their needs to meet balance of payments difficulties and long-term developmental needs. Both of these entities affect U.S. banks by the direct and unique contributions they can provide to meet the urgent needs of many countries and thereby provide a more orderly and stable international financial environment.

QUESTIONS

1. What does the Eximbank do?
2. What does the World Bank do?
3. What does the International Monetary Fund do?
4. Why do other countries have agencies comparable to the Eximbank?

PROBLEM

Locate current newspaper or magazine articles that are about work being done by the Eximbank, World Bank, and International Monetary Fund. How does this demonstrate the goals and purposes for which each organization is set up?

Notes

1. The World Bank, *World Debt Tables*, 1988-89 Edition, Vol. I (Washington, D.C., 1988), p. xvii.

2. Charles E. Gaba, "Export Finance and the Role of the Export-Import Bank of the United States," *International Banking: U.S. Laws and Regulations* (Washington, D.C.: American Bankers Association, 1984), pp. 6-11.

3. *Ibid.*, pp. 6-12.

4. *Export-Import Bank Act of 1945*, Section 2(b) (1) (A), 12 U.S.C. sec. 635.

5. *Official U.S. and International Financing Institutions*, (Washington, D.C.: U.S. Department of Commerce, 1985), p. 4.

6.   *The New York Times*, February 6, 1990, p. C7.

7.   *Official U.S. and International Financing Institutions, op. cit.*, p. 6.

8.   Gaba, *op. cit.*, pp. 6-27.

9.   Peter McPherson, "We weren't looking for a quick fix," *The New York Times*, Nov. 23, 1986, Sec. 3, p. 2.

10.   *Annual Report*, The World Bank, 1990, p. 3.

11.   *Ibid.*, p. 225.

12.   *Ibid.*, p. 3.

13.   Warren C. Baum and Stokes M. Tolbert, *Investing in Development* (New York: World Bank/Oxford University Press, 1985), p. 8.

14.   *Institutional Investor*, September 1986, p. 88.

15.   *The Economist*, September 27, 1986, p. 19.

16.   *Ibid.*, p. 33.

17.   The World Bank, *op. cit.*, p. 13.

18.   *Ibid.*, p. 3.

19.   *Ibid.*

20.   International Finance Corporation, *Annual Report 1990*, p. 3.

21.   *World Bank Annual Report*, p. 103.

22.   International Monetary Fund, *Annual Report* (Washington, D.C., 1986), p. 31.

23.   International Monetary Fund, *International Financial Statistics: Supplement on Fund Accounts* (Washington, D.C., 1982), p. iii.

24.   International Monetary Fund, *Annual Report 1990*, p. 47.

25.   International Monetary Fund, *International Financial Statistics: Supplement on Fund Accounts* (Washington, D.C., 1982), p. iii.

26.   International Monetary Fund, *Annual Report 1989*, p. 34-35.

27.   International Monetary Fund, *Annual Report 1990*, pp. 52, 57.

28.   *The Economist*, April 21, 1990, p. 85.

29.   *The Economist*, March 20, 1982, Survey, p. 27.

17

The Debt Crisis

The international banking activities and expectations of U.S. banks have undergone substantial and critical changes during the 1980s. When the decade began, many banks had active international departments that were optimistic about the potential for global business growth. Loan syndications were a major activity, raising billions of dollars from hundreds of banks for manufacturing expansions, infrastructure development, natural resource processing, and other major projects that could make possible important improvements in the standards of living in many developing countries. Commercial bankers were confident that they could marshall the world's financial resources, particularly drawing on the huge oil revenues of the OPEC countries, and lend these monies to developing countries to turn the potential for economic growth into real development. Regional and small banks were attracted to international syndications, often relying on the syndicate manager banks with their large international banking staffs and expertise.

Reality turned out to be less favorable. If, in retrospect, one had to pick the date when it changed, it was during the weeks of mid-August 1982. The crisis focused on Mexico and climaxed, after days of financial turmoil, with Mexico's public statement to the world's leading bankers that it could not, at that time, repay the current installments on its debts (see table 17.1 for a profile of Mexico's debt situation from 1970 to 1988).

In the months that followed, lending banks reacted, reassessed their overall policies, and began to withdraw from new international lendings. Within a few years, most international banking departments reduced their activities and personnel.

Countries that had been dependent on foreign sources of funds for their economic growth now were cut off from new money. This became known as the *international debt crisis.* It has changed how international banking is conducted by commercial banks. Millions of people in both developing and developed countries have been adversely affected, and governments and international organizations are still concentrating on finding solutions.

The search for a solution has proven to be very difficult since there are, in actuality, two problems, and solving one does not solve the other. The first problem is how to relieve the present burden on the debtor countries of the repayment for their past borrowings; that has been the urgent focus since 1982. The second problem is how to reactivate a new flow of loans and other capital that is vital for the future of the developing countries. That solution has proven to be a tortuous struggle with very little success.

The debt crisis did not affect all the developing countries. "A majority of developing countries have been able to service their external debt in the 1980s, and their development process in this decade has not been much different from that in earlier periods. . . . International capital markets, bilateral lenders, and multilateral institutions have rewarded this group of countries that have avoided debt servicing problems through continued access to external resources in the quantity and on the terms sufficient for their sustained growth."[1] The World Bank classifies 46 of 111 developing countries as being severely indebted; however, among those 46 are the largest borrowers.

The objectives of this chapter are to
- examine the trends that led to the growth of developing country debt
- analyze the causes of the debt crisis
- examine the search for solutions
- consider the consequences of the debt crisis for both borrowers and lenders

Table 17.1 Country Debt Profile: Mexico

(US$ millions, unless otherwise indicated)

	1970	1980	1981	1982	1983	1984	1985	1986	1987	1988
1. SUMMARY DEBT DATA										
TOTAL DEBT STOCKS (EDT)	..	57,378	78,215	86,019	92,964	94,822	96,875	100,876	109,292	101,566
Long-term debt (LDOD)	5,966	41,215	53,232	59,651	81,565	86,022	88,456	90,916	98,329	88,665
Public and publicly guaranteed	3,196	33,915	43,032	51,551	66,765	69,726	72,711	75,813	84,181	81,207
Private nonguaranteed	2,770	7,300	10,200	8,100	14,800	16,296	15,745	15,103	14,148	7,458
Use of IMF credit	0	0	0	221	1,260	2,360	2,969	4,060	5,163	4,804
Short-term debt	..	16,163	24,983	26,147	10,139	6,440	5,450	5,900	5,800	8,097
Interest arrears on LDOD	..	0	0	0	0	0	0	0	0	0
TOTAL DEBT FLOWS										
Disbursements	..	11,581	17,003	12,721	8,259	8,515	5,348	6,285	7,978	8,614
Long-term debt	1,375	11,581	17,003	12,500	7,186	7,281	5,047	4,965	7,192	5,846
IMF purchases	0	0	0	222	1,072	1,234	300	870	786	470
Principal repayments	..	4,894	4,574	4,531	4,828	5,656	6,062	4,580	3,998	6,805
Long-term debt	1,017	4,760	4,504	4,531	4,828	5,656	5,072	4,433	3,531	6,242
IMF repurchases	0	134	70	0	0	0	0	147	367	563
Net flows	..	6,686	12,429	8,190	3,431	2,859	-714	1,704	3,979	1,809
Interest payments (INT)	..	6,068	9,766	11,153	9,994	11,302	10,220	8,376	8,325	8,759
Long-term debt (LINT)	283	4,580	6,117	7,769	8,140	10,250	9,382	7,676	7,691	7,590
IMF charges	0	4	0	0	26	115	202	266	283	339
Short-term debt	..	1,484	3,649	3,384	1,828	938	636	434	350	830
Net transfers	..	618	2,662	-2,963	-6,563	-8,443	-10,935	-6,672	-4,345	-6,951
Total debt service (TDS)	..	10,962	14,340	15,684	14,822	16,958	16,283	12,956	12,323	15,564
Long-term debt (LTDS)	1,300	9,340	10,622	12,300	12,968	15,906	14,454	12,109	11,223	13,832
IMF	0	138	70	0	26	115	202	413	650	903
Short-term debt	..	1,484	3,649	3,384	1,828	938	1,626	434	450	830
2. MAJOR ECONOMIC AGGREGATES										
Gross national product (GNP)	36,869	189,155	240,877	163,815	140,089	165,962	176,380	122,557	140,469	175,203
Exports of goods & services (XGS)	2,935	22,133	27,765	27,618	28,689	32,555	29,717	23,864	30,106	32,093
Imports of goods & services (MGS)	4,058	33,028	44,001	34,130	23,477	28,594	29,414	25,821	26,545	35,349
International reserves (RES)	756	4,175	4,971	1,778	4,794	8,019	5,679	6,674	13,692	6,327
Current account balance	-1,068	-10,750	-16,061	-6,307	5,403	4,194	1,130	-1,673	3,968	-2,927
3. PRINCIPAL RATIOS										
TOTAL EXTERNAL DEBT (%)										
EDT /XGS	..	259.2	281.7	311.5	324.0	291.3	326.0	422.7	363.0	316.5
EDT/ GNP	..	30.3	32.5	52.5	66.4	57.1	54.9	82.3	77.8	58.0
TDS/ XGS	..	49.5	51.6	56.8	51.7	52.1	54.8	54.3	40.9	48.5
INT/ XGS	..	27.4	35.2	40.4	34.8	34.7	34.4	35.1	27.7	27.3
INT/ GNP	..	3.2	4.1	6.8	7.1	6.8	5.8	6.8	5.9	5.0
RES/EDT	..	7.3	6.4	2.1	5.2	8.5	5.9	6.6	12.5	6.2
RES/MGS (months)	2.2	1.5	1.4	0.6	2.5	3.4	2.3	3.1	6.2	2.1
Short-term / EDT	..	28.2	31.9	30.4	10.9	6.8	5.6	5.8	5.3	8.0
Concessional / EDT	..	1.0	0.8	0.6	0.6	0.5	0.5	0.5	0.5	0.5
Multilateral / EDT	..	5.6	4.7	5.5	4.5	4.6	6.2	8.1	9.5	10.2
LONG-TERM DEBT (%)										
LDOD/XGS	203.3	186.2	191.7	216.0	284.3	264.2	297.7	381.0	326.6	276.3
LDOD/GNP	16.2	21.8	22.1	36.4	58.2	51.8	50.2	74.2	70.0	50.6
LTDS/XGS	44.3	42.2	38.3	44.5	45.2	48.9	48.6	50.7	37.3	43.1
LTDS/GNP	3.5	4.9	4.4	7.5	9.3	9.6	8.2	9.9	8.0	7.9
LINT/XGS	9.6	20.7	22.0	28.1	28.4	31.5	31.6	32.2	25.5	23.6
LINT/GNP	0.8	2.4	2.5	4.7	5.8	6.2	5.3	6.3	5.5	4.3
RES/LDOD	12.7	10.1	9.3	3.0	5.9	9.3	6.4	7.3	13.9	7.1
4. LONG-TERM DEBT										
DEBT OUTSTANDING (LDOD)	5,966	41,215	53,232	59,651	81,565	86,022	88,456	90,916	98,329	88,665
Public and publicly guaranteed	3,196	33,915	43,032	51,551	66,765	69,726	72,711	75,813	84,181	81,207
Official creditors	1,149	4,481	5,385	6,958	6,713	6,996	8,840	12,080	15,687	16,022
Multilateral	748	3,189	3,660	4,761	4,203	4,393	6,016	8,177	10,380	10,333
Concessional	505	375	328	280	231	188	150	140	122	103
IDA	0	0	0	0	0	0	0	0	0	0
Nonconcessional	243	2,814	3,332	4,481	3,972	4,205	5,866	8,037	10,258	10,230
IBRD	582	2,063	2,417	2,692	2,870	2,852	4,034	5,566	7,346	7,427
Bilateral	401	1,291	1,726	2,197	2,509	2,603	2,823	3,903	5,307	5,690
Concessional	122	182	260	279	334	310	315	360	409	371
Private creditors	2,047	29,434	37,647	44,592	60,053	62,730	63,871	63,733	68,494	65,185
Bonds	405	3,128	4,335	5,187	4,589	3,962	3,708	3,376	2,797	4,184
Commercial banks	1,267	25,608	32,402	38,542	50,234	53,972	55,676	55,397	60,499	55,926
Other private	375	698	909	864	5,230	4,796	4,486	4,960	5,198	5,074
Private nonguaranteed	2,770	7,300	10,200	8,100	14,800	16,296	15,745	15,103	14,148	7,458
Memo: total commercial bank	4,037	32,908	42,602	46,642	65,034	70,268	71,421	70,500	74,647	63,384

THE INTERNATIONAL DEBT CRISIS

The current use of the term debt crisis generally refers to the inability of a developing country to meet its debt repayments on the original schedule. But there is nothing new about a borrower being unable to repay a loan to a bank on time. Bankers know from experience that in spite of their best analysis, some borrowers will require a new repayment schedule, modified terms, and in some cases added financing to get through a difficult time. Countries are just like other borrowers. Often the causes of the country's problems are reflected in a deterioration in its balance of payments (see chapter 3). This has happened with countries many times before. Brazil, for example, had rescheduled its foreign debt in 1964-65.

What caused the events in 1982 to be perceived as a crisis was that it was unexpected by many, the amount of debt was so huge, and so many countries eventually were affected. What also made this crisis unique was that it predominately involved commercial banks. Before this, from the nineteenth century to the late 1940s, term lending to developing foreign governments and for projects such as building railroads, had been done by merchant banks (see chapter 2) and investors who knew from the outset that their own money was at risk. Previous debt crises had meant that these bondholders were the ones who were exposed to losses.

To illustrate: In the mid-nineteenth century a major investor in Latin America had been the merchant bankers, Baring Brothers. In spite of one difficult loan renegotiation with Argentina "Barings were disposed to lend more money. . . . The fact was that Argentina enjoyed immense natural wealth and that though incompetence, corruption, and political instability might from time to time put foreign investors at risk, in the long run their profit was likely to be secure. The very fact that the risks were there meant that the profits would be greater than those secured in more stable areas. Up to 18 percent interest could be secured on a well secured short-term loan. Handled with discretion, investments in Argentina would be an eminently satisfactory enterprise. Barings lost a great deal of money there, but that should not be allowed to obscure the fact that they made a great deal, too. They were in a position of peculiar responsibility. The British investor was ignorant of almost everything to do with Latin America, confusing Argentina with Chile and Mexico and wholly unable to follow the intricacies of Argentina internal politics. They depended on the judgement of Barings as to whether or not the money would be safe. On the whole their confidence was justified."[2]

Background

For most countries, economic development became a goal after World War II in order to raise the standard of living of its people. Economic development is associated with establishing industries, building utilities, and shifting away from concentrating on exporting commodities and raw materials. The symbolic shift from being a supplier of crude raw materials and crops to the supplier of technologically more advanced products can usually mean greater export earnings and better living standards. It was the difference, for example, between being a miner of iron ore or the producer of steel, which for many developing countries in the 1950s and 1960s had great significance.

The countries in Latin America, Africa, and much of Asia saw the achievements that industry brought to the United States, Western Europe, and Japan. By emulating these countries, the underdeveloped countries sought to raise their economies and achieve the same benefits. The world was in the midst of a "revolution of rising expectations." It has been said that one of the greatest incentives for economic development in underdeveloped countries has been people seeing the life-style of industrialized countries as depicted in motion pictures.

Economists created development programs for these countries that required sources of capital to make the investments. One source could be from the savings of the people and businesses within that country. However, most developing countries lack such sufficient internal savings and capital markets. The catalyst for these plans, therefore, was that the country would attract capital from the developed countries and use it to build industrial plants and the associated support systems (often called *infrastructure*—all-weather roads, power systems, transport systems, and so forth). The model was often the United States, which, for example, had followed just such a pattern, using British investments and loans to build railroads and the great manufacturing plants, and then was able to buy out the investors from the wealth the industrial development had created.

The foreign capital could come from investments, borrowings, or gifts. When the capital came to the country as a direct investment, it was money from a corporation brought in to build a specific manufacturing plant, for example. The supplier of the capital would be rewarded as the venture prospered by a future flow of dividends. "Bond markets offering long-term, fixed-interest monies were largely closed to developing countries."[3] So, some of the capital would be funds lent by multinational institutions such as the World Bank or directly from other governments through grants, loans, or export guarantee programs such as those of the Export-Import Bank of the United States (chapter 16).

During the 1960s the source of development funds began to shift with a majority coming from bank loans. In Latin America, for example, outstanding long-term debt in 1970 was $27.8 billion with about half from commercial banks and the other half split between official sources—governments (direct and through international agencies)—and private investors. By 1980 the outstanding debt was $172.8 billion with 70 percent from commercial banks and only 18 percent from official sources.[4]

Initially, a bank would, by itself, make a loan to a borrower, but as the amounts needed became larger, groups of banks formed syndicates to provide joint financing. In all cases the loans had a schedule for repayment. Lending banks required that the borrower demonstrate expectations of a cash flow from the project that could repay the loan interest and principal and that the country would have the ability to earn enough foreign exchange so that the borrower could convert the local currency profits into dollars, marks, yen, sterling, or some other so-called hard currency, which is basically the currency of the lending country. By contrast, an investment had no schedule for return of the capital, and earnings went from the developing country only when the enterprise succeeded. Many countries, however, were suspicious of foreign investors, and bank loans were preferred because the foreign bankers had no interest in ownership and, once the loan was repaid, had no control over the company.

During the 1960s and 1970s such lending became a growing activity for banks. Loans were made, they were repaid, and more loans were made for other country and company development. As these developing economies grew, the countries identified more projects they wanted to do, and it was expected that progress could continue.

The key element in a country's continued ability to borrow was its demonstrated capability to repay, either from its export earnings or its reserves. Countries that were growing because of their expanding industrial base were the most sought-after borrowers. These countries had export earnings that created the foreign exchange needed. At the same time, many other countries that were poor and lacked a source of major export earnings did not attract investments or bank loans and were dependent on foreign-aid grants from the industrial countries and programs of establishments, such as the International Development Agency (chapter 16).

The Situation in the 1970s

The 1970s saw a great spurt in the projects that the developing countries wanted to build and, at the same time, a tremendous interest by bankers to lend. With the sudden rise in the price of oil, some petroleum-exporting countries acquired massive surpluses of funds, which they deposited in banks through the Eurodollar market (chapter 15). The banks put these funds to work in a process that came to be called recycling. This simply meant that banks assumed the risk of putting these dollars back into the developing countries by making more loans. It is not a coincidence that the great increase in international loans for new manufacturing plants, infrastructure, and mineral development came at the same time that a huge surplus of funds was being deposited in the global banking system.

There were warning signs that trouble could come. Zaire, for example, had borrowed heavily in the early 1970s. When the world price for copper, almost its only major export earner, dropped, Zaire found that it could not earn enough dollars to pay its foreign debts, which accounted for 40 percent of its gross domestic product.[5] In 1973 and 1974, when Zaire was borrowing, copper prices were 80 cents to 93 cents a pound. In 1976 and 1977, when it asked for rescheduling of its debt, the price was 59 cents to 63 cents a pound.[6]

Concerns also developed that some countries were borrowing so fast that previous loans were being repaid from the new borrowings. Banks only had incomplete information about the total amount some countries were borrowing in both the public and private sectors and how much foreign exchange was going to be needed in the future to service this debt. Sometimes even the countries themselves did not have accurate and complete information.

The Crisis

Mexico triggered the international debt crisis.[7] It was not the largest international borrower at the time; Brazil was. Nor was it the first large debtor country to have problems. This had come the year before, when Poland had requested a moratorium on its debt repayments. Mexico, however, was very much a U.S. customer. Two-thirds of its exports and imports were with the United States. As a neighbor, U.S. banks had made substantial credit available to both the public sector (the government and government-owned companies) and the private sector (privately owned corporations). When Poland had encountered problems, German banks suffered; with Mexico, it was the U.S. banks. Poland had owed over $25 billion to all its creditors; Mexico owed over $70 billion.

Mexico was a developing country that was making the transition to industrialization. Its natural resources were being developed and it had a population that produced entrepreneurs, workers who were moving from agriculture to industry, and a growing middle class with the skills and desire to work to improve their standard of living. Illiteracy was low. In 1921, Mexico had been the second largest oil producer in the world, but shortly thereafter became a net oil importer. Since World War II, Mexico had steadily expanded its industry into steel, chemicals, and other types of manufacturing. It was politically stable, financially conservative, but with a rapidly expanding population that needed by 1976 to create 800,000 jobs annually.[8]

Then, in the 1970s, Mexico discovered huge new reserves of oil. It decided to export at a level of 1.1 million barrels a day. This came at the same time OPEC forced the increase in oil prices and as the industrialized countries projected an upward trend of

---

Oral History of Jesus Silva Herzog, Former Finance Minister of Mexico

What became known as the beginning of the debt crisis took place Friday, the twentieth of August 1982, when we called a meeting of the most prominent representatives of international banking in the building of the Federal Reserve Bank of New York. That morning there were about 180 people, representatives of the world's banks, to whom we said Mexico did not have sufficient resources to continue paying the service on its foreign debt. That day Mexico had little more than $180 million in liquid reserves, and the following Monday, August 23, we had to make payments of almost $300 million to international banks.

We had faced very serious problems for several months. In February 1982 we had devalued the peso after suffering, in the second half of 1981, an increase in interest rates, a fall in the prices of our exports and an enormous and dramatic flight of capital—the product of uncertainty in Mexico, an overvalued exchange rate and a lack of confidence. Several weeks later we made an adjustment of salaries throughout the country that sent the sig-

nal that the adjustment needed after a devaluation was not going to be sufficiently strong. And capital flight continued and accelerated, probably worsening during June and July of 1982. Those were truly dramatic moments, in which the financial authorities felt a great impotence to prevent or detain capital flight. We took some compensatory measures to restore confidence, but the crisis was such we could not detain capital flight. There were times when Mexico lost $200 and $300 million in a single day.

We carried out various emergency measures, among them a support of $700 million from the Federal Reserve Bank of New York, which was nearly used up in a week. We signed the last "jumbo" credit, headed by Bank of America, in June of 1982 for $2.5 billion. That was also used up after a few days.

We felt we needed new conditions of repayment periods to be able to continue meeting our financial obligations. The impact brought about by our meeting with the bankers was very perceptible. That first day, the stocks of the principal

Continued

banks of New York fell on the New York Stock Exchange. Here in Mexico people talked of a possible collapse of the international financial system, of a run on the principal banks of the U.S. and a domino effect throughout Latin America.

The problem that arose on the twentieth of August was a surprise for the great majority of participants in the international financial market. Neither the high officials of the governments of the industrial countries, nor the most prominent bankers, and least of all the financial academics, foresaw the debt crisis. I don't think any of us attending the August 20 meeting realized the consequences of what was happening in those moments. We knew, of course, that it was a delicate, important, far-reaching moment, but we never thought—at least I did not think—that it would begin the so-called debt crisis in the developing world.

We erred—the debtors as well as the creditors—in interpreting the essence of the debt problem. At that moment, August 20, 1982, we in the debtor nations and equally the creditor nations and the international organizations thought it was a liquidity problem. In other words, we believed that it was a short-term problem that would be resolved through restructuring the existing debt, obtaining new resources and adopting internal austerity measures in each of the debtor countries. As finance minister, I myself made a public statement upon my return to Mexico—which was often repeated—pointing out that we were facing a cash-flow problem. I was wrong; five years later, no one speaks of the debt as a liquidity problem. Rather, it is a deeper problem of a more structural nature and tied more to the basic economic problems of debtor countries and to international economic relations in general.

future consumption. Thus Mexico anticipated a rising income for years. Faced with a need to create new jobs and a need to maintain momentum to keep the standard of living of its people rising, which was politically important as the middle class grew, Mexico made a decision to build the new manufacturing plants and government projects it needed. To do this, it borrowed principally from banks. With its projected future oil income, neither Mexico nor its bankers anticipated any cash flow problems when these loans came due.

Other countries, such as Nigeria, made similar decisions based on similar projections. Brazil was another heavy borrower at that time but not based on expectations of oil income, since it had comparatively little. Said Brazil's Minister of Finance: "We had a planned policy to increase the [foreign] debt and at the same time to have investments that would create additional exports and reduce the demand for imports; so as a result, we would be able to service the debt."[9]

What went wrong for Mexico, and Nigeria, was that neither the demand nor the price for oil continued to rise. They stabilized, and then actually fell. Basic economic tenets were proved once again: Rising supply and falling demand will result in falling prices. Mexico had less than expected income when it came time to repay the money it had borrowed to make its big industrialization push.

The shock that an oil producer had run out of foreign exchange caused bankers around the world to become very hesitant to lend to any developing country. Brazil was the next to be affected when it could not borrow what it needed to continue its plan for creating export industries. Bank syndications virtually stopped. Country after country found itself unable to borrow at long term for any purpose, unable to complete development projects, and unable to repay the loan installments coming due.

Their problem could be understood by looking at Nigeria. "Much of the $20 billion in debt was incurred in the early 1980s after economists predicted that the $26 billion Nigeria earned from oil in 1980 would swell to $40 billion in 1986. But oil revenues, which account for almost all of the country's export earnings, were crippled when world prices plummeted and are . . . just $5 billion [in 1986]."[10]

In August 1982, some thought the problem was only a short-term cash flow shortage that could be easily corrected. Instead, many countries had to ask for new repayment schedules and assistance. They had over-borrowed; the banks had over-lent. Within each country there continued to be many borrowers and projects that were maintaining their profitability, but when they went to the central bank for foreign exchange, they became part of the crisis.

THE SEARCH FOR SOLUTIONS

In the month's following Mexico's announcement on August 20, 1982, of their repayment problem, a series of steps were initiated. The banks extended the loan installments that were immediately falling due. Mexico sought a loan from the IMF for $4.65 billion. The United States advanced money against future oil purchases and made credit available through the Eximbank. Central banks of the industrialized countries, coordinated through the Bank for International Settlements, made an interim (*bridge*) loan. The commercial banks formed a creditors' committee to begin work with the Mexican government: first, to define the size of the problem, then to assess the causes, and finally to develop a program to resolve it. During 1982 Mexico's international reserves dropped from over $4 billion to $800 million.

Mexico was to be the prototype program for other developing countries who subsequently announced their difficulties in meeting their current loan repayments. Between 1982 and 1985 "some

$210 billion of third-world debt has been rescheduled or rolled over."[11]

Eventually, the IMF made its loan in return for Mexico's agreement to cut inflation, restrain imports, reduce the government's deficit, and devalue the currency. As their part of the IMF's agreement, commercial banks rescheduled the next years of Mexico's debt repayments and agreed to make new loans. *Rescheduling* or *restructuring* means taking loan installments that are now due but are not being paid and creating a new schedule for these to be repaid in installments over a number of years, such as five or seven, providing new grace periods, and often lower interest rates.

The search for a solution became very difficult. The first steps that were taken proved to be inadequate and negotiators spent the next years repeating their work. They moved from year-by-year restructurings to *multiyear restructuring arrangements* (MYRA). The burden fell heavily on the bank loans. At the same time, new direct investments from corporations, which could have provided new capital, declined precipitously.

Companies in both the creditor and debtor countries were severely affected. There had been translation losses (see chapter 12) for existing investments in subsidiaries in the borrowing countries when those countries devalued their currencies. Companies in the debtor countries that had borrowed in foreign currency now found that the cost, in local currency terms, of paying interest and principal increased while their local earnings declined. Within their countries, most companies found that the government's programs to reduce inflation led to business recessions, declining sales, and business losses. It became extremely difficult, and in some cases impossible, for them to obtain new term financing abroad.

Some companies simply did not survive these pressures. Also affected were companies in the industrialized countries that had been selling their products to the debtor countries where foreign exchange now became scarce and imports were restricted. Many American companies lost some of their major export markets.

DUAL PROBLEMS

It soon became apparent that there was not one major problem, but two and within each of these other complexities that needed to be addressed. The first of the major problems was the ongoing need to reschedule repayments from previous term loans as they fell due with the goal of easing the strain on each country's balance of payments so that current account earnings would not be completely consumed by repayments of principal and interest. New syndicated bank loans were unavailable, which meant that each country was now heavily dependent on its own capacity to generate foreign earnings. The commercial banks recognized the necessity for short-term trade financing to be extended to give a country the capability to have export earnings. Analyzing a country's balance of payments was discovered to be inadequate since it did not show the timing of the actual foreign exchange receipts or payments. This meant developing a greater capacity within each country to capture this data so that recovery plans could be made.

The second major problem was that almost no new net capital was coming into these countries to complete development programs or to start new ones. Economies stagnated, unemployment rose, and standards of living fell. In Latin America from 1980 to 1985, a period spanning the onset of the debt crisis, per capital output declined 8 percent overall, with some countries suffering a drop of 10 to 15 percent while unemployment was 10 percent higher. Although many of the restructurings included what was described as new money, this turned out in many instances to be what was needed by the country to pay the interest on its existing bank loans. As figure 17.1 shows, more money was going to the industrialized countries than the developing countries were receiving! In addition, there was an indeterminate amount of capital flight that added to the burden.

By the late 1980s the term *debt fatigue* was being used. Negotiating teams and senior officers from the commercial banks were exhausted from these years of searching for formulae to solve both the problems; many banks that had participated in syndicated loans disposed of or otherwise wrote off their outstandings at a loss and withdrew from any further activities. Whereas, as previously noted, official creditors in 1980 accounted for only 18 percent of the $172.8 billion long-term debt to Latin America, by 1990 official creditors had grown to account for 34 percent of the now $339 billion debt (see figure 17.2).[12]

Developing country governments were likewise exhausted; their populace angry by the decline in living standards without any apparent resolution of the crisis; some governments simply stopped paying the interest due or restricted the amount to a percentage of their export earnings. De facto debt moratoriums occurred.

**Figure 17.1 Long-Term Net Flows and Transfers to Highly
Indebted Countries.** For the 17 most highly indebted countries,
the bar graphs show net flows by category of lender: new loan
disbursements minus principal repayments; net transfers show
net flows minus interest payments. The trend continued in subsequent years.

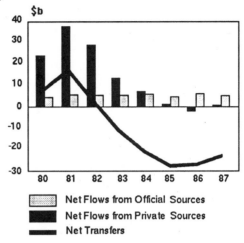

Reprinted with permission. The World Bank, *World Debt Tables
1988-89 edition, Volume 1* (Washington, D.C.: The World Bank),
p. xvii.

Figure 17.2 Developing Countries External Debt

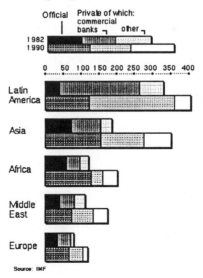

Reprinted with permission. *The Economist Newspaper Ltd.*,
June 9, 1990, p. 105

Over the years, proposals were made by senior government officials in the industrialized countries, such as that by U.S. Treasury Secretary Nicholas Brady, seeking to break the stalemate of the crisis (see box). This prompted new rounds of negotiations between the banks and the debtor countries centered on reducing the debt servicing strain through forgiving part of the debt, reducing the interest rate on existing debt, or making new loans, usually accompanied by some external guarantees for the repayment of some of the remaining debt. Such an agreement for Mexico, for example, achieved the effect of a reduction of "about $14.5 billion in the present value of [its] debt to commercial banks,"[13] which had been about $48.5 billion in medium- and long-term debt. (Mexico's total foreign debt was about $90 billion at this time.) The reduction was achieved through actually forgiving of loan principal and lowering the interest rate on the remaining principal.

The additional problem of renewing a new flow of development capital has proven considerably more elusive.

DEBT REDUCTION TECHNIQUES

As the debt crisis continued, a small secondary market developed where outstanding loans to developing countries could be traded. The source of these loans were many banks who wished to dispose of their loans. Purchasers included various types of investors and speculators, aware that historically some defaulted bonds eventually had been redeemed at or near their face value. The debt was traded at discount, which in some cases was in excess of 75 percent. Occasionally, this market was used by a borrowing country as a way of buying back their debt at a discount or by debtor country residents as a way to repatriate flight capital. Debt reduction techniques, such as the following basic types, were often included as part of the restructuring negotiations.

Debt-for-debt swaps: In this transaction, the bank exchanges its loans to a developing country with another bank or in exchange for bonds the country issues. In the early years of the debt crisis, a bank with a small amount of loans to country A and a larger amount to country B might exchange the loans to country A with another bank for more loans to country B, thereby reducing its involvement to only one country restructuring—or to concentrate on those countries where the bank had greater long-term interests. In later years, debt-for-debt swaps involved exchanging a loan at a discount for a bond issued by the developing country, which usually included some form of collateral or guaranteed source of repayment at a future time, thereby improving the quality of the bank's nondiscounted debt. Mexico, for example, in 1988 offered to exchange some of its existing bank debt at a discount for new bonds collateralized by 20-year U.S. Treasury dollar bonds, which they purchased as a guarantee of a source of repayment at the end of that time.

Debt-for-equity swaps: In this kind of transaction, some developing countries would permit local investments to be made with its foreign debt. The investor would purchase the country's loans at a discount in the foreign market, turn that loan into the developing country's central bank who would pay for it with local currency that the investor would then use to make its investment. The advantage: for the investor, this could be cheaper than making the investment directly; for the developing country, it reduces their foreign debt by paying local currency. The disadvantage for the developing country is that it does not receive the full amount of the foreign currency that it otherwise would have. Many developing countries therefore put restrictions or limits on the amount of such swaps. As an example, the government of Argentina sold two major nationalized industries to foreign investors in 1990 and accepted a combination of its debt paper and cash. The debt thus retired was $7 billion (out of total bank debt of $40 billion), which was estimated would save the country about $800 million a year in debt servicing costs.[14]

ACCOUNTING

Bank accounting practices have been an important factor in the debt restructuring negotiations.

Interest: Banks use the accrual method of accounting for earnings. "Interest income should be recorded when earned, although not collected in cash . . . on the daily balances of the principal amount outstanding throughout the life of the loan."[15] When the cash payment is not made after 90 days of the due date, the general practice is to stop accruing, reverse from the bank's earnings what has been accrued but not yet collected, and then to report the interest as earnings only when it is actually paid. This can cause considerable distortion in a bank's overall earnings, as happened with Brazil. In February 1987 Brazil declared a moratorium on its interest repayments. In late 1988 "under an agreement reached earlier in the year, banks issued new credits permitting Brazil to resume interest payments on its U.S. bank debt. This enabled banks to book nearly $3 billion of accumulated interest during the fourth quarter. As a result, net interest income of the largest banks was 26.7 percent higher in the fourth quarter than in the same quarter in 1987."[16] Banks were willing to make new loans to a number of countries so that interest payments could be made and thus protect the bank's earnings. This had the same basic effect as capitalizing the interest.

Allowance for Loan Losses: As the debt crisis stretched over years, the likelihood for full repayment of many loans became questionable. Banks increased their allowance for loan losses from each year's income so that when any loss would be recognized it would not all have to be charged to that one year's earnings. It became an important criteria for outside investors to see how much allowance a bank had built up. Until the loss was actually realized, the bank could count this loan loss reserve (except an Allocated Transfer Risk Reserve—see chapter 3) as part of its capital, although the risk-based capital guidelines limits this.

Loss: In addition to the normal practice of charging off a loan when it was determined to be uncollectible, banks had a loss whenever they sold a loan at a discount. Thus, a bank that sold a loan in the market, agreed to a debt-for-debt swap at a discount, or forgave some debt under a Brady Plan negotiation, had to recognize that amount below the face amount as a loss.

SUMMARY

The debt crisis that began in mid-1982 has resulted in losses for all the participants. For the developing countries it has cut off most of the long-term flow of funds that they have depended on for the development of their industry and economies. While struggling with the immediate problem to meet their obligations for the money they borrowed during the 1970s, these countries have experienced declines in their standards of living with the resulting danger to the maintenance of political democracy. For the commercial banks that made loans that are not being repaid, there have been losses that have had major impacts on their overall business. For businesses in both the borrowing and lending countries, loss of markets has occurred with the resulting impact on sales, profits, and growth.

The search for solutions has involved governments, banks, and international organizations, all of whom are acutely aware that the continuation of the debt crisis has serious implications for the world economic community. In spite of a decade of efforts, such long-term solutions continue to be elusive.

The Brady Plan

Any new approach must continue to emphasize the importance of stronger growth in debtor nations, as well as the need for debtor reforms and adequate financial support to achieve that growth. We will have success only if our efforts are truly cooperative. And, to succeed we must have the commitment and involvement of all parties.

First and foremost, debtor nations must focus particular attention on the adoption of policies which can better encourage new investment flows, strengthen domestic savings, and promote the return of flight capital. This requires sound growth policies which foster confidence in both domestic and foreign investors. These are essential ingredients for reducing the future stock of debt and sustaining strong growth. Specific policy measures in these areas should be part of any new IMF and World Bank programs. It is worth noting that total capital flight for most major debtors is roughly comparable to their total debt.

Second, the creditor community—the commercial banks, international financial institutions, and creditor governments—should provide more effective and timely financial support. A number of steps are needed in this area.

Commercial banks need to work with debtor nations to provide a broader range of alternatives for financial support, including greater efforts to achieve both debt and debt service reduction and to provide new lending. The approach to this problem must be realistic. The path towards greater creditworthiness and return to the markets for many debtor countries needs to involve debt reduction. Diversified forms of financial support need to flourish and constraints should be relaxed. To be specific, the sharing and negative pledge clauses included in existing loan agreements are a substantial barrier to debt reduction. In addition, the banking community's interests have become more diverse in recent years. This needs to be recognized by both banks and debtors to take advantage of various preferences.

A key element of this approach, therefore, would be the negotiation of a general waiver of the sharing and negative pledge clauses for each performing debtor, to permit an orderly process whereby banks which wish to do so, negotiate debt or debt service reduction transactions. Such waivers might have a three-year life, to stimulate activity within a short but measurable time frame. We expect these waivers to accelerate sharply the pace of debt reduction and pass the benefits directly to the debtor nations. We would expect debtor nations also to maintain viable debt/equity swap programs for the duration of this endeavor, and would encourage them to permit domestic nationals to engage in such transactions.

Of course, banks will remain interested in providing new money, especially if creditworthiness improves over the three-year period. They should be encouraged to do so, for new financing will still be required. In this connection, consideration could be given in some cases to ways of differentiating new from old debt.

The international financial institutions will need to continue to play central roles. The heart of their effort would be to promote sound policies in the debtor countries through advice and financial support. With steady performance under IMF and World Bank programs, these institutions can catalyze new financing. In addition, to support and encourage debtor and commercial bank efforts to reduce debt and debt service burdens, the IMF and World Bank could provide funding, as part of their policy-based lending programs, for debt or debt service reduction purposes. This financial support would be available to countries which elect to undertake a debt reduction program. A portion of their policy-based loans could be used to finance specific debt reduction plans. These funds could support collateralized debt for bond exchanges involving a significant discount on outstanding debt. They could also be used to replenish reserves following a cash buyback.

Continued

Moreover, both institutions could offer new, additional financial support to collateralize a portion of interest payments for debt or debt service reduction transactions. By offering direct financial support for debt and debt service operations, the IMF and the World Bank could provide new incentives, which would act simultaneously to strengthen prospects for greater creditworthiness and to restore voluntary private financing in the future. This could lead to considerable improvements in the cash flow positions of the debtor countries.

While the IMF and World Bank will want to set guidelines on how their funds are used, the negotiation of transactions will remain in the market place—en-couraged and supported but not managed by the international institutions.

Creditor governments should continue to reschedule or restructure their own exposure through the Paris Club, and to maintain export credit cover for countries with solid reform programs. In addition, creditor countries which are in a position to provide additional financing in support of this effort may wish to consider doing so.

Extract from Remarks by the Secretary of the Treasury, Nicholas F. Brady, March 10, 1989.

QUESTIONS

1. What is the international debt crisis?
2. How does a rescheduling affect the borrowing country?
3. What is the Brady Plan?
4. Describe a debt-equity swap.

Notes

1. The World Bank, *World Debt Tables 1989-90, Volume 1* (Washington, D.C.: The World Bank, 1989), pp. 7-8.

2. Philip Ziegler, *The Sixth Great Power: Barings 1762-1929* (London: Collins, 1988), pp. 233-234.

3. Irving S. Friedman, *The World Debt Dilemma: Managing Country Risk* (Philadelphia: Robert Morris Associates, 1983), p. xiii.

4. The World Bank, *World Debt Tables 1989-90, Volume 1* (Washington, D.C.: The World Bank, 1989), p. 94.

5. Friedman, *op. cit.*, p. 137.

6. International Monetary Fund, *Primary Commodities* (Washington, D.C., May 1986), p. 57.

7. *The Economist*, "Mexico: The Fork in the Road," April 5, 1986, p. 20.

8. Howard Burmess, *Mexico: Crisis of Confidence*, Harvard Business School Case Study 9-383-148 (Boston: President and Fellows of Harvard College, 1984), p. 8.

9. The Editors of *Institutional Investor, The Way It Was: An Oral History of Finance 1967-1987* (New York: William Morrow and Co., 1988), p. 453.

10. *The New York Times*, "Nigeria, Rich in Oil, Juggles Its Huge Debt," December 22, 1986, p. 28.

11. *The Economist*, "Debtors Hope for Growth, Yearn For Cash—And Fear the Worst," October 12, 1985, p. 75.

12. The World Bank, *World Debt Tables 1990-91, Volume 1*, (Washington, D.C.: The World Bank, 1990), p. 142.

13. International Monetary Fund, *Annual Report 1990*, p. 28.

14. *The New York Times*, "Argentina Closes Sale of State-Owned Airline" November 23, 1990, p. C2.

15. Fred M. Frankston, Charles D. Mecimore, and Michael F. Cornick, *Bank Accounting* (Washington, D.C.: American Institute of Banking, 1984), p. 150.

16. FDIC, *Quarterly Banking Profile*, 4th Quarter, 1988, p. 2.

EPILOGUE

A Final Word

We end as we began with the recognition that the United States is inextricably involved economically with the world. United States business is global; the United States market is open to virtually every country's business. As *Business Week* summed it up, "Our analysis shows that all Americans are affected by trade and forever jettisons the notion that it is possible to hide from the global economy. . . . If Americans don't embrace the global marketplace and become better and bigger participants in it, U.S. stature will only erode further."[1]

While many United States banks may have said they want to get away from international banking, the reality is that they cannot because their customers have not retreated from global competition. The U.S. bank that hesitates to serve their customer's needs will likely find that someone else will and that someone is likely to be a foreign bank with the skills to manage differentiated global risks.

What has changed in the United States bank, however, is who is the international banker. As was said at the outset of this book, the banker is likely not to be a specialist doing only international business. Many banks have found that they simply cannot afford to have two departments while, at the same time, the business of the world is making it harder to distinguish between domestic and international. New financial products span domestic as well as international needs.

Today's banker must see global risks and commitments as indistinguishable from domestic ones. That is how customers conduct their business; their banker must do likewise.

---

1.   *Business Week*, "The Global Economy—Can You Compete," December 17, 1990, p. 63.

SUGGESTED READING LIST

The student interested in more information on a particular topic may find it in the various sources cited in the notes at the end of each chapter. In addition, the following are other publications that can increase one's knowledge and depth of the world in which international banking takes place.

Baughn, William H., and Donald R. Mandich, eds. *The International Banking Handbook.* Homewood, Illinois: Dow Jones-Irwin, 1983.

Braudel, Fernand. *Civilization and Capitalism, 15th-18th Century*, 3 vol. (The Structure of Everyday Life, The Wheels of Commerce, and The Perspective of the World) New York: Harper and Row, 1981. A fascinating and readable economic history from which the reader can see the origin of many activities of international banking. It is, however, a total of about 2,000 pages. For the specifics of international trade and finance, see Vol. 3, The Perspective of the World.

Harfield, Henry. *Bank Credits and Acceptances*, Fifth Edition. New York: The Ronald Press, 1974. A key book on the legal underpinnings of bankers' acceptances and letters of credit.

International Monetary Fund, Washington, D.C. A series of publications offering detailed current data and information on international finance. These include *International Financial Statistics, World Economic and Financial Surveys, and Occasional Papers* on such topics as capital markets, trade policies, and area studies.

Pocket Banker and *Pocket Economist.* London: The Economist, 1983, 1985. Two slightly irreverent reference books that nonetheless accurately and concisely explain many terms and practices of international finance.

318

Porter, Michael E. *The Competitive Advantage of Nations*. New York: The Free Press, 1990. An original insight into the relationship between successful global industries and their national base. One reviewer's comment: He "has done for international capitalism what Marx did for the class struggle."

Shaterian, William S. *Export-Import Banking*. New York: The Ronald Press, 1956. Although an older book, still continues as a basic guide to letters of credit.

Stigum, Marcia. *The Money Market*, Third Edition. Homewood, Illinois: Business One Irwin, 1990. The latest edition of a series describing those money market instruments used by international bankers. There is simply nothing better nor more readable on this topic.

World Bank, Washington, D.C. A number of studies on development. Of particular interest is an annual *World Development Report*, which covers general topics and then concentrates on one major international financial topic.

GLOSSARY

Acceptance

A time draft (bill of exchange) on the face of which the drawee has written the word "accepted" and the date it is payable, and which the drawee has signed, thereby acknowledging a commitment to pay at the future date. (*See* bankers' acceptance, trade acceptance.)

Affiliate

A business organization sharing with another organization some aspect of common ownership and control.

Agency

A banking office of a foreign bank in the United States that is restricted to accepting deposits in its own name.

American Depository Receipt (ADR)

A certificate representing shares of a foreign stock that is issued by a U.S. depository bank.

Arbitrage

A technique for buying and selling of the same currency in different markets to take advantage of price differentials.

Authority to Purchase

An instrument similar to a letter of credit, except that the draft is drawn on the foreign buyer. Authorities to purchase are used primarily in Asia.

Aval

A form of guarantee established by signing on a promissory note, which is acceptable in some countries.

Back-to -Back Letter of Credit

A letter of credit with identical documentary requirements and covering the same merchandise as another letter of credit, except for a difference in the price of the merchandise as shown by the invoice and the draft. The second letter of credit can be negotiated only after the first is negotiated.

Balance of Payments

A statement that shows all of a country's receipts from and payments to foreign countries during a given period of time.

Balance of Trade	The difference between a nation's merchandise exports and imports over a given period of time.
Balance on Goods and Services	The difference between exports and imports of goods and services. It includes merchandise trade and invisible items.
Bankers' Acceptance	An acceptance drawn on and accepted by a bank that thereby becomes primarily liable to pay on the maturity date. In the U.S. it must cover certain specified underlying transactions in accordance with Federal Reserve requirements to be eligible for discount at a Federal Reserve Bank.
Banques d'affaires	French form of merchant bank.
Barter	The trade of goods without an exchange of money.
Beneficiary	The person in whose favor a letter of credit is issued.
Bilateral Net Credit Limit	The maximum dollar amount a bank participating in a U.S. payment network (for example, CHIPS) will permit in net transfers during a day (value of receives in excess of value of sends).
Bill of Exchange	*See* Draft.
Bill of Lading	A document issued by a transportation company that acknowledges the receipt of specified goods for transportation to a certain place, sets forth the contract between the shipper and the carrier, and provides for delivery of the goods.
Branch	A separate banking unit that is part of a U.S. or foreign bank.
Capital Account	(1) The net worth, capital investment, or owner's equity of an enterprise. Capital account is the difference between an entity's assets and liabilities. (2) The account used to record the flow of investment (long-term) capital to and from a nation.
Capital Flight	A transfer of money from one nation to another as a hedge against poor economic or political conditions.
Carter Bonds	Two- to four-year bonds issued by the U.S. in 1978-80 denominated in DM and Swiss Francs to supplement foreign currency resources for U.S. intervention.
Cash Letter	The cover letter used by banks in sending checks to a correspondent, sometimes in another country, for clearance.
Cash Letter of Credit	A letter addressed by a bank to a correspondent asking that a specified amount of funds be made available to the party named in the letter within a certain time.
Certificate of Analysis	*See* Inspection Certificate.

Certificate of Origin	A document that certifies to the country of origin of the goods.
CHIPS	Acronym for New York's Clearing House Interbank Payments System, an automated large item payment's system.
Clearing Agreement	An agreement between two or more countries that the payment of all trade between them will be passed through special accounts in their central banks and will be kept generally in balance.
Collateral	Value, such as securities, that are pledged as an alternate source of repayment of a loan.
Collection	The process of presenting a negotiable instrument to the maker for payment.
Confirmed Letter of Credit	A letter of credit issued by the local bank of the importer and to which another bank, usually in the country of the exporter, has added its commitment to honor drafts and documents presented in accordance with the terms of the credit.
Consignment Shipment	A shipment for sale that is available to the importer in his location, at which time payment is made to the exporter.
Consular Invoice	An invoice for merchandise shipped from one country to another, prepared by the shipper, and certified at the shipping point by a consul of the country of destination.
Correspondent Bank	A bank with which a second bank in another area has an account relationship and that helps the second bank to conduct business.
Cost and Freight (C.&F.)	A shipping term under which the seller quotes a price, including the cost of transportation to the named point of destination.
Cost, Insurance, and Freight (C.I.F.)	A shipping term under which the seller quotes a price including the cost of the goods, insurance, and all transportation charges to the named point of destination.
Country Risk	The risk that borrowers within a country cannot repay their obligations to foreign creditors because of political or general economic factors, such as lack of exchange, prevailing in their country.
Cross-Rate	The exchange rate between each pair of three or more currencies.
Current Account	The value of all invisible and visible trade between nations (goods, services, income, and unilateral transfers).
Customs Invoice	A document that contains a declaration by the seller, the shipper, or the agent of either as to the value of the goods covered.
Deferred Payment Letter of Credit	A letter of credit under which the seller agrees to full or partial payment over six months or more after shipment.

Developing Country	An ill-defined term to identify that group of countries that have not attained a high degree of industrialization, sometimes referred to as less developed countries (LDC) or the Third World.
Direct Investments	Investments in foreign corporations where the investors have a controlling interest in the overseas firm.
Documents	Items presented along with the draft under a letter of credit. These may include bill of lading, invoice, customs invoice, marine insurance policy or certificate, certificate of origin, weight list, packing list, and inspection certificate (or certificate of analysis).
Documents Against Acceptance (D/A) Draft	A time draft to which title documents are attached. The documents are surrendered to the drawee when the drawee has accepted the corresponding draft, acknowledging the obligation to pay at the future date.
Documents Against Payment (D/P) Draft	A sight draft to which title documents are attached. The documents are surrendered to the drawee only when the drawee has paid the corresponding draft.
Draft	A signed order by one party, the drawer, addressed to another, the drawee, directing the drawee to pay a specified sum of money to the order of a third person, the payee.
Drawback	Rebate of U.S. customs duty for imported goods that are subsequently exported.
Dual Currency Account	An account kept by a bank with a bank in a foreign country in the foreign currency (Due From account).
Due From Account	A deposit account maintained in another bank.
Due To Account	A deposit account maintained by another bank.
Edge Act Corporation	A national chartered corporation established under section 25(a) of the Federal Reserve Act to engage in international banking and investment.
Eurodollars	U.S. dollars deposited in a banking office outside the United States.
Export Trading Company (ETC)	A company under the Export Trading Company Act of 1982 permitting banks to function as agents in international trade.
Exports	Goods and services that a nation sells abroad.
Fedwire	Automated system for effecting payments between banks through their accounts at a Federal Reserve Bank.
Floating Rate	The absence of fixed rates of exchange. Each currency rate is determined by the supply and demand.

Foreign Currency	The money of another country.
Foreign Draft	A draft drawn by a bank on a foreign correspondent bank.
Foreign Drawings and Remittance Service	A service through which major banks make their Due From accounts available to their correspondents for use in arranging money transfers overseas.
Foreign Exchange	(1) The money of another country. (2) The process of converting the currency of one country for that of another country.
Foreign Exchange Rate	The price relationship between the currencies of two countries.
Foreign Exchange Trading	The buying and selling of the currency of one country for that of another.
Foreign Trade	The exchange of goods between nations.
Forward Delivery	The contracting for the transfer of foreign exchange at a specified future date.
Free Alongside (F.A.S.)	A shipping term under which the seller quotes a price including delivery of the goods alongside the ocean vessel and within reach of its loading tackle.
Free On Board (F.O.B.)	A shipping term under which the price quoted applies only at shipping point, and the seller is responsible for all charges only until the merchandise is loaded on the vessel.
General Average	A marine insurance concept whereby all the shippers on a given voyage reimburse those shippers whose cargo was jettisoned in bad weather, for example, to save the ship.
Gross National Product (GNP)	The total value of the goods and services produced in a nation during a specific period and also comprising the total of expenditures by consumers and government plus gross private investment plus exports minus imports.
Group of 7 (G-7) countries	Informal term for Canada, France, Germany, Great Britain, Italy, Japan, and the U.S.
Group of 10 (G-10) countries	Informal term for Belgium, Canada, France, Germany, Italy, Japan, Netherlands, Sweden, United Kingdom, and the U.S. Switzerland later joined in 1984, making it in fact 11 countries, but name remains as is.
Guarantee	A written promise by one party to be liable for the debt of another party.
Guarantor	One who extends a guarantee.

Hedging	The purchase or sale of foreign exchange, usually on a forward basis, to avoid any loss in the event of a change in the foreign exchange rate.
Imports	Goods and services that a nation buys from abroad.
Incoterms	Commonly accepted definition for trade price items.
Inspection Certificate	A certificate issued by an independent third party when outside examination is called for in the merchandise contract in international trade.
Interest Rate Arbitrage	The movement of funds from one money market to another through the foreign exchange market to obtain a higher rate of interest.
International Banking Facility	A separate set of asset and liability books established within a banking office in the U.S. that domiciles Eurodollar loans and deposits.
Investments	The flow of funds, usually for a long term, to build or acquire assets.
Invisible Trade	The foreign trade of services, such as travel and transportation, and interest from investments abroad.
Invoice	A statement prepared by the seller addressed to the buyer showing the details of the sale.
Letter of Credit	An instrument issued by a bank to a seller by which the bank substitutes its own credit for that of the buyer.
LIBID	Acronym for London interbank bid rate for Eurodollar time deposits of a given tenor.
LIBOR	Acronym for London interbank offered rate, which is the interest rate a bank agrees to pay on a Eurodollar deposit to another bank.
LIMEAN	Acronym for the average of LIBOR and LIBID of a given tenor.
Merchant Bank	A European form of an investment bank.
Most Favored Nation	A convention in foreign trade treaties that a designated nation will not be charged a tariff rate any higher than the most preferential rate the granting nation gives to anyone else.
Negotiation Credit	A letter of credit that expires in the location of the exporter, thereby permitting drafts to be negotiated through any bank.
Netting by novation	Trading contracts, such as in foreign exchange, which by agreement may be amalgamated with all other contracts with the same

	customer of same value date and currency and legally substitute one single net amount for the previous gross obligations.
Nostro Account	An old term meaning "our account with you." (Due From account.)
Option Contract	A foreign exchange contract that matures not on a stated date but any date between two dates at the option of the one party.
Par Value	The basic value of its currency, declared by a country in accordance with the requirements of the International Monetary Fund.
Parastatal	A government-owned corporation.
Position	A bank's net balance of purchases and sales in a foreign currency at the end of a business day.
Prime Rate	A bank's base lending rate of interest.
Promissory Note	A written promise that commits the signer to repay a certain sum to the payee at a fixed future date, usually with interest.
Protest	The legal process of demanding payment of a negotiable item from the maker or drawee who has refused to pay.
Quota	A restriction on the quantity of an import.
Red Clause Letter of Credit	A letter of credit that provides for advance payments prior to the presentation of documents.
Reserves	(1) Profits of a business that have been set aside for a specific purpose, for example, reserves for depreciation, bad debts, and contingencies. (2) Cash on hand or deposited with the Federal Reserve, used by depository institutions to meet legal reserve requirements. (3) A nation's holding of gold, SDRs, convertible currencies, and other foreign assets.
Revocable Letter of Credit	A letter of credit that may be withdrawn from the beneficiary at any time without prior notice to the beneficiary.
Revolving Letter of Credit	A letter of credit that provides for renewed credit to become available as soon as the opening bank has advised the negotiating or paying bank that the drafts already drawn by the beneficiary have been reimbursed to the opening bank by the buyer.
Schedule of Charges	A schedule showing the rates charged by an international department for handling various transactions.
Sender Net Debit Cap	The maximum dollar amount a bank participating in a U.S. payment network (for example, CHIPS) will permit in daylight overdraft (the value of all sends in excess of the value of all receives).

Settlement	(1) A transfer of funds to complete a transaction. (2) The conclusion of a transaction: completing all necessary documentation, making the necessary payments, and, where appropriate, transferring title.
Sight Draft	A draft that is payable upon presentation to the drawee on sight or on demand.
Signature Book	A book containing facsimiles of the signatures of the authorized officers of a bank who may commit that bank.
Sovereign Risk	The risk that a foreign government (as distinct from a business in that country) may default on its borrowings. See country risk.
Special Drawing Rights (SDR)	An international reserve asset created by the International Monetary Fund, the value of which is based on a basket of currencies.
Spot Delivery	The transfer of foreign exchange within two business days.
Spread	The difference between the buying rate and the selling rate of a foreign currency.
Standby Letter of Credit	A letter of credit that can be drawn against only if another business transaction is not performed.
Straight Credit	A letter of credit instrument under which the beneficiary is paid by a bank in the beneficiary's area that has been designated by the bank opening the credit.
Subsidiary	A company that is owned by another company, either wholly or by holding a majority of the stocks.
Swap	(1) The purchase or sale of foreign exchange for delivery on one date, with the offsetting simultaneous sale or purchase of the equivalent exchange for delivery on another date. (2) An agreement between two parties exchanging the obligation to pay interest on each other's debt.
Swap Line	A mutual credit facility between governments for the short-term purchase and sale of foreign exchange.
S.W.I.F.T.	Acronym for Society for Worldwide Interbank Financial Telecommunications, a cooperative for a standardized automated international funds transfer information system between banks.
Tariff	A customs tax on goods being imported.

Tenor	The time between the date of issue or acceptance of a note or draft and the maturity date.
Test Key	A code established between banks for authenticating tele-communication messages, usually for the transfer of funds.
Time Draft	A draft that is payable at a fixed or determinable future time.
Trade Acceptance	A draft drawn by the seller of goods on the buyer and accepted by the buyer for payment at a specified future date.
Trade Balance	The net balance of exports and imports of a country's merchandise (physical goods, not including services).
Transferable Letter of Credit	A letter of credit that enables the beneficiary to transfer the credit to another party, thereby authorizing the other party to present documents and a draft.
Traveler's Check	A special check supplied by banks and other companies to enable travelers to carry money without fear of loss or theft.
Traveler's Letter of Credit	A letter of credit addressed by a bank to its correspondent banks, authorizing the person named in the letter to draw drafts on the correspondent banks to the extent of the credit specified.
Trust Receipt	An agreement between a bank and a borrower in which the bank releases documents, merchandise, or other property without releasing its title to the property.
Value Date	The date when a sum of money is transferred.
Visible Trade	Merchandise exports and imports.
Vostro Account	An old term used by foreign banks, meaning "your account with us." *See also* Due To Account.
Weight List	A list that itemizes the weights of individual parcels or bales (in the case of bulk commodities, it covers an entire cargo).

APPENDIX A

Incoterms
ICC Publication No. 460
Effective July 1, 1990

PURPOSE OF INCOTERMS

1. The purpose of "Incoterms" is to provide a set of international rules for the interpretation of the most commonly used trade terms in foreign trade. Thus, the uncertainties of different interpretations of such terms in different countries can be avoided or at least reduced to a considerable degree.

2. Frequently parties to a contract are unaware of the different trading practices in their respective countries. This can give rise to misunderstandings, disputes and litigation with all the waste of time and money that this entails. In order to remedy these problems the International Chamber of Commerce first published in 1936 a set of international rules for the interpretation of trade terms. These rules were known as "Incoterms 1936". Amendments and additions were later made in 1953, 1967, 1976, 1980 and presently 1990 in order to bring the rules in line with current international trade practices.

WHY NEW INCOTERMS?

3. The main reason for the 1990 revision of Incoterms was the desire to adapt terms to the increasing use of electronic data interchange (EDI). In the present 1990 version of Incoterms this is possible when the parties have to provide various documents (such as commercial invoices, documents needed for customs

clearance or documents in proof of delivery of the goods as well as transport documents). Particular problems arise when the seller has to present a negotiable transport document and notably the bill of lading which is frequently used for the purposes of selling the goods while they are being carried. In these cases it is of vital importance, when using EDI messages, to ensure that the buyer has the same legal position as he would have obtained if he had received a bill of lading from the seller.

NEW TRANSPORTATION TECHNIQUES	4. A further reason for the revision stems from changed transportation techniques, particularly the unitisation of cargo in containers, multimodal transport and roll on-roll off traffic with road vehicles and railway wagons in "short-sea" maritime transport. In Incoterms 1990 the term "Free carrier . . . named place" (FCA) has now been adapted to suit all types of transport irrespective of the mode and combination of different modes. As a consequence, the terms which appear in the previous version of Incoterms dealing with some particular modes of transport (FOR/FOT and FOB Airport) have been removed.
NEW METHOD OF PRESENTING INCOTERMS	5. In connection with the revision work within the ICC Working Party, suggestions were made to present the trade terms in another manner for the purpose of easier reading and understanding. The terms have been grouped in four basically different categories; namely starting with the only term whereby the seller makes the goods available to the buyer at the seller's own premises (the "E"-term Ex works); followed by the second group whereby the seller is called upon to deliver the goods to a carrier appointed by the buyer (the "F"-terms FCA, FAS and FOB); continuing with the "C"-terms where the seller has to contract for carriage, but without assuming the risk of loss of or damage to the goods or additional costs due to events occurring after shipment and dispatch (CFR, CIF, CPT and CIP); and, finally, the "D"-terms whereby the seller has to bear all costs and risks needed to bring the goods to the country of destination (DAF, DES, DEQ, DDU and DDP). A chart setting out this new classification is given hereafter.

INCOTERMS 1990

Group E Departure	EXW	Ex Works
Group F Main cordage unpaid	FCA	Free Carrier
	FAS	Free Alongside Ship
	FOB	Free On Board
Group C Main carriage paid	CFR	Cost and Freight
	CIF	Cost, Insurance and Freight
	CPT	Carriage Paid To
	CIP	Cordage and Insurance Paid To
Group D Arrival	DAF	Delivered At Frontier
	DES	Delivered Ex Ship
	DEQ	Delivered Ex Quay
	DDU	Delivered Duty Unpaid
	DDP	Delivered Duty Paid

Further, under all terms, the respective obligations of the parties have been grouped under 10 headings where each heading on the seller's side "mirrors" the position of the buyer with respect to the same subject matter. Thus, if for instance according to A.3. the seller has to arrange and pay for the contract of carriage we find the words "No obligation" under the heading "Contract of carriage" in B.3. setting forth the buyer's position. Needless to say, this does not mean that the buyer would not in his own interest make such contracts as may be needed to bring the goods to the desired destination, but he has no "obligation" to the seller to do so. However, with respect to the division between the parties of duties, taxes and other official charges, as well as the costs of carrying out customs formalities, the terms explain for the sake of clarity how such costs are divided between the parties although, of course, the seller might not have any interest at all in the buyer's further disposal of the goods after they have been delivered to him. Conversely, under some terms such as the "D"-terms, the buyer is not interested in costs which the seller might incur in order to bring the goods all the way to the agreed destination point.

CUSTOMS OF THE PORT OR OF A PARTICULAR TRADE	6. Since the trade terms must necessarily be possible to use in different trades and regions it is impossible to set forth the obligations of the parties with precision. To some extent it is therefore necessary to refer to the custom of the particular trade place or to the practices which the parties themselves may have established in their previous dealings (cf. Article 9 of the 1980 United Nations Convention on Contracts for the International Sale of Goods). It is of course desirable that sellers and buyers keep themselves duly informed of such customs of the trade when they negotiate their contract and that, whenever uncertainty arises, clarify their legal position by appropriate clauses in their contract of sale. Such special provisions in the individual contract would supersede or vary anything which is set forth as a rule of interpretation in the various Incoterms.
THE BUYER'S OPTIONS	7. In some situations, it may not be possible at the time when the contract of sale is entered into to decide precisely on the exact point or even the place where the goods should be delivered by the seller for carriage or at the final destination. For instance reference might have been made at this stage merely to a "range" or to a rather large place, e.g. seaport, and it is then usually stipulated that the buyer can have the light or duty to name later on the more precise point within the range or the place. If the buyer has a duty to name the precise point as aforesaid his failure to do so might result in liability to bear the risks and additional costs resulting from such failure. In addition, the buyer's failure to use his light to indicate the point may give the seller the right to select the point which best suits his purpose.
CUSTOMS CLEARANCE	8. It is normally desirable that customs clearance is arranged by the party domiciled in the country where such clearance should take place or at least by somebody acting there on his behalf. Thus, the exporter should normally clear the goods for export, while the importer should clear the goods for import. However,

under some trade terms, the buyer might undertake to clear the goods for export in the seller's country (EXW, FAS) and, in other terms, the seller might undertake to clear the goods for import into the buyer's country (DEQ and DDP). Needless to say in these cases the buyer and the seller respectively must assume any risk of export and import prohibition. Also they must ascertain that a customs clearance performed by, or on behalf of, a party not domiciled in the respective country is accepted by the authorities. Particular problems ease when the seller undertakes to deliver the goods into the buyer's country in places which cannot be reached until the goods have been cleared for import but where his ability to reach that place is adversely affected by the buyer's failure to fulfil his obligation to clear the goods for import (see further the comment to DDU below).

It may well be that a buyer would wish to collect the goods at the seller's premises under the term EXW or to receive the goods alongside a ship under the trade term FAS, but would like the seller to clear the goods for export. If so, the words "cleared for export" could be added after the respective trade term. Conversely, it may be that the seller is prepared to deliver the goods under the trade term DEO or DDP, but without assuming wholly or partly the obligation to pay the duty or other taxes or official charges levied upon importation of the goods. If so, the words "duty unpaid" might be added after DEQ; or the particular taxes or charges which the seller does not wish to pay may be specifically excluded, e.g. DEQ or DDP "VAT unpaid".

It has also been observed that in many countries it is difficult for a foreign company to obtain not only the import licence, but also duty reliefs (VAT deduction, etc.). "Delivered, Duty Unpaid", can solve these problems by removing from the seller the obligation to clear the goods for import.

In some cases, however, the seller whose obligation of carriage extends to the buyer's premises in the country of import, wants to carry out customs formalities without paying the duties. If so, the DDU term should be added with words to that effect such as "DDU, cleared". Corresponding additions may be used with other "D" terms, e.g. "DDP, VAT unpaid DEQ, duty unpaid".

PACKAGING

9. In most cases, the parties would know beforehand which packaging is required for the safe carriage of the goods to the destination. However, since the seller's obligation to pack the goods may well vary according to the type and duration of the

transport envisaged, it has been felt necessary to stipulate that the seller is obliged to pack the goods in such a manner as is required for the transport, but only to the extent that the circumstances relating to the transport are made known to him before the contract of sale is concluded (cf. Articles 35.1. and 35.2.b. of the 1980 United Nations Convention on Contracts for the International Sale of Goods where the goods, including packaging, must be "fit for any particular purpose expressly or impliedly made known to the seller at the time of the conclusion of the contract, except where the circumstances show that the buyer did not rely, or that it was unreasonable for him to rely, on the seller's skill and judgement").

INSPECTION OF GOODS

10. In many cases, the buyer may be well advised to arrange for inspection of the goods before or at the time they are handed over by the seller for carriage (so-called preshipment inspection or PSI). Unless the contract stipulates otherwise, the buyer would himself have to pay the cost for such inspection which is arranged in his own interest. However, if the inspection has been made in order to enable the seller to comply with any mandatory rules applicable to the export of the goods in his own country he would have to pay for that inspection.

FREE CARRIER... NAMED PLACE (FCA)

11. As has been said, the FCA-term could be used whenever the seller should fulfil his obligation by handing over the goods to a carrier named by the buyer. It is expected that this term will also be used for maritime transport in all cases where the cargo is not handed to the ship in the traditional method over the ship's rail. Needless to say, the traditional FOB-term is inappropriate where the seller is called upon to hand over the goods to a cargo terminal before the ship arrives, since he would then have to bear the risks and costs after the time when he has no possibility to control the goods or to give instructions with respect to their custody.

It should be stressed that under the "F"-terms, the seller should hand over the goods for carriage as instructed by the buyer, since the buyer would make the contract of carriage and name the carrier. Thus, it is not necessary to spell out in the trade term precisely how the goods should be handed over by the seller to the carrier. Nevertheless, in order to make it possible for traders to use FCA as an "overiding" "F" -term, explanations are given with respect to the customary modalities of delivery for the different modes of transport.

In the same manner, it may well be superfluous to introduce a definition of "carrier", since it is for the buyer to instruct the seller to whom the goods should be delivered for carriage. However, since the carrier and the document of transport are of great importance to traders, the preamble to the FCA-term contains a definition of "carrier". In this context, it should be noted that the term "carrier" not only refers to an enterprise actually performing the carriage but it also includes an enterprise merely having undertaken to perform or to procure the performance of the carriage as long as such enterprise assumes liability as a carrier for the carriage. In other words, the term "carrier" comprises performing as well as contracting carriers. Since the position in this respect of the freight forwarder varies from country to country and according to practices in the freight forwarding industry, the preamble contains a reminder that the seller must, of course, follow the buyer's instructions to deliver the goods to a freight forwarder even if the freight forwarder would have refused to accept carrier liability and thus fall outside the definition of "carrier".

The "C" Terms (CFR, CIF, CPT and CIP)

12. Under the "C"-terms, the seller must contract for carriage on usual terms at his own expense. Therefore, a point up to which he would have to pay transportation costs must necessarily be indicated after the respective "C"-term. Under the CIF and CIP terms the seller also has to take out insurance and bear the insurance cost.

Since the point for the division of costs refers to the country of destination, the "C"-terms are frequently mistakenly believed to be arrival contracts, whereby the seller is not relieved from any risks or costs until the goods have actually arrived at the agreed point. However, it must be stressed over and over again that the "C"-terms are of the same nature as the "F"-terms in that the seller fulfils the contract in the country of shipment or dispatch. Thus, the contracts of sale under the "C"-terms, like the contracts under the "F"-terms, fall under the category of shipment contracts. While the seller would have to pay the normal transportation cost for the carriage of the goods by a usual route and in a customary manner to the agreed place of destination, the risk for loss of or damage to the goods, as well as additional costs resulting from events occurring after the goods having been handed over for carriage, fall upon the buyer. Hence, the "C"-terms as distinguished from all other terms contain two "critical" points, one for the division of costs and another one for the division of risks. For this reason, the greatest caution must be observed when adding obligations of the seller to the "C"-terms referring to a time after the aforementioned "critical" point for the division of risk. It is the very essence of the "C"-terms to relieve the seller from any further risk and cost after he has duly fulfilled his contract by contracting for carriage and handing over the goods to the carrier and by providing for insurance under the CIF- and CIP-terms.

It should also be possible for the seller to agree with the buyer to collect payment under a documentary credit by presenting the agreed shipping documents to the bank. It would be quite contrary to this common method of payment in international trade if the seller were to have to bear further risks and costs after the moment when payment had been made under documentary credits or otherwise upon shipment and dispatch of the goods. Needless to say, however, the seller would have to pay every cost which is due to the carrier irrespective of whether freight should be pre-paid upon shipment or is payable at destination (freight collect), except such additional costs which may result from events occurring subsequent to shipment and dispatch.

If it is customary to procure several contracts of carriage involving transhipment of the goods at intermediate places in order to reach the agreed destination, the seller would have to pay all these costs, including any costs when the goods are transhipped from one means of conveyance to the other. If, however, the carrier exercised his rights under a transhipment—or similar clause—in order to avoid unexpected hindrances (such as ice, congestion, labour disturbances, government orders, war or warlike operations) then any additional cost resulting therefrom would be for the account of the buyer.

13. It happens quite often that the parties wish to clarify to which extent the seller should procure a contract of carriage including the costs of discharge. Since such costs are normally covered by the freight when the goods are carried by regular shipping lines, the contract of sale would frequently stipulate that the goods would have to be so carried or at least that they should be carried under "liner terms". In other cases, the word "landed" is added after CFR or CIF. Nevertheless, it is advisable not to use abbreviations added to the "C"-terms unless, in the relevant trade, the meaning of the abbreviations is clearly understood and accepted by the contracting parties or under any applicable law or custom of the trade. In any event, the seller should not—and

indeed could not—without changing the very nature of the "C"-terms undertake any obligation with respect to the arrival of the goods at destination, since the risk for any delay during the carriage is borne by the buyer. Thus, any obligation with respect to time must necessarily refer to the place of shipment or dispatch, e.g. "shipment (dispatch) not later than. . . ". An agreement e.g."CFR Hamburg not later than. . ." is really a misnomer and thus open to different possible interpretations. The parties could be taken to have meant either that the goods must actually arrive at Hamburg at the specified date, in which case the contract is not a shipment contract but an arrival contract or, alternatively, that the seller must ship the goods at such a time that they would normally arrive at Hamburg before the specified date unless the carriage would have been delayed because of unforeseen events.

14. It happens in commodity trades that goods are bought while they are carried at sea and that, in such cases, the word "afloat" is added after the trade term. Since the risk for loss of or damage to the goods would then, under the CFR- and CIF-terms, have passed from the seller to the buyer, difficulties of interpretation might arise. One possibility would be to maintain the ordinary meaning of the CFR- and CIF-terms with respect to the division of risk between seller and buyer which would mean that the buyer might have to assume risks which have already occurred at the time when the contract of sale has entered into force. The other possibility would be to let the passing of the risk coincide with the time when the contract of sale is concluded. The former possibility might well be practical, since it is usually impossible to ascertain the condition of the goods while they are being carried. For this reason the 1980 UN Convention on Contracts for the International Sale of Goods Article 68 stipulates that "if the circumstances so indicate, the risk is assumed by the buyer from the time the goods were handed over to the carrier who issued the documents embodying the contract of carriage". There is, however, an exception to this rule when "the seller knew or ought to have known that the goods had been lost or damaged and did not disclose this to the buyer". Thus, the interpretation of a CFR- or CIF-term with the addition of the word "afloat" will depend upon the law applicable to the contract of sale. The parties are advised to ascertain the applicable law and any solution which might follow therefrom. In case of doubt, the parties are advised to clarify the matter in their contract.

"INCOTERMS" AND THE CONTRACT OF CARRIAGE

15. It should be stressed that Incoterms only relate to trade terms used in the contract of sale and thus do not deal with terms—sometimes of the same or similar wording—which may be used in contracts of carriage, particularly as terms of various charterparties. Charterparty terms are usually more specific with respect to costs of loading and discharge and the time available for these operations (so-called "demurrage" provisions). Parties to contracts of sale are advised to consider this problem by specific stipulations in their contracts of sale so that it is made clear as exactly as possible how much time would be available for the seller to load the goods on a ship or other means of conveyance provided by the buyer and for the buyer to receive the goods from the carrier at destination and, further, to specify to which extent the seller would have to bear the risk and cost of loading operations under the "F"-terms and discharging operations under the "C"-terms. The mere fact that the seller might have procured a contract of carriage, e.g. under the charterparty term "free out" whereby the carrier in the contract of carriage would be relieved from the discharging operations, does not necessarily mean that the risk and cost for such operations would fall upon the buyer under the contract of sale, since it might follow from the stipulations of the latter contract, or the custom of the port, that the contract of carriage procured by the seller should have included the discharging operations.

THE "ON BOARD REQUIREMENT" UNDER FOB, CFR AND CIF

16. The contract of carriage would determine the obligations of the shipper or the sender with respect to handing over the goods for carriage to the carrier. It should be noted that FOB, CFR and CIF all retain the traditional practice to deliver the goods on board the vessel. While, traditionally, the point for delivery of the goods according to the contract of sale coincided with the point for handing over the goods for carriage, contemporary transportation techniques create a considerable problem of "synchronisation" between the contract of carriage and the contract of sale. Nowadays goods are usually delivered by the seller to the carrier before the goods are taken on board or sometimes even before the ship has arrived in the seaport. In such cases, merchants are advised to use such "F"- or "C"-terms which do not attach the handing over of the goods for carriage to shipment on board, namely FCA, CPT or CIP instead of FOB, CFR and CIF.

THE "D"-TERMS (DAF, DES, DEO, DDU AND DDP)

17. As has been said, the "D"-terms are different in nature from the "C"-terms, since the seller according to the "D"-terms is responsible for the arrival of the goods at the agreed place or point of destination. The seller must bear all risks and costs in bringing the goods thereto. Hence, the "D"-terms signify arrival contracts, while the "C"-terms evidence shipment contracts.

The "D"-terms fall into two separate categories. Under DAF, DES and DDU the seller does not have to deliver the goods cleared for import, while under DEQ and DDP he would have to do so. Since DAF is frequently used in railway traffic, where it is practical to obtain a through document from the railway covering the entire transport to the final destination and to arrange insurance for the same period, DAF contains a stipulation in this respect in A.8.. It should be stressed, however, that the seller's duty to assist the buyer in obtaining such a through document of transport is done at the buyer's risk and expense. Similarly, any costs of insurance relating to the time subsequent to the seller's delivery of the goods at the frontier would be for the account of the buyer.

The term DDU has been added in the present 1990 version of Incoterms. The term fulfils an important function whenever the seller is prepared to deliver the goods in the country of destination without clearing the goods for import and paying the duty. Whenever clearance for import does not present any problem—such as within the European Common Market—the term may be quite desirable and appropriate. However, in countries where import clearance may be difficult and time consuming, it may be risky for the seller to undertake an obligation to deliver the goods beyond the customs clearance point. Although, according to DDU B.5. and B.6., the buyer would have to bear the additional risks and costs which might follow from his failure to fulfil his obligations to clear the goods for import, the seller is advised not to use the term DDU in countries where difficulties might be expected in clearing the goods for import.

THE BILL OF LADING AND EDI PROCEDURES

18. Traditionally, the on board bill of lading has been the only acceptable document to be presented by the seller under the terms CFR and CIF. The bill of lading fulfils three important functions, namely

-proof of delivery of the goods on board the vessel
-evidence of the contract of carriage

-a means of transferring rights to the goods in transit by the transfer of the paper document to another party.

Transport documents other than the bill of lading would fulfil the two first-mentioned functions, but would not control the delivery of the goods at destination or enable a buyer to sell the goods in transit by surrendering the paper document to his buyer. Instead, other transport documents would name the party entitled to receive the goods at destination. The fact that the possession of the bill of lading is required in order to obtain the goods from the carrier at destination makes it particularly difficult to replace by EDI procedures.

Further, it is customary to issue bills of lading in several originals but it is, of course, of vital importance for a buyer or a bank acting upon his instructions in paying the seller to ensure that all originals are surrendered by the seller (so-called "full set"). This is also a requirement under the ICC Rules for Documentary Credits (the so-called Uniform Customs and Practice, "UCP", ICC Publication 400).

The transport document must evidence not only delivery of the goods to the carrier but also that the goods, as far as could be ascertained by the carrier, were received in good order and condition. Any notation on the transport document which would indicate that the goods had not been in such condition would make the document "unclean" and thus make it unacceptable under UCP (Art. 18; see also ICC Publication 473). In spite of the particular legal nature of the bill of lading it is expected that it will be replaced by EDI procedures in the near future. The 1990 version of Incoterms has taken this expected development into proper account.

NON-NEGOTIABLE TRANSPORT DOCUMENTS INSTEAD OF BILLS OF LADING

19. In recent years, a considerable simplification of documentary practices has been achieved. Bills of lading are frequently replaced by non-negotiable documents similar to those which are used for other modes of transport than carriage by sea. These documents are called "sea waybills", "liner waybills", "freight receipts", or variants of such expressions. These non-negotiable documents are quite satisfactory to use except where the buyer wishes to sell the goods in transit by surrendering a paper document to the new buyer. In order to make this possible, the obligation of the seller to provide a bill of lading under CFR and CIF must necessarily be retained. However, when the contracting parties know that the buyer does not contemplate selling the

goods in transit, they may specifically agree to relieve the seller from the obligation to provide a bill of lading, or, alternatively, they may use CPT and CIP where there is no requirement to provide a bill of lading.

**Mode of Transport and the
Appropriate Incoterm 1990**

Any Mode of Transport including Multimodal	EXW	Ex Works (...named place)
	FCA	Free Carrier (...named place)
	CPT	Carriage Paid To (...named place of destination)
	CIP	Carriage and Insurance Paid To ...named place of destination)
	DAF	Delivered At Frontier (...named place)
	DDU	Delivered Duty Unpaid (...named place of destination)
	DDP	Delivered Duty Paid (...named place of destination)
Air Transport	FCA	Free Carrier (...named place)
Rail Transport	FCA	Free Carrier (...named place)
Sea and Inland Waterway Transport	FAS	Free Alongside Ship (...named port of shipment)
	FOB	Free On Board (...named port of shipment)
	CFR	Cost and Freight (...named port of destination)
	CIF	Cost, Insurance and Freight (... named port of destination)
	DES	Delivered Ex Ship (...named port of destination)
	DEO	Delivered Ex Quay (... named port of destination)

THE RIGHT TO GIVE INSTRUCTIONS TO THE CARRIER	20. A buyer paying for the goods under a "C"-term should ensure that the seller upon payment is prevented from disposing of the goods by new instructions to the carrier. Some transport documents used for particular modes of transport (air, road or rail) offer the contracting parties a possibility to estop the seller from giving such new instructions to the carrier by providing the buyer with a particular original or duplicate of the waybill. These waybills will have a "no-disposal" clause. However, the documents used instead of bills of lading for maritime carriage do not normally contain such an "estoppel" function. Work is in progress within the Comite Maritime International to remedy this shortcoming of the above-mentioned documents by introducing "Uniform Rules for Sea Waybills". However, until this work has materialised, and been followed through in practice, the buyer should avoid paying against these non-negotiable documents whenever he has any reason to mistrust his seller.
PASSING OF RISKS AND COSTS RELATING TO THE GOODS	21. The risk for loss of or damage to the goods, as well as the obligation to bear the costs relating to the goods, passes from the seller to the buyer when the seller has fulfilled his obligation to deliver the goods. Since the buyer should not be given the possibility to delay the passing of the risks and costs, all terms stipulate that the passing of risks and costs may occur even before delivery, if the buyer does not take delivery as agreed or fails to give such instructions (with respect to time for shipment and/or place for delivery) as the seller may require in order to fulfil his obligation to deliver the goods. It is a requirement for such premature passing of risk and costs that the goods have been identified as intended for the buyer or, as is stipulated in the terms, set aside for him (appropriation). This requirement is particularly important under EXW, since under all other terms the goods would normally have been identified as intended for the buyer when measures have been taken for their shipment or dispatch ("F"- and "C"-terms) or their delivery at destination ("D"-terms). In exceptional cases, however, the goods may have been sent from the seller in bulk without identification of the quantity for each buyer and, if so, passing of risk and cost does not occur before the goods have been appropriated as aforesaid (cf. also Article 69.3 of the 1980 UN Convention on the International Sale of Goods).

REFERENCE TO INCOTERMS	22. Merchants wishing to use these rules should now specify that their contracts will be governed by "Incoterms 1990".

ICC ARBITRATION	Contracting parties that wish to have the possibility of resorting to ICC Arbitration in the event of a dispute with their contracting partner should specifically and clearly agree upon ICC Arbitration in their contract or, in the event no single contractual document exists, in the exchange of correspondence which constitutes the agreement between them. The fact of incorporating one or more Incoterms in a contract or the related correspondence does NOT by itself constitute an agreement to have resort to ICC Arbitration.

The following standard arbitration clause is recommended by the ICC:

"All disputes arising in connection with the present contract shall be finally settled under the Rules of Conciliation and Arbitration of the International Chamber of Commerce by one or more arbitrators appointed in accordance with the said Rules."

EX WORKS (...named place)	"Ex works" means that the seller fulfils his obligation to deliver when he has made the goods available at his premises (i.e. works, factory, warehouse, etc.) to the buyer. In particular, he is not responsible for loading the goods on the vehicle provided by the buyer or for clearing the goods for export, unless otherwise agreed. The buyer bears all costs and risks involved in taking the goods from the seller's premises to the desired destination. This term thus represents the minimum obligation for the seller. This term should not be used when the buyer cannot carry out directly or indirectly the export formalities. In such circumstances, the FCA term should be used.

A. THE SELLER MUST:	1. Provision of goods in conformity with the contract Provide the goods and the commercial invoice, or its equivalent electronic message, in conformity with the contract of sale and any other evidence of conformity which may be required by the contract. 2. Licences, authorisations and formalities Render the buyer, at the latter's request, risk and expense, every

assistance in obtaining any export licence or other official authorisation necessary for the exportation of the goods.

3.   Contract of carriage and insurance
   a) Contract of carriage
   No obligation.
   b) Contract of insurance
   No obligation.

4.   Delivery
Place the goods at the disposal of the buyer at the named place of delivery on the date or within the period stipulated or, if no such place or time is stipulated, at the usual place and time for delivery of such goods.

5.   Transfer of risks
Subject to the provisions of B.5., bear all risks of loss of or damage to the goods until such time as they have been placed at the disposal of the buyer in accordance with A.4.

6.   Division of costs
Subject to the provisions of B.6., pay all costs relating to the goods until such time as they have been placed at the disposal of the buyer in accordance with A.4.

7.   Notice to the buyer
Give the buyer sufficient notice as to when and where the goods will be placed at his disposal.

8.   Proof of delivery, transport document or equivalent electronic message
No obligation.

9.   Checking - packaging - marking
Pay the costs of those checking operations (such as checking quality, measuring, weighing, counting) which are necessary for the purpose of placing the goods at the disposal of the buyer.

Provide at his own expense packaging (unless it is usual for the particular trade to make the goods of the contract description available unpacked) which is required for the transport of the goods, to the extent that the circumstances relating to the transport (e.g. modalities, destination) are made known to the seller before the contract of sale is concluded. Packaging is to be marked appropriately.

10. Other obligations
Render the buyer at the latter's request, risk and expense, every assistance in obtaining any documents or equivalent electronic

messages issued or transmitted in the country of delivery and/or of origin which the buyer may require for the exportation and/or importation of the goods, and, where necessary, for their transit through another country.

Provide the buyer, upon request, with the necessary information for procuring insurance.

THE BUYER MUST:

1.   Payment of the price
Pay the price as provided in the contract of sale.

2.   Licenses, authorisations and formalities
Obtain at his own risk and expense any export and import licence or other official authorisation and carry out all customs formalities for the exportation and importation of the goods and, where necessary, for their transit through another country.

3.   Contract of carriage
No obligation.

4.   Taking delivery
Take delivery of the goods as soon as they have been placed at his disposal in accordance with A.4.

5.   Transfer of risks
Bear all risks of loss of or damage to the goods from the time they have been placed at his disposal in accordance with A.4. Should he fail to give notice in accordance with B.7., bear all risks of loss of or damage to the goods from the agreed date or the expiry date of any period fixed for taking delivery provided, however, that the goods have been duly appropriated to the contract, that is to say clearly set aside or otherwise identified as the contract goods.

6.   Division of costs
Pay all costs relating to the goods from the time they have been placed at his disposal in accordance with A.4.

Pay any additional costs incurred by failing either to take delivery of the goods when they have been placed at his disposal, or to give appropriate notice in accordance with B.7. provided, however, that the goods have been duly appropriated to the contract, that is to say clearly set aside or otherwise identified as the contract goods.

Pay all duties, taxes and other official charges as well as the costs of carrying out customs formalities payable upon exportation and importation of the goods and, where necessary, for their transit through another country.

Reimburse all costs and charges incurred by the seller in rendering assistance in accordance with A.2.

7. Notice to the seller
Whenever he is entitled to determine the time within a stipulated period and/or the place of taking delivery, give the seller sufficient notice thereof.

8. Proof of delivery, transport document or equivalent electronic message
Provide the seller with appropriate evidence of having taken delivery.

9. Inspection of goods
Pay, unless otherwise agreed, the costs of pre-shipment inspection (including inspection mandated by the authorities of the country of exportation).

10. Other obligations
Pay all costs and charges incurred in obtaining the documents or equivalent electronic messages mentioned in A.10. and reimburse those incurred by the seller in rendering his assistance in accordance therewith.

FREE CARRIER (... named place)

"Free Carrier" means that the seller fulfils his obligation to deliver when he has handed over the goods, cleared for export, into the charge of the carrier named by the buyer at the named place or point. If no precise point is indicated by the buyer, the seller may choose within the place or range stipulated where the carrier shall take the goods into his charge. When, according to commercial practice, the seller's assistance is required in making the contract with the carrier (such as in rail or air transport) the seller may act at the buyer's risk and expense.

This term may be used for any mode of transport, including multimodal transport.

"Carrier" means any person who, in a contract of carriage, undertakes to perform or to procure the performance of carriage by rail, road, sea, air, inland waterway or by a combination of such modes. If the buyer instructs the seller to deliver the cargo to a person, e.g. a freight forwarder who is not a "carrier", the seller is deemed to have fulfilled his obligation to deliver the goods when they are in the custody of that person.

"Transport terminal" means a railway terminal, a freight station, a container terminal or yard, a multi-purpose cargo terminal or any similar receiving point.

"Container" includes any equipment used to unitise cargo, e.g. all types of containers and/or flats, whether ISO accepted or not, trailers, swap bodies, ro-ro equipment, igloos, and applies to all modes of transport.

A. THE SELLER MUST:

1. Provision of goods in conformity with the contract
Provide the goods and the commercial invoice, or its equivalent electronic message, in conformity with the contract of sale and any other evidence of conformity which may be required by the contract.

2. Licences, authorisations and formalities
Obtain at his own risk and expense any export licence or other official authorisation and carry out all customs formalities necessary for the exportation of the goods.

3. Contract of carriage and insurance
   a) Contract of carriage

No obligation. However, if requested by the buyer or if it is commercial practice and the buyer does not give an instruction to the contrary in due time, the seller may contract for carriage on usual terms at the buyer's risk and expense. The seller may decline to make the contract and, if he does, shall promptly notify the buyer accordingly.
   b) Contract of insurance
   No obligation.

4. Delivery
Deliver the goods into the custody of the carrier or another person (e.g. a freight forwarder) named by the buyer, or chosen by the seller in accordance with A.3.a), at the named place or point (e.g. transport terminal or other receiving point) on the date or within the period agreed for delivery and in the manner agreed or customary at such point. If no specific point has been agreed, and if there are several points available, the seller may select the point at the place of delivery which best suits his purpose. Failing precise instructions from the buyer, the seller may deliver the goods to the carrier in such a manner as the transport mode of that carrier and the quantity and/or nature of the goods may require.
   i) In the case of rail transport when the goods constitute a wagon load (or a container load carried by rail) the seller has to load the wagon or container in the appropriate manner. Delivery is completed when the loaded wagon or container is taken over by the railway or by another person acting on its behalf.

When the goods do not constitute a wagon or container load, delivery is completed when the seller has handed over the goods at the railway receiving point or loaded them into a vehicle provided by the railway.

ii) In the case of road transport when loading takes place at the seller's premises, delivery is completed when the goods have been loaded on the vehicle provided by the buyer.

When the goods are delivered to the carrier's premises, delivery is completed when they have been handed over to the road carrier or to another person acting on his behalf.

iii) In the case of transport by inland waterway when loading takes place at the seller's premises, delivery is completed when the goods have been loaded on the carrying vessel provided by the buyer.

When the goods are delivered to the carrier's premises, delivery is completed when they have been handed over to the inland waterway carrier or to another person acting on his behalf.

iv) In the case of sea transport when the goods constitute a full container load (FCL), delivery is completed when the loaded container is taken over by the sea carrier. When the container has been carried to an operator of a transport terminal acting on behalf of the carrier, the goods shall be deemed to have been taken over when the container has entered into the premises of that terminal.

When the goods are less than a container load (LCL), or are not to be containerised, the seller has to carry them to the transport terminal. Delivery is completed when the goods have been handed over to the sea carrier or to another person acting on his behalf.

v) In the case of *air transport*, delivery is completed when the goods have been handed over to the air carrier or to another person acting on his behalf.

vi) In the case of *unnamed transport*, delivery is completed when the goods have been handed over to the carrier or to another person acting on his behalf.

vii) In the case of *multimodal transport*, delivery is completed when the goods have been handed over as specified in I) - VI), as the case may be.

5.   Transfer of risks
Subject to the provisions of B.5., bear all risks of loss of or damage to the goods until such time as they have been delivered in accordance with A.4.

6.   Division of costs
Subject to the provisions of B.6.

- pay all costs relating to the goods until such time as they have been delivered to the carrier in accordance with A.4.;

- pay the costs of customs formalities as well as all duties, taxes, and other official charges payable upon exportation.

7. Notice to the buyer

Give the buyer sufficient notice that the goods have been delivered into the custody of the carrier. Should the carrier fail to take the goods into his charge at the time agreed, the seller must notify the buyer accordingly.

8. Proof of delivery, transport document or equivalent electronic message

Provide the buyer at the seller's expense, if customary, with the usual document in proof of delivery of the goods in accordance with A.4.

Unless the document referred to in the preceding paragraph is the transport document, render the buyer at the latter's request, risk and expense, every assistance in obtaining a transport document for the contract of carriage (for example, a negotiable bill of lading, a non-negotiable sea waybill, an inland waterway document, an air waybill, a railway consignment note, a road consignment note, or a multimodal transport document).

When the seller and the buyer have agreed to communicate electronically, the document referred to in the preceding paragraph may be replaced by an equivalent electronic data interchange (EDI) message.

9. Checking - packaging - marking

Pay the costs of those checking operations (such as checking quality, measuring, weighing, counting) which are necessary for the purpose of delivering the goods to the carrier.

Provide at his own expense packaging (unless it is usual for the particular trade to send the goods of the contract description unpacked) which is required for the transport of the goods, to the extent that the circumstances relating to the transport (e.g. modalities, destination) are made known to the seller before the contract of sale is concluded. Packaging is to be marked appropriately.

10. Other obligations

Render the buyer at the latter's request, risk and expense, every assistance in obtaining any documents or equivalent electronic messages (other than those mentioned in A.8.) issued or transmitted in the country of delivery and/or of origin which the buyer may require for the importation of the goods and, where necessary, for their transit through another country. Provide the buyer, upon request, with the necessary information for procuring insurance.

B. THE BUYER MUST:

1. Payment of the price
Pay the price as provided in the contract of sale.

2. Licences, authorisations and formalities
Obtain at his own risk and expense any import licence or other official authorisation and carry out all customs formalities for the importation of the goods and, where necessary, for their transit through another country.

3. Contract of carriage
Contract at his own expense for the carriage of the goods from the named place, except as provided for in A.3.a).

4. Taking delivery
Take delivery of the goods in accordance with A.4.

5. Transfer of risks
Bear all risks of loss of or damage to the goods from the time they have been delivered in accordance with A.4.

Should he fail to give notice in accordance with B.7., or should the carrier named by him fail to take the goods into his charge, bear all risks of loss of or damage to the goods from the agreed date or the expiry date of any period stipulated for delivery provided, however, that the goods have been duly appropriated to the contract, that is to say, clearly set aside or otherwise identified as the contract goods.

6. Division of costs
Pay all costs relating to the goods from the time when they have been delivered in accordance with A.4.

Pay any additional costs incurred, either because he fails to name the carrier, or the carrier named by him fails to take the goods into his charge at the agreed time, or because he has failed to give appropriate notice in accordance with B.7. provided, however, that the goods have been duly appropriated to the contract, that is to say, clearly set aside or otherwise identified as the contract goods.

Pay all duties, taxes and other official charges as well as the costs of carrying out customs formalities payable upon importation of the goods and, where necessary, for their transit through another country.

7. Notice to the seller
Give the seller sufficient notice of the name of the carrier and, where necessary, specify the mode of transport, as well as the date or period for delivering the goods to him and, as the case may be, the point within the place where the goods should be delivered to the carrier.

8. Proof of delivery, transport document or equivalent electronic message
Accept the proof of delivery in accordance with A.8.

9. Inspection of goods
Pay, unless otherwise agreed, the costs of pre-shipment inspection except when mandated by the authorities of the country of exportation.

10. Other obligations
Pay all costs and charges incurred in obtaining the documents or equivalent electronic messages mentioned in A.10. and reimburse those incurred by the seller in rendering his assistance in accordance therewith and in contracting for carriage in accordance with A.3.a).

Give the seller appropriate instructions whenever the seller's assistance in contracting for carriage is required in accordance with A.3.a).

FREE ALONGSIDE SHIP (... named port of shipment)	"Free Alongside Ship" means that the seller fulfils his obligation to deliver when the goods have been placed alongside the vessel on the quay or in lighters at the named port of shipment. This means that the buyer has to bear all costs and risks of loss of or damage to the goods from that moment. The FAS term requires the buyer to clear the goods for export. It should not be used when the buyer cannot carry out directly or indirectly the export formalities. This term can only be used for sea or inland waterway transport.

A. THE SELLER MUST:	1. Provision of goods in conformity with the contract Provide the goods and the commercial invoice, or its equivalent electronic message, in conformity with the contract of sale and any other evidence of conformity which may be required by the contract. 2. Licences, authorisations and formalities

Render the buyer, at the latter's request, risk and expense, every assistance in obtaining any export licence or other official authorisation necessary for the exportation of the goods.

3.   Contract of carriage and insurance

a) Contract of carriage
No obligation.
b) Contract of insurance
No obligation.

4.   Delivery
Deliver the goods alongside the named vessel at the loading place named by the buyer at the named port of shipment on the date or within the period stipulated and in the manner customary at the port.

5.   Transfer of risks
Subject to the provisions of B.5., bear all risks of loss of or damage to the goods until such time as they have been delivered in accordance with A.4.

6.   Division of costs
Subject to the provisions of B.6., pay all costs relating to the goods until such time as they have been delivered in accordance with A.4.

7.   Notice to the buyer
Give the buyer sufficient notice that the goods have been delivered alongside the named vessel.

8.   Proof of delivery, transport document or equivalent electronic message
Provide the buyer at the seller's expense with the usual document in proof of delivery of the goods in accordance with A.4.

Unless the document referred to in the preceding paragraph is the transport document, render the buyer at the latter's request, risk and expense, every assistance in obtaining a transport document (for example, a negotiable bill of lading, a non-negotiable sea waybill, an inland waterway document).

When the seller and the buyer have agreed to communicate electronically, the document referred to in the preceding paragraphs may be replaced by an equivalent electronic data interchange (EDI) message.

9.   Checking - packaging - marking
Pay the costs of those checking operations (such as checking quality, measuring, weighing, counting) which are necessary for the purpose of placing the goods at the disposal of the buyer. Provide at his own expense packaging (unless it is usual for the

particular trade to ship the goods of the contract description unpacked) which is required for the transport of the goods, to the extent that the circumstances relating to the transport (e.g. modalities, destination) are made known to the seller before the contract of sale is concluded. Packaging is to be marked appropriately.

10. Other obligations
Render the buyer at the latter's request, risk and expense, every assistance in obtaining any documents or equivalent electronic messages (other than those mentioned in A.8.) issued or transmitted in the country of shipment and/or of origin which the buyer may require for the exportation and/or importation of the goods and, where necessary, for their transit through another country. Provide the buyer, upon request, with the necessary information for procuring insurance.

B. THE BUYER MUST:

1. Payment of the price
Pay the price as provided in the contract of sale.

2. Licences, authorisations and formalities
Obtain at his own risk and expense any export and import licence or other official authorisation and carry out all customs formalities for the exportation and importation of the goods and, where necessary, for their transit through another country.

3. Contract of carriage
Contract at his own expense for the carriage of the goods from the named port of shipment.

4. Taking delivery
Take delivery of the goods in accordance with A.4.

5. Transfer of risks
Bear all risks of loss of or damage to the goods from the time they have been delivered in accordance with A.4.
Should he fail to fulfil his obligations in accordance with B.2., bear all additional risks of loss of or damage to the goods incurred thereby and should he fail to give notice in accordance with B.7., or should the vessel named by him fail to arrive on time, or be unable to take the goods, or close for cargo earlier than the stipulated time, bear all risks of loss of or damage to the goods from the agreed date or the expiry date of the period stipulated for delivery provided, however, that the goods have been duly appropriated to the contract, that is to say, clearly set aside or otherwise identified as the contract goods.

6. Division of costs

Pay all costs relating to the goods from the time they have been delivered in accordance with A.4.

Pay any additional costs incurred, either because the vessel named by him has failed to arrive on time, or will be unable to take the goods, or will close for cargo earlier than the stipulated time, or because the buyer has failed to fulfil his obligations in accordance with B.2., or to give appropriate notice in accordance with B.7. provided, however, that the goods have been duly appropriated to the contract, that is to say, clearly set aside or otherwise identified as the contract goods.

Pay all duties, taxes and other official charges as well as the costs of carrying out customs formalities payable upon exportation and importation of the goods and, where necessary, for their transit through another country.

Pay all costs and charges incurred by the seller in rendering assistance in accordance with A.2.

7. Notice to the seller

Give the seller sufficient notice of the vessel name, loading place and required delivery time.

8. Proof of delivery, transport document or equivalent electronic message

Accept the proof of delivery in accordance with A.8.

9. Inspection of goods

Pay, unless otherwise agreed, the costs of pre-shipment inspection (including inspection mandated by the authorities of the country of exportation).

10. Other obligations

Pay all costs and charges incurred in obtaining the documents or equivalent electronic messages mentioned in A.10. and reimburse those incurred by the seller in rendering his assistance in accordance therewith.

FREE ON BOARD (... named port of shipment)

"Free on Board" means that the seller fulfils his obligation to deliver when the goods have passed over the ship's rail at the named port of shipment. This means that the buyer has to bear all costs and risks of loss of or damage to the goods from that point. The FOB term requires the seller to clear the goods for export.

This term can only be used for sea or inland waterway transport. When the ship's rail serves no practical purpose, such as in the case of roll-on/roll-off or container traffic, the FCA term is more appropriate to use.

A. THE SELLER MUST:

1. **Provision of goods in conformity with the contract**
Provide the goods and the commercial invoice, or its equivalent electronic message, in conformity with the contract of sale and any other evidence of conformity which may be required by the contract.

2. **Licences, authorisations and formalities**
Obtain at his own risk and expense any export licence or other official authorisation and carry out all customs formalities necessary for the exportation of the goods.

3. **Contract of carriage and insurance**
   a) Contract of carriage
   No obligation.
   b) Contract of insurance
   No obligation.

4. **Delivery**
Deliver the goods on board the vessel named by the buyer at the named port of shipment on the date or within the period stipulated and in the manner customary at the port.

5. **Transfer of risks**
Subject to the provisions of B.5., bear all risks of loss of or damage to the goods until such time as they have passed the ship's rail at the named port of shipment.

6. **Division of costs**
Subject to the provisions of 6-6.

   • pay all costs relating to the goods until such time as they have passed the ship's rail at the named port of shipment;

   • pay the costs of customs formalities necessary for exportation as well as all duties, taxes and other official charges payable upon exportation.

7. **Notice to the buyer**
Give the buyer sufficient notice that the goods have been delivered on board.

8. **Proof of delivery, transport document or equivalent electronic message**

Provide the buyer at the seller's expense with the usual document in proof of delivery in accordance with A.4.

Unless the document referred to in the preceding paragraph is the transport document, render the buyer, at the latter's request, risk and expense, every assistance in obtaining a transport document for the contract of carriage (for example, a negotiable bill of lading, a non-negotiable sea waybill, an inland waterway document, or a multimodal transport document).

Where the seller and the buyer have agreed to communicate electronically, the document referred to in the preceding paragraph may be replaced by an equivalent electronic data interchange (EDI) message.

9. Checking - packaging - marking

Pay the costs of those checking operations (such as checking quality, measuring, weighing, counting) which are necessary for the purpose of delivering the goods in accordance with A.4.

Provide at his own expense packaging (unless it is usual for the particular trade to ship the goods of the contract description unpacked) which is required for the transport of the goods, to the extent that the circumstances relating to the transport (e.g. modalities, destination) are made known to the seller before the contract of sale is concluded. Packaging is to be marked appropriately.

10. Other obligations

Render the buyer at the latter's request, risk and expense, every assistance in obtaining any documents or equivalent electronic messages (other than those mentioned in A.8.) issued or transmitted in the country of shipment and/or of origin which the buyer may require for the importation of the goods and, where necessary, for their transit through another country. Provide the buyer, upon request, with the necessary information for procuring insurance.

B. THE BUYER MUST:

1. Payment of the price
Pay the price as provided in the contract of sale.

2. Licences, authorisations and formalities
Obtain at his own risk and expense any import licence or other official authorisation and carry out all customs formalities for the importation of the goods and, where necessary, for their transit through another country.

3. Contract of carriage
Contract at his own expense for the carriage of the goods from the named port of shipment.

4. Taking delivery
Take delivery of the goods in accordance with A.4.

5. Transfer of risks
Bear all risks of loss of or damage to the goods from the time they have passed the ship's rail at the named port of shipment. Should he fail to give notice in accordance with B.7., or should the vessel named by him fail to arrive on time, or be unable to take the goods, or close for cargo earlier than the stipulated time, bear all risks of loss of or damage to the goods from the agreed date or the expiry date of the period stipulated for delivery provided, however, that the goods have been duly appropriated to the contract, that is to say, clearly set aside or otherwise identified as the contract goods.

6. Division of costs
Pay all costs relating to the goods from the time they have passed the ship's rail at the named port of shipment.

Pay any additional costs incurred, either because the vessel named by him has failed to arrive on time, or is unable to take the goods, or will close for cargo earlier than the stipulated date, or because the buyer has failed to give appropriate notice in accordance with B.7. provided, however, that the goods have been duly appropriated to the contract, that is to say, clearly set aside or otherwise identified as the contract goods.

Pay all duties, taxes and other official charges as well as the costs of carrying out customs formalities payable upon importation of the goods and, where necessary, for their transit through another country.

7. Notice to the seller
Give the seller sufficient notice of the vessel name, loading point and required delivery time.

8. Proof of delivery, transport document or equivalent electronic message
Accept the proof of delivery in accordance with A.8.

9. Inspection of goods
Pay, unless otherwise agreed, the costs of pre-shipment inspection except when mandated by the authorities of the country of export.

10. Other obligations
Pay all costs and charges incurred in obtaining the documents or equivalent electronic messages mentioned in A.10. and reimburse those incurred by the seller in rendering his assistance in accordance therewith.

COST AND FREIGHT
(... named port of
destination)

"Cost and Freight" means that the seller must pay the costs and freight necessary to bring the goods to the named port of destination but the risk of loss of or damage to the goods, as well as any additional costs due to events occurring after the time the goods have been delivered on board the vessel, is transferred from the seller to the buyer when the goods pass the ship's rail in the port of shipment.

The CFR term requires the seller to clear the goods for export. This term can only be used for sea and inland waterway transport. When the ship's rail serves no practical purpose, such as in the case of roll-on/roll-off or container traffic, the CPT term is more appropriate to use.

A. THE SELLER MUST:

1. Provision of goods in conformity with the contract
Provide the goods and the commercial invoice, or its equivalent electronic message, in conformity with the contract of sale and any other evidence of conformity which may be required by the contract.

2. Licences, authorisations and formalities
Obtain at his own risk and expense any export licence or other official authorisation and carry out all customs formalities necessary for the exportation of the goods.

3. Contract of carriage and insurance
   a) Contract of carriage

Contract on usual terms at his own expense for the carriage of the goods to the named port of destination by the usual route in a seagoing vessel (or inland waterway vessel as appropriate) of the type normally used for the transport of goods of the contract description.

   b) Contract of insurance
   No obligation.

4. Delivery
Deliver the goods on board the vessel at the port of shipment on the date or within the period stipulated.

5. Transfer of risks
Subject to the provisions of 8.5., bear all risks of loss of or damage to the goods until such time as they have passed the ship's rail at the port of shipment.

6. Division of costs
Subject to the provisions of B.6.

- pay all costs relating to the goods until they have been delivered in accordance with A.4. as well as the freight and all other costs resulting from A.3.a), including costs of loading the goods on board and any charges for unloading at the port of discharge which may be levied by regular shipping lines when contracting for carriage;

- pay the costs of customs formalities necessary for exportation as well as all duties, taxes and other official charges payable upon exportation.

7. Notice to the buyer
Give the buyer sufficient notice that the goods have been delivered on board the vessel as well as any other notice required in order to allow the buyer to take measures which are normally necessary to enable him to take the goods.

8. Proof of delivery, transport document or equivalent electronic message
Unless otherwise agreed, at his own expense provide the buyer without delay with the usual transport document for the agreed port of destination.

This document (for example, a negotiable bill of lading, a non-negotiable sea waybill or an inland waterway document) must cover the contract goods, be dated within the period agreed for shipment, enable the buyer to claim the goods from the carrier at destination and, unless otherwise agreed, enable the buyer to sell the goods in transit by the transfer of the document to a subsequent buyer (the negotiable bill of lading) or by notification to the carrier.

When such a transport document is issued in several originals, a full set of originals must be presented to the buyer. If the transport document contains a reference to a charter party, the seller must also provide a copy of this latter document.

Where the seller and the buyer have agreed to communicate electronically, the document referred to in the preceding paragraphs may be replaced by an equivalent electronic data interchange (EDI) message.

9.   Checking - packaging - marking
Pay the costs of those checking operations (such as checking quality, measuring, weighing, counting) which are necessary for the purpose of delivering the goods in accordance with A.4.

Provide at his own expense packaging (unless it is usual for the particular trade to ship the goods of the contract description unpacked) which is required for the transport of the goods arranged by him. Packaging is to be marked appropriately.

10. Other obligations
Render the buyer at the latter's request, risk and expense, every assistance in obtaining any documents or equivalent electronic messages (other than those mentioned in A.8.) issued or transmitted in the country of shipment and/or of origin which the buyer may require for the importation of the goods and, where necessary, for their transit through another country. Provide the buyer, upon request, with the necessary information for procuring insurance.

B. THE BUYER MUST: 1.   Payment of the price
Pay the price as provided in the contract of sale.

2.   Licences, authorisations and formalities
Obtain at his own risk and expense any import licence or other official authorisation and carry out all customs formalities for the importation of the goods and, where necessary, for their transit through another country.

3.   Contract of carriage
No obligation.

4.   Taking delivery
Accept delivery of the goods when they have been delivered in accordance with A.4. and receive them from the carrier at the named port of destination.

5.   Transfer of risks
Bear all risks of loss of or damage to the goods from the time they have passed the ship's rail at the port of shipment.

Should he fail to give notice in accordance with B.7., bear all risks of loss of or damage to the goods from the agreed date or the expiry date of the period fixed for shipment provided, however, that the goods have been duly appropriated to the contract, that is to say, clearly set aside or otherwise identified as the contract goods.

6.   Division of costs
Subject to the provisions of A.3., pay all costs relating to the goods from the time they have been delivered in accordance with A.4. and, unless such costs and charges have been levied by regular shipping lines when contracting for carriage, pay all costs and charges relating to the goods whilst in transit until their arrival at the port of destination, as well as unloading costs including lighterage and wharfage charges.

Should he fail to give notice in accordance with B.7., pay the additional costs thereby incurred for the goods from the agreed date or the expiry date of the period fixed for shipment provided, however, that the goods have been duly appropriated to the contract, that is to say, clearly set aside or otherwise identified as the contract goods.

Pay all duties, taxes and other official charges as well as the costs of carrying out customs formalities payable upon importation of the goods and, where necessary, for their transit through another country.

7.   Notice to the seller
Whenever he is entitled to determine the time for shipping the goods and/or the port of destination, give the seller sufficient notice thereof.

8.   Proof of delivery, transport document or equivalent electronic message
Accept the transport document in accordance with A.8. if it is in conformity with the contract.

9.   Inspection of goods
Pay, unless otherwise agreed, the costs of pre-shipment inspection except when mandated by the authorities of the country of exportation.

10. Other obligations
Pay all costs and charges incurred in obtaining the documents or equivalent electronic messages mentioned in A.10. and reimburse those incurred by the seller in rendering his assistance in accordance therewith.

COST, INSURANCE AND FREIGHT (... named port of destination)	"Cost, Insurance and Freight" means that the seller has the same obligations as under CFR but with the addition that he has to procure marine insurance against the buyer's risk of loss of or damage to the goods during the carriage. The seller contracts for insurance and pays the insurance premium.

"Cost, Insurance and Freight" means that the seller has the same obligations as under CFR but with the addition that he has to procure marine insurance against the buyer's risk of loss of or damage to the goods during the carriage. The seller contracts for insurance and pays the insurance premium.

The buyer should note that under the CIF term the seller is only required to obtain insurance on minimum coverage. The CIF term requires the seller to clear the goods for export.

This term can only be used for sea and inland waterway transport. When the ship's rail serves no practical purposes such as in the case of roll-on/roll-off or container traffic, the CIP term is more appropriate to use.

A. THE SELLER MUST:

1.   Provision of goods in conformity with the contract
Provide the goods and the commercial invoice, or its equivalent electronic message, in conformity with the contract of sale and any other evidence of conformity which may be required by the contract.

2.   Licences, authorisations and formalities
Obtain at his own risk and expense any export licence or other official authorisation and carry out all customs formalities necessary for the exportation of the goods.

3.   Contract of carriage and insurance
a) Contract of carriage

Contract on usual terms at his own expense for the carriage of the goods to the named port of destination by the usual route in a seagoing vessel (or inland waterway vessel as appropriate) of the type normally used for the transport of goods of the contract description.
b) Contract of insurance

Obtain at his own expense cargo insurance as agreed in the contract, that the buyer, or any other person having an insurable interest in the goods, shall be entitled to claim directly from the insurer and provide the buyer with the insurance policy or other evidence of insurance cover.

The insurance shall be contracted with underwriters or an insurance company of good repute and, failing express agreement to the contrary, be in accordance with minimum cover of the Institute Cargo Clauses (institute of London Underwriters) or any similar set of clauses. The duration of insurance cover shall be in accordance with B.5. and B.4. When required by the buyer, the seller shall provide at the buyer's expense war, strikes, riots and civil commotion risk insurances if procurable. The minimum insurance shall cover the price provided in the contract plus ten per cent (i.e. 110 %) and shall be provided in the currency of the contract.

4. Delivery
Deliver the goods on board the vessel at the port of shipment on the date or within the period stipulated.

5. Transfer of risks
Subject to the provisions of 6.5., bear all risks of loss of or damage to the goods until such time as they have passed the ship's rail at the port of shipment.

6. Division of costs
Subject to the provisions of B.6.

- pay all costs relating to the goods until they have been delivered in accordance with A.4. as well as the freight and all other costs resulting from A.3., including costs of loading the goods on board and any charges for unloading at the port of discharge which may be levied by regular shipping lines when contracting for carriage;

- pay the costs of customs formalities necessary for exportation as well as all duties, taxes and other official charges payable upon exportation.

7. Notice to the buyer
Give the buyer sufficient notice that the goods have been delivered on board the vessel as well as any other notice required in order to allow the buyer to take measures which are normally necessary to enable him to take the goods.

8. Proof of delivery, transport document or equivalent electronic message
Unless otherwise agreed, at his own expense provide the buyer without delay with the usual transport document for the agreed port of destination.

This document (for example, a negotiable bill of lading, a non-negotiable sea waybill or an inland waterway document) must cover the contract goods, be dated within the period agreed for shipment, enable the buyer to claim the goods from the carrier at destination and, unless otherwise agreed, enable the buyer to sell the goods in transit by the transfer of the document to a subsequent buyer (the negotiable bill of lading) or by notification to the carrier.

When such a transport document is issued in several originals, a full set of originals must be presented to the buyer. If the transport document contains a reference to a charter party, the seller must also provide a copy of this latter document.

Where the seller and the buyer have agreed to communicate electronically, the document referred to in the preceding paragraphs may be replaced by an equivalent electronic data interchange (EDI) message.

9.   Checking - packaging - marking
Pay the costs of those checking operations (such as checking quality, measuring, weighing, counting) which are necessary for the purpose of delivering the goods in accordance with A.4.

Provide at his own expense packaging (unless it is usual for the particular trade to ship the goods of the contract description unpacked) which is required for the transport of the goods arranged by him. Packaging is to be marked appropriately.

10. Other obligations
Render the buyer at the latter's request, risk and expense, every assistance in obtaining any documents or equivalent electronic messages (other than those mentioned in A.8.) issued or transmitted in the country of shipment and/or of origin which the buyer may require for the importation of the goods and, where necessary, for their transit through another country.

B. THE BUYER MUST: 1.   Payment of the price
Pay the price as provided in the contract of sale.

2.   Licences, authorisations and formalities
Obtain at his own risk and expense any import licence or other official authorisation and carry out all customs formalities for the importation of the goods and, where necessary, for their transit through another country.

3.   Contract of carriage
No obligation.

4.   Taking delivery
Accept delivery of the goods when they have been delivered in accordance with A.4. and receive them from the carrier at the named port of destination.

5. Transfer of risks

Bear all risks of loss of or damage to the goods from the time they have passed the ship's rail at the port of shipment.

Should he fail to give notice in accordance with B.7., bear all risks of loss of or damage to the goods from the agreed date or the expiry date of the period fixed for shipment provided, however, that the goods have been duly appropriated to the contract, that is to say, clearly set aside or otherwise identified as the contract goods.

6. Division of costs

Subject to the provisions of A.3., pay all costs relating to the goods from the time they have been delivered in accordance with A.4. and, unless such costs and charges have been levied by regular shipping lines when contracting for carriage, pay all costs and charges relating to the goods whilst in transit until their arrival at the port of destination, as well as unloading costs including lighterage and wharfage charges.

Should he fail to give notice in accordance with B.7., pay the additional costs thereby incurred for the goods from the agreed date or the expiry date of the period fixed for shipment provided, however, that the goods have been duly appropriated to the contract, that is to say, clearly set aside or otherwise identified as the contract goods.

Pay all duties, taxes and other official charges as well as the costs of carrying out customs formalities payable upon importation of the goods and, where necessary, for their transit through another country.

7. Notice to the seller

Whenever he is entitled to determine the time for shipping the goods and/or the port of destination, give the seller sufficient notice thereof.

8. Proof of delivery, transport document or equivalent electronic message

Accept the transport document in accordance with A.8. if it is in conformity with the contract.

9. Inspection of goods

Pay, unless otherwise agreed, the costs of pre-shipment inspection except when mandated by the authorities of the country of exportation.

10. Other obligations

Pay all costs and charges incurred in obtaining the documents or equivalent electronic messages mentioned in A.10. and reimburse those incurred by the seller in rendering his assistance in accordance therewith.

Provide the seller, upon request, with the necessary information for procuring insurance.

CARRIAGE PAID TO
(... named place of
destination)

"Carriage paid to. . ." means that the seller pays the freight for the carriage of the goods to the named destination. The risk of loss of or damage to the goods, as well as any additional costs due to events occurring after the time the goods have been delivered to the carrier, is transferred from the seller to the buyer when the goods have been delivered into the custody of the carrier. "Carrier" means any person who, in a contract of carriage, undertakes to perform or to procure the performance of carriage, by rail, road, sea, air, inland waterway or by a combination of such modes.

If subsequent carriers are used for the carriage to the agreed destination, the risk passes when the goods have been delivered to the first carrier.

The CPT term requires the seller to clear the goods for export. This term may be used for any mode of transport including multimodal transport.

A. THE SELLER MUST:

1.   Provision of goods in conformity with the contract
Provide the goods and the commercial invoice, or its equivalent electronic message, in conformity with the contract of sale and any other evidence of conformity which may be required by the contract.

2.   Licences, authorisations and formalities
Obtain at his own risk and expense any export licence or other official authorisation and carry out all customs formalities necessary for the exportation of the goods.

3.   Contract of carriage and insurance
a)   Contract of carriage

Contract on usual terms at his own expense for the carriage of the goods to the agreed point at the named place of destination by a usual route and in a customary manner. If a point is not agreed or is not determined by practice, the seller may select the point at the named place of destination which best suits his purpose.
b) Contract of insurance
No obligation.

4. Delivery

Deliver the goods into the custody of the carrier or, if there are subsequent carriers, to the first carrier, for transportation to the named place of destination on the date or within the period stipulated.

5. Transfer of risks

Subject to the provisions of B.5., bear all risks of loss of or damage to the goods until such time as they have been delivered in accordance with A.4.

6. Division of costs

Subject to the provisions of B.6.

- pay all costs relating to the goods until they have been delivered in accordance with A.4. as well as the freight and all other costs resulting from A.3.a), including costs of loading the goods and any charges for unloading at the place of destination which may be included in the freight or incurred by the seller when contracting for carriage;

- pay the costs of customs formalities necessary for exportation as well as all duties, taxes or other official charges payable upon exportation.

7. Notice to the buyer

Give the buyer sufficient notice that the goods have been delivered in accordance with A.4. as well as any other notice required in order to allow the buyer to take measures which are normally necessary to enable him to take the goods.

8. Proof of delivery, transport document or equivalent electronic message

Provide the buyer at the seller's expense, if customary, with the usual transport document (for example a negotiable bill of lading, a non-negotiable sea waybill, an inland waterway document, an air waybill, a railway consignment note, a road consignment note, or a multimodal transport document).

Where the seller and the buyer have agreed to communicate electronically, the document referred to in the preceding paragraph may be replaced by an equivalent electronic data interchange (EDI) message.

9. Checking - packaging - marking

Pay the costs of those checking operations (such as checking quality, measuring, weighing, counting) which are necessary for the purpose of delivering the goods in accordance with A.4.

Provide at his own expense packaging (unless it is usual for the particular trade to send the goods of the contract description unpacked) which is required for the transport of the goods arranged by him. Packaging is to be marked appropriately.

10. Other obligations
Render the buyer at the latter's request, risk and expense, every assistance in obtaining any documents or equivalent electronic messages (other than those mentioned in A.8.) issued or transmitted in the country of dispatch and/or of origin which the buyer may require for the importation of the goods and, where necessary, for their transit through another country. Provide the buyer, upon request, with the necessary information for procuring insurance.

B. THE BUYER MUST: 1. Payment of the price
Pay the price as provided in the contract of sale.

2. Licences, authorisations and formalities
Obtain at his own risk and expense any import licence or other official authorisation and carry out all customs formalities for the importation of the goods and, where necessary, for their transit through another country.

3. Contract of carriage
No obligation.

4. Taking delivery
Accept delivery of the goods when they have been delivered in accordance with A.4. and receive them from the carrier at the named place of destination.

5. Transfer of risks
Bear all risks of loss of or damage to the goods from the time they have been delivered in accordance with A.4.
Should he fail to give notice in accordance with B.7., bear all risks of the goods from the agreed date or the expiry date of the period fixed for delivery provided, however, that the goods have been duly appropriated to the contract, that is to say, clearly set aside or otherwise identified as the contract goods.

6. Division of costs
Subject to the provisions of A.3.a), pay all costs relating to the goods from the time they have been delivered in accordance with A.4. and, unless such costs and charges have been included in the

freight or incurred by the seller when contracting for carriage in accordance with A.3.a), pay all costs and charges relating to the goods whilst in transit until their arrival at the agreed place of destination, as well as unloading costs.

Should he fail to give notice in accordance with B.7., pay the additional costs thereby incurred for the goods from the agreed date or the expiry date of the period fixed for dispatch provided, however, that the goods have been duly appropriated to the contract, that is to say, clearly set aside or otherwise identified as the contract goods.

Pay all duties, taxes and other official charges as well as the costs of carrying out customs formalities payable upon importation of the goods and, where necessary, for their transit through another country.

7. Notice to the seller
Whenever he is entitled to determine the time for dispatching the goods and/or the destination, give the seller sufficient notice thereof.

8. Proof of delivery, transport document or equivalent electronic message
Accept the transport document in accordance with A.8. if it is in conformity with the contract.

9. Inspection of goods
Pay, unless otherwise agreed, the costs of pre-shipment inspection except when mandated by the authorities of the country of exportation.

10. Other obligations
Pay all costs and charges incurred in obtaining the documents or equivalent electronic messages mentioned in A.10. and reimburse those incurred by the seller in rendering his assistance in accordance therewith.

CARRIAGE AND INSURANCE PAID TO (... named place of destination)

"Carriage and insurance paid to. . ." means that the seller has the same obligations as under CPT but with the addition that the seller has to procure cargo insurance against the buyer's risk of loss of or damage to the goods during the carriage. The seller contracts for insurance and pays the insurance premium.

The buyer should note that under the CIP term the seller is only required to obtain insurance on minimum coverage. The CIP term requires the seller to clear the goods for export. This term may be used for any mode of transport including multimodal transport.

A. THE SELLER MUST:

1.   Provision of goods in conformity with the contract
Provide the goods and the commercial invoice, or its equivalent electronic message, in conformity with the contract of sale and any other evidence of conformity which may be required by the contract.

2.   Licences, authorisations and formalities
Obtain at his own risk and expense any export licence or other official authorisation and carry out all customs formalities necessary for the exportation of the goods.

3.   Contract of carriage and insurance
a)   Contract of carriage

Contract on usual terms at his own expense for the carriage of the goods to the agreed point at the named place of destination by a usual route and in a customary manner. If a point is not agreed or is not determined by practice, the seller may select the point at the named place of destination which best suits his purpose.
b)   Contract of insurance

Obtain at his own expense cargo insurance as agreed in the contract, that the buyer, or any other person having an insurable interest in the goods, shall be entitled to claim directly from the insurer and provide the buyer with the insurance policy or other evidence of insurance cover.

The insurance shall be contracted with underwriters or an insurance company of good repute and, failing express agreement to the contrary, be in accordance with minimum cover of the Institute Cargo Clauses (Institute of London Underwriters) or any similar set of clauses. The duration of insurance cover shall be in accordance with B.5. and B.4. When required by the buyer, the seller shall provide at the buyer's expense war, strikes, riots and civil commotion risk insurances if procurable. The minimum insurance shall cover the price provided in the contract plus ten per cent (i.e. 110%) and shall be provided in the currency of the contract.

4.   Delivery
Deliver the goods into the custody of the carrier or, if there are subsequent carriers, to the first carrier, for transportation to the

named place of destination on the date or within the period
stipulated.

5.   Transfer of risks
Subject to the provisions of B.5., bear all risks of loss of or
damage to the goods until such time as they have been delivered
in accordance with A.4.

6.   Division of costs
Subject to the provisions of B.6.

- pay all costs relating to the goods until they have been
  delivered in accordance with A.4. as well as the freight and
  all other costs resulting from A.3., including costs of loading
  the goods and any charges for unloading at the place of
  destination which may be included in the freight or incurred
  by the seller when contracting for carriage;

- pay the costs of customs formalities necessary for exportation
  as well as all duties, taxes or other official charges payable
  upon exportation.

7.   Notice to the buyer
Give the buyer sufficient notice that the goods have been
delivered in accordance with A.4. as well as any other notice
required in order to allow the buyer to take measures which are
normally necessary to enable him to take the goods.

8.   Proof of delivery, transport document or equivalent
electronic message
Provide the buyer at the seller's expense, if customary, with the
usual transport document (for example, a negotiable bill of
lading, a non-negotiable sea waybill, an inland waterway document, an air waybill, a railway consignment note, a road consignment note or a multimodal transport document).

   Where the seller and the buyer have agreed to communicate
electronically, the document referred to in the preceding paragraph may be replaced by an equivalent electronic data interchange (EDI) message.

9.   Checking - packaging - marking
Pay the costs of those checking operations (such as checking
quality, measuring, weighing, counting) which are necessary for
the purpose of delivering the goods in accordance with A.4.

   Provide at his own expense packaging (unless it is usual for
the particular trade to send the goods of the contract description
unpacked) which is required for the transport of the goods arranged by him. Packaging is to be marked appropriately.

10. Other obligations

Render the buyer at the latter's request, risk and expense, every assistance in obtaining any documents or equivalent electronic messages (other than those mentioned in A.8.) issued or transmitted in the country of dispatch and/or of origin, which the buyer may require for the importation of the goods and where necessary, for their transit through another country.

B. THE BUYER MUST:

1. Payment of the price

Pay the price as provided in the contract of sale.

2. Licences, authorisations and formalities

Obtain at his own risk and expense any import licence or other official authorisation and carry out all customs formalities for the importation of the goods and, where necessary, for their transit through another country.

3. Contract of carriage

No obligation.

4. Taking delivery

Accept delivery of the goods when they have been delivered in accordance with A.4. and receive them from the carrier at the named port of destination.

5. Transfer of risks

Bear all risks of loss of or damage to the goods from the time they have been delivered in accordance with A.4.

Should he fail to give notice in accordance with B.7., bear all risks of the goods from the agreed date or the expiry date of the period fixed for delivery provided, however, that the goods have been duly appropriated to the contract, that is to say, clearly set aside or otherwise identified as the contract goods.

6. Division of costs

Subject to the provisions of A.3., pay all costs relating to the goods from the time they have been delivered in accordance with A.4. and, unless such costs and charges have been included in the freight or incurred by the seller when contracting for carriage in accordance with A.3.a), pay all costs and charges relating to the goods whilst in transit until their arrival at the agreed place of destination, as well as unloading costs.

Should he fail to give notice in accordance with B.7., pay the additional costs thereby incurred for the goods from the agreed date or the expiry date of the period fixed for dispatch provided, however, that the goods have been duly appropriated to the contract, that is to say, clearly set aside or otherwise identified as the contract goods.

Pay all duties, taxes and other official charges as well as the costs of carrying out customs formalities payable upon importation of the goods and, where necessary, for their transit through another country.

7. Notice to the seller
Whenever he is entitled to determine the time for dispatching the goods and/or the destination, give the seller sufficient notice thereof.

8. Proof of delivery, transport document or equivalent electronic message
Accept the transport document in accordance with A.8. if it is in conformity with the contract.

9. Inspection of goods
Pay, unless otherwise agreed, the costs of pre-shipment inspection except when mandated by the authorities of the country of exportation.

10. Other obligations
Pay all costs and charges incurred in obtaining the documents or equivalent electronic messages mentioned in A.10. and reimburse those incurred by the seller in rendering his assistance in accordance therewith.

Provide the seller, upon request, with the necessary information for procuring insurance.

DELIVERED AT FRONTIER (... **named place**)	"Delivered at Frontier" means that the seller fulfils his obligation to deliver when the goods have been made available, cleared for export, at the named point and place at the frontier, but before the customs border of the adjoining country. The term "frontier" may be used for any frontier including that of the country of export. Therefore, it is of vital importance that the frontier in question be defined precisely by always naming the point and place in the term. The term is primarily intended to be used when goods are to be carried by rail or road, but it may be used for any mode of transport.
A. THE SELLER MUST:	1. Provision of goods in conformity with the contract Provide the goods and the commercial invoice, or its equivalent

electronic message, in conformity with the contract of sale and any other evidence of conformity which may be required by the contract.

2.   Licences, authorisations and formalities

Obtain at his own risk and expense any export licence or other official authorisation or other document necessary for placing the goods at the buyer's disposal. Carry out all customs formalities for the exportation of the goods to the named place of delivery at the frontier and, where necessary, for their prior transit through another country.

3.   Contract of carriage and insurance
a)   Contract of carriage

Contract at his own expense for the carriage of the goods by a usual route and in a customary manner to the named point at the place of delivery at the frontier (including, if necessary, for their transit through another country).

If a point at the named place of delivery at the frontier is not agreed or is not determined by practice, the seller may select the point at the named place of delivery which best suits his purpose.
b)   Contract of insurance
No obligation.

4.   Delivery

Place the goods at the disposal of the buyer at the named place of delivery at the frontier on the date or within the period stipulated.

5.   Transfer of risks

Subject to the provisions of B.5., bear all risks of loss of or damage to the goods until such time as they have been delivered in accordance with A.4.

6.   Division of costs

Subject to the provisions of B.6.

- pay all costs of the goods until they have been delivered in accordance with A.4. as well as, in addition to costs resulting from A.3.a), the expenses of discharge operations (including lighterage and handling charges), if it is necessary or customary for the goods to be discharged on their arrival at the named place of delivery at the frontier, in order to place them at the buyer's disposal;

- pay the costs of customs formalities necessary for exportation as well as all duties, taxes or other official charges payable upon exportation and, where necessary, for their transit through another country prior to delivery in accordance with A.4.

7. Notice to the buyer

Give the buyer sufficient notice of the dispatch of the goods to the named place at the frontier as well as any other notice required in order to allow the buyer to take measures which are normally necessary to enable him to take the goods.

8. Proof of delivery, transport document or equivalent electronic message

Provide the buyer at the seller's expense with the usual document or other evidence of the delivery of the goods at the named place at the frontier.

Provide the buyer at the latter's request, risk and expense, with a through document of transport normally obtained in the country of dispatch covering on usual terms the transport of the goods from the point of dispatch in that country to the place of final destination in the country of importation named by the buyer.

Where the seller and the buyer have agreed to communicate electronically, the document referred to in the preceding paragraph may be replaced by an equivalent electronic data interchange (EDI) message.

9. Checking - packaging - marking

Pay the costs of those checking operations (such as checking quality, measuring, weighing, counting) which are necessary for the purpose of delivering the goods in accordance with A.4.

Provide at his own expense packaging (unless it is usual for the particular trade to deliver the goods of the contract description unpacked) which is required for the delivery of the goods at the frontier and for the subsequent transport to the extent that the circumstances (e.g. modalities, destination) are made known to the seller before the contract of sale is concluded. Packaging is to be marked appropriately.

10. Other obligations

Render the buyer at the latter's request, risk and expense, every assistance in obtaining any documents or equivalent electronic messages (other than those mentioned in A.8.) issued or transmitted in the country of dispatch and/or origin which the buyer may require for the importation of the goods and, where necessary, for their transit through another country. Provide the buyer, upon request, with the necessary information for procuring insurance.

B. THE BUYER MUST:

1.   Payment of the price
Pay the price as provided in the contract of sale.

2.   Licences, authorisations and formalities
Obtain at his own risk and expense any import licence or other official authorisation and carry out all customs formalities at the named point of delivery at the frontier or elsewhere for the importation of the goods and, where necessary, for their subsequent transport.

3.   Contract of carriage
No obligation.

4.   Taking delivery
Take delivery of the goods as soon as they have been placed at his disposal in accordance with A.4.

5.   Transfer of risks
Bear all risks of loss of or damage to the goods from the time they have been placed at his disposal in accordance with A.4. Should he fail to give notice in accordance with B.7., bear all risks of loss of or damage to the goods from the agreed date or the expiry date of the period stipulated for delivery provided, however, that the goods have been duly appropriated to the contract, that is to say, clearly set aside or otherwise identified as the contract goods.

6.   Division of costs
Pay all costs relating to the goods from the time they have been placed at his disposal in accordance with A.4.

Should he fail to take delivery of the goods when they have been placed at his disposal in accordance with A.4., or to give notice in accordance with B.7., bear all additional costs incurred thereby provided, however, that the goods have been appropriated to the contract, that is to say, clearly set aside or otherwise identified as the contract goods.

Pay all duties, taxes and other official charges as well as the costs of carrying out customs formalities payable upon importation of the goods and, where necessary, for their subsequent transport.

7.   Notice to the seller
Whenever he is entitled to determine the time within a stipulated period and/or the place of taking delivery, give the seller sufficient notice thereof.

8.   Proof of delivery, transport document or equivalent electronic message

Accept the transport document and/or other evidence of delivery in accordance with A.8.

9. Inspection of goods
Pay, unless otherwise agreed, the costs of pre-shipment inspection except when mandated by the authorities of the country of exportation.

10. Other obligations
Pay all costs and charges incurred in obtaining the documents or equivalent electronic messages mentioned in A.10. and reimburse those incurred by the seller in rendering his assistance in accordance therewith.

If necessary, provide the seller at his request and the buyer's risk and expense with exchange control authorisation, permits, other documents or certified copies thereof, or with the address of the final destination of the goods in the country of importation for the purpose of obtaining the through document of transport or any other document contemplated in A.8.

DELIVERED EX SHIP
(... named port of destination)

"Delivered Ex Ship" means that the seller fulfils his obligation to deliver when the goods have been made available to the buyer on board the ship uncleared for import at the named port of destination. The seller has to bear all the costs and risks involved in bringing the goods to the named port of destination.

This term can only be used for sea or inland waterway transport.

A. THE SELLER MUST:

1. Provision of goods in conformity with the contract
Provide the goods and the commercial invoice, or its equivalent electronic message, in conformity with the contract of sale and any other evidence of conformity which may be required by the contract.

2. Licences, authorisations and formalities
Obtain at his own risk and expense any export licence or other official authorisation and carry out all customs formalities necessary for the exportation of the goods and, where necessary, for their transit through another country.

3. Contract of carriage and insurance
a) Contract of carriage

Contract at his own expense for the carriage of the goods by a usual route and in a customary manner to the named place at the named port of destination. If a point is not agreed or is not determined by practice, the seller may select the point at the named port of destination which best suits his purpose.
b) Contract of insurance
No obligation.

4. Delivery
Place the goods at the disposal of the buyer on board the vessel at the usual unloading point in the named port of destination uncleared for import on the date or within the period stipulated, in such a way as to enable them to be removed from the vessel by unloading equipment appropriate to the nature of the goods.

5. Transfer of risks
Subject to the provisions of B.5., bear all risks of loss of or damage to the goods until such time as they have been delivered in accordance with A.4.

6. Division of costs
Subject to the provisions of B.6.

- in addition to costs resulting from A.3.a), pay all costs relating to the goods until such time as they have been delivered in accordance with A.4.;

- pay the costs of customs formalities necessary for exportation as well as all duties, taxes or other official charges payable upon exportation and, where necessary, for their transit through another country prior to delivery in accordance with A.4.

7. Notice to the buyer
Give the buyer sufficient notice of the estimated time of arrival of the named vessel in accordance with A.4. as well as any other notice required in order to allow the buyer to take measures which are normally necessary to enable him to take the goods.

8. Proof of delivery, transport document or equivalent electronic message
Provide the buyer at the seller's expense with the delivery order and/or the usual transport document (for example a negotiable bill of lading, a non-negotiable sea waybill, an inland waterway document, or a multimodal transport document) to enable the buyer to take delivery of the goods.

Where the seller and the buyer have agreed to communicate electronically, the document referred to in the preceding paragraph may be replaced by an equivalent electronic data interchange (EDI) message.

9. Checking - packaging - marking
Pay the costs of those checking operations (such as checking quality, measuring, weighing, counting) which are necessary for the purpose of delivering the goods in accordance with A.4.

Provide at his own expense packaging (unless it is usual for the particular trade to deliver the goods of the contract description unpacked) which is required for the delivery of the goods. Packaging is to be marked appropriately.

10. Other obligations
Render the buyer at the latter's request, risk and expense, every assistance in obtaining any documents or equivalent electronic messages (other than those mentioned in A.8.) issued or transmitted in the country of dispatch and/or of origin which the buyer may require for the importation of the goods. Provide the buyer, upon request, with the necessary information for procuring insurance.

B. THE BUYER MUST:

1. Payment of the price
Pay the price as provided in the contract of sale.

2. Licences, authorisations and formalities
Obtain at his own risk and expense any import licence or other official authorisation and carry out all customs formalities necessary for the importation of the goods.

3. Contract of carriage
No obligation.

4. Taking delivery
Take delivery of the goods as soon as they are placed at his disposal in accordance with A.4.

5. Transfer of risks
Bear all risks of loss of or damage to the goods from the time they have been placed at his disposal in accordance with A.4. Should he fail to give notice in accordance with B.7., bear all risks of loss of or damage to the goods from the agreed date or the expiry date of the period stipulated for delivery provided, however, that the goods have been duly appropriated to the contract, that is to say, clearly set aside or otherwise identified as the contract goods.

6.   Division of costs
Pay all costs relating to the goods including unloading from the time they have been placed at his disposal in accordance with A.4.

Should he fail to take delivery of the goods when they have been placed at his disposal in accordance with A.4., or to give notice in accordance with B.7., bear all additional costs incurred thereby provided, however, that the goods have been appropriated to the contract, that is to say, clearly set aside or otherwise identified as the contract goods.

Pay all duties, taxes and other official charges as well as the costs of carrying out customs formalities payable upon importation of the goods.

7.   Notice to the seller
Whenever he is entitled to determine the time within a stipulated period and/or the place of taking delivery, give the seller sufficient notice thereof.

8.   Proof of delivery, transport document or equivalent electronic message
Accept the delivery order or the transport document in accordance with A.8.

9.   Inspection of goods
Pay, unless otherwise agreed, the costs of pre-shipment inspection except when mandated by the authorities of the country of exportation.

10. Other obligations
Pay all costs and charges incurred in obtaining the documents or equivalent electronic messages mentioned in A.10. and reimburse those incurred by the seller in rendering his assistance in accordance therewith.

DELIVERED EX QUAY PAID (... named port of destination)

"Delivered Ex Quay (duty paid)" means that the seller fulfils his obligation to deliver when he has made the goods available to the buyer on the quay (wharf) at the named port of destination, cleared for importation. The seller has to bear all risks and costs including duties, taxes and other charges of delivering the goods thereto.

This term should not be used if the seller is unable directly or indirectly to obtain the import licence.

If the parties wish the buyer to clear the goods for importation and pay the duty the words "duty unpaid" should be used instead of "duty paid".

If the parties wish to exclude from the seller's obligations some of the costs payable upon importation of the goods (such as value added tax (VAT)), this should be made clear by adding words to this effect: "Delivered ex quay, VAT unpaid (... named port of destination)".

This term can only be used for sea or inland waterway transport.

A. THE SELLER MUST:

1. Provision of goods in conformity with the contract
Provide the goods and the commercial invoice, or its equivalent electronic message, in conformity with the contract of sale and any other evidence of conformity which may be required by the contract.

2. Licences, authorisations and formalities
Obtain at his own risk and expense any export and import licence or other official authorisation and carry out all customs formalities for the exportation and importation of the goods and, where necessary, for their transit through another country.

3. Contract of carriage and insurance
a) Contract of carriage

Contract at his own expense for the carriage of the goods by a usual route and in a customary manner to the quay at the named port of destination. If a point is not agreed or is not determined by practice, the seller may select the point at the named port of destination which best suits his purpose.

b) Contract of insurance
No obligation.

4. Delivery
Place the goods at the disposal of the buyer on the quay or wharf at the agreed port of destination and on the date or within the period stipulated.

5. Transfer of risks
Subject to the provisions of B.5., bear all risks of loss of or damage to the goods until such time as they have been delivered in accordance with A.4.

6. Division of costs
Subject to the provisions of B.6.

- in addition to costs resulting from A.3.a), pay all costs relating to the goods until such time as they are delivered in accordance with A.4.;

- pay the costs of customs formalities as well as all duties, taxes and other official charges payable upon exportation and importation of the goods, unless otherwise agreed and, where necessary, for their transit through another country prior to delivery in accordance with A.4.

7.   Notice to the buyer

Give the buyer sufficient notice of the estimated time of arrival of the named vessel in accordance with A.4., as well as any other notice required in order to allow the buyer to take measures which are normally necessary to enable him to take the goods.

8.   Transport document or equivalent electronic message

Provide the buyer at the seller's expense with the delivery order and/or the usual transport document (for example, a negotiable bill of lading, a non-negotiable sea waybill, an inland waterway document or a multimodal transport document) to enable him to take the goods and remove them from the quay.

Where the seller and the buyer have agreed to communicate electronically, the document referred to in the preceding paragraph may be replaced by an equivalent electronic data interchange (EDI) message.

9.   Checking - packaging - marking

Pay the costs of those checking operations (such as checking quality, measuring, weighing, counting) which are necessary for the purpose of delivering the goods in accordance with A.4.

Provide at his own expense packaging (unless it is usual for the particular trade to deliver the goods of the contract description unpacked) which is required for the delivery of the goods. Packaging is to be marked appropriately.

10. Other obligations

Pay all costs and charges incurred in obtaining the documents or equivalent electronic messages mentioned in B.10. and reimburse those incurred by the buyer in rendering his assistance therewith. Provide the buyer, upon request, with the necessary information for procuring insurance.

B. THE BUYER MUST:

1.   Payment of the price

Pay the price as provided in the contract of sale.

2. Licences, authorisations and formalities
Render the seller at the latter's request, risk and expense, every assistance in obtaining any import licence or other official authorisation necessary for the importation of the goods.

3. Contract of carriage
No obligation.

4. Taking delivery
Take delivery of the goods as soon as they have been placed at his disposal in accordance with A.4.

5. Transfer of risks
Bear all risks of loss of or damage to the goods from the time they have been placed at his disposal in accordance with A.4. Should he fail to give notice in accordance with B.7., bear all risks of loss of or damage to the goods from the agreed date or the expiry date of the period stipulated for delivery provided, however, that the goods have been duly appropriated to the contract, that is to say, clearly set aside or otherwise identified as the contract goods.

6. Division of costs
Pay all costs relating to the goods from the time they have been placed at his disposal in accordance with A.4.

Should he fail to take delivery of the goods when they have been placed at his disposal in accordance with A.4., or to give notice in accordance with B.7., bear all additional costs incurred thereby provided, however, that the goods have been appropriated to the contract, that is to say, clearly set aside or otherwise identified as the contract goods.

7. Notice to the seller
Whenever he is entitled to determine the time within a stipulated period and/or the place of taking delivery, give the seller sufficient notice thereof.

8. Proof of delivery, transport document or equivalent electronic message
Accept the delivery order or transport document in accordance with A.8.

9. Inspection of goods
Pay, unless otherwise agreed, the costs of pre-shipment inspection except when mandated by the authorities of the country of exportation.

10. Other obligations
Render the seller, at the latter's request, risk and expense, every assistance in obtaining any documents or equivalent electronic

messages issued or transmitted in the country of importation which the seller may require for the purpose of placing the goods at the disposal of the buyer in accordance with these rules.

DELIVERED DUTY UNPAID (... named place of destination)	"Delivered duty unpaid" means that the seller fulfils his obligation to deliver when the goods have been made available at the named place in the country of importation. The seller has to bear the costs and risks involved in bringing the goods thereto (excluding duties, taxes and other official charges payable upon importation as well as the costs and risks of carrying out customs formalities). The buyer has to pay any additional costs and to bear any risks caused by his failure to clear the goods for import in time. If the parties wish the seller to carry out customs formalities and bear the costs and risks resulting therefrom, this has to be made clear by adding words to this effect. If the parties wish to include in the seller's obligations some of the costs payable upon importation of the goods (such as value added tax (VAT)), this should be made clear by adding words to this effect: "Delivered duty unpaid, VAT paid, (. . . named place of destination)". This term may be used irrespective of the mode of transport.

A. THE SELLER MUST:	**1. Provision of the goods in conformity with the contract** Provide the goods and the commercial invoice, or its equivalent electronic message, in conformity with the contract of sale and any other evidence of conformity which may be required by the contract. **2. Licences, authorisations and formalities** Obtain at his own risk and expense any export licence and other official authorisation and carry out all customs formalities for the exportation of the goods and, where necessary, for their transit through another country. **3. Contract of carriage and insurance** a) Contract of carriage Contract on usual terms at his own expense for the carriage of the goods by a usual route and in the customary manner to the agreed point at the named place of destination. If a point is not agreed or is not determined by practice, the seller may select the point at the named place of destination which best suits his purpose.

b) Contract of insurance
No obligation.

4. Delivery
Place the goods at the disposal of the buyer in accordance with A.3. on the date or within the period stipulated.

5. Transfer of risks
Subject to the provisions of B.5., bear all risks of loss of or damage to the goods until such time as they have been delivered in accordance with A.4.

6. Division of costs
Subject to the provisions of B.6.

- in addition to costs resulting from A.3.a), pay all costs relating to the goods until such time as they have been delivered in accordance with A.4.;

- pay the costs of customs formalities necessary for exportation as well as all duties, taxes and other official charges payable upon exportation and, where necessary, for their transit through another country prior to delivery in accordance with A.4.

7. Notice to the buyer
Give the buyer sufficient notice of the dispatch of the goods as well as any other notice required in order to allow the buyer to take measures which are normally necessary to enable him to take the goods.

8. Proof of delivery, transport document or equivalent electronic message
Provide at his own expense the delivery order and/or the usual transport document (for example a negotiable bill of lading, a non-negotiable sea waybill, an inland waterway document, an air waybill, a railway consignment note, a road consignment note, or a multimodal transport document) which the buyer may require to take delivery of the goods.

Where the seller and the buyer have agreed to communicate electronically, the document referred to in the preceding paragraph may be replaced by an equivalent electronic data interchange (EDI) message.

9. Checking - packaging - marking
Pay the costs of those checking operations (such as checking quality, measuring, weighing, counting) which are necessary for the purpose of delivering the goods in accordance with A.4.

Provide at his own expense packaging (unless it is usual for the particular trade to deliver the goods of the contract description unpacked) which is required for the delivery of the goods. Packaging is to be marked appropriately.

10. Other obligations

Render the buyer at the latter's request, risk and expense, every assistance in obtaining any documents or equivalent electronic messages other than those mentioned in A.8. issued or transmitted in the country of dispatch and/or of origin which the buyer may require for the importation of the goods.

Provide the buyer, upon request, with the necessary information for procuring insurance.

B. THE BUYER MUST:

1. Payment of the price
Pay the price as provided in the contract of sale.

2. Licences, authorisations and formalities
Obtain at his own risk and expense any import licence or other official authorisation and carry out all customs formalities necessary for the importation of the goods.

3. Contract of carriage
No obligation.

4. Taking delivery
Take delivery of the goods as soon as they have been placed at his disposal in accordance with A.4.

5. Transfer of risks
Bear all risks of loss of or damage to the goods from the time they have been placed at his disposal in accordance with A.4. Should he fail to fulfil his obligations in accordance with B.2., bear all additional risks of loss of or damage to the goods incurred thereby and should he fail to give notice in accordance with B.7., bear all risks of loss of or damage to the goods from the agreed date or the expiry date of the period stipulated for delivery provided, however, that the goods have been duly appropriated to the contract, that is to say, clearly set aside or otherwise identified as the contract goods.

6. Division of costs
Pay all costs relating to the goods from the time they have been placed at his disposal at the named point of destination in accordance with A.4.

Should he fail to fulfil his obligations in accordance with B.2., or to take delivery of the goods when they have been placed at his disposal in accordance with A.4., or to give notice in accordance with B.7., bear all additional costs incurred thereby provided, however. that the goods have been duly appropriated to the contract, that is to say, clearly set aside or otherwise identified as the contract goods.

Pay all duties, taxes and other official charges as well as the costs of carrying out customs formalities payable upon importation of the goods.

7. Notice to the seller
Whenever he is entitled to determine the time within a stipulated period and/or the place of taking delivery, give the seller sufficient notice thereof.

8. Proof of delivery, transport document or equivalent electronic message
Accept the appropriate delivery order or transport document in accordance with A-8.

9. Inspection of goods
Pay, unless otherwise agreed, the costs of pre-shipment inspection except when mandated by the authorities of the country of exportation.

10. Other obligations
Pay all costs and charges incurred in obtaining the documents or equivalent electronic messages mentioned in A.10 and reimburse those incurred by the seller in rendering his assistance in accordance therewith.

DELIVERED DUTY PAID (... named place of destination)

"Delivered duty paid" means that the seller fulfils his obligation to deliver when the goods have been made available at the named place in the country of importation. The seller has to bear the risks and costs, including duties, taxes and other charges of delivering the goods thereto, cleared for importation. Whilst the EXW term represents the minimum obligation for the seller, DDP represents the maximum obligation.

This term should not be used if the seller is unable directly or indirectly to obtain the import licence.

If the parties wish the buyer to clear the goods for importation and to pay the duty, the term DDU should be used.

If the parties wish to exclude from the seller's obligations some of the costs payable upon importation of the goods (such as value added tax (VAT)), this should be made clear by adding words to this effect: "Delivered duty paid, VAT unpaid (. . . named place of destination)".

This term may be used irrespective of the mode of transport.

A. THE SELLER MUST:

1.   Provision of the goods in conformity with the contract
Provide the goods and the commercial invoice, or its equivalent electronic message, in conformity with the contract of sale and any other evidence of conformity which may be required by the contract.

2.   Licences, authorisations and formalities
Obtain at his own risk and expense any export and import licence and other official authorisation and carry out all customs formalities for the exportation and importation of the goods and, where necessary, for their transit through another country.

3.   Contract of carriage and insurance
a) Contract of carriage

Contract at his own expense for the carriage of the goods by a usual route and in a customary manner to the agreed point at the named place of destination. If a point is not agreed or is not determined by practice, the seller may select the point at the named place of destination which best suits his purpose.
b)   Contract of insurance
No obligation.

4.   Delivery
Place the goods at the disposal of the buyer in accordance with A.3. on the date or within the period stipulated.

5.   Transfer of risks
Subject to the provisions of B.5., bear all risks of loss of or damage to the goods until such time as they have been delivered in accordance with A.4.

6.   Division of costs
Subject to the provisions of B.6.

- in addition to costs resulting from A.3.a), pay all costs relating to the goods until such time as they have been delivered in accordance with A.4.;

- pay the costs of customs formalities as well as all duties, taxes and other official charges payable upon exportation and importation of the goods, unless otherwise agreed and, where necessary, their transit through another country prior to delivery in accordance with A.4.

7.   Notice to the buyer
Give the buyer sufficient notice of the dispatch of the goods as well as any other notice required in order to allow the buyer to take measures which are normally necessary to enable him to take the goods.

8.   Proof of delivery, transport document or equivalent electronic message
Provide the buyer at the seller's expense with the delivery order and/or the usual transport document (for example, a negotiable bill of lading, a non-negotiable sea waybill, an inland waterway document, an air waybill, a railway consignment note, a road consignment note, or a multimodal transport document) which the buyer may require to take the goods.

Where the seller and the buyer have agreed to communicate electronically, the document referred to in the preceding paragraph may be replaced by an equivalent electronic data interchange (EDI) message.

9.   Checking - packaging - marking
Pay the costs of those checking operations (such as checking quality, measuring, weighing, counting) which are necessary for the purpose of delivering the goods in accordance with A.4.

Provide at his own expense packaging (unless it is usual for the particular trade to deliver the goods of the contract description unpacked) which is required for the delivery of the goods. Packaging is to be marked appropriately.

10. Other obligations
Pay all costs and charges incurred in obtaining the documents or equivalent electronic messages mentioned in B.10. and reimburse those incurred by the buyer in rendering his assistance therewith. Provide the buyer, upon request, with the necessary information for procuring insurance.

B. THE BUYER MUST:

1.   Payment of the price
Pay the price as provided in the contract of sale.

2.   Licences, authorisations and formalities
Render the seller at the latter's request, risk and expense every assistance in obtaining any import licence and other official authorisation necessary for the importation of the goods.

3. Contract of carriage
No obligation.

4. Taking delivery
Take delivery of the goods as soon as they have been placed at his disposal in accordance with A.4.

5. Transfer of risks
Bear all risks of loss of or damage to the goods from the time they have been placed at his disposal in accordance with A.4. Should he fail to give notice in accordance with B.7., bear all risks of loss of or damage to the goods from the agreed date or the expiry date of the period stipulated for delivery provided, however, that the goods have been duly appropriated to the contract, that is to say, clearly set aside or otherwise identified as the contract goods.

6. Division of costs
Pay all costs relating to the goods from the time they have been placed at his disposal in accordance with A.4.

Should he fail to take delivery of the goods when they have been placed at his disposal in accordance with A.4., or to give notice in accordance with B.7., bear all additional costs incurred thereby provided, however, that the goods have been appropriated to the contract, that is to say, clearly set aside or otherwise identified as the contract goods.

7. Notice to the seller
Whenever he is entitled to determine the time within a stipulated period and/or the place of taking delivery, give the seller sufficient notice thereof.

8. Proof of delivery, transport document or equivalent electronic message
Accept the appropriate delivery order or transport document in accordance with A.8.

9. Inspection of goods
Pay, unless otherwise agreed, the costs of pre-shipment inspection except when mandated by the authorities of the country of exportation.

10. Other obligations
Render the seller, at his request, risk and expense, every assistance in obtaining any documents or equivalent electronic messages issued or transmitted in the country of importation which the seller may require for the purpose of placing the goods at the disposal of the buyer in accordance with these rules.

APPENDIX B

Uniform Rules for Collections
ICC Publication No. 322
Effective January 1, 1979

GENERAL PROVISIONS AND DEFINITIONS

A. These provisions and definitions and the following articles apply to all collections as defined in (B) below and are binding upon all parties thereto unless otherwise expressly agreed or unless contrary to the provisions of a national, state or local law and/or regulation which cannot be departed from.

B. For the purpose of such provisions, definitions and articles:

1. i. "Collection" means the handling by banks, on instructions received, of documents as defined in (ii) below, in order to

   a) obtain acceptance and/or, as the case may be, payment, or

   b) deliver commercial documents against acceptance and/or, as the case may be, against payment, or

   c) deliver documents on other terms and conditions.

   ii. "Documents" means financial documents and/or commercial documents:

   a) "financial documents" means bills of exchange, promissory notes, cheques, payment receipts or other similar instruments used for obtaining the payment of money;

b) "commercial documents" means invoices, shipping documents, documents of title or other similar documents, or any other documents whatsoever, not being financial documents.

iii. "Clean collection" means collection of financial documents not accompanied by commercial documents.

iv. "Documentary collection" means collection of

a) financial documents accompanied by commercial documents;

b) commercial documents not accompanied by financial documents.

2. The "parties thereto" are:

i. The "principal" who is the customer entrusting the operation of collection to his bank;

ii. The "remitting bank" which is the bank to which the principal has entrusted the operation of collection;

iii. The "collecting bank" which is any bank, other than the remitting bank, involved in processing the collection order;

iv. The "presenting bank" which is the collecting bank making presentation to the drawee.

3. The "drawee" is the one to whom presentation is to be made according to the collection order.

C. All documents sent for collection must be accompanied by a collection order giving complete and precise instructions. Banks are only permitted to act upon the instructions given in such collection order, and in accordance with these Rules.

If any bank cannot, for any reason, comply with the instructions given in the collection order received by it, it must immediately advise the party from whom it received the collection order.

LIABILITIES AND RESPONSIBILITIES

Article 1

Banks will act in good faith and exercise reasonable care.

Article 2

Banks must verify that the documents received appear to be as listed in the collection order and must immediately advise the party from whom the collection order was received of any documents missing.

Banks have no further obligation to examine the documents.

Article 3

For the purpose of giving effect to the instructions of the principal, the remitting bank will utilize as the collecting bank:

i. the collecting bank nominated by the principal or, in the absence of such nomination,

ii. any bank, of its own or another bank's choice, in the country of payment or acceptance, as the case may be.

The documents and the collection order may be sent to the collecting bank directly or through another bank as intermediary.

Banks utilizing the services of other banks for the purpose of giving effect to the instructions of the principal do so for the account of and at the risk of the latter.

The principal shall be bound by and liable to indemnity the banks against all obligations and responsibilities imposed by foreign laws or usages.

Article 4

Banks concerned with a collection assume no liability or responsibility for the consequences arising out of delay and/or loss in transit of any messages, letters or documents, or for delay, mutilation or other errors arising in the transmission of cables, telegrams, telex, or communication by electronic systems, or for errors in translation or interpretation of technical terms.

Article 5

Banks concerned with a collection assume no liability or responsibility for consequences arising out of the interruption of their business by Acts of God, riots, civil commotions, insurrection, wars, or any other causes beyond their control or by strikes or lockouts.

Article 6

Goods should not be dispatched directly to the address of a bank or consigned to a bank without prior agreement on the part of that bank.

In the event of goods being dispatched directly to the address of a bank or consigned to a bank for delivery to a drawee against payment or acceptance or upon other terms without prior agreement on the part of the bank, the bank has no obligation to take delivery of the goods, which remain at the risk and responsibility of the party dispatching the goods.

PRESENTATION

Article 7

Documents are to be presented to the drawee in the form in which they are received, except that the remitting and collecting banks are authorized to affix any necessary stamps, at the expense of the principal unless otherwise instructed, and to make any necessary endorsements or place any rubber stamps or other identifying marks or symbols customary to or required for the collection operation.

Article 8

Collection orders should bear the complete address of the drawee or of the domicile at which presentation is to be made. If the address is incomplete or incorrect, the collecting bank may, without obligation and responsibility on its part, endeavor to ascertain the proper address.

Article 9

In the case of documents payable at sight the presenting bank must make presentation for payment without delay.

In the case of documents payable at a tenor other than sight the presenting bank must, where acceptance is called for, make presentation for acceptance without delay, and where payment is called for, make presentation for payment not later than the appropriate maturity date.

Article 10

In respect of a documentary collection including a bill of exchange payable at a future date, the collection order should state whether the commercial documents are to be released to the drawee against acceptance (D/A) or against payment (D/P).

In the absence of such statement, the commercial documents will be released only against payment.

PAYMENT

Article 11

In the case of documents payable in the currency of the country of payment (local currency), the presenting bank must, unless otherwise instructed in the collection order, only release the documents to the drawee against payment in local currency which is immediately available for disposal in the manner specified in the collection order.

Article 12

In the case of documents payable in a currency other than that of the country of payment (foreign currency), the presenting bank must, unless otherwise instructed in the collection order, only release the documents to the drawee against payment in the relative foreign currency which can immediately be remitted in accordance with the instructions given in the collection order.

Article 13

In respect of clean collections partial payments will be accepted if and to the extent to which and on the conditions on which partial payments are authorized by the law in force in the place of payment. The documents will only be released to the drawee when full payment thereof has been received.

In respect of documentary collections partial payments will only be accepted if specifically authorized in the collection order. However, unless otherwise instructed, the presenting bank will only release the documents to the drawee after full payment has been received.

In all cases, partial payments will only be accepted subject to compliance with the provisions of either Article 11 or Article 12 as appropriate.

Partial payment, if accepted, will be dealt with in accordance with the provisions of Article 14.

Article 14

Amounts collected (less charges and/or disbursements and/or expenses where applicable) must be made available without delay to the bank from which the collection order was received in accordance with the instructions contained in the collection order.

ACCEPTANCE

Article 15

The presenting bank is responsible for seeing that the form of the acceptance of a bill of exchange appears to be complete and correct, but is not responsible for the genuineness of any signature or for the authority of any signatory to sign the acceptance.

PROMISSORY NOTES, RECEIPTS AND OTHER SIMILAR INSTRUMENTS

Article 16

The presenting bank is not responsible for the genuineness of any signature or for the authority of any signatory to sign a promissory note, receipt, or other similar instrument.

PROTEST

Article 17

The collection order should give specific instructions regarding protest (or other legal process in lieu thereof), in the event of non-acceptance or non-payment.

In the absence of such specific instructions the banks concerned with the collection have no obligation to have the documents protested (or subjected to other legal process in lieu thereof) for non-payment or non-acceptance.

Any charges and/or expenses incurred by banks in connection with such protest or other legal process will be for the account of the principal.

**CASE-OF-NEED
(PRINCIPAL'S
REPRESENTATIVE) AND
PROTECTION OF GOODS**

Article 18

If the principal nominates a representative to act as case-of-need in the event of non-acceptance and/or non-payment the collection order should clearly and fully indicate the powers of such case-of-need.

In the absence of such indication banks will not accept any instructions from the case-of-need.

Article 19

Banks have no obligation to take any action in respect of the goods to which a documentary collection relates.

Nevertheless, in the case that banks take action for the protection of the goods, whether instructed or not, they assume no liability or responsibility with regard to the fate and/or condition of the goods and/or for any acts and/or omissions on the part of any third parties entrusted with the custody and/or protection of the goods. However, the collecting bank must immediately advise the bank from which the collection order was received of any such action taken.

Any charges and/or expenses incurred by banks in connection with any action for the protection of the goods will be for the account of the principal.

ADVICE OF FATE, ETC.

Article 20

Collecting banks are to advise fate in accordance with the following rules:

i. Form of advice. All advices or information from the collecting bank to the bank from which the collection order was received, must bear appropriate detail including, in all cases, the latter bank's reference number of the collection order.

ii. Method of advice. In the absence of specific instructions, the collecting bank must send all advices to the bank from which the collection order was received by quickest mail but, if the collecting bank considers the matter to be urgent, quicker methods such as cable, telegram, telex, or communication by electronic systems, etc., may be used at the expense of the principal.

iii a) Advice of payment. The collecting bank must send without delay advice of payment to the bank from which the collection order was received, detailing the amount or amounts collected, charges and/or disbursements and/or expenses deducted, where appropriate, and method of disposal of the funds.

b) Advice of acceptance. The collecting bank must send without delay advice of acceptance to the bank from which the collection order was received.

c) Advice of non-payment or non-acceptance. The collecting bank must send without delay advice of non-payment or advice of non-acceptance to the bank from which the collection order was received.

The presenting bank should endeavor to ascertain the reasons for such non-payment or non-acceptance and advise accordingly the bank from which the collection order was received.

On receipt of such advice the remitting bank must, within a reasonable time, give appropriate instructions as to the further handling of the documents. If such instructions are not received by the presenting bank within 90 days from its advice of non-payment or non-acceptance, the documents may be returned to the bank from which the collection order was received.

INTEREST, CHARGES AND EXPENSES

Article 21

If the collection order includes an instruction to collect interest which is not embodied in the accompanying financial document(s), if any, and the drawee refuses to pay such interest, the presenting bank may deliver the document(s) against payment or acceptance as the case may be without collecting such interest, unless the collection order expressly states that such interest may not be waived. Where such interest is to be collected the collection order must bear an indication of the rate of interest and the period covered. When payment of interest has been refused the presenting bank must inform the bank from which the collection order was received accordingly.

If the documents include a financial document containing an unconditional and definitive interest clause, the interest amount is deemed to form part of the amount of the documents to be collected. Accordingly, the interest amount is payable in addition to the principal amount shown in the financial document and may not be waived unless the collection order so authorizes.

Article 22

If the collection order includes an instruction that collection charges and/or expenses are to be for the account of the drawee and the drawee refuses to pay them, the presenting bank may deliver the document(s) against payment or acceptance as the case may be without collecting charges and/or expenses unless the collection order expressly states that such charges and/or expenses may not be waived. When payment of collection charges and/or expenses has been refused the presenting bank must inform the bank from which the collection order was received accordingly. Whenever collection charges and/or expenses are so waived they will be for the account of the principal, and may be deducted from the proceeds.

Should a collection order specifically prohibit the waiving of collection charges and/or expenses then neither the remitting nor collecting nor presenting bank shall be responsible for any costs or delays resulting from this prohibition.

Article 23

In all cases where in the express terms of a collection order, or under these Rules, disbursements and/or expenses and/or collection charges are to be borne by the principal, the collecting bank(s) shall be entitled promptly to recover outlays in respect of disbursements and expenses and charges from the bank from which the collection order was received and the remitting bank shall have the right promptly to recover from the principal any amounts so paid out by it, together with its own disbursements, expenses and charges, regardless of the fate of the collection.

ICC SERVICES TO BUSINESS

The International Chamber of Commerce is the world business organization. It acts to promote the greater freedom of world trade, to harmonize and facilitate business and trade practices, and to represent the business community at international levels. Paris based, the ICC is represented by National Committees and Councils in over 50 countries and also has members in over 40 others.

The ICC Banking Commission

The Uniform Rules for Collection found in this brochure were developed by the ICC Commission on Banking Technique and Practice. This Commission brings together bankers from throughout the world with the aim of:

- defining, simplifying and harmonizing the practices and terminology used in international banking;

- expressing the views of bankers before relevant international organizations, in particular the United Nations Commission on International Trade Law (UNCITRAL);

- serving as a meeting ground for the bankers of the world to discuss common problems.

ADDITIONAL PUBLICATIONS

Guide to Documentary Credit Operations

This new guide explains the role of documentary credits and, in a practical, step-by-step manner, how they work. International businessmen and bankers will find it invaluable in their daily professional life. It includes the Uniform Customs and Practice contained in publication No. 290.

English and French editions.   **No. 305**

Standard Forms for Issuing Documentary Credits

With help of banking authorities throughout the world, the ICC has recently completed work on new standard forms for issuing documentary credits. In addition, practical advice for their use is given in an explanatory booklet. The increasing use of ICC standard credit forms is a further contribution to uniform documentary credit practice.

English and French editions.   **No. 323**

Uniform Rules for Contract Guarantees

The result of 12 years of work by the ICC Commissions on Banking and Commercial Practice, this new brochure presents Rules designed to regulate contract guarantees as well as an introduction explaining their use. The Rules cover tender bonds, performance guarantees and repayment guarantees given by banks, insurance companies and other guarantors to ensure the fulfillment of a tender or a contract. They invest these guarantees with a moral content and strive to achieve a fair balance between the legitimate interests of the parties involved.

English and French editions. **No. 325**

APPENDIX C

Uniform Customs and Practice for Documentary Credits
ICC Publication No. 400 Effective October 1, 1984

A. GENERAL PROVISIONS AND DEFINITIONS

Article 1

These articles apply to all documentary credits, including, to the extent to which they may be applicable, standby letters of credit, and are binding on all parties thereto unless otherwise expressly agreed. They shall be incorporated into each documentary credit by wording in the credit indicating that such credit is issued subject to Uniform Customs and Practice for Documentary Credits, 1983 revision, ICC Publication No. 400.

Article 2

For the purposes of these articles, the expressions "documentary credit(s)" and "standby letter(s) of credit" used herein (hereinafter referred to as "credit(s)"), mean any arrangement, however named or described, whereby a bank (the issuing bank), acting at the request and on the instructions of a customer (the applicant for the credit),

 i.   is to make a payment to or to the order of a third party (the beneficiary), or is to pay or accept bills of exchange (drafts) drawn by the beneficiary, or

ii.   authorizes another bank to effect such payment, or to pay, accept or negotiate such bills of exchange (drafts), against stipulated documents, provided that the terms and conditions of the credit are complied with.

Article 3

Credits, by their nature, are separate transactions from the sales or other contract(s) on which they may be based and banks are in no way concerned with or bound by such contract(s), even if any reference whatsoever to such contract(s) is included in the credit.

Article 4

In credit operations all parties concerned deal in documents, and not in goods, services and/or other performances to which the documents may relate.

Article 5

Instructions for the issuance of credits, the credits themselves, instructions for any amendments thereto and the amendments themselves must be complete and precise.

In order to guard against confusion and misunderstanding, banks should discourage any attempt to include excessive detail in the credit or in any amendment thereto.

Article 6

A beneficiary can in no case avail himself of the contractual relationships existing between the banks or between the applicant for the credit and the issuing bank.

B. FORM AND NOTIFICATION OF CREDITS

Article 7

a. Credits may be either

i. revocable, or

ii. irrevocable.

b.   All credits, therefore, should clearly indicate whether they are revocable or irrevocable.

c.   In the absence of such indication the credit shall be deemed to be revocable.

Article 8

A credit may be advised to a beneficiary through another bank (the advising bank) without engagement on the part of the advising bank, but that bank shall take reasonable care to check the apparent authenticity of the credit which it advises.

Article 9

a.   A revocable credit may be amended or cancelled by the issuing bank at any moment and without prior notice to the beneficiary.

b.   However, the issuing bank is bound to:

i.   reimburse a branch or bank with which a revocable credit has been made available for sight payment, acceptance or negotiation, for any payment, acceptance or negotiation made by such branch or bank prior to receipt by it of notice of amendment or cancellation, against documents which appear on their face to be in accordance with the terms and conditions of the credit.

ii.   reimburse a branch or bank with which a revocable credit has been made available for deferred payment, if such branch or bank has, prior to receipt by it of notice of amendment or cancellation, taken up documents which appear on their face to be in accordance with the terms and conditions of the credit.

Article 10

a.   An irrevocable credit constitutes a definite undertaking of the issuing bank, provided that the stipulated documents are presented and that the terms and conditions of the credit are complied with:

i.   if the credit provides for sight payment-to pay, or that payment will be made;

ii.   if the credit provides for deferred payment-to pay, or that payment will be made, on the date(s) determinable in accordance with the stipulations of the credit;

iii.   if the credit provides for acceptance-to accept drafts drawn by the beneficiary if the credit stipulates that they are to be drawn on the issuing bank, or to be responsible for their acceptance and payment at maturity if the credit stipulates that they are to be drawn on the applicant for the credit or any other drawee stipulated in the credit;

iv.   if the credit provides for negotiation-to pay without recourse to drawers and/or bona fide holders, draft(s) drawn by the beneficiary, at sight or at a tenor, on the applicant for the credit or on any other drawee stipulated in the credit other than the issuing bank itself, or to provide for negotiation by another bank and to pay, as above, if such negotiation is not effected.

b.   When an issuing bank authorizes or requests another bank to confirm its irrevocable credit and the latter has added its confirmation, such confirmation constitutes a definite undertaking of such bank (the confirming bank), in addition to that of the issuing bank, provided that the stipulated documents are presented and that the terms and conditions of the credit are complied with:

i.   if the credit provides for sight payment-to pay, or that payment will be made;

ii.   if the credit provides for deferred payment-to pay, or that payment will be made, on the date(s) determinable in accordance with the stipulations of the credit;

iii.   if the credit provides for acceptance-to accept drafts drawn by the beneficiary if the credit stipulates that they are to be drawn on the confirming bank, or to be responsible for their acceptance and payment at maturity if the credit stipulates that they are to be drawn on the applicant for the credit or any other drawee stipulated in the credit;

iv.   if the credit provides for negotiation-to negotiate without recourse to drawers and/or bona fide holders, draft(s) drawn by the beneficiary, at sight or at a tenor, on the issuing bank or on the applicant for the credit or on any other drawee stipulated in the credit other than the confirming bank itself.

c.   If a bank is authorized or requested by the issuing bank to add its confirmation to a credit but is not prepared to do so, it must so inform the issuing bank without delay. Unless the issuing bank specifies otherwise in its confirmation authorization or request, the advising bank will advise the credit to the beneficiary without adding its confirmation.

d.   Such undertakings can neither be amended nor cancelled without the agreement of the issuing bank, the confirming bank (if any), and the beneficiary. Partial acceptance of amendments contained in one and the same advice of amendment is not effective without the agreement of all the above named parties.

Article 11

a.   All credits must clearly indicate whether they are available by sight payment, by deferred payment, by acceptance or by negotiation.

b.   All credits must nominate the bank (nominated bank) which is authorized to pay (paying bank), or to accept drafts (accepting bank), or to negotiate (negotiating bank), unless the credit allows negotiation by any bank (negotiating bank).

c.   Unless the nominated bank is the issuing bank or the confirming bank, its nomination by the issuing bank does not constitute any undertaking by the nominated bank to pay, to accept, or to negotiate.

d.   By nominating a bank other than itself, or by allowing for negotiation by any bank, or by authorizing or requesting a bank to add its confirmation, the issuing bank authorizes such bank to pay, accept or negotiate, as the case may be, against documents which appear on their face to be in accordance with the terms and conditions of the credit, and undertakes to reimburse such bank in accordance with the provisions of these articles.

Article 12

a.   When an issuing bank instructs a bank (advising bank) by any teletransmission to advise a credit or an amendment to a credit, and intends the mail confirmation to be the operative credit instrument, or the operative amendment, the teletransmission must state "full details to follow" (or words of similar effect), or that the mail confirmation will be the operative credit instrument or the operative amendment. The issuing bank must forward the operative credit instrument or the operative amendment to such advising bank without delay.

b.   The teletransmission will be deemed to be the operative credit instrument or the operative amendment, and no mail confirmation should be sent, unless the teletransmission states "full details to follow" (or words of similar effect), or states that the mail confirmation is to be the operative credit instrument or the operative amendment.

c.   A teletransmission intended by the issuing bank to be the operative credit instrument should clearly indicate that the credit is issued subject to Uniform Customs and Practice for Documentary Credits, 1983 revision, ICC Publication No. 400.

d.   If a bank uses the services of another bank or banks (the advising bank) to have the credit advised to the beneficiary, it must also use the services of the same bank(s) for advising any amendments.

e.   Banks shall be responsible for any consequences arising from their failure to follow the procedures set out in the preceding paragraphs.

Article 13

When a bank is instructed to issue, confirm or advise a credit similar in terms to one previously issued, confirmed or advised (similar credit) and the previous credit has been the subject of amendment(s), it shall be understood that the similar credit will not include any such amendment(s) unless the instructions specify clearly the amendment(s) which is/are to apply to the similar credit. Banks should discourage instructions to issue, confirm or advise a credit in this manner.

Article 14

If incomplete or unclear instructions are received to issue, confirm, advise or amend a credit, the bank requested to act on such instructions may give preliminary notification to the beneficiary for information only and without responsibility. The credit will be issued, confirmed, advised or amended only when the necessary information has been received and if the bank is then prepared to act on the instructions. Banks should provide the necessary information without delay.

C. LIABILITIES AND RESPONSIBILITIES

Article 15

Banks must examine all documents with reasonable care to ascertain that they appear on their face to be in accordance with the terms and conditions of the credit. Documents which appear on their face to be inconsistent with one another will be considered as not appearing on their face to be in accordance with the terms and conditions of the credit.

Article 16

a. If a bank so authorized effects payment, or incurs a deferred payment undertaking, or accepts, or negotiates against documents which appear on their face to be in accordance with the terms and conditions of a credit, the party giving such authority shall be bound to reimburse the bank which has effected payment, or incurred a deferred payment undertaking, or has accepted, or negotiated, and to take up the documents.

b. If, upon receipt of the documents, the issuing bank considers that they appear on their face not to be in accordance with the terms and conditions of the credit, it must determine, on the basis of the documents alone, whether to take up such documents, or to refuse them and claim that they appear on their face not to be in accordance with the terms and conditions of the credit.

c. The issuing bank shall have a reasonable time in which to examine the documents and to determine as above whether to take up or to refuse the documents.

d. If the issuing bank decides to refuse the documents, it must give notice to that effect without delay by telecommunication or, if that is not possible, by other expeditious means, to the bank from which it received the documents (the remitting bank), or to the beneficiary, if it received the documents directly from him. Such notice must state the discrepancies in respect of which the issuing bank refuses the documents and must also state whether it is holding the documents at the disposal of, or is returning them to, the presentor (remitting bank or the beneficiary, as the case may be). The issuing bank shall then be entitled to claim from the remitting bank refund of any reimbursement which may have been made to that bank.

e. If the issuing bank fails to act in accordance with the provisions of paragraphs (c) and (d) of this article and/or fails to hold the documents at the disposal of, or to return them to, the presentor, the issuing bank shall be precluded from claiming that the documents are not in accordance with the terms and conditions of the credit.

f.   If the remitting bank draws the attention of the issuing bank to any discrepancies in the documents or advises the issuing bank that it has paid, incurred a deferred payment undertaking, accepted or negotiated under reserve or against an indemnity in respect of such discrepancies, the issuing bank shall not be thereby relieved from any of its obligations under any provision of this article. Such reserve or indemnity concerns only the relations between the remitting bank and the party toward whom the reserve was made, or from whom, or on whose behalf, the indemnity was obtained.

Article 17

Banks assume no liability or responsibility for the form, sufficiency, accuracy, genuineness, falsification or legal effect of any documents, or for the general and/or particular conditions stipulated in the documents or superimposed thereon; nor do they assume any liability or responsibility for the description, quantity, weight, quality, condition, packing, delivery, value or existence of the goods represented by any documents, or for the good faith or acts and/or omissions, solvency, performance or standing of the consignor, the carriers, or the insurers of the goods, or any other person whomsoever.

Article 18

Banks assume no liability or responsibility for the consequences arising out of delay and/or loss in transit of any messages, letters or documents, or for delay, mutilation or other errors arising in the transmission of any telecommunication. Banks assume no liability or responsibility for errors in translation or interpretation of technical terms, and reserve the right to transmit credit terms without translating them.

Article 19

Banks assume no liability or responsibility for consequences arising out of the interruption of their business by Acts of God, riots, civil commotions, insurrections, wars or any other causes beyond their control, or by any strikes or lockouts. Unless specifically authorized, banks will not, upon resumption of their business, incur a deferred payment undertaking, or effect payment, acceptance or negotiation under credits which expired during such interruption of their business.

Article 20

a.   Banks utilizing the services of another bank or other banks for the purpose of giving effect to the instructions of the applicant for the credit do so for the account and at the risk of such applicant.

b.   Banks assume no liability or responsibility should the instructions they transmit not be carried out, even if they have themselves taken the initiative in the choice of such other bank(s).

c.   The applicant for the credit shall be bound by and liable to indemnity the banks against all obligations and responsibilities imposed by foreign laws and usages.

Article 21

a.   If an issuing bank intends that the reimbursement to which a paying, accepting or negotiating bank is entitled shall be obtained by such bank claiming on another branch or office of the issuing bank or on a third bank (all hereinafter referred to as the reimbursing bank) it shall provide such reimbursing bank in good time with the proper instructions or authorization to honor such reimbursement claims and without making it a condition that the bank entitled to claim reimbursement must certify compliance with the terms and conditions of the credit to the reimbursing bank.

b.   An issuing bank will not be relieved from any of its obligations to provide reimbursement itself if and when reimbursement is not effected by the reimbursing bank.

c.   The issuing bank will be responsible to the paying, accepting or negotiating bank for any loss of interest if reimbursement is not provided on first demand made to the reimbursing bank, or as otherwise specified in the credit, or mutually agreed, as the case may be.

D. DOCUMENTS

Article 22

a.   All instructions for the issuance of credits and the credits themselves and, where applicable, all instructions for amendments thereto and the amendments themselves, must state precisely the document(s) against which payment, acceptance or negotiation is to be made.

b.   Terms such as "first class", "well known", "qualified", "independent", "official", and the like shall not be used to describe the issuers of any documents to be presented under a credit. If such terms are incorporated in the credit terms, banks will accept the relative documents as presented, provided that they appear on their face to be in accordance with the other terms and conditions of the credit.

c.   Unless otherwise stipulated in the credit, banks will accept as originals documents produced or appearing to have been produced:

  i.   by reprographic systems;

  ii.   by, or as the result of, automated or computerized systems;

  iii.   as carbon copies,

if marked as originals, always provided that, where necessary, such documents appear to have been authenticated.

Article 23

When documents other than transport documents, insurance documents and commercial invoices are called for, the credit should stipulate by whom such documents are to be issued and their wording or data content. If the credit does not so stipulate, banks will accept such documents as presented, provided that their data content makes it possible to relate the goods and/or services referred to therein to those referred to in the commercial invoice(s) presented, or to those referred to in the credit if the credit does not stipulate presentation of a commercial invoice.

Article 24

Unless otherwise stipulated in the credit, banks will accept a document bearing a date of issuance prior to that of the credit, subject to such document being presented within the time limits set out in the credit and in these articles.

D.I. Transport documents (documents indicating loading on board or dispatch or taking in charge)

Article 25

Unless a credit calling for a transport document stipulates as such document a marine bill of lading (ocean bill of lading or a bill of lading covering carriage by sea), or a post receipt or certificate of posting:

a.   Banks will, unless otherwise stipulated in the credit, accept a transport document which:

   i.   appears on its face to have been issued by a named carrier, or his agent, and

   ii.   indicates dispatch or taking in charge of the goods, or loading on board, as the case may be, and

   iii.   consists of the full set of originals issued to the consignor if issued in more than one original, and

   iv.   meets all other stipulations of the credit.

b.   Subject to the above, and unless otherwise stipulated in the credit, banks will not reject a transport document which:

   i.   bears a title such as "Combined transport bill of lading", "Combined transport document", "Combined transport bill of lading or port-to-port bill of lading", or a title or a combination of titles of similar intent and effect, and/or

   ii.   indicates some or all of the conditions of carriage by reference to a source or document other than the transport document itself (short form/blank back transport document), and/or

   iii.   indicates a place of taking in charge different from the port of loading and/or a place of final destination different from the port of discharge, and/or

   iv.   relates to cargoes such as those in containers or on pallets, and the like, and/or

   v.   contains the indication "intended", or similar qualification, in relation to the vessel or other means of transport, and/or the port of loading and/or the port of discharge.

c.   Unless otherwise stipulated in the credit in the case of carriage by sea or by more than one mode of transport but including carriage by sea, banks will reject a transport document which:

    i.   indicates that it is subject to a charter party, and/or

    ii.   indicates that the carrying vessel is propelled by sail only.

d.   Unless otherwise stipulated in the credit, banks will reject a transport document issued by a freight forwarder unless it is the FIATA Combined Transport Bill of Lading approved by the International Chamber of Commerce or otherwise indicates that it is issued by a freight forwarder acting as a carrier or agent of a named carrier.

Article 26

If a credit calling for a transport document stipulates as such document a marine bill of lading:

a.   Banks will, unless otherwise stipulated in the credit, accept a document which:

    i.   appears on its face to have been issued by a named carrier, or his agent, and

    ii.   indicates that the goods have been loaded on board or shipped on a named vessel, and

    iii.   consists of the full set of originals issued to the consignor if issued in more than one original, and

    iv.   meets all other stipulations of the credit.

b.   Subject to the above, and unless otherwise stipulated in the credit, banks will not reject a document which:

    i.   bears a title such as "Combined transport bill of lading", "Combined transport document", "Combined transport bill of lading or port-to-port bill of lading", or a title or a combination of titles of similar intent and effect, and/or

    ii.   indicates some or all of the conditions of carriage by reference to a source or document other than the transport document itself (short form/blank back transport document), and/or

    iii.   indicates a place of taking in charge different from the port of loading, and/or a place of final destination different from the port of discharge, and/or

iv.   relates to cargoes such as those in containers or on pallets, and the like.

c.   Unless otherwise stipulated in the credit, banks will reject a document which:

i.   indicates that it is subject to a charter party, and/or

ii.   indicates that the carrying vessel is propelled by sail only, and/or

iii.   contains the indication "intended", or similar qualification in relation to

- the vessel and/or the port of loading—unless such document bears an on board notation in accordance with article 27 (b) and also indicates the actual port of loading, and/or

- the port of discharge—unless the place of final destination indicated on the document is other than the port of discharge, and/or

iv.   is issued by a freight forwarder, unless it indicates that it is issued by such freight forwarder acting as a carrier, or as the agent of a named carrier.

Article 27

a.   Unless a credit specifically calls for an on board transport document, or unless inconsistent with other stipulation(s) in the credit, or with article 26, banks will accept a transport document which indicates that the goods have been taken in charge or received for shipment.

b.   Loading on board or shipment on a vessel may be evidenced either by a transport document bearing wording indicating loading on board a named vessel or shipment on a named vessel, or, in the case of a transport document stating "received for shipment", by means of a notation of loading on board on the transport document signed or initiated and dated by the carrier or his agent, and the date of this notation shall be regarded as the date of loading on board the named vessel or shipment on the named vessel.

Article 28

a.   In the case of carriage by sea or by more than one mode of transport but including carriage by sea, banks will refuse a transport document stating that the goods are or will be loaded on deck, unless specifically authorized in the credit.

b.   Banks will not refuse a transport document which contains a provision that the goods may be carried on deck, provided it does not specifically state that they are or will be loaded on deck.

Article 29

a.   For the purpose of this article transhipment means a transfer and reloading during the course of carriage from the port of loading or place of dispatch or taking in charge to the port of discharge or place of destination either from one conveyance or vessel to another conveyance or vessel within the same mode of transport or from one mode of transport to another mode of transport.

b.   Unless transhipment is prohibited by the terms of the credit, banks will accept transport documents which indicate that the goods will be transhipped, provided the entire carriage is covered by one and the same transport document.

c.   Even if transhipment is prohibited by the terms of the credit, banks will accept transport documents which:

    i.   incorporate printed clauses stating that the carrier has the right to tranship, or

    ii.   state or indicate that transhipment will or may take place, when the credit stipulates a combined transport document, or indicates carriage from a place of taking in charge to a place of final destination by different modes of transport including a carriage by sea, provided that the entire carriage is covered by one and the same transport document, or

    iii.   state or indicate that the goods are in a container(s), trailer(s), "LASH" barge(s), and the like and will be carried from the place of taking in charge to the place of final destination in the same container(s), trailer(s), "LASH" barge(s), and the like under one and the same transport document.

    iv.   state or indicate the place of receipt and/or of final destination as "C.F.S." (container freight station) or "C.Y."

(container yard) at, or associated with, the port of loading and/or the port of destination.

Article 30

If the credit stipulates dispatch of goods by post and calls for a post receipt or certificate of posting, banks will accept such post receipt or certificate of posting if it appears to have been stamped or otherwise authenticated and dated in the place from which the credit stipulates the goods are to be dispatched.

Article 31

a.   Unless otherwise stipulated in the credit, or inconsistent with any of the documents presented under the credit, banks will accept transport documents stating that freight or transportation charges (hereinafter referred to as "freight") have still to be paid.

b.   If a credit stipulates that the transport document has to indicate that freight has been paid or prepaid, banks will accept a transport document on which words clearly indicating payment or prepayment of freight appear by stamp or otherwise, or on which payment of freight is indicated by other means.

c.   The words "freight prepayable" or "freight to be prepaid" or words of similar effect, if appearing on transport documents, will not be accepted as constituting evidence of the payment of freight.

d.   Banks will accept transport documents bearing reference by stamp or otherwise to costs additional to the freight charges, such as costs of, or disbursements incurred in connection with, loading, unloading or similar operations, unless the conditions of the credit specifically prohibit such reference.

Article 32

Unless otherwise stipulated in the credit, banks will accept transport documents which bear a clause on the face thereof such as "shipper's load and count" or "said by shipper to contain" or words of similar effect.

Article 33

Unless otherwise stipulated in the credit, banks will accept transport documents indicating as the consignor of the goods a party other than the beneficiary of the credit.

Article 34

a.   A clean transport document is one which bears no superimposed clause or notation which expressly declares a defective condition of the goods and/or the packaging.

b.   Banks will refuse to transport documents bearing such clauses or notations unless the credit expressly stipulates the clauses or notations which may be accepted.

c.   Banks will regard a requirement in a credit for a transport document to bear the clause "clean on board" as complied with if such transport document meets the requirements of this article and of article 27(b).

D2.   Insurance documents

Article 35

a.   Insurance documents must be as stipulated in the credit, and must be issued and/or signed by insurance companies or underwriters, or their agents.

b.   Cover notes issued by brokers will not be accepted, unless specifically authorized by the credit.

Article 36

Unless otherwise stipulated in the credit, or unless it appears from the insurance document(s) that the cover is effective at the latest from the date of loading on board or dispatch or taking in charge of the goods, banks will refuse insurance documents presented which bear a date later than the date of loading on board or dispatch or taking in charge of the goods as indicated by the transport document(s).

Article 37

a.   Unless otherwise stipulated in the credit, the insurance document must be expressed in the same currency as the credit.

b.   Unless otherwise stipulated in the credit, the minimum amount for which the insurance document must indicate the insurance cover to have been effected is the CIF (cost, insurance and freight . . . "named port of destination") or CIP (freight/carriage and insurance paid to "named point of destination") value of the goods, as the case may be, plus 10%. However, if banks cannot determine the CIF or CIP value, as the case may be, from the documents on their face, they will accept as such minimum amount the amount for which payment, acceptance or negotiation is requested under the credit, or the amount of the commercial invoice, whichever is the greater.

Article 38

a.   Credits should stipulate the type of insurance required and, if any, the additional risks which are to be covered. Imprecise terms such as "usual risks" or "customary risks" should not be used; if they are used, banks will accept insurance documents as presented, without responsibility for any risks not being covered.

b.   Failing specific stipulations in the credit, banks will accept insurance documents as presented, without responsibility for any risk not being covered.

Article 39

Where a credit stipulates "insurance against all risks", banks will accept an insurance document which contains any "all risks" notation or clause, whether or not bearing the heading "all risks", even if indicating that certain risks are excluded, without responsibility for any risk(s) not being covered.

Article 40

Banks will accept an insurance document which indicates that the cover is subject to a franchise or an excess (deductible), unless it is specifically stipulated in the credit that the insurance must be issued irrespective of percentage.

D3. Commercial Invoice

Article 41

a.   Unless otherwise stipulated in the credit, commercial invoices must be made out in the name of the applicant for the credit.

b.   Unless otherwise stipulated in the credit, banks may refuse commercial invoices issued for amounts in excess of the amount permitted by the credit. Nevertheless, if a bank authorized to pay, incur a deferred payment undertaking, accept, or negotiate under a credit accepts such invoices, its decision will be binding upon all parties, provided such bank has not paid, incurred a deferred payment undertaking, accepted or effected negotiation for an amount in excess of that permitted by the credit.

c.   The description of the goods in the commercial invoice must correspond with the description in the credit. In all other documents, the goods may be described in general terms not inconsistent with the description of the goods in the credit.

D4. Other documents

Article 42

If a credit calls for an attestation or certification of weight in the case of transport other than by sea, banks will accept a weight stamp or declaration of weight which appears to have been superimposed on the transport document by the carrier or his agent unless the credit specifically stipulates that the attestation or certification of weight must be by means of a separate document.

E. MISCELLANEOUS PROVISIONS

Quantity and amount

Article 43

a.   The words "about", "circa" or similar expressions used in connection with the amount of the credit or the quantity or the unit price stated in the credit are to be construed as allowing a difference not to exceed 10% more or 10% less than the amount or the quantity or the unit price to which they refer.

b.   Unless a credit stipulates that the quantity of the goods specified must not be exceeded or reduced, a tolerance of 5% more or 5% less will be permissible, even if partial shipments are not permitted, always provided that the amount of the drawings does not exceed the amount of the credit. This tolerance does not apply when the credit stipulates the quantity in terms of a stated number of packing units or individual items.

Partial drawings and/or shipments

Article 44

a.   Partial drawing and/or shipments are allowed, unless the credit stipulates otherwise.

b.   Shipments by sea, or by more than one mode of transport but including carriage by sea, made on the same vessel and for the same voyage, will not be regarded as partial shipments, even if the transport documents indicating loading on board bear different dates of issuance and/or indicate different ports of loading on board.

c.   Shipments made by post will not be regarded as partial shipments if the post receipts or certificates of posting appear to have been stamped or otherwise authenticated in the place from which the credit stipulates the goods are to be dispatched, and on the same date.

d.   Shipments made by modes of transport other than those referred to in paragraphs (b) and (c) of this article will not be regarded as partial shipments, provided the transport documents are issued by one and the same carrier or his agent and indicate the same date of issuance, the same place of dispatch or taking in charge of the goods, and the same destination.

Drawings and/or shipments by Instalments

Article 45

If drawings and/or shipments by instalments within given periods are stipulated in the credit and any instalment is not drawn and/or shipped within the period allowed for that instalment, the credit ceases to be available for that and any subsequent instalments, unless otherwise stipulated in the credit.

Expiry date and presentation

Article 46

a.   All credits must stipulate an expiry date for presentation of documents for payment, acceptance or negotiation.

b.   Except as provided in article 48 (a), documents must be presented on or before such expiry date.

c.   If an issuing bank states that the credit is to be available "for one month", "for six months" or the like, but does not specify the date from which the time is to run, the date of issuance of the credit by the issuing bank will be deemed to be the first day from which such time is to run. Banks should discourage indication of the expiry date of the credit in this manner.

Article 47

a.   In addition to stipulating an expiry date for presentation of documents, every credit which calls for a transport document(s) should also stipulate a specified period of time after the date of issuance of the transport document(s) during which presentation of documents for payment, acceptance or negotiation must be made. If no such period of time is stipulated, banks will refuse documents presented to them later than 21 days after the date of issuance of the transport document(s). In every case, however, documents must be presented not later than the expiry date of the credit.

b.   For the purpose of these articles, the date of issuance of a transport document(s) will be deemed to be:

i.   in the case of a transport document evidencing dispatch, or taking in charge, or receipt of goods for shipment by a mode of transport other than by air—the date of issuance indicated on the transport document or the date of the reception stamp thereon whichever is the later.

ii.   in the case of a transport document evidencing carriage by air—the date of issuance indicated on the transport document or, if the credit stipulates that the transport document shall indicate an actual flight date, the actual flight date as indicated on the transport document.

iii.   in the case of a transport document evidencing loading on board a named vessel—the date of issuance of the transport document or, in the case of an on board notation in accordance with article 27(b), the date of such notation.

iv.   in cases to which article 44(b) applies, the date determined as above of the latest transport document issued.

Article 48

a.   If the expiry date of the credit and/or the last day of the period of time after the date of issuance of the transport document(s) for presentation of documents stipulated by the credit or applicable by virtue of article 47 falls on a day on which the bank to which presentation has to be made is closed for reasons other than those referred to in article 19, the stipulated expiry date and/or the last day of the period of time after the date of issuance of the transport document(s) for presentation of documents, as the case may be, shall be extended to the first following business day on which such bank is open.

b.   The latest date for loading on board, or dispatch, or taking in charge shall not be extended by reason of the extension of the expiry date and/or the period of time after the date of issuance of the transport document(s) for presentation of document(s) in accordance with this article. If no such latest date for shipment is stipulated in the credit or amendments thereto, banks will reject transport documents indicating a date of issuance later than the expiry date stipulated in the credit or amendments thereto.

c.   The bank to which presentation is made on such first following business day must add to the documents its certificate that the documents were presented within the time limits extended in accordance with article 48(a) of the Uniform Customs and Practice for Documentary Credits, 1983 revision, ICC Publication No. 400.

Article 49

Banks are under no obligation to accept presentation of documents outside their banking hours.

Loading on board, dispatch and taking in charge (shipment)

Article 50

a.   Unless otherwise stipulated in the credit, the expression "shipment" used in stipulating an earliest and/or a latest shipment date will be understood to include the expressions "loading on board", "dispatch" and "taking in charge".

b.   The date of issuance of the transport document determined in accordance with article 47(b) will be taken to be the date of shipment.

c.   Expressions such as "prompt", "immediately", "as soon as possible", and the like should not be used. If they are used, banks will interpret them as a stipulation that shipment is to be made within thirty days from the date of issuance of the credit by the issuing bank.

d.   If the expression "on or about" and similar expressions are used, banks will interpret them as a stipulation that shipment is to be made during the period from five days before to five days after the specified date, both end days included.

Date terms

Article 51

The words "to", "until", "till", "from", and words of similar import applying to any date term in the credit will be understood to include the date mentioned. The word "after" will be understood to exclude the date mentioned.

Article 52

The terms "first half", "second half" of a month shall be construed respectively as from the 1st to the 15th, and the 16th to the last day of each month, inclusive.

Article 53

The terms "beginning", "middle", or "end" of a month shall be construed respectively as from the 1st to the 10th, the 11th to the 20th, and the 21st to the last day of each month, inclusive.

F. TRANSFER

Article 54

a.   A transferable credit is a credit under which the beneficiary has the right to request the bank called upon to effect payment or acceptance or any bank entitled to effect negotiation to make the credit available in whole or in part to one or more other parties (second beneficiaries).

b.   A credit can be transferred only if it is expressly designated as "transferable" by the issuing bank. Terms such as "divisible", "fractionable", "assignable", and "transmissible" add nothing to the meaning of the term "transferable" and shall not be used.

c.   The bank requested to effect the transfer (transferring bank), whether it has confirmed the credit or not, shall be under no obligation to effect such transfer except to the extent and in the manner expressly consented to by such bank.

d.   Bank charges in respect of transfers are payable by the first beneficiary unless otherwise specified. The transferring bank shall be under no obligation to effect the transfer until such charges are paid.

e.   A transferable credit can be transferred once only. Fractions of a transferable credit (not exceeding in the aggregate the amount of the credit) can be transferred separately, provided partial shipments are not prohibited, and the aggregate of such transfers will be considered as constituting only one transfer of the credit. The credit can be transferred only on the terms and conditions specified in the original credit, with the exception of the amount of the credit, of any unit prices stated therein, of the period of validity, of the last date for presentation of documents in accordance with article 47 and the period for shipment, any or all of which may be reduced or curtailed, or the percentage for which insurance cover must be effected, which may be increased in such a way as to provide the amount of cover stipulated in the original credit, or these articles. Additionally, the name of the first beneficiary can be substituted for that of the applicant for the credit, but if the name of the applicant for the credit is specifically required by the original credit to appear in any document other than the invoice, such requirement must be fulfilled.

f.   The first beneficiary has the right to substitute his own invoices (and drafts if the credit stipulates that drafts are to be drawn on the applicant for the credit) in exchange for those of the second beneficiary, for amounts not in excess of the original amount stipulated in the credit and for the original unit prices if stipulated in the credit, and upon such substitution of invoices (and drafts) the first beneficiary can draw under the credit for the difference, if any, between his invoices and the second beneficiary's invoices. When a credit has been transferred and the first beneficiary is to supply his own invoices (and drafts) in exchange for the second beneficiary's invoices (and drafts) but fails to do so on first demand, the paying, accepting or negotiating bank has the right to deliver to the issuing bank the documents received under the credit, including the second beneficiary's invoices (and drafts) without further responsibility to the first beneficiary.

9.   Unless otherwise stipulated in the credit, the first beneficiary of a transferable credit may request that the credit be transferred to a second beneficiary in the same country, or in another country. Further, unless otherwise stipulated in the credit, the first beneficiary shall have the right to request that payment or negotiation be effected to the second beneficiary at the place to which the credit has been transferred, up to and including the expiry date of the original credit, and without prejudice to the first beneficiary's right subsequently to substitute his own invoices and drafts (if any) for those of the second beneficiary and to claim any difference due to him.

Assignment of proceeds

Article 55

The fact that a credit is not stated to be transferable shall not affect the beneficiary's right to assign any proceeds to which he may be, or may become, entitled under such credit, in accordance with the provisions of the applicable law.

Appendix D: Risk-Based Capital Guidelines

Federal Reserve Bulletin, March 1989, pp. 157-170.

I.   *Overview*

The Board of Governors of the Federal Reserve System has adopted a risk-based capital measure to assist in the assessment of the capital adequacy of state member banks. The principal objectives of this measure are to:

(i)   make regulatory capital requirements more sensitive to differences in risk profiles among banks;

(ii) factor off-balance sheet exposures into the assessment of capital adequacy;

(iii) minimize disincentives to holding liquid, low-risk assets; and

(iv) achieve greater consistency in the evaluation of the capital adequacy of major banks throughout the world.

The risk-based capital guidelines include both a definition of capital and a framework for calculating weighted risk assets by assigning assets and off-balance sheet items to broad risk categories. A bank's risk-based capital ratio is calculated by dividing its qualifying capital (the numerator of the ratio) by its weighted risk assets (the denominator). The definition of qualifying capital is outlined below in Section II, and the procedures for calculating weighted risk assets are discussed in Section III. Attachment I illustrates a sample calculation of weighted risk assets and the risk-based capital ratio.

The risk-based capital guidelines also establish a schedule for achieving a minimum supervisory standard for the ratio of qualifying capital to weighted risk assets and provide for transitional arrangements during a phase-in period to facilitate adoption and implementation of the measure at the end of 1992. These interim standards and transitional arrangements are set forth in Section IV.

The risk-based guidelines apply to all state member banks on a consolidated basis. They are to be used in the examination and supervisory process as well as in the analysis of applications acted upon by the Federal Reserve. Thus, in considering an application filed by a state member bank, the Federal Reserve will take into account the bank's risk-based capital ratio, the reasonableness of its capital plans, and the degree of progress it has demonstrated toward meeting the interim and final risk-based capital standards.

The risk-based capital ratio focuses principally on broad categories of credit risk, although the framework for assigning assets and off-balance sheet items to risk categories does incorporate elements of transfer risk, as well as limited instances of interest rate and market risk. The risk-based ratio does not, however, incorporate other factors that can affect a bank's financial condition. These factors include overall interest rate exposure; liquidity, funding and market risks; the quality and level of earnings; investment or loan portfolio concentrations; the quality of loans and investments; the effectiveness of loan and investment policies; and management's ability to monitor and control financial and operating risks.

In addition to evaluating capital ratios, an overall assessment of capital adequacy must take account of these other factors, including, in particular, the level and severity of problem and classified assets. For this reason, the final supervisory judgment on a bank's capital adequacy may differ significantly from conclusions that might be drawn solely from the level of its risk-based capital ratio.

The risk-based capital guidelines establish *minimum* ratios of capital to weighted risk assets. In light of the considerations just discussed, banks generally are expected to operate well above the *minimum* risk-based ratios. In particular, banks contemplating significant expansion proposals are expected to maintain strong capital levels substantially above the *minimum* ratios and should not allow significant diminution of financial strength below these strong levels to fund their expansion plans. Institutions with high or inordinate levels of risk are also expected to operate well above minimum capital standards. In all cases, institutions should hold capital commensurate with the level and nature of the risks to which they are exposed. Banks that do not meet the minimum risk-based standard, or that are otherwise considered to be inadequately capitalized, are expected to develop and implement plans acceptable to the Federal Reserve for achieving adequate levels of capital within a reasonable period of time.

The Board will monitor the implementation and effect of these guidelines in relation to domestic and international developments in the banking industry. When necessary and appropriate, the Board will consider the need to modify the guidelines in light of any significant changes in the economy, financial markets, banking practices, or other relevant factors.

II.   Definition of Qualifying Capital for the Risk-Based Capital Ratio

A bank's qualifying total capital consists of two types of capital components: "core capital elements" (comprising Tier I capital) and "supplementary capital elements" (comprising Tier 2 capital). These capital elements and the various limits, restrictions, and deductions to which they are subject, are discussed below and are set forth in Attachment II.

To qualify as an element of Tier I or Tier 2 capital, a capital instrument may not contain or be covered by any covenants, terms, or restrictions that are inconsistent with safe and sound banking practices.

Redemptions of permanent equity or other capital instruments before stated maturity could have a significant impact on a bank's overall capital structure. Consequently, a bank considering such a step should consult with the Federal Reserve before redeeming any equity or debt capital instrument (prior to maturity) if such redemption could have a material effect on the level or composition of the institution's capital base.

A.   The Components of Qualifying Capital.

1.   Core capital elements (Tier I capital). The Tier I component of a bank's qualifying capital must represent at least 50 percent of qualifying total capital and may consist of the following items that are defined as core capital elements:

(i) Common stockholders' equity.

(ii) Qualifying noncumulative perpetual preferred stock (including related surplus).

(iii) Minority interest in the equity accounts of consolidated subsidiaries.

Tier I capital is generally defined as the sum of the core capital elements less goodwill. (See Section II (B) below for a more detailed discussion of the treatment of goodwill, including an explanation of certain limited grandfathering arrangements.)

a.   *Common stockholders'equity.*   Common stockholders' equity includes: common stock; related surplus; and retained earnings, including capital reserves and adjustments for the cumulative effect of foreign currency translation, net of any treasury stock.

b.   *Perpetual preferred stock.*   Perpetual preferred stock is defined as preferred stock that does not have a maturity date, that cannot be redeemed at the option of the holder of the instrument, and that has no other provisions that will require future redemption of the issue. In general, preferred stock will qualify for inclusion in capital only if it can absorb losses while the issuer operates as a going concern (a fundamental characteristic of equity capital) *and* only if the issuer has the ability and legal right to defer or eliminate preferred dividends.

The only form of perpetual preferred stock that state member banks may consider as an element of Tier 1 capital is noncumulative perpetual preferred.   While the guidelines allow for the inclusion of noncumulative perpetual preferred stock in Tier 1, it is desirable from a supervisory standpoint that voting common stockholders' equity remain the dominant form of Tier 1 capital. Thus, state member banks should avoid over-reliance on preferred stock or non-voting equity elements within Tier 1.

Perpetual preferred stock in which the dividend is reset periodically based, in whole or in part, upon the bank's current credit standing (that is, auction rate perpetual preferred stock, including so-called Dutch auction, money market, and remarketable preferred) will not qualify for inclusion in Tier 1 capital. Such instruments, however, qualify for inclusion in Tier 2 capital.

c.   *Minority interest in equity accounts of consolidated subsidiaries.* This element is included in Tier 1 because, as a general rule, it represents equity that is freely available to absorb losses in operating subsidiaries. While not subject to an explicit sublimit within Tier 1, banks are expected to avoid using minority interest in the equity accounts of consolidated subsidiaries as an avenue for introducing into their capital structures elements that might not otherwise qualify as Tier 1 capital or that would, in effect, result in an excessive reliance on preferred stock within Tier 1.

2.   *Supplementary capital elements (Tier 2 capital).*   The Tier 2 component of a bank's qualifying total capital may consist of the following items that are defined as supplementary capital elements:

(i) Allowance for loan and lease losses (subject to limitations discussed below).

(ii) Perpetual preferred stock and related surplus (subject to conditions discussed below).

(iii) Hybrid capital instruments (as defined below) and mandatory convertible debt securities.

(iv) Term subordinated debt and intermediate-term preferred stock, including related surplus (subject to limitations discussed below).

The maximum amount of Tier 2 capital that may be included in a bank's qualifying total capital is limited to 100 percent of Tier 1 capital (net of goodwill).

a.   *Allowance for loan and lease losses.* Allowances for loan and lease losses are reserves that have been established through a charge against earnings to absorb future losses on loans or lease financing receivables. Allowances for loan and lease losses exclude "allocated transfer risk reserves," and reserves created against identified losses.

During the transition period, the risk-based capital guidelines provide for reducing the amount of this allowance that may be included in an institution's total capital. Initially, it is unlimited. However, by year-end 1990, the amount of the allowance for loan and lease losses that will qualify as capital will be limited to 1.5 percent of an institution's weighted risk assets. By the end of the transition period, the amount of the allowance qualifying for inclusion in Tier 2 capital may not exceed 1.25 percent of weighted risk assets.

b.   *Perpetual preferred stock.* Perpetual preferred stock, as noted above, is defined as preferred stock that has no maturity date, that cannot be redeemed at the option of the holder, and that has no other provisions that will require future redemption of the issue. Such instruments are eligible for inclusion in Tier 2 capital without limit.

c.   Hybrid capital instruments and mandatory convertible debt securities. Hybrid capital instruments include instruments that are essentially permanent in nature and that have certain characteristics of both equity and debt. Such instruments may be included in Tier 2 without limit. The general criteria hybrid capital instruments must meet in order to qualify for inclusion in Tier 2 capital are listed below:

(1) The instrument must be unsecured; fully paid-up; and subordinated to general creditors and must also be subordinated to claims of depositors.

(2) The instrument must not be redeemable at the option of the holder prior to maturity, except with the prior approval of the Federal Reserve. (Consistent with the Board's criteria for perpetual debt and mandatory convertible securities, this requirement implies that holders of such instruments may not accelerate the payment of principal except in the event of bankruptcy, insolvency, or reorganization.)

(3) The instrument must be available to participate in losses while the issuer is operating as a going concern. (Term subordinated debt would not meet this requirement.) To satisfy this requirement, the instrument must convert to common or perpetual preferred stock in the event that the accumulated losses exceed the sum of the retained earnings and capital surplus accounts of the issuer.

(4) The instrument must provide the option for the issuer to defer interest payments if: (a) the issuer does not report a profit in the preceding annual period (defined as combined profits for the most recent four quarters), *and* (b) the issuer eliminates cash dividends on common and preferred stock.

Mandatory convertible debt securities in the form of equity contract notes that meet the criteria set forth in 12 C.F.R. Part 225, Appendix B, also qualify as unlimited elements of Tier 2 capital. In accordance with that appendix, equity commitment notes issued prior to May 15, 1985 also qualify for inclusion in Tier 2.

d.   Subordinated debt and intermediate-term preferred stock. The aggregate amount of term subordinated debt (excluding mandatory convertible debt) and intermediate-term preferred stock that may be treated as supplementary capital is limited to 50 percent of Tier 1 capital (net of goodwill). Amounts in excess of these limits may be issued and, while not included in the ratio calculation, will be taken into account in the overall assessment of a bank's funding and financial condition.

Subordinated debt and intermediate-term preferred stock must have an original weighted average maturity of at least five years to qualify as supplementary capital. (If the holder has the option to require the issuer to redeem, repay, or repurchase the instrument prior to the original stated maturity, maturity would be defined, for risk-based capital purposes, as the earliest possible date on which the holder can put the instrument back to the issuing bank.)

In the case of subordinated debt, the instrument must be unsecured and must clearly state on its face that it is not a deposit and is not insured by a Federal agency. To qualify as capital in banks, debt must be subordinated to general creditors and claims of depositors. Consistent with current regulatory requirements, if a state member bank wishes to redeem subordinated debt before the stated maturity, it must receive prior approval of the Federal Reserve.

e.   *Discount of supplementary capital instruments.*   As a limited-life capital instrument approaches maturity it begins to take on characteristics of a short-term obligation. For this reason, the outstanding amount of term subordinated debt and any long- or intermediate-life, or term, preferred stock eligible for inclusion in Tier 2 is reduced, or discounted, as these instruments approach maturity: one-fifth of the original amount, less any redemptions, is excluded each year during the instrument's last five years before maturity.

f.   *Revaluation reserves.* Such reserves reflect the formal balance sheet restatement or revaluation for capital purposes of asset carrying values to reflect current market values. In the United States, banks, for the most part, follow GAAP when preparing their financial statements, and GAAP generally does not permit the use of market-value accounting. For this and other reasons, the Federal banking agencies generally have not included unrealized asset values in capital ratio calculations, although they have long taken such values into account as a separate factor in assessing the overall financial strength of a bank.

Consistent with long-standing supervisory practice, the excess of market values over book values for assets held by state member banks will generally not be recognized in supplementary capital or in the calculation of the risk-based capital ratio. However, all banks are encouraged to disclose their equivalent of premises (building) and equity revaluation reserves. Such values will be taken into account as additional considerations in assessing overall capital strength and financial condition.

B.   Deductions from Capital and Other Adjustments.

Certain assets are deducted from a bank's capital for the purpose of calculating the risk-based capital ratio. These assets include:

(i) Goodwill-deducted from the sum of core capital elements.

(ii) Investments in banking and finance subsidiaries that are not consolidated for accounting or supervisory purposes and, on a case-by-case basis, investments in other designated subsidiaries or associated companies at the discretion of the Federal Reserve—deducted from total capital components.

(iii) Reciprocal holdings of capital instruments of banking organizations—deducted from total capital components.

1.   Goodwill and other intangible assets.

a.   Goodwill. Goodwill is an intangible asset that represents the excess of the purchase price over the fair market value of identifiable assets acquired less liabilities assumed in acquisitions accounted for under the purchase method of accounting. State member banks generally have not been allowed to include goodwill in regulatory capital under current supervisory policies. Consistent with this policy, all goodwill in state member banks will be deducted from Tier 1 capital.

b.   Other intangible assets. The Federal Reserve is not proposing, as a matter of general policy, to deduct automatically any other intangible assets from the capital of state member banks. The Federal Reserve, however, will continue to monitor closely the level and quality of other intangible assets—including purchased mortgage servicing rights, leaseholds, and core deposit value and take them into account in assessing the capital adequacy and overall asset quality of banks.

Generally, banks should review all intangible assets at least quarterly and, if necessary, make appropriate reductions in their carrying values. In addition, in order to conform with prudent banking practice, an institution should reassess such values during its annual audit. Banks should use appropriate amortization methods and assign prudent amortization periods for intangible assets. Examiners will review the carrying value of these assets, together with supporting documentation, as well as the appropriateness of including particular intangible assets in a bank's capital calculation. In making such evaluations, examiners will consider a number of factors, including:

(1) The reliability and predictability of any cash flows associated with the asset and the degree of certainty that can be

achieved in periodically determining the asset's useful life and value;

(2) The existence of an active and liquid market for the asset; and

(3) The feasibility of selling the asset apart from the bank or from the bulk of its assets.

While all intangible assets will be monitored, intangible assets (other than goodwill) in excess of 25 percent of Tier 1 capital (which is defined net of goodwill) will be subject to particularly close scrutiny, both through the examination process and by other appropriate means. Whenever necessary—in particular, when assessing applications to expand or to engage in other activities that could entail unusual or higher-than-normal risks—the Board will, on a case-by-case basis, continue to consider the level of an individual bank's tangible capital ratios (after deducting all intangible assets), together with the quality and value of the bank's tangible and intangible assets, in making an overall assessment of capital adequacy.

Consistent with long-standing Board policy, banks experiencing substantial growth, whether internally or by acquisition, are expected to maintain strong capital positions substantially above minimum supervisory levels, without significant reliance on intangible assets.

2.   *Investments in certain subsidiaries.* The aggregate amount of investments in banking or finance subsidiaries whose financial statements are not consolidated for accounting or bank regulatory reporting purposes will be deducted from a bank's total capital components. Generally, investments for this purpose are defined as equity and debt capital investments and any other instruments that are deemed to be capital in the particular subsidiary.

Advances (that is, loans, extensions of credit, guarantees, commitments, or any other forms of credit exposure) to the subsidiary that are not deemed to be capital will generally not be deducted from a bank's capital. Rather, such advances generally will be included in the bank's consolidated assets and be assigned to the 100 percent risk category, unless such obligations are backed by recognized collateral or guarantees, in which case they will be assigned to the risk category appropriate to such collateral or guarantees. These advances may, however, also be deducted from the bank's capital if, in the judgment of the Federal Reserve, the risks stemming from such advances are comparable to the risks associated with capital investments or if the advances involve other risk factors that warrant such an adjustment to capital for supervisory purposes. These other factors could include, for example, the absence of collateral support.

Inasmuch as the assets of unconsolidated banking and finance subsidiaries are not fully reflected in a bank's consolidated total assets, such assets may be viewed as the equivalent of off-balance sheet exposures since the operations of an unconsolidated subsidiary could expose the bank to considerable risk. For this reason, it is generally appropriate to view the capital resources invested in these unconsolidated entities as primarily supporting the risks inherent in these off-balance sheet assets, and not generally available to support risks or absorb losses elsewhere in the bank.

The Federal Reserve may, on a case-by-case basis, also deduct from a bank's capital, investments in certain other subsidiaries in order to determine if the consolidated bank meets minimum supervisory capital requirements without reliance on the resources invested in such subsidiaries.

The Federal Reserve will not automatically deduct investments in other unconsolidated subsidiaries or investments in joint ventures and associated companies. Nonetheless, the resources invested in these entities, like investments in unconsolidated banking and finance subsidiaries, support assets not consolidated with the rest of the bank's activities and, therefore, may not be generally available to support additional leverage or absorb losses elsewhere in the bank. Moreover, experience has shown that banks stand behind the losses of affiliated institutions, such as joint ventures and associated companies, in order to protect the reputation of the organization as a whole. In some cases, this has led to losses that have exceeded the investments in such organizations.

For this reason, the Federal Reserve will monitor the level and nature of such investments for individual banks and, on a case-by-case basis may, for risk-based capital purposes, deduct such investments from total capital components, apply an appropriate risk-weighted capital charge against the bank's proportionate share of the assets of its associated companies, require a line-by-line consolidation of the entity (in the event that the bank's control over the entity makes it the functional equivalent of a subsidiary), or otherwise require the bank to operate with a risk-based capital ratio above the minimum.

In considering the appropriateness of such adjustments or actions, the Federal Reserve will generally take into account whether:

(1) The bank has significant influence over the financial or managerial policies or operations of the subsidiary, joint venture, or associated company;

(2) The bank is the largest investor in the affiliated company; or

(3) Other circumstances prevail that appear to closely tie the activities of the affiliated company to the bank.

3.   Reciprocal holdings of banking organizations' capital instruments. Reciprocal holdings of banking organizations' capital instruments (that is, instruments that qualify as Tier 1 or Tier 2 capital) will be deducted from a bank's total capital components for the purpose of determining the numerator of the risk-based capital ratio.

Reciprocal holdings are cross-holdings resulting from formal or informal arrangements in which two or more banking organizations swap, exchange, or otherwise agree to hold each other's capital instruments. Generally, deductions will be limited to intentional cross-holdings. At present, the Board does not intend to require banks to deduct non-reciprocal holdings of such capital instruments.

III.   Procedures for Computing Weighted Risk Assets and Off-Balance Sheet Items

A.   Procedures.

Assets and credit equivalent amounts of off-balance sheet items of state member banks are assigned to one of several broad risk categories, according to the obligor, or, if relevant, the guarantor or the nature of the collateral. The aggregate dollar value of the amount in each category is then multiplied by the risk weight associated with that category. The resulting weighted values from each of the risk categories are added together, and this sum is the bank's total weighted risk assets that comprise the denominator of the risk-based capital ratio. Attachment I provides a sample calculation.

Risk weights for all off-balance sheet items are determined by a two-step process. First, the "credit equivalent amount" of off-balance sheet items is determined, in most cases by multiplying the off-balance sheet item by a credit conversion factor. Second, the credit equivalent amount is treated like any balance sheet asset and generally is assigned to the appropriate risk category according to the obligor, or, if relevant, the guarantor or the nature of the collateral.

In general, if a particular item qualifies for placement in more than one risk category, it is assigned to the category that has the lowest risk weight. A holding of a U.S. municipal revenue bond that is fully guaranteed by a U.S. bank, for example, would be assigned the 20 percent risk weight appropriate to claims guaranteed by U.S. banks, rather than the 50 percent risk weight appropriate to U.S. municipal revenue bonds.

The terms "claims" and "securities" used in the context of the discussion of risk weights, unless otherwise specified, refer to loans or debt obligations of the entity on whom the claim is held. Assets in the form of stock or equity holdings in commercial or financial firms are assigned to the 100 percent risk category, unless some other treatment is explicitly permitted.

B.   Collateral, Guarantees, and Other Considerations.

1.   Collateral. The only forms of collateral that are formally recognized by the risk-based capital framework are: cash on deposit in the bank; securities issued or guaranteed by the central governments of the OECD-based group of countries, U.S. Government agencies, or U.S. Government-sponsored agencies; and securities issued by multilateral lending institutions or regional development banks. Claims fully secured by such collateral are assigned to the 20 percent risk weight category.

The extent to which qualifying securities are recognized as collateral is determined by their current market value. If a claim is only partially secured, that is, the market value of the pledged securities is less than the face amount of a balance sheet asset or an off-balance sheet item, the portion that is covered by the market value of the qualifying collateral is assigned to the 20 percent risk category, and the portion of the claim that is not covered by collateral in the form of cash or a qualifying security is assigned to the risk category appropriate to the obligor or, if relevant, the guarantor. For example, to the extent that a claim on a private sector obligor is collateralized by the current market value of U.S. Government securities, it would be placed in the 20 percent risk category, and the balance would be assigned to the 100 percent risk category.

2. *Guarantees.* Guarantees of the OECD and non-OECD central governments, U.S. Government agencies, U.S. Government-sponsored agencies, state and local governments of the OECD-based group of countries, multilateral lending institutions and regional development banks, U.S. depository institutions, and foreign banks are also recognized. If a claim is partially guaranteed, that is, coverage of the guarantee is less than the face amount of a balance sheet asset or an off-balance sheet item, the portion that is not fully covered by the guarantee is assigned to the risk category appropriate to the obligor or, if relevant, to any collateral. The face amount of a claim covered by two types of guarantees that have different risk weights, such as a U.S. Government guarantee and a state guarantee, is to be apportioned between the two risk categories appropriate to the guarantors.

The existence of other forms of collateral or guarantees that the risk-based capital framework does not formally recognize may be taken into consideration in evaluating the risks inherent in a bank's loan portfolio—which, in turn, would affect the overall supervisory assessment of the bank's capital adequacy.

3. *Mortgage-backed securities.* Mortgage-backed securities, including pass-throughs and collateralized mortgage obligations (but not stripped mortgage-backed securities), that are *issued* or *guaranteed* by a U.S. Government agency or U.S. Government-sponsored agency are assigned to the risk weight category appropriate to the issuer or guarantor. Generally, a privately-issued mortgage-backed security meeting certain criteria set forth in the accompanying footnote, is treated as essentially an indirect holding of the underlying assets, and assigned to the same risk category as the underlying assets, but in no case to the zero percent risk category. Privately-issued mortgage-backed securities whose structures do not qualify them to be regarded as indirect holdings of the underlying assets are assigned to the 100 percent risk category. During the examination process, privately-issued mortgage-backed securities that are assigned to a lower risk weight category will be subject to examiner review to ensure that they meet the appropriate criteria.

While the risk category to which mortgage-backed securities is assigned will generally be based upon the issuer or guarantor or, in the case of privately-issued mortgage-backed securities, the assets underlying the security, any class of a mortgage-backed security that can absorb more than its *pro rata* share of loss without the whole issue being in default (for example, a so-called subordinated class or residual interest), is assigned to the 100 percent risk category. Furthermore, all stripped mortgage-backed securities, including interest-only strips (IOs), principal-only strips (POs), and similar instruments are also assigned to the 100 percent risk weight category, regardless of the issuer or guarantor.

4.   Maturity. Maturity is generally not a factor in assigning items to risk categories with the exception of claims on non-OECD banks, commitments, and interest rate and foreign exchange rate contracts.

Except for commitments, short-term is defined as one year or less *remaining* maturity and long-term is defined as over one year *remaining* maturity. In the case of commitments, short-term is defined as one year or less *original* maturity and long-term is defined as over one year original maturity.

C.   Risk Weights.

Attachment III contains a listing of the risk categories, a summary of the types of assets assigned to each category and the weight associated with each category, that is, 0 percent, 20 percent, 50 percent, and 100 percent. A brief explanation of the components of each category follows.

1.   Category 1: zero percent. This category includes cash (domestic and foreign) owned and held in all offices of the bank or in transit and gold bullion held in the bank's own vaults or in another bank's vaults on an allocated basis, to the extent it is offset by gold bullion liabilities. The category also includes all direct claims (including securities, loans, and leases) on, and the portions of claims that are directly and unconditionally guaranteed by, the central governments of the OECD countries and U.S. Government agencies, as well as all direct local currency claims on, and the portions of local currency claims that are directly and unconditionally guaranteed by, the central governments of non-OECD countries, to the extent that the bank has liabilities booked in that currency. A claim is not considered to be unconditionally guaranteed by a central government if the validity of the guarantee is dependent upon some affirmative action by the holder or a third party. Generally, securities guaranteed by the U.S. Government or its agencies that are actively traded in financial markets, such as GNMA securities, are considered to be unconditionally guaranteed.

2.   Category 2: 20 percent. This category includes cash items in the process of collection, both foreign and domestic; short-term claims (including demand deposits) on, and the portions of short-term claims that are guaranteed by, U.S. depository institutions and foreign banks; and long-term claims on, and the portions of long-term claims that are guaranteed by, U.S. depository institutions and OECD banks.

This category also includes the portions of claims that are conditionally guaranteed by OECD central governments and U.S. Government agencies, as well as the portions of local currency claims that are conditionally guaranteed by non-OECD central governments, to the extent that the bank has liabilities booked in that currency. In addition, this category includes claims on, and the portions of claims that are guaranteed by, U.S. Government-sponsored agencies and claims on, and the portions of claims guaranteed by, the International Bank for Reconstruction and Development (World Bank), the Interamerican Development Bank, the Asian Development Bank, the African Development Bank, the European Investment Bank, and other multilateral lending institutions or regional development banks in which the U.S. Government is a shareholder or contributing member. General obligation claims on, or portions of claims guaranteed by the full faith and credit of, states or other political subdivisions of the U.S. or other countries of the OECD-based group are also assigned to this category.

This category also includes the portions of claims (including repurchase agreements) collateralized by cash on deposit in the bank; by securities issued or guaranteed by OECD central governments, U.S. Government agencies, or U.S. Government-sponsored agencies; or by securities issued by multilateral lending institutions or regional development banks in which the U.S. Government is a shareholder or contributing member.

3.   *Category 3: 50 percent.* This category includes loans fully secured by first liens on 1-4 family residential properties, either owner-occupied or rented, provided that such loans have been made in accordance with prudent underwriting standards, including a conservative loan-to-value ratio; are performing in accordance with their original terms; and are not 90 days or more past due or carried in nonaccrual status. Also included in this category are privately-issued mortgage-backed securities provided that:

(1)   the structure of the security meets the criteria described in section III (B)(3) above;

(2)   if the security is backed by a pool of conventional mortgages, each underlying mortgage meets the criteria described above in this section for eligibility for the 50 percent risk weight category at the time the pool is originated; and (3) if the security is backed by privately-issued mortgage-backed securities, each underlying security qualifies for the 50 per-

cent risk category. Privately-issued mortgage-backed securities that do not meet these criteria or that do not qualify for a lower risk weight are generally assigned to the 100 percent risk weight category.

Also assigned to this category are *revenue* (nongeneral obligation) bonds or similar obligations, including loans and leases, that are obligations of states or other political subdivisions of the U.S. (for example, municipal revenue bonds) or other countries of the OECD-based group, but for which the government entity is committed to repay the debt with revenues from the specific projects financed, rather than from general tax funds.

Credit equivalent amounts of interest rate and foreign exchange rate contracts involving standard risk obligors (that is, obligors whose loans or debt securities would be assigned to the 100 percent risk category) are included in the 50 percent category, unless they are backed by collateral or guarantees that allow them to be placed in a lower risk category.

4.   *Category 4: 100 percent.* All assets not included in the categories above are assigned to this category, which comprises standard risk assets. The bulk of the assets typically found in a loan portfolio would be assigned to the 100 percent category.

This category includes long-term claims on, or guaranteed by, non-OECD banks, and all claims on non-OECD central governments that entail some degree of transfer risk. This category also includes all claims on foreign and domestic private sector obligors not included in the categories above (including loans to non-depository financial institutions and bank holding companies); claims on commercial firms owned by the public sector; customer liabilities to the bank on acceptances outstanding involving standard risk claims; investments in fixed assets, premises, and other real estate owned; common and preferred stock of corporations, including stock acquired for debts previously contracted; commercial and consumer loans (except those assigned to lower risk categories due to recognized guarantees or collateral and loans for residential property that qualify for a lower risk weight); mortgage-backed securities that do not meet criteria for assignment to a lower risk weight (including any classes of mortgage-backed securities that can absorb more than their *pro rata* share of loss without the whole issue being in default); and all stripped mortgage-backed and similar securities.

Also included in this category are industrial development bonds and similar obligations issued under the auspices of states or political subdivisions of the OECD-based group of countries for the benefit of a private party or enterprise where that party or enterprise, not the government entity, is obligated to pay the principal and interest, and all obligations of states or political subdivisions of countries that do not belong to the OECD-based group.

The following assets also are assigned a risk weight of 100 percent if they have not been deducted from capital: investments in unconsolidated companies, joint ventures or associated companies; instruments that qualify as capital issued by other banking organizations; and any intangibles, including grandfathered goodwill.

D.   Off-Balance Sheet Items.

The face amount of an off-balance sheet item is incorporated into the risk-based capital ratio by multiplying it by a credit conversion factor. The resultant credit equivalent amount is assigned to the appropriate risk category according to the obligor, or, if relevant, the guarantor or the nature of the collateral. Attachment IV sets forth the conversion factors for various types of off-balance sheet items.

1.   Items with a 100 percent conversion factor. A 100 percent conversion factor applies to direct credit substitutes, which include guarantees, or equivalent instruments, backing financial claims, such as outstanding securities, loans, and other financial liabilities, or that back off-balance sheet items that require capital under the risk-based capital framework. Direct credit substitutes include, for example, financial standby letters of credit, or other equivalent irrevocable undertakings or surety arrangements, that guarantee repayment of financial obligations such as: commercial paper, tax-exempt securities, commercial or individual loans or debt obligations, or standby or commercial letters of credit. Direct credit substitutes also include the acquisition of risk participations in bankers acceptances and standby letters of credit, since both of these transactions, in effect, constitute a guarantee by the acquiring bank that the underlying account party (obligor) will repay its obligation to the originating, or issuing, institution. (Standby letters of credit that are performance-related are discussed below and have a credit conversion factor of 50 percent.)

The full amount of a direct credit substitute is converted at 100 percent and the resulting credit equivalent amount is assigned to the risk category appropriate to the obligor or, if relevant, the guarantor or the nature of the collateral. In the case of a direct credit substitute in which a risk participation has been conveyed, the full amount is still converted at 100 percent. However, the credit equivalent amount that has been conveyed is assigned to whichever risk category is lower: the risk category appropriate to the obligor, after giving effect to any relevant guarantees or collateral, or the risk category appropriate to the institution acquiring the participation. Any remainder is assigned to the risk category appropriate to the obligor, guarantor, or collateral. For example, the portion of a direct credit substitute conveyed as a risk participation to a U.S. domestic depository institution or foreign bank is assigned to the risk category appropriate to claims guaranteed by those institutions, that is, the 20 percent risk category. This approach recognizes that such conveyances replace the originating bank's exposure to the obligor with an exposure to the institutions acquiring the risk participations.

In the case of direct credit substitutes that take the form of a syndication as defined in the instructions to the commercial bank Call Report, that is, where each bank is obligated only for its *pro rata* share of the risk and there is no recourse to the originating bank, each bank will only include its *pro rata* share of the direct credit substitute in its risk-based capital calculation.

Financial standby letters of credit are distinguished from loan commitments (discussed below) in that standbys are irrevocable obligations of the bank to pay a third-party beneficiary when a customer (account party) *fails to repay* an outstanding loan or debt instrument (direct credit substitute). Performance standby letters of credit (performance bonds) are irrevocable obligations of the bank to pay a third-party beneficiary when a customer (account party) *fails to perform* some other contractual non-financial obligation.

The distinguishing characteristic of a standby letter of credit for risk-based capital purposes is the combination of irrevocability with the fact that funding is triggered by some failure to repay or perform an obligation. Thus, any commitment (by whatever name) that involves an *irrevocable* obligation to make a payment to the customer or to a third party in the event the customer *fails to repay* an outstanding debt obligation or *fails to perform* a contractual obligation is treated, for risk-based capital purposes, as respectively, a financial guarantee standby letter of credit or a performance standby.

A loan commitment, on the other hand, involves an obligation (with or without a material adverse change or similar clause) of the bank to fund its customer *in the normal course* of business should the customer seek to draw down the commitment.

Sale and repurchase agreements and asset sales with recourse (to the extent not included on the balance sheet) and forward agreements also are converted at 100 percent. The risk-based capital definition of the sale of assets with recourse, including the sale of 1-4 family residential mortgages, is the same as the definition contained in the instructions to the commercial bank Call Report. So-called "loan strips" (that is, short-term advances sold under long-term commitments without direct recourse) are defined in the instructions to the commercial bank Call Report and for risk-based capital purposes as assets sold with recourse.

Forward agreements are legally binding contractual obligations to purchase assets with certain drawdown at a specified future date. Such obligations include forward purchases, forward forward deposits placed, and partly-paid shares and securities; they do not include commitments to make residential mortgage loans or forward foreign exchange contracts.

Securities lent by a bank are treated in one of two ways, depending upon whether the lender is at risk of loss. If a bank, as agent for a customer, lends the customer's securities and does not indemnify the customer against loss, then the transaction is excluded from the risk-based capital calculation. If, alternatively, a bank lends its own securities or, acting as agent for a customer, lends the customer's securities and indemnifies the customer against loss, the transaction is converted at 100 percent and assigned to the risk weight category appropriate to the obligor, to any collateral delivered to the lending bank, or, if applicable, to the independent custodian acting on the lender's behalf.

2.   *Items with a 50 percent conversion factor.* Transaction-related contingencies are converted at 50 percent. Such contingencies include bid bonds, performance bonds, warranties, standby letters of credit related to particular transactions, and performance standby letters of credit, as well as acquisitions of risk participations in performance standby letters of credit. Performance standby letters of credit represent obligations backing the performance of nonfinancial or commercial contracts or undertakings. To the extent permitted by law or regulation, performance standby letters of credit include arrangements backing, among other things, subcontractors' and suppliers' performance, labor and materials contracts, and construction bids.

The unused portion of commitments with an original maturity exceeding one year, including underwriting commitments, and commercial and consumer credit commitments also are converted at 50 percent. Original maturity is defined as the length of time between the date the commitment is issued and the earliest date on which:

(1) the bank can, at its option, unconditionally (without cause) cancel the commitment, and

(2) the bank is scheduled to (and as a normal practice actually does) review the facility to determine whether or not it should be extended.

Such reviews must continue to be conducted at least annually for such a facility to qualify as a short-term commitment.

Commitments are defined as any legally binding arrangements that obligate a bank to extend credit in the form of loans or leases; to purchase loans, securities, or other assets; or to participate in loans and leases. They also include overdraft facilities, revolving credit, home equity and mortgage lines of credit, and similar transactions.

Normally, commitments involve a written contract or agreement and a commitment fee, or some other form of consideration. Commitments are included in weighted risk assets regardless of whether they contain "material adverse change" clauses or other provisions that are intended to relieve the issuer of its funding obligation under certain conditions. In the case of commitments structured as syndications, where the bank is obligated solely for its *pro rata* share, only the bank's proportional share of the syndicated commitment is taken into account in calculating the risk-based capital ratio.

Facilities that are unconditionally cancellable (without cause) at any time by the bank are not deemed to be commitments, provided the bank makes a separate credit decision before each drawing under the facility. Commitments with an original maturity of one year or less are deemed to involve low risk and, therefore, are not assessed a capital charge. Such short-term commitments are defined to include the unused portion of lines of credit on retail credit cards and related plans (as defined in the instructions to the commercial bank Call Report) if the bank has the unconditional right to cancel the line of credit at any time, in accordance with applicable law.

Once a commitment has been converted at 50 percent, any portion that has been conveyed to other U.S. depository institutions or OECD banks as participations in which the originating bank retains the full obligation to the borrower if the participating bank fails to pay when the instrument is drawn, is assigned to the 20 percent risk category. This treatment is analogous to that accorded to conveyances of risk participations in standby letters of credit. The acquisition of a participation in a commitment by a bank is converted at 50 percent and assigned to the risk category appropriate to the account party obligor or, if relevant, the nature of the collateral or guarantees.

Revolving underwriting facilities (RUFs), note issuance facilities (NIFs), and other similar arrangements also are converted at 50 percent regardless of maturity. These are facilities under which a borrower can issue on a revolving basis short-term paper in its own name, but for which the underwriting banks have a legally binding commitment either to purchase any notes the borrower is unable to sell by the roll-over date or to advance funds to the borrower.

3.   Items with a 20 percent conversion factor. Short-term, self-liquidating trade-related contingencies which arise from the movement of goods are converted at 20 percent. Such contingencies generally include commercial letters of credit and other documentary letters of credit collateralized by the underlying shipments.

4.   Items with a zero percent conversion factor. These include unused portions of commitments with an original maturity of one year or less, or which are unconditionally cancellable at any time, provided a separate credit decision is made before each drawing under the facility.

Unused portions of lines of credit on retail credit cards and related plans are deemed to be short-term commitments if the bank has the unconditional right to cancel the line of credit at any time, in accordance with applicable law.

E.   Interest Rate and Foreign Exchange Rate Contracts.

1.   Scope. Credit equivalent amounts are computed for each of the following off-balance sheet interest rate and foreign exchange rate instruments:

I.   Interest Rate Contracts

A.   Single currency interest rate swaps.

B.   Basis swaps.

C.   Forward rate agreements.

D.   Interest rate options purchased (including caps, collars, and floors purchased).

E.   Any other instrument that gives rise to similar credit risks (including when-issued securities and forward deposits accepted).

II.   Exchange Rate Contracts

A.   Cross-currency interest rate swaps.

B.   Forward foreign exchange contracts.

C.   Currency options purchased.

D.   Any other instrument that gives rise to similar credit risks.

Exchange rate contracts with an original maturity of fourteen calendar days or less and instruments traded on exchanges that require daily payment of variation margin are excluded from the risk-based ratio calculation. Over-the-counter options purchased, however, are included and treated in the same way as the other interest rate and exchange rate contracts.

2.   *Calculation of credit equivalent amounts.* Credit equivalent amounts are calculated for each individual contract of the types listed above. To calculate the credit equivalent amount of its off-balance sheet interest rate and exchange rate instruments, a bank sums these amounts:

(1)   the mark-to-market value (positive values only) of each contract (that is, the current exposure); and

(2)   an estimate of the potential future credit exposure over the remaining life of each contract.

The potential future credit exposure on a contract, including contracts with negative mark-to-market values, is estimated by multiplying the notional principal amount by one of the following credit conversion factors, as appropriate:

Remaining Interest Rate
Maturity Contracts

One year or less...	0	1.0%
Over one year...	0.5%	5.0%

Examples of the calculation of credit equivalent amounts for these instruments are contained in Attachment V.

Because exchange rate contracts involve an exchange of principal upon maturity, and exchange rates are generally more volatile than interest rates, higher conversion factors have been established for foreign exchange contracts than for interest rate contracts.

No potential future credit exposure is calculated for single currency interest rate swaps in which payments are made based upon two floating rate indices, so-called floating/floating or basis swaps; the credit exposure on these contracts is evaluated solely on the basis of their mark-to-market values.

3.   *Risk weights.* Once the credit equivalent amount for interest rate and exchange rate instruments has been determined, that amount is assigned to the risk weight category appropriate to the counterparty, or, if relevant, the nature of any collateral or guarantees. However, the maximum weight that will be applied to the credit equivalent amount of such instruments is 50 percent.

4.   *Avoidance of double counting.* In certain cases, credit exposures arising from the interest rate and exchange instruments covered by these guidelines may already be reflected, in part, on the balance sheet. To avoid double counting such exposures in the assessment of capital adequacy and, perhaps, assigning inappropriate risk weights, counterparty credit exposures arising from the types of instruments covered by these guidelines may need to be excluded from balance sheet assets in calculating banks' risk-based capital ratios.

5.   *Netting.* Netting of swaps and similar contracts is recognized for purposes of calculating the risk-based capital ratio *only* when accomplished through netting by novation. While the Federal Reserve encourages any reasonable arrangements designed to reduce the risks inherent in these transactions, other types of netting arrangements are not recognized for purposes of calculating the risk-based ratio at this time.

IV.   Minimum Supervisory Ratios and Standards

The interim and final supervisory standards set forth below specify minimum supervisory ratios based primarily on broad credit risk considerations. As noted above, the risk-based ratio does not take explicit account of the quality of individual asset portfolios or the range of other types of risks to which banks may be exposed, such as interest rate, liquidity, market or operational risks. For this reason, banks are generally expected to operate with capital positions above the minimum ratios. This is particularly true for institutions that are undertaking significant expansion or that are exposed to high or unusual levels of risk.

Upon adoption of the risk-based framework, any bank that does not meet the interim or final supervisory ratios, or whose capital is otherwise considered inadequate, is expected to develop and implement a plan acceptable to the Federal Reserve for achieving an adequate level of capital consistent with the provisions of these guidelines or with the special circumstances affecting the individual institution. In addition, such banks should avoid any actions, including increased risk-taking or unwarranted expansion, that would lower or further erode their capital positions.

A.   Minimum Risk-Based Ratio After Transition Period

As reflected in Attachment VI, by year-end 1992, all state member banks should meet a minimum ratio of qualifying total capital to weighted risk assets of 8 percent, of which at least 4.0 percentage points should be in the form of Tier 1 capital net of goodwill. (Section II above contains detailed definitions of capital and related terms used in this section.) The maximum amount of supplementary capital elements that qualifies as Tier 2 capital is limited to 100 percent of Tier 1 capital net of goodwill. In addition, the combined maximum amount of subordinated debt and intermediate-term preferred stock that qualifies as Tier 2 capital is limited to 50 percent of Tier 1 capital. The maximum amount of the allowance for loan and lease losses that qualifies as Tier 2 capital is limited to 1.25 percent of gross weighted risk assets. Allowances for loan and lease losses in excess of this limit may, of course, be maintained, but would not be included in a bank's total capital. The Federal Reserve will continue to require banks to maintain reserves at levels fully sufficient to cover losses inherent in their loan portfolios.

Qualifying total capital is calculated by adding Tier 1 capital and Tier 2 capital (limited to 100 percent of Tier 1 capital) and then deducting from this sum certain investments in banking or finance subsidiaries that are not consolidated for accounting or supervisory purposes, reciprocal holdings of banking organization capital securities, or other items at the direction of the Federal Reserve. These deductions are discussed above in Section II(B).

INDEX

INTERNATIONAL BANKING TEXTBOOK QUESTIONNAIRE

Date:_____

This questionnaire is designed to get your opinion of the <u>International Banking</u> textbook on which this course is based. This is **NOT** an evaluation of your instructor or experience in class. Please take a few minutes to answer the following questions and return this self-mailing questionnaire. Your comments will be used to improve future editions of this textbook.

I. About the Textbook

Please rate your opinions of the textbook by checking the appropriate comment.

A. Thoroughness
___Covers too little   ___Sufficient content   ___Covers too much

B. Difficulty of content
___Too difficult   ___Appropriate   ___Too easy

C. Readability (language, style, etc.)
___Easy to read   ___Fairly readable   ___Hard to read

D. Practicality (usefulness to your job)
___Too theoretical   ___Practical   ___Not practical but useful

E. Organization of subjects
___Very well organized   ___Organized   ___Not well organized

F. Textbook's ability to address stated learning objectives
___Always addressed   ___Mostly addressed   ___Seldom addressed

G. Graphics/examples
___Always appropriate   ___Sometimes appropriate   ___Seldom appropriate

H. Overall rating of the text (circle rating)
Very effective   Ineffective
5   4   3   2   1

II. Background Information

A. Bank Position: _____

B. Major Job Responsibility: _____

C. Asset Size of Bank:
___Under $100m   ___$100-$500m   ___$501m-$1bil   ___Over $1bil

D. Highest Education Level
___High School   ___Some College   ___BA/BS Degree   ___Advanced

E. Age:
___Under 25   ___25-35   ___36-45   ___Over 45

F. Years in Banking:
___0-2   ___3-5   ___6-10   ___Over 10

III. Comments

A. What specific suggestions can you make for improving this textbook?

B. If we may call you for more comments, please provide your name and phone number below:

Name:_____   Phone Number: _____

FOLD IN HALF AND STAPLE

FOLD HERE

BUSINESS REPLY MAIL
FIRST CLASS PERMIT NO. 10579   WASHINGTON, DC

POSTAGE WILL BE PAID BY ADDRESSEE

American Bankers Association
American Institute of Banking
Education Policy & Development Group
1120 Connecticut Avenue, N.W.
Washington, D.C. 20077-5760